State, Society and the Environment in South Asia

NORDIC INSTITUTE OF ASIAN STUDIES

Man & Nature in Asia

Series Editor: Arne Kalland
Senior Research Associate, Centre for Development
and the Environment, University of Oslo

The implication that environmental degradation has only occurred in Asia as a product of Westernization ignores the fact that Asia, too, has degradation and disaster in its history. The principal aim of this series, then, is to encourage critical research into the human–nature relationship in Asia. The series' multidisciplinary approach invites studies in a number of topics: how people make a living from nature; their knowledge and perception of their natural environment and how this is reflected in their praxis; indigenous systems of resource management; environmental problems, movements and campaigns; and many more.

The series will be of particular interest to anthropologists, geographers, historians, political scientists and sociologists as well as to policy-makers and those interested in development and environmental issues in Asia.

Recent Titles

Japanese Images of Nature: Cultural Perspectives
Pamela J. Asquith and Arne Kalland (eds)

Environmental Challenges in South-East Asia
Victor T. King (ed.)

Environmental Movements in Asia
Arne Kalland and Gerard Persoon (eds)

State, Society and the Environment in South Asia
Stig Toft Madsen (ed.)

State, Society and the Environment in South Asia

Edited by
Stig Toft Madsen

CURZON

Nordic Institute of Asian Studies
Man & Nature in Asia Series, No. 3

First published in 1999
by Curzon Press
15 The Quadrant, Richmond
Surrey TW9 1BP

Typesetting by the Nordic Institute of Asian Studies
Printed and bound in Great Britain by
Biddles Ltd, Guildford and King's Lynn

British Library Catalogue in Publication Data

State, society and the environment in South Asia. - (Man & nature in
Asia ; no. 3)
  1.Economic Development - Environmental aspects - South Asia
  2.Natural resources - South Asia - Management
  3.Environmental degradation - South Asia
  I.Madsen, Stig Toft
  333.7'0954

ISBN 0-7007-0614-3

Contents

	Preface	vii
	List of Contributors	viii
	List of Abbreviations	ix
	Editor's Note on Transliteration	xi
1	Introduction *Stig Toft Madsen*	1
2	From Wild Pigs to Foreign Trees: Oral Histories of Environmental Change in Rajasthan *Ann Grodzins Gold*	20
3	The Use of Metaphor in Himalayan Resource Management *Tor Aase*	59
4	A Community Management Plan: The Van Gujjars and the Rajaji National Park *Pernille Gooch*	79
5	The Role of Voluntary Organizations in Environmental Service Provision *Håkan Tropp*	113
6	International Production of Pesticides: Case Study of Gujarat, India *Petter Lindstad*	146
7	Linkages between Income Distribution and Environmental Degradation in Rural India *Rabindra Nath Chakraborty*	165
8	Deforestation and Entrepreneurship in the North-West Frontier Province, Pakistan *Are J. Knudsen*	200
9	The Irrigating Public: The State and Local Management in Colonial Irrigation *David Gilmartin*	236

10   When the Wells Ran Dry: Tragedy of
     Collective Action among Farmers in South India   266
     Staffan Lindberg

11   Nature, State and Market: Implementing
     International Regimes in India   297
     Ronald Herring

     Index   333

Tables

3.1   Metaphorization of land allocation   72
7.1   Structural asymmetries between Indian
      rural rich and poor   173
7.2   Mechanisms of environmental degradation   189
8.1   Legal classification of forests in Pakistan   206
8.2   Reduction in forest cover   218

Maps

3.1   The northern areas of Pakistan   61
3.2   Sai catchment area   67
3.3   Topography of the Sai catchment area   69
4.1   Proposed Rajaji National Park   90
8.1   North-West Frontier Province, Pakistan   201

Figures

3.1   Shina land types   64
3.2   Water discharge (cu ft/sec) in Sai Nalah   74

Preface

This book is the outcome of the conference 'Rural and Urban Environments in South Asia' organized by the Nordic Association for South Asian Studies (NASA) in Oslo from 18 to 22 May 1995. The book has been edited by Stig Toft Madsen in consultation with Sidsel Hansson, editorial assistant, and Pamela G. Price, the convener of the conference.

We would like to thank the following for supporting the conference and this publication: the Department of History, University of Oslo; the Norwegian Research Council; the Norwegian Agency for Development Cooperation (NORAD); the Nordic Academy for Advanced Study (NORFA); the Danish Council for Development Research; the Swedish Agency for Research Cooperation with Developing Countries (SAREC); the Centre for Development Research (CDR), Copenhagen; and the Nordic Institute of Asian Studies (NIAS), Copenhagen. Finally, we would like to thank the participants of the conference, including the authors of the articles appearing in this volume, the copyeditor Sandra Jones and the editorial staff at NIAS.

Stig Toft Madsen

List of Contributors

Tor Halfdan Aase PhD in anthropology, professor, Department of Geography, University of Bergen, Norway.

Rabindra Nath Chakraborty Economist working as a research staff member at the German Development Institute, Berlin, Germany.

David Gilmartin Professor of history, North Carolina State University.

Ann Grodzins Gold PhD in anthropology, professor of religion at Syracuse University, New York, USA.

Pernille Gooch PhD in social anthropology, lecturer and researcher at the Department of Human Ecology, University of Lund, Sweden.

Ronald Herring Professor in the fields of international relations and government; director, The Mario Einaudi Center for International Studies, Cornell University, New York, USA.

Are J. Knudsen Social anthropologist, research fellow and PhD student, Chr. Michelsen Institute, Bergen, Norway.

Staffan Lindberg Professor of sociology, University of Lund, Sweden.

Petter Lindstad Masters degree in social geography, senior executive officer at Oslo College, Faculty of Fine Arts and Drama.

Stig Toft Madsen Research associate at NIAS (the Nordic Institute of Asian Studies), Copenhagen, Denmark.

Håkan Tropp Political scientist, PhD student at the Department of Water and Environmental Studies, Linköping University, Sweden.

Abbreviations, Acronyms and Special Terms

AIADMK	All-India Anna Dravida Munnetra Kazagam
BHC	an insecticide similar to DDT
CBO	Community-Based Organization
CE	Civic Exnora
CFM-PA	Community Forest Management in Protected Areas
CITES	Convention on International Trade in Endangered Species of Flora and Fauna
CPI	Communist Party of India
CPR	Common Property Resource
crore	Indian word for the amount 10,000,000
CSE	Centre for Science and Environment
cum	cubic meter
DFO	Divisional Forest Officer
DMK	Dravida Munnetra Kazagam
FAO	Food and Agriculture Organization of the UN
FATA	Federally Administered Tribal Areas
FCS	Forest Cooperative Society
FD	Forest Department
FDC	Forest Development Cooperation
FSI	Forest Survey of India
FSMP	Forestry Sector Master Plan
GONGO	Government Organized Non-Governmental Organization
GPCB	Gujarat Pollution Control Board
HJP	Himalayan Jungle Project
ICSSR	Indian Council of Social Science Research
ITTA	International Tropical Timber Agreement
IUCN	International Union for the Conservation of Nature and Natural Resources
IWGIA	International Work Group for Indigenous Affairs
JFM	Joint Forest Management
KIDP	Kalam Integrated Development Project
lakh	Indian word for the amount 100,000

lpcd	liter per capita per day
M.G.R	M.G. Ramachandran
MIDS	Madras Institute of Development Studies
MLA	Member of the Legislative Assembly
MMA	Madras Metropolitan Area
MW	megawatt
NAPWD	Northern Areas Public Works Department
NCS	National Conservation Strategy
NDZ	No-Development Zone
NGO	Non-Governmental Organization
NORAD	Norwegian Agency for Development Cooperation
NWFP	North-West Frontier Province
paisa	monetary unit; 100 paise or Np = 1 rupee
PFI	Pakistan Forest Institute
RLEK	Rural Litigation and Entitlement Kendra
Rs	rupees (41 Pakistani rupees equivalent to 1 US$ as of September 1997, 43 Indian rupees equivalent to 1 US$ as of August 1998)
SAREC	Swedish Agency for Research Cooperation with Developing Countries
SDPI	Sustainable Development Policy Institute
SEN	Standard Environmental Narrative
SPCS	Sarhad Provincial Conservation Strategy
TNAA	Tamil Nadu Agriculturists' Association
TNC	Transnational Corporation
TNED	Tamil Nadu Electricity Board
UP	Uttar Pradesh
VO	Voluntary Organization
VS	Tamilaga Vyvasayigal Samgam
WAPDA	Pakistan Water and Power Development Agency
WHC	World Heritage Convention

Editor's Note on Transliteration

Transliterated Hindi words appear with diacritical marks in Chapter 2. These marks have not been employed in any other chapter. Moreover, double vowels sometimes used to indicate a long vowel have not been used in these chapters, e.g. instead of *sifareesh, sifarish* has been used.

1 | Introduction

Stig Toft Madsen

Nature and Social Science

Over the last few decades environmental concerns have moved centre stage. The natural sciences have contributed prominently to this movement. One of the major works so far has been written by the neo-Darwinist and sociobiologist Edward O. Wilson. In his book *The Diversity of Life* (1992), Wilson asserts that biological wealth is as important for humans as cultural and material wealth. The threat to biological wealth or biodiversity, he argues, is already great, and the next fifty to one hundred years will increase that threat. Operating with a time-frame which extends back to the origin of life on this planet, Wilson describes our time as the sixth period of mass extinction. In contrast to earlier periods, the current phase of mass extinction is largely caused by humans. During the next fifty to a hundred years, more than 25 per cent of all the species on earth may disappear. To limit extinctions to about 10 per cent of all species, Wilson proposes that areas of exceptionally high biodiversity be identified and protected from the onslaught of humanity. Eighteen such areas have been identified by Norman Myers. Three of these hotspots are in South Asia: one in the south-western parts of Sri Lanka; another along India's west coast in the Western Ghats; and a third stretches along the Eastern Himalayas into China (Myers 1990; Wilson 1992: 249–51).

In contrast to Wilson and other neo-Darwinists, most social scientists operate within a time-frame comprising decades, or, at the most, a century or two. Social scientists studying environmental history in South Asia have typically moved into the field

1

from rural sociology and agrarian history. In their previous studies they have concentrated on village settlements and on the cultivated fields surrounding these settlements. Few have studied social life in relation to village grazing areas, 'wastelands', jungles and rivers. Thus, they have brought into the study of social ecology the view from the village, rather than the view from the jungle.[1] Further, as has been noted by Gadgil and Guha, social scientists studying the environment tend to neglect the demographic dimension of social life, which might otherwise link the natural and the social sciences (Guha 1994a: 13; Gadgil and Guha 1995: 178).

While social scientists tend to eschew the natural sciences, some natural scientists have the ambition of applying evolutionary theory to social and cultural systems. Thus, in a socio-biological perspective, human cultures are regarded as mechanisms whose evolution makes them more or less successful in aiding the adaptation of human societies to their surrounding environments, thereby favouring the chances for survival of one population or another. This underlying genetic dimension is generally absent in the social sciences, which view culture, rather than genes, as the substratum that underlies and informs the multitude of observable living forms. In this book, the dominant view of life is located squarely within the social sciences and humanities. It may be noted, however, that several scholars working in South Asia are seeking to bridge the gap between social and natural sciences.

The Standard Environmental Narrative (SEN)

Within the emergent field of social studies addressing the environment in South Asia, one school of thought has become dominant. Its leading propositions are contained in a narrative that has been dubbed the *Standard Environmental Narrative* by Paul Greenough (see Sinha and Herring 1993). The Standard Environmental Narrative (or SEN) tells us that in the days of yore vibrant local communities lived largely in balance with nature, prudently managing their common property resources to satisfy a variety of needs of the community. The British, however, expropriated the common property resources without compensating the local stake-holders in order to exploit these resources commercially, thereby

2

undermining the resource base of the local communities. Through no fault of their own, these communities subsequently have had to exploit whatever resources they had access to, in a less sustainable manner. After Independence, the state and its main agent, the Forest Department, have been increasingly corrupted by politicians, forest contractors and timber mafias. According to the SEN, this has caused the contemporary environmental crisis. Consequently, the forest-dwellers and tribals must reassert their control over the commons to manage it on the basis of their indigenous knowledge, and in cooperation with NGOs (Madsen 1996: 210–11; see also Sivaramakrishnan 1995 and Jeffery *et al.* 1996).

Phrased in this manner, the SEN offers a geographically and historically differentiated view of South Asian environmental issues. It constitutes a nationalist critique of colonial and post-colonial policies and practices foregrounding the interplay of statal, societal and market forces to postulate certain abusive environmental consequences set in contrast to the benign agendas and prudent practices presumably characterizing indigenous and pre-colonial societies.

As indicated by the phrase 'Standard Environmental Narrative', the SEN takes the form of an easily understood, yet profound and meaningful set of propositions spun into a story suitable for narration in a variety of fora. The SEN shares these characteristics with other environmental narratives elsewhere in the world. For example, Hoben has identified a powerful environmental narrative in Africa connecting human imprudence to soil erosion, desertification and environmental crisis (Hoben 1997). According to Hoben, environmental narratives that are simple, clear-cut and dramatic are politically efficient because they enable decision-makers to coordinate their interventions in situations of high uncertainty, complexity and stress. Such situations characterize international development work. Hence, the international development discourse is replete with standardized development narratives.

In South Asia, however, the SEN is not primarily a policy narrative designed to secure international funds for eco-restoration projects. Rather, the SEN is an anti-colonial narrative, which also implies a criticism of post-colonial governmentality. Historically, the SEN may well have its origins in colonial environmental narratives (similar to the environmental narratives in Africa), blaming environmental degradation on the age-old practices of pastoralists and farmers. But by turning the colonial narrative on its head, the SEN has erected a framework for understanding the South Asian environmental situation from a critical anti-colonial angle.

One of the central concepts of the SEN is the notion of *common property resources* (CPRs). CPRs are resources that are not individually owned, but individually used in accordance with rules agreed to by one or more local communities. The concept of CPRs does not come from South Asia, but it has entered the environmental debate in the region in a major way. As noted by Henderson, the notion of CPRs is mainly supported by those who believe in democratically or consensually structured popular institutions, and who mistrust state interventions (Henderson 1996). In India, this means that CPR-oriented analysis often resonates with neo-Gandhians, and with scholars who employ a Marxist mode of analysis.

Among the well-known Indian authors employing the SEN and stressing CPRs may be mentioned Anil Agarwal, Madhav Gadgil, Ramachandra Guha, Vandana Shiva and the late Chhatrapati Singh. Several of these scholars are not trained in the social sciences. Agarwal is an engineer, who has been inspired *inter alia* by Gandhi and Gunnar Myrdal. Gadgil is an ecologist interested in mathematical ecology, population biology and human ecology (see Gadgil 1996; Achar 1997). Interestingly, it is these Indian scholars and activists who most clearly try to bridge the gap between the social and the natural sciences.

The SEN and caste

The Standard Environmental Narrative and its connection to evolutionary ecology may be illustrated by recounting the analysis of caste made by Gadgil, Guha and K.C. Malhotra. Following the SEN axiom that strong social institutions protecting the environment have existed on the subcontinent from time immemorial, Gadgil and Malhotra (1994) propose that one such institution is caste. The caste system, they argue, achieves prudence of management by *resource partitioning*, i.e. by authoritatively allocating resources on the basis of caste and hedging access to specific resources with taboos and sanctions. Turning around Leach's argument that caste is a system whereby kinship groups monopolize various economic functions (Leach 1960), Gadgil and Malhotra offer a view of caste as an adaptive institution promoting sustainability by erecting a variety of local non-market barriers to the over-exploitation of the environment. By raising transaction and communication costs, the institution of caste has contained the forces of both market and state in order to secure for local societies a high degree of environmental stability and control. Caste, in other words, has provided the cultural matrix for successful adaptation to the environment.

Gadgil and Malhotra's study of caste has been extended by Gadgil and Guha in their book *This Fissured Land: An Ecological History of India*. In this book from 1992, the authors rewrite Indian history as an essay in social ecology. In the process they foreground indigenous caste-based knowledge to an extent that makes me wonder if they are presenting an idealized version of the past. Is it really true that the caste system – which allows some segments to monopolize strategic knowledge to an extraordinary degree – has been capable of prudently adapting to changing natural circumstances over the centuries (Rahul 1994; Freeman 1998)?

Versatility and constraints of the SEN

The versatility of the SEN also extends in other directions. The affinity of the SEN with Marxism means that modern environmental studies lend themselves to 'naturalization' within subaltern studies. Subaltern studies generally take the form of a critique of the colonial state from the point of view of the marginalized colonial subject. In other words, it is based on the idea of a deep antinomy between state and society. With this background, it is not unnatural that the *Subaltern Studies* series includes several articles about conflicts over the natural environment during British rule. These include David Arnold's study of *adivasi* tribes near

Godavari River in Andhra Pradesh (Arnold 1982), Ramachandra Guha's article on the Kumaun Hills (Guha 1985), and David Hardiman's work on *adivasis* in the Dangs in Gujarat (Hardiman 1994).[2]

As far as India is concerned, the SEN view of history is presently very well established. However, it is increasingly being supplemented by a kindred, but somewhat differently weighted, framework of research. Since the late 1980s, this paradigm has focused our interest on the relative strength, the functional autonomy and the mutual embeddedness of state, society and market. Given the opposition inherent in the SEN between the colonial or post-colonial state and the subordinated civil society, the SEN may well be inscribed within this paradigm. However, due to its subsistence-model of the rural economy, studies in the SEN mode have had little to contribute to the analysis of the market. As Rangarajan has pointed out, much environmentalist thinking and activism in India fails precisely when it comes to 'deeper market forces that may corrode the resource base' (Rangarajan 1996: 2403).

The SEN mode of analysis generally takes a bleak and pessimistic view of the present state of the environment in South Asia and elsewhere. It shares this mood of crisis with the neo-Darwinist perspective referred to initially. In contrast, the 'state–society–market paradigm' is relatively less predicated on the idea of a current crisis. Being 'crisis-neutral' it rather attempts to explain why outcomes vary in different countries or societies. This perspective is common within the discipline of political science, and also lends itself to the analysis of environmental issues.

The present book loosely adheres to a state, society and market framework of analysis. Being conscious of the SEN view of life, the authors of this book vary in their endorsement of the SEN. Thus, the book may be read as a garland of studies critically relating to the SEN mode of analysis, written by scholars based in Europe and North America and focusing on India and Pakistan. The book presents an attempt to expand the SEN by, *inter alia*, a closer attention to the role of market forces in South Asia.

The State and Social Institutions

The first article is by Ann Gold. As her title will indicate, wild pigs used to be the major predators on agricultural fields in the part of Rajasthan which Gold studied. In this respect this area is similar to the rest of the subcontinent (Sukumar 1994), but while in many areas villagers have hunted wild pigs, the pre-independence ruler of the small state in this part of Rajasthan forbade his subjects to hunt pigs. He also took effective steps to limit use of the forests for grazing and wood cutting. Gold's article is woven around villagers' accounts of this princely order, its eventual decline and fall, and the introduction of a more just, but less governable, democratic order. Her article shows that villagers are acutely conscious of the environmental and social trade-offs arising out of political and economic change. Contemporary rural society now remembers the feudal rule as a period with an abundance of wildlife and trees and also as a period of injustice and poverty.

The integration of princely states into India and Pakistan and the subsequent abolition of landlordism in the 1950s, known in India as the Zamindari Abolition, marked the first step in the rise to power of the class of cultivating owner-proprietors. This wave of reform also drastically changed the ownership of the forests, hunting grounds and orchards previously under the control of princes and landlords. On the one hand, it expanded the area of reserved forests under the control of the Forest Department, allowing several national parks to be created. On the other hand, it meant that cultivators could work areas hitherto under extensive landlord management more intensively, while at the same time staking claims on the forest areas over which the Forest Department was gaining control. Gold's paper allows us to follow this process, which has hitherto been strangely neglected.[3]

Gold's research also affords us a vantage point for a closer look at pre-colonial times. In most accounts of environmental change, it is presumed that nineteenth-century colonialism effectively destroyed pre-colonial ways, but in this case the native order came to an end within living memory. The subaltern voices, therefore, speak that much louder and clearer – in a kind of participatory rural evaluation – about the kind of mechanisms which earlier

7

secured prudence, and about the mechanisms which later resulted in environmental crisis.

As Simon Schama has reminded us, landscapes often serve as tableaux of memory (Schama 1995). In his contribution to this volume (chapter 3), Tor Aase looks at landscapes precisely as repositories of collective memories. The case that he discusses provides evidence that village institutions continue to have the strength to devise pragmatic solutions to problems with the allocation of resources, problems which in this specific instance arise from a new hydro-electric scheme. The scheme is one that will make it possible to irrigate previously uncultivated land, thus creating a new and valuable resource. According to Aase, villagers in these mountain areas of Pakistan have responded to this potential conflict situation by using the historical precedent of a royal order relating to porterage duties as a metaphor to determine to whom the newly cultivable land would belong. The new land would belong to those who used to carry royal loads to the area now being converted to agricultural land. Thus, the memory of the royal directive appears to have been read off and back into the landscape to serve as *ratio decidendi* to resolve the issue at hand.

In the parts of Northern Pakistan considered by Aase, British influence was marginal and even the present state is weakly institutionalized. Given the reputation that men in these areas have of taking to the gun easily, the high degree of willingness to seek a compromise begs an explanation. One could argue that the very likelihood of armed conflict may account for the willingness to compromise: the risks of following a confrontational strategy may be too high. However, Aase seeks his explanation by examining environmental perceptions. In the process, he shows us local communities not as conceptually self-sufficient, but as *bricoleurs* in the sense of Lévi-Strauss, making use of apt similes and other abstractions associated with the state to solve specific problems.[4]

Like Aase's contribution, that of Pernille Gooch (chapter 4) is based on intensive fieldwork. Gooch is arguing that where state capacity is weak and corruption rampant, it is right and reasonable to count on the social capital and indigenous knowledge of local communities to manage even national parks. In her study of the pastoral *Van* Gujjar tribe in Uttar Pradesh, she describes the symbiotic relation between this marginalized tribe and an NGO fighting on its behalf. Through its deft handling of the print media, this NGO has invested the tribe with the inherent – yet partly unfolded – capacity to produce a whole range of political, eco-nomical and ecological goods. These assets, it is argued, make it incumbent upon the state to allow the tribe to exercise control over the national park in which it lives for most of the year.

Urban Environments

The subsequent two contributions to the present book turn to urban and industrial pollution. Even though the rate of urbaniza-tion in South Asia has been relatively low, the cities in the region face a host of increasingly grave environmental problems, including air, water and noise pollution. With regard to air pollution, Delhi is now often rated the fourth most polluted city in the world (*Down to Earth* 1996). Equally alarming, the air in Kathmandu and Dhaka is also heavily polluted. As regards water pollution, the wastes produced in the South Asian cities are an increasing hazard to the surrounding countryside. Thus, in 1985 some twenty-nine large cities accounted for almost 90 per cent of the untreated sewage emptied into the Ganges River (Tewari 1987: 194). Kanpur city is one of the worst polluters along the river, passing on the wastes from eighty tanneries and seventy other industrial plants as well 400 million litres of raw sewage. At Varanasi, the river has had a coliform count of 100,000 per 100 ml as against the WHO standard for drinking water of 10 per 100 ml of water (Sampat 1996). The Ganges Action Plan initiated in the mid-1980s may have improved conditions at some sites, and in Kanpur many factories have been closed following a court order. But by any standard the Ganges is highly polluted, and so are many other rivers on the subcontinent.

Already environmental pollution is a major cause of disease and death in South Asia. There is no agreement as to how to measure the economic costs of water, air and soil degradation, but a study relating to India has put the costs at IRs 34,000 crore, the equivalent of US$ 9.7 billion or 4.5 per cent of the GDP in 1992 (Brandon and Hommann 1996). According to this estimate, water-borne diseases alone account for a loss of IRs 19,950 crore. Anil Agarwal has criticized the study for underestimating the true cost of environmental degradation (Agarwal 1996). In any case, the figures convey a clear message regarding the state of India's rural and urban environments.

The Garden City òf Madras dealt with by Håkan Tropp in chapter 5 bears witness to the abject neglect of pollution control characterizing the subcontinent as a whole. However, neighbour-hood groups in Madras (now Chennai) have formed voluntary associations to collect and remove garbage. Several of these organizations have a middle-class base. Possessing a degree of social capital, they have been able to negotiate with the civic authorities regarding garbage collection and cleaning of the two main waterways in the city.

The contribution by Petter Lindstad (chapter 6) about the production of pesticides also deals with urban and industrial pollution. The difference between the two articles is that in Lindstad's case, the workers, who suffer poisoning by pesticides, have not been able to press demands regarding occupational health and safety. In his article, Lindstad graphically portrays the pesticide industry in the 450 km 'Golden Corridor' between Ahmedabad and Bombay (now Mumbai). Most of the pesticide factories are licensed, and some have tie-ups with multinationals. Laws governing the production of pesticides in India should apply, but in reality they have been flouted. The High Court in Gujarat has taken steps to control industrial pollution, but as Lindstad's analysis shows, there is a long way to go before the state will be able to monitor and control pollution in this area. It is worth noting that in the case of Gujarat, the institution that has intervened is the state High Court. This indicates that inter-vention from the centre is not a necessary precondition for reform. In Tamil Nadu and Delhi, however, it has been mainly the Supreme Court, and not the respective High Courts, which has exercised a degree of judicial activism to control polluters. Thanks mainly to the judiciary, around 10,000 industrial units in India were 'either shut down, warned, asked to relocate or given an ultimatum to clean up' in 1996 (Halarnkar and Koppikar 1996; see also Iyer 1995).

Classes and Stakeholders

Currently, the world's population is nearing 6 billion. By 2020 it will be around 7.1 or 7.4 billion, and by 2050, the population may be anywhere between 7.9 billion and 11.9 billion, or more (Catley-Carlson 1995: 60). South Asia has one of the major concentrations of people living under conditions of poverty. India, Pakistan and Bangladesh are among the ten countries with the largest number of poor people. India is home to about a quarter of all poor people on earth, and a third or more of the absolute poor.

Since the late 1960s, food production in South Asia has increased rapidly thanks to the Green Revolution. Whether the South Asian output of food crops will keep pace with its growing population is not certain. As regards India, the International Food Policy Research Institute believes that it may be able to export both rice and wheat by 2020, while Worldwatch Institute believes that India will have to import 45 million tonnes of cereals by the year 2030. Pakistan will probably have a food shortage for many years ahead. The key question remains: 'How can people in developing countries achieve a decent living from the land without destroying it?' (Wilson 1992: 309). This question has been intensively discussed since the publication of the Brundtland report (World Commission on Environment and Development 1987). A number of scholars have forcefully argued that poverty 'traps' the poor in a vicious circle, forcing poor people to degrade their environment. This hypothesis directly contrasts with the SEN, which holds that rural communities, including poor rural communities, are likely to be much better stewards of natural resources than private sector companies or the state, because 'ecosystem people' would be the first to suffer from the consequences of any imprudence on their part.[5]

In chapter 7, Rabindra Nath Chakraborty presents a model of rural resource use and abuse based on individual calculations and class positions. He concludes that the rural rich are in a better position to eschew negative environmental practices, but that they more often degrade their environment in order to cash in on new economic opportunities. By contrast, rural poor have little option but to resort to abusive resource use. Unless the poor are reached by poverty alleviation programmes, or otherwise brought out of their present dependency, rural poverty will continue to be a factor in the destruction of the environment.

This problem is further illuminated by Are Knudsen (chapter 8), who details why local communities of stakeholders enter into environmentally destructive deals with forest contractors. In some valleys in Northern Pakistan, villagers, or village leaders, sell their shares in the local forest to forest contractors. This significantly reduces the income which would otherwise accrue to the village communities, if the process of harvesting went according to auction rules. Knudsen explains this apparently self-defeating behaviour by the need on the part of the villagers for immediate monetary benefits and for risk minimization in an environment where the government machinery is perceived to be unlikely to perform according to rules. The role of contractors in subcontinental forestry history has been touched upon by others, including Tucker (1979: 283) and Guha (1983; 1994b: 33). By integrating an actor-oriented approach with an institutional analysis, Knudsen adds to their discussion significantly.

From Colonialism to Democracy

In chapter 9, the focus shifts to one of the main institutional actors, i.e. the colonial state. In his paper on the management and operation of irrigation canals in Punjab, David Gilmartin shows that the British rulers acted as if state and society were separate worlds, each governed and governable by its own logic – only to find that they were not. Over the years, the state repeatedly changed its policy on how to define and relate to 'the irrigating public' in the Punjab. While authors adhering to the SEN see the state as exterior to society, Gilmartin's study, based on a close reading of colonial archives, shows the inevitability of the state–society imbrication in the case of irrigation schemes: the state in Punjab not only framed new rules, it intervened in the game, too.

One of the most important new rules in the history of the subcontinent is democracy. In this book, the contributions by Ann Gold and Staffan Lindberg both help us to increase our understanding of the environmental impact of formal democracy. Most often, this issue has been discussed at local *panchayat* level (see e.g. Sinha and Herring 1993: 1428), but Lindberg's study (chapter 10) deals with mass mobilization over much wider areas, and the political response to these movements. In brief, Lindberg details the relation between technological change, political mobilization, democracy and the environment by giving a blow-by-blow account of a series of campaigns launched by the Tamil Nadu irrigating public for lower electricity tariffs. Without a strong scientific establishment able to direct state policy in an ecologically sound direction, political parties operating in a democratic set-up contributed to the over-exploitation of that vital resource, groundwater, by deciding to provide electricity for energized wells free of charge. Lindberg is not the first to have pointed out the possible negative environmental consequences of democracy, but his contribution starkly actualizes the need for an effective policy narrative about environmental risks to temper what he refers to as 'competitive populism'.

As the reader will discover by comparing Pernille Gooch's article with Ronald Herring's, this anthology does not present a uniform view. While Gooch sees little role for the state, Herring acknowledges that there is a case for state property in nature and for state regulation of trade and industry. However, he shares Gooch's rather pessimistic view of the *capacity* of the Government of India to put such a regime of control in place. The lack of state capacity is clearly evident in the failure of the Indian authorities to apprehend the ivory and sandalwood smuggler Veerappan operating in Karnataka and Tamil Nadu for years (*India Today* 1996), in their failure to bring to book Sansar Chand, a key person in the trade in endangered animals, including tigers (Swami 1995), and in their failure to bring the Jammu and Kashmir Wildlife Protection Act in line with the rest of the country (Vinayak 1997). As time passes, the groups engaged in tiger poaching seem to have become even more daring, which leads to a further decimation of the Indian tiger population (Thapa 1997).

In his exhaustive article, Ronald Herring argues that the issue of state capacity is all the more crucial in the present context of liberalization and decentralization. Though decentralization is often seen as a good and efficient way to structure a polity under conditions of democracy (Crook and Manor 1995: 311), it may have mixed environmental consequences under conditions of economic liberalization. Thus, decentralization may lead to increased competition between provinces or states, each of which may want to relax or ignore environmental standards to attract investments and enhance revenue. Herring's argument contrasts with that of the World Bank, which tends to argue that developing countries do not generally try to attract 'dirty' industries by lowering their environmental standards. The main reason for this, according to a World Bank study, is that environmental costs are a small share of output value (World Bank 1992: 67). Because South Asian countries are currently opening up to private and international investment, the issue of state capacity and autonomy is likely to remain central (see Bidwai 1996).

Battlefields

Nature is everywhere evaluated in terms of the benefits it produces, as well as the costs and risks it imposes. Because costs and benefits are not equally shared, because risks are hard to assess and agree on, and because ethical, economical and ecological goods are difficult to compare, nature inevitably becomes a battleground of knowledge and action. In addition there is the timescale problem alluded to above: The fact that our natural environment has a much longer history than mere human history makes it extremely difficult to put into proper perspective contemporary human concerns, which are transitory as measured by geological time but vital for living individuals (see Gould 1993; Driver and Chapman 1996). To compound the difficulties, serious doubts can be raised about the empirical basis of theories relating to the environment. This applies both to the social sciences and the natural sciences. Thus, even the neo-Darwinist paradigm, which clearly aspires to the status of 'hard' science, may rest on an uncertain empirical basis as regards its estimates of the decline in biodiversity. The present volume will not settle these issues. Nevertheless, by exploring specific themes, such as the limits of popular stakeholding, the challenges to state capacity and the environmental consequences of democracy and decentralization, the following studies will make the reader better armed for the battle![6]

Acknowledgements

I would like to thank Tor Aase, R.N. Chakraborty, Robert Cribb, Harish Gaonkar, Kate Toft Madsen and Sanjeev Prakash for their comments.

Notes

1. See Guha (1994a: 1–4) on the marginal role social scientists have played in social ecology.

2. The symbiosis between the subalternists and environmental historians is not unquestioned. In his review of one of the later volumes of the *Subaltern Studies* series, Ramachandra Guha has been critical of what he feels is an increasingly elitist orientation of the subalternists (Guha 1995).

3. See, however, Farmer's account of agricultural colonization (1974), Jewitt on Bihar in the 1950s (1995: 79), Poffenberger (1996: 149–53) on a royal felling craze in the 1950s West Bengal, Jodha's studies on the effect of economic and political reform (1986), and Madsen (1996: 261, n. 21).

4. The capacity of local institutions in these areas to act as brokers of compromise has also been noted by the Aga Khan Rural Support Programme (World Bank 1987). For an analysis of the evolution of legal precedents, see Heiner (1986).

5. For the concept of ecosystem people, see e.g. Gadgil (1996: 346). For a critique of the poverty trap thesis, see Prakash (1997).

6. Preliminary versions of this introduction were presented at a seminar at the Nordic Institute of Asian Studies on 19 March 1996; at a conference on 'Civil Society, Public Sphere, and Organizational Behaviour: Approaches to the Study of State–Society Relations in the Non-Western World' in Oslo, 22–23 April 1996; and at a workshop on 'Organizational Cultures and Administrative Practices in Institutional Development in South Asia' in Lund, 28–30 May 1996.

References

Achar, K. Prabhakar (1997) 'Peeping into Western Ghats for Life Resources', *Times of India*, 19 January, p. 2.

Agarwal, Anil (1996) 'Pay-offs to Progress', *Down to Earth*, 15 October, pp. 31–39.

Arnold, David (1982) 'Rebellious Hillmen, 1839–1924', in Ranajit Guha (ed.) *Subaltern Studies I*, Delhi: Oxford University Press, pp. 88–142.

Bidwai, Praful (1996). 'India's Grave Environmental Crisis. Dangers of Neo-liberal Industrialism', *Frontline*, 29 November 1996, pp. 103–104.

Brandon, Carter and Kirsten Hommann (1996) *The Cost of Inaction: Valuing the Economy-Wide Cost of Environmental Degradation in India*, Washington DC: The World Bank.

Catley-Carlson, Margaret (1995) 'The World's Population in Flux: Issues and Prescriptions to 2020', *A 2020 Vision for Food, Agriculture, and the Environment*. Conference hosted by the International Food Policy Research Institute and the National Geographic Society, Washington, DC, 13–15 June, pp. 59–66.

Crook, R.C. and James Manor (1995) 'Democratic Decentralization and Institutional Performance: Four Asian and African Experiences Compared', *Journal of Commonwealth and Comparative Politics*, vol. 33, no. 3, pp. 309–34.

Down to Earth (1996) 'Smog Inc.', 15 November, pp. 26–39.

Driver, Thackwray S. and Graham P. Chapman (eds) (1996) *Time-scales and Environmental Change*, London and New York: Routledge.

Farmer, B.H. (1974) *Agricultural Colonization in India since Independence*, The Royal Institute of International Affairs, London: Oxford University Press.

Freeman, Rich (1998) 'Folk-Models of the Forest Environment in Highland Malabar', in Roger Jeffery (ed.), *The Social Construction of Indian Forests*, Edinburgh: Centre for South Asian Studies and New Delhi: Manohar, pp. 55–78.

Gadgil, Madhav (1996) 'Managing Biodiversity', in Kevin J. Gaston (ed.), *Biodiversity. A Biology of Numbers and Difference*, Oxford: Blackwell Science, pp. 345–66.

—— and Ramachandra Guha (1992) *This Fissured Land. An Ecological History of India*, Delhi: Oxford University Press.

—— and Ramachandra Guha (1995) *Ecology and Equity. The Use and Abuse of Nature in Contemporary India*, London and New York: Routledge.

—— and K.C. Malhotra (1994 [1983]). 'The Ecological Significance of Caste', in Ramachandra Guha (ed.), *Social Ecology, Oxford in India Readings in Sociology and Social Anthropology*, Delhi: Oxford University Press, pp. 27–41.

Gould, Stephen Jay (1993) 'Modified Grandeur. A Crumbling Pedestal Supports Our Arrogant View of Life', *Natural History* vol. 102, no. 3, pp. 14–20.

Guha, Ramachandra (1983) 'Forestry in British and Post-British India: A Historical Analysis', *Economic and Political Weekly*, 29 October, pp. 1882–96.

—— (1985) 'Forestry and Social Protest in Kumaun', in Ranajit Guha (ed.), *Subaltern Studies IV*, Delhi: Oxford University Press, pp. 54–100.

—— (ed.) (1994a) *Social Ecology, Oxford in India Readings in Sociology and Social Anthropology*, Delhi: Oxford University Press.

—— (1994b) 'Fighting for the Forest. State Forestry and Social Change in Tribal India', in Oliver Mendelsohn and Upendra Baxi (eds), *The Rights of Subordinated Peoples*, Delhi: Oxford University Press, pp. 20–37.

—— (1995) 'Subaltern and Bhadralok Studies', *Economic and Political Weekly*, 19 August 1995, pp. 2056–58. (Review of *Subaltern Studies VIII: Essays in Honour of Ranajit Guha* edited by David Arnold and David Hardiman, and of *Event, Memory, Metaphor: Chauri Chaura, 1922–1992* by Shahid Amin.)

Halarnkar, Samar and Smruti Koppikar (1996) 'More Pain than Gain', *India Today*, 15 July, pp. 48–52.

Hardiman, David (1994) 'Power in the Forest: The Dangs, 1820–1940', in David Arnold and David Hardiman (eds) *Subaltern Studies VIII. Essays in Honour of Ranajit Guha*, Delhi: Oxford University Press, pp. 89–147.

Heiner, Ronald A. (1986) 'Imperfect Decisions and the Law: On the Evolution of Legal Precedent and Rules', *The Journal of Legal Studies*, vol. 15, no. 2, pp. 227–61.

Henderson, Carol (1996) 'Claiming Common Property: The Experience of Organizations in India'. Paper prepared for the 25th Annual Conference on South Asian Studies, Madison, Wisconsin, 18 October.

Hoben, Allan (1998) 'The Role of Development Discourse in the Construction of Environmental Policy in Africa', in Henrik Secher Marcussen and Signe Arnfred (eds), *Concepts and Metaphors: Ideologies, Narratives and Myths in Development Discourse*, Occasional paper 19, International Development Studies, Roskilde University, pp. 122–145.

India Today (1996) 'Still at Large', 15 November, p. 14.

Iyer, Meera (1995) 'Blood on Its Hands', *Down to Earth*, 31 October, pp. 22–23.

Jeffery, Roger, Nandini Sundar, Pradeep Tharakan, Neeraj Peter and Abha Mishra (1996) 'A Move from Minor to Major: Competing Discourses of Non-Timber Forest Products in India'. Paper presented at the 14th European Conference on Modern South Asian Studies, Copenhagen, 21–24 August.

Jewitt, Sarah L. (1995) 'Europe's "Others"? Forestry Policy and Practices in Colonial and Postcolonial India', *Environment and Planning D: Society and Space*, vol. 13, pp. 67–90.

Jodha, N.S. (1986) 'Common Property Resources and Rural Poor in Dry Regions of India', *Economic and Political Weekly*, vol. 21, no. 27, 5 July, pp. 1169–81.

Leach, E.R. (1960) 'What Should We Mean by Caste?' In E.R. Leach (ed.), *Aspects of Caste in South India, Ceylon and Northwest Pakistan*, Cambridge Papers in Social Anthropology, vol. 2, pp. 1–10.

Madsen, Stig Toft (1996) *State, Society and Human Rights in South Asia*, New Delhi: Manohar.

Myers, Norman (1990) 'The Biodiversity Challenge: Expanded Hot-Spots Analysis', *The Environmentalist*, vol. 10, no. 4, pp. 243–56.

Poffenberger, Mark (1996) 'The Struggle for Forest Control in the Jungle Mahals of West Bengal, 1750–1990', in Mark Poffenberger and Betsy McGean (eds), *Village Voices, Forest Choices. Joint Forest Management in India*, Delhi: Oxford University Press, pp. 132–61.

Prakash, Sanjeev (1997) 'Poverty and Environmental Linkages in Mountains and Uplands: Reflections on the "Poverty Trap" Thesis', CREED Working Paper no. 12, International Institute for the Environment and Development, London and Institute for Environmental Studies, Amsterdam.

Rahul (1994) 'Looking Back in Wonder, in Search of Our Ecological Roots', *Economic and Political Weekly*, 30 July, pp. 2006–09.

Rangarajan, Mahesh (1996) 'The Politics of Ecology. The Debate on Wildlife and People in India, 1970–95', *Economic and Political Weekly*, special number, (September), pp. 2391–409.

Sampat, Payal (1996) 'The River Ganges' Long Decline', *World Watch* (July/August), pp. 25–32.

Schama, Simon (1995) *Landscape and Memory*, London: Harper Collins.

Sinha, Subir and Ronald Herring (1993) 'Common Property, Collective Action and Ecology', *Economic and Political Weekly*, 3–10 July, pp. 1425–32.

Sivaramakrishnan, K. (1995) 'Colonialism and Forestry in India: Imagining the Past in Present Politics', *Comparative Studies in Society and History*, vol. 37, no. 1, pp. 3–40.

Sukumar, R. (1994) 'Wildlife–Human Conflict in India: An Ecological and Social Perspective', in Ramachandra Guha (ed.), *Social Ecology, Oxford in India Readings in Sociology and Social Anthropology*, Delhi: Oxford University Press, pp. 302–17.

Swami, Praveen (1995) 'Wildlife Villain, Sansar Chand, North India's Veerappan?', *Frontline*, 25 August, pp. 92–94.

Tewari, D.N. (1987) *Victims of Environmental Crisis*, Dehra Dun: EBD Educational Private Ltd.

Thapa, Vijay Jung (1997) 'Tigers. Predator as Prey', *India Today*, 29 December, pp. 34–35.

Tucker, Richard (1979) 'Forest Management and Imperial Politics: Thana District, Bombay, 1823–1887', *The Indian Economic and Social History Review*, vol. 16, no. 3, pp. 273–300.

Vinayak, Ramesh (1997) 'Trapped in Loopholes', *India Today International*, 15 September, pp. 44–45.

Wilson, Edward O. (1992) *The Diversity of Life*, Cambridge, Mass.: Harvard University Press.

World Bank (1987) *The Aga Khan Rural Support Program in Pakistan, A Second Interim Evaluation*, Washington, DC: A World Bank Operations Evaluation Study.

—— (1992) *World Development Report 1992. Development and the Environment*, Oxford: Oxford University Press.

World Commission on Environment and Development (1987) *Our Common Future*, Oxford: Oxford University Press.

2

From Wild Pigs to Foreign Trees: Oral Histories of Environmental Change in Rajasthan

Ann Grodzins Gold

Preface: Memories and Histories

[T]here is a key mediating term between individual and society, and it is memory (Tonkin 1992: 98).

Memory cannot be strictly individual, inasmuch as it is symbolic and hence intersubjective. Nor can it be literally collective, since it is not superorganic but embodied (Boyarin 1994: 26).

How, then, do we *do* an ethnography of the historical imagination? How do we contextualize the fragments of human worlds, redeeming them without losing their fragile uniqueness and ambiguity? (Comaroff and Comaroff 1992: 31)

In December 1992 I went to Rajasthan to study cultural constructions of the environment. My specific focus was to be the intertwining of rural North Indian Hindu practice with agriculture and herding. I returned to a place, Ghatiyali in Ajmer District, where I had lived over a decade earlier (Gold 1988). In imagining this new fieldwork I conjectured that rituals surrounding production (planting, harvest, livestock health and so forth) in the harsh, semi-arid environment would reveal something about the ways religious ideas conditioned people's treatment and conceptions of their natural surroundings. I hoped to take recent insights on the mutual infusion, or fusion, of praxis and meaning to an understanding of a farming community's ecological relationships.[1] However, as I struggled to find the right people to ask the right questions, I soon discovered that the ritual cycles I had thought to study were in a particularly accelerated transitional flux – a flux intrinsic to and conditioned by broader historical patterns.[2] Thus I found myself increasingly gripped by narratives of change.

I knew vaguely from casual comments people had made during my earlier residence in this area, and from the general literature on deforestation and the decline of common property resources in Rajasthan, that the landscape had undergone radical transformations within the last half-century, and thus within living memories.[3] I recalled persons telling me in 1980 of a dense, dark and frightening forest inhabited by dangerous wild animals where now we saw scrubby, barren, largely open land.[4] I had found this hard to imagine, and paid it little attention then.[5]

In 1993, hard in search of ideas about nature, but a little baffled by where to find them, my closest collaborator in the village, Bhoju Ram Gujar, and I began to ask old people about the vanished trees.[6] In the memories and histories our questions evoked, we encountered a consistent and powerful discourse of environmental, agricultural, social, religious and moral change. This vision is ecological in its sensitivity to the web-like interconnectedness of concurrent transformations; historical, in its attentiveness to sequence, causality and passage; emotional in that linked transformations in polity and landscape engage human feelings intensely.[7]

Recent decades have seen a rapprochement of anthropology with history, for which memory is pivotal.[8] This essay is not just based on, but constructed from oral histories elicited in interviews with aging North Indian villagers. Each of its four parts takes recounted memories as source and substance.[9] In these memories environmental change interweaves with changes in politics, economy, society and religion to reveal richly textured, if partial, histories of a rather small place. I stress the partial nature of the accounts that follow for two reasons. First, I have not yet done any comparative archival work that might enrich or offer alternative perspectives to these oral narratives based on memories. Second, even for the oral narratives I only am able to transmit a few voices from among those I consulted, and those I consulted are only a few.

1. **Wild pigs**[10] – I begin with a tale serendipitously critical to my
   fieldwork as hearing it the first time made me realize
   (though not immediately) that I had accidentally begun to
   'do' oral history. I subsequently heard the same event retold
   repeatedly, but in different ways. I am prepared to argue that
   it is paradigmatic for the rememberers, who are its tellers, as
   much as a prod to the outsider-listener. I'll offer you two radically divergent versions of this tale of 'The Farmers, the Pigs,
   and the King'.
2. **Politics of deforestation** – I turn to the ways villagers today
   explain the political and pragmatic causes of deforestation,
   as they live with its consequences.
3. **Foreign trees** – Over the last few decades, reforestation projects
   have made the dominant tree species around Ghatiyali an
   aesthetically unpleasing, stubby mimosa locally dubbed 'foreign *bambūl*' (*vilāyatī bambūl*), and often simply referred to as
   'foreign'. This chapter segment concerns the advent of foreign trees and the ways they are emblematic of other kinds of
   invasions and adjustments.
4. **Moral ecologies for the *Kali Yuga*** – I consider in conclusion
   the various ways people associate loss of indigenous tree cover
   with a perceived change in climate, a deterioration in interpersonal relationships and divine anger. I note that these histories, in that they are resonant with ancient texts on the one
   hand, and modern ecological activist ideologies on the other,
   might suggest a kind of moral ecology for the *Kali Yuga*.[11]

Wild Pigs

Feudal culture in the Indian subcontinent also waxed fat on
signs systematized into codes of authority and deferential
response (Ranajit Guha 1983: 37).

[A]lternative meanings, alternative values, alternative versions
of a people's history are available as a potential challenge to the
dominant (Roseberry 1989: 27).

[T]he oral traditions neither spoke from, nor envisioned, a field
free of power. But while speaking the language of hierarchy and
dependent relations, they made it dissonant, ... (Prakash 1991:
147).

I must briefly preface the first wild pig story with a little information particular to its setting. For while many of the experiences
and images of change that unfolded in our interviews undoubt-
edly reflect patterns existing in many parts of Rajasthan and
throughout North India, it was often hard to keep this in mind.
As stories of Ghatiyali's past unfolded, they made it appear unique:
the stories of a singular place, its named localities and inhabitants.

A key player in Ghatiyali's remembered past was a strong
personality: the *thākur* or local ruler, Vansh Pradip Singh. In our
interviews, he is usually referred to as 'the court' (*darbār*) – a term
of reference commonly applied to rulers of big and little
kingdoms in Rajasthan. Vansh Pradip Singh reigned over the
very small kingdom of Sawar and its twenty-seven subordinate
villages (including Ghatiyali), for more than thirty years, from
his ascension to the throne in 1914, until his death in 1947.[12]
This well-remembered *darbār* had a strong interest in all kinds of
religious actions, and was a fervent protector of the forest and of
wildlife (Mathur 1977). Indeed, everyone old enough to remember
him told with varying degrees of bitterness, astonishment and
admiration, how he had scattered popcorn for the wild pigs who
destroyed his subjects' crops, and caused persons who harmed
any forest animals or cut reserved trees, to be ignominiously
beaten and fined. Some described his authority and its sanctions
as the 'Rule of the shoe'. An untouchable sweeper was employed
in the Fort to administer a 'shoe-beating' to any who defied the
court – including pig poachers and tree cutters. His implement
was an oversized embroidered leather shoe with bells on its
pointed toe. Any infractor's abject humiliation would, I was told,
thus be made public knowledge, as the little bells rang.

In my earlier fieldwork I had lived with Rajputs and spent
much of my time with religious experts; I learned my history out
of a book published by the royal family. Thus, when I first spoke
with Kalyan Mali about the formerly wooded hills, and the wildlife that thrived there in the past, I had no sense of the oppressions
of former times. I knew almost nothing of this. Kalyanji was
almost always to be found sitting on the stoop in front of his

house, which was quite close to Bhoju Ram's house. He wore thick glasses held together at the nose with soiled adhesive tape. In his eighties, he was a little deaf as well as dim-sighted. The tale he told us on 3 January 1993 emerged with minimal probing – evoked by a simple question about the jungle that used to be. It was a spontaneous, free association on the topic of wild animals. Judging from the way he spoke and the way his small audience responded, it was a story he had told more than once. Not only did he use the textured, rhythmic speech style of a storyteller, but one of the bystanders – Bhoju Ram's father, Sukh Devji (referred to below as SD), who was of the same generation – spontaneously and rapidly assumed the role of *hūṅkar* or respondent, a role crucial to any non-musical oral performance in the village (see Gold 1992: 21–22). Sukh Devji's occasional promptings contributed substantially to the tale's lucidity.

Kalyan Mali's wild pig story

AG: Do you remember the wild animals, tigers and every-thing?

BG: She is saying, did you see wild animals, tigers, wild pigs, lions, panthers? [Bhoju thus cues him to 'pigs'.]

KM: I saw lots of them, I saw them and I chased them away.

BG: Now where have they gone?

KM: There were so many wild pigs … and we made a com-plaint: 'Come with me, to see.' He [later to be identified as one of the king's agents, a man of the merchant caste named Jivan Lalji] went over there [that is, to KM's field] to see, and the pigs had eaten up everything.

SD: They ate up everything.

KM: Our small piece of land near the village …

SD: A piece of land near the village …

KM: Yes, a fine piece of land, they ate everything up, and afterwards he went along the road. Who? The king's agent [*kāmdār*, RSK: a large *jāgīrdār*, *seṭh* or king's *prabandhkartā*], and he put his hand on my shoulder [this is rude, pre-

sumptuous] ... he put his hand on my shoulder, and I said,
'All night, I chase them and chase them again, but they eat
everything up, and aren't you ashamed, you ... ?'

SD: He had no pity.

KM: That Jivan Lalji. I spent the whole night guarding
against wild pigs. 'Aren't you ashamed? You don't listen to
me.' I got angry and shouted at him. I said, 'Half the
women in the village are widows [*rāṇḍ*; unspoken: because
the men have to sleep in the fields because of the pigs.
There may also be a suggestion that women alone in the
house are tempted to infidelities, the other common meaning of *rāṇḍ* being 'slut'. The use of this term heightens the
drama considerably.]

SD: Oh ho!

KM: In my Ghatiyali.

SD: They're widows!

KM: And only the women who sleep in the fields with their
husbands are auspiciously married (*suhāg*) ... So, talking
in this way we went and sat down at Four Arms Temple.[13]
... We gathered, and sat ... the village people gathered in
a group. We said, 'Our bodies are suffering.'

SD: Yes, our bodies were suffering, and we gathered in a
group.

KM: We were suffering, and we were gathered, and then
'Let us have our justice, this sorrow should be decreased.'

SD: Oh ho!

KM: And just at this moment, *Jaganāth Lakāro* came by,
carrying his mattress.

SD: On his head, Oh ho, good. [This is now comical.]

KM: And his wife was going with him, walking along behind.

SD: She was going.

KM: They were going to protect the crops. 'Look!' And
they looked.

SD: Such was our condition.

KM: Yes, such was our condition. [The agent said:] 'So, tomorrow, you come to Sawar.'

SD: Good.

KM: Come to Sawar, and tell the Court (*darbār*). On the next day ... this was the tenth ... Tejaji's tenth.[14] Next day was the eleventh, and they went over there.

SD: They [a large group] went to Sawar.

KM: They went, but [the king said] 'How can I? Today is the eleventh, and I don't hold court, today, I have none.'[15] [Here the *darbār* briefly holds the moral high ground with his Eleventh Fast about which his subjects have forgotten; or is he just obviously stalling for time?]

SD: 'I can't see them, how could I see them?'

KM: 'I can't see you, so come tomorrow.'

SD: 'Come tomorrow.'

KM: So, two hundred people were there, had come there. But later, the next day, just five or ten chief people, leaders ...

SD: ... went.

KM: Went, and so they went, the next day, the clients. And he said, 'Let the *public[16] stay below ...

SD: Oh ho.

KM: 'And five or seven leaders may come.' [It was explained to me later that the *darbār* mistakenly thinks the entire group of two hundred has come again. He is misled by the leaders so that he continues to believe this, and his being thus duped adds to their triumph.]

SD: They came.

KM: They came. So, five or seven leaders went, and he [the king] said, 'I fell from the sky and the earth caught me, the earth caught me, and I have no children, nothing at all ...' [This is a phrase straight out of epic poetry; it may mean that one is detached from families in a religiously superior way, like a renouncer; or it may mean that one is pathetically alone, as helpless as an orphan, without recourse.

26

For an example of this built-in ambiguity, see Gold (1992: 196): 'You were thrown down from the sky and caught by Earth Mother.']

SD: Oh ho.

KM: 'And I am lame' [the *darbār*'s biography tells us he once received a bullet wound in the foot, in a hunting accident].

SD: Good.

KM: 'And … spreading from village to village, my … '

SD: His bad name (*badnām*) was spreading.

KM: … was spreading. 'What do you want?'

SD: Oh ho.

KM: 'Go, ask the public. You ask the others: "What do you want?" Then I'll take food and water, but not before.' [Here again, the *darbār* is represented deploying his religious virtue and attempting to establish both sympathy and power through refusing food – the time-honoured strategy used by Gandhi – while his people are troubled.]

So I went back for a little while, to the portal [pretending to consult with the non-existent public], and then I went back and said, "The *public has this to say, 'Let us kill them!'"

'Well, fine! These are my subjects. But don't give me a bad name, don't let my bad name be heard.'

SD: 'My bad name would be heard.'

KM: 'I would get a bad name. But all right, sure, kill! But don't harm the wood, for which I will punish, don't cut the trees or destroy anything else.'

So the very next day, the people of the village rushed out in a hurry, and in one day they killed ninety animals.

SD: Ninety.

KM: Ninety, killed in one day. And those that were born in the rainy season …

SD: The newborn piglets, the babies …

KM: The babies couldn't be counted, but on the next day we went and killed sixty, and ...

SD: Good, everybody killed a pig.

KM: We killed them, and our suffering was decreased. And the Chasta Brahmin said, 'The pigs are our enemies,' so even the Brahmin killed a piglet.

The nuances of this telling – which I have had both to condense and annotate excessively in order to make it accessible – are rich and subtle. The characters and speeches reported from approximately fifty years back are surely stylized, but acutely so. The insufferable insolence of the king's agent is portrayed with a single brush stroke when he claps his hand familiarly on the angry farmer's shoulder. The king's agents – as many other interviews were to show – were easy to hate. They were the ones who exploited the people intimately on a day-to-day basis. By contrast, except for rare moments such as the one in this story, the *darbār* usually appears remote.

The *darbār*'s strategic and complicated pose of full authority, yet near-abject humility – as Kalyan Mali describes it – deserves some reflection. He speaks as if he inhabits 'legend' rather than 'history', describing himself in terms appropriate to a helpless orphan or world-renouncer. Kalyanji's portrait of villagers' interactions with Vansh Pradip Singh projects a mixture of gleeful trickery and genuine pathos. The *darbār* is not without majesty and principles, yet he is palpably self-inflated, clearly dupable, and possibly pitiable.

It was this interview, which took place only a few weeks after my arrival in Rajasthan, that set us thinking about ways in which a history of trees and wild animals in Ghatiyali is intricately bound up with a history of royalty and of resistance to its often unreasonable power – a power which nonetheless protected the trees.[17] The *darbār* wants to maintain a wildlife preserve to uphold his reputation (and of course to secure his own hunting pleasure). The people want to save their crops and their own dignity. The mattress on the head, and the wife trailing behind, are images of utter indignity. Thus clashes are, as usual, not merely over power, or means of subsistence (though both are evidently salient), but also over coded signs and the feelings they evoke.

Kalyan Mali's wild pig story was the beginning of the somewhat sporadic and rarely linear attempts by Bhoju and myself, over the months that followed, to understand the political, economic, social and moral dimensions of environmental change. From this day we grew ever more deeply involved in the past and its web of relationships with the present.

For many months we concentrated our interviews among the majority castes of agriculturists and pastoralists – Gujars, Malis, Lodas, Regars and Chamars – because of their direct work with the land. What began as a collage of memories gathered in bits and pieces over the months between January and July gradually revealed patterns as a still patchy canvas of history. As my research period neared its close, we initiated, somewhat too late, a concerted effort to include diverse perspectives in our historical vision, seeking out senior persons belonging to smaller caste groups: Brahmins, shopkeepers, carpenters and potters. Many small vignettes combine as scenes of a larger social drama; many different voices offer a surprisingly consistent picture of pre-democratic environment and society. Nonetheless, caste identity, economic status and gender difference evidently inform accounts, and now and then give rise to clashing colours, conflicting memories and double exposures.[18] Then 'contested history' – the trendy term – is fleshed out in real people's words and lives. For Ghatiyali, this phenomenon emerged nowhere as vividly as in another interview, which elicited another wild pig story.

In our investigation of the relationships among farmers, herders, rulers and the changing landscape, we had deliberately avoided talking with members of the Rajput caste – the former power-holders. The few attempts we made were disappointing; our interviewees were evasive and defensive. Worst of all, Bhoju felt our topic of inquiry inevitably saddened them, brought pain to their faces. He was reluctant to remind these still proud persons of their heavy losses.[19]

Moreover, I had been privately advised by several friends specifically not to raise some of our concerns with Rajputs. For example, Kalyan Mali's pig story, I was told by another man who had been present at the January telling, would disturb members of the royal family (from whom my family and I were renting our home). 'Don't play it for them, or let them see the transcript,' he warned in earnest.[20]

However, one day at the end of June, at my urging, we went to visit Himmat Singh, a retired school-teacher with whose family I had established an amicable relationship. Himmat Singh's father and uncle were commonly understood to be the illegitimate sons of the tragically 'childless' Vansh Pradip Singh. Moreover, they had been two of the Court's most prominent agents (*kāmdār*) in the last decades before Independence, and figured prominently in many stories of those days. Their mother was a *Darogā* – a member of the 'royal servant' caste, whose women were traditionally sexually available to Rajput men, thus producing royal but disinherited children.

Bhoju Ram felt a certain diffidence in this household, and I took a greater role in questioning than usual. Himmat Singh, in his schoolmaster Hindi so different from Kalyan Mali's dialect, gave us the Rajput party line on the good old days: 'The *darbār* and the farmers had a relationship just like that of father to son (*pitra-pūtra*).' Finally I came round to asking Himmat Singh about the wild pigs. And he, without excessive urging, began to narrate a story:

Himmat Singh's wild pig story

HS: So, the people were in great difficulty, the wild pigs were destroying the fields. So the people gathered together, and all went to the *darbār*, they went to the fort. [Around here, HS falls into a performative, storytelling style, just as Kalyan Mali did.] Having gone to the fort ...

The *darbār* said, 'What's the problem, people?'

And they said [Himmat Singh drops his voice here, seems almost to whisper, perhaps evoking the extreme respect of subjects to ruler], 'Well it's like this, there are many wild pigs ... '

He called four or five men to him, and said, 'What is the matter?'

'Sir, this is the matter … '

He said, 'People, if you didn't have me you wouldn't have pigs either, nor would the jungle remain … ' So he told them he would not count what was destroyed by the pigs [when assessing the grain tax on their fields].

[I suddenly realize I have just heard what began as the same story Kalyan Mali told, but with a different ending.]

AG [excitedly]: What? He didn't accept what the people said, he forbade killing the pigs anyway?

HS: Yes, he accepted *dharma*. Just like we give grain to pigeons, he gave grain to pigs. What he did was forgive (*māf kiyā*) two maunds [80 kg].

AG [still incredulous]: Forgive? [I knew well this term which was used when royal grace decreed that certain taxes not be collected; HS assumes incomprehension rather than amazement and substitutes a different verb.]

HS: He removed (*haṭā thā*) two maunds. For some people two maunds, for some people three maunds … Yes, he was a good man … In many places he built small water reservoirs (*nāḍī*) …

For Vansh Pradip Singh, and for his heirs and kin, the protection of trees and wildlife was bound up with royal reputation and with *dharma*. Both stories make this clear. But the farmer's tale ends in a free-for-all pig slaughter which assaults the ruler's dignity, religious status and reputation even as it affirms the farmers' successful manipulative strategies. Himmat Singh's story very deliberately insists that such an outcome is unthinkable.[21]

These vividly conflicting versions of the wild pig protest story in fact frame my incomplete field research chronologically. Conceptually they engage many of the theoretical issues involved in doing ethnographic history, and perhaps in any endeavour to interpret the past. Moreover, I believe they contribute to recent attempts to trace a counterpoint subaltern history, however scant its direct record may be.[22]

Rather than pursue these lines of thought, however, I continue to plot through interview texts the ambiguous moral implications of rulers who protected trees and animals apparently at the expense of their subjects' well-being, and the consequences, for nature and society, that followed the sudden decline of those rulers' powers.

Politics of Deforestation

[T]rees have life since they feel pain and pleasure and grow though cut.

[T]he king should award [fines] against those who wrongfully cut a tree ... (Kane 1974, vol. II, part 2: 895).

Once restraint becomes illegitimate and excess laudable, the desire to protect nature also becomes suspect, and has to be justified by purely instrumental arguments (Banuri and Marglin 1993: 19).

Vansh Pradip Singh's death without progeny in 1947 resulted in a succession dispute to the Sawar throne which lasted until 1951. Beginning in this four-year interregnum (which coincided with a tumultuous period in India's history), there was a rapid decimation of trees. Within a single decade, the densely wooded hills where wild animals, including large herds of pigs, once found sustenance and shelter were stripped almost bare.[23] Shortly after a successor to the Sawar royal seat was enthroned, a series of land reform bills radically disempowered the former princes. In Ghatiyali, as these initial recollections hint, there is a strong association in people's minds between the former kings, old growths of indigenous trees and wild animals. These three came to an end together, and as the tales are told, it appears this was both a sweet and bitter transformation.

The Rajasthani term usually employed for the designated 'cattle-guard' whose job is to protect the trees from grazing livestock and firewood cutters is the same today as in the past: *syāṇā*. But the sanctions that today's government-appointed *syāṇā* wields, and his status in the village, are very different from those attributed to past guards who were agents of the king. For while these strong-arms abused their powers and exploited the people, the authority behind them was royal. They were perhaps more hated, but less despised than today's cattle-guards.

Dayal Gujar, a former herder, probably in his sixties, forced by ill health to stay at home, explicitly connects the changed landscape with the changed political regime. Others with whom we spoke believed, along with Dayal Gujar, that no one charged with law enforcement in the present era possessed or could exercise an authoritative power in any way comparable to that of the 'great kings' – the *rājā mahārājā*.[24] This does not mean that people lament their passing, but they are aware of its consequences for local government's effectiveness.

BG: For how many years did you graze goats?

DG: For forty years.

BG: Between this time and that, what are the differences?

DG: Four *ānās* to a rupee [that is, the present is only 25 per cent of the past].[25]

BG: What are all the differences?

DG: At that time there were many wild pigs, many *roj* [the Rajasthani term for Hindi *nīlgāy*, a species of deer], many *hiraṇ* [deer or antelope], living in herds of hundreds, such large groups. There were ... *sāmbhar* [another species of deer-like animal]; and the wild pigs and the tigers even came right up to the village.

Just as the *rājā mahārājā* are now finished (*khatm*) the jungle too is finished ... the kings were finished, their time (*vakt*) was finished, then people started to cut the trees because there was no responsible authority (*zimmedārī*).

BG: But what about the Forestry Department, the cattle-guard (*syāṇā*)?

DG: No ... the Congress came and they are all government workers, so there is no responsible authority.

Violence against trees was perpetuated at several levels of the social order and in varied settings. While villagers stripped the uncultivated commons to store up firewood, the new *ṭhākur's* family sold off the roadside trees for cash. It was common knowledge in Ghatiyali that the royal family members themselves had destroyed the shade trees along the 7 km Sawar–Ghatiyali road. Vansh Pradip Singh had ordered trees to be planted – a meritorious act recommended for kings in ancient Hindu texts. His heirs (who were not his descendants) had them cut and sold. This selling of shade trees people viewed as an exemplary act of amoral selfishness. It is regularly described in metaphors of consumption.

Bhoju discusses these linked events with an elderly and educated Brahmin, Suva Lal Chasta, and his somewhat younger castefellow Bhairu Lal Chasta:

> SL: Those who were to protect the jungle ate it. And besides that, the *rājā mahārājā* thought, 'The jungle is ours.' So, after Independence, they thought, 'It is our property,' so they arranged to have it cut and to sell it fast.
>
> Along the Sawar–Ghatiyali road, there were so many trees, every ten minutes on both sides. When they knew that the government was taking things over, they thought, 'We planted these trees and they are ours.'
>
> BL: They weren't sorry. They had planted and watered them and raised them, and their rule was over, so they cut them.

A burden of sin is ascribed to the rulers who had the trees cut and sold. This lapse into amoral behaviour is emblematic of similar moral decay in society at large, just as the cutting and selling of roadside shade trees is of the greater commons problem and subsequent deforestation.

Today's forestry agent is perceived not only as amoral but as ineffective. Haidar Ali, a Muslim shopkeeper, contrasts the current Forestry Department's work with the enforcement carried out in the Kings' era:

> HA: The kinds of trees that once existed no longer remain. The government servants sold them all and ate them; and people think it is just a game of sin (*pāp-līlā*).[26] In the time of the *rājā mahārājā* there were twenty forestry guards; and now the government sends only one man.

Suppose we build a thorn wall around our field but it starts to eat the field, how will it protect what it eats? [He follows this thought with a traditional saying:] 'The hedge of thorns will eat the field, so how will the field be protected?' (*bāṛ khet ko khāyegī to khet kī rakṣā kaise hogī?*)[27]

However, not everyone blames the government. Rup Lal Khati, an older man of the carpenter caste, reflective and intelligent, attributes the major share of blame to the community. He described the situation for us in terms of a classic commons problem (once Leviathan, in the form of the *darbār* and his agents, is removed):

RK: Before people needed firewood and today they need firewood, but when they saw that the wood was being used up, everyone thought 'I need some for myself', and they cut it even faster. They stored in *advance.[28]

And if at that time people had only taken what they needed, then the jungle wouldn't have been finished and everyone, and the cows, goats and buffaloes, all could have lived at ease.

The destruction of trees understood as sinful is embedded in other concurrent degenerations both ecological and moral. Haidar Ali's portrayal of the forestry agent, and all those who negotiate with him, as engaged in a 'sin-game' (*pāp līlā*) effectively expresses this convergence of wanton and irrational environmental destruction and lack of moral sensibilities.

Foreign Trees

For the poetics of history lie also in mute meanings transacted through goods and practices, through icons and images dispersed in the landscape of the everyday (Comaroff and Comaroff 1992: 35).

'Foreign *bambūl*' (*vilāyatī bambūl*) – often simply referred to as *vilāyatī* ('foreign') – is very thorny and fast-growing. Its presence in relative abundance has averted a severe firewood shortage in the area around Ghatiyali, and government planners continue to promote its propagation in plantations on otherwise barren land.[29] Initially introduced and accepted by farmers as an organic hedge to protect their fields and mark their boundaries, *vilāyatī* has become an unwelcome and hard-to-remove colonizer of agricultural land. Puncture wounds and splinters from its thorns cause dangerous infections, and play havoc with bicycle tyres. It grows so well because its leaves are unappealing to goats.[30] Goats eat the seed pods, however, and new trees sprout from their dung. While seedlings of almost every other kind of tree must be protected from livestock with elaborate improvised structures, and watered for several years as well, *vilāyatī* needs no human assistance.

The perceived ecological colonization of foreign *bambūl* intermeshes, conceptually and actually, with other kinds of gross and subtle invasions and replacements that have so transformed these Rajasthanis' lives in the second half of the twentieth century. *Vilāyatī* is strongly associated with a reduced quality of life which people note in many related areas. That this decline should be thus linked to the spread of something 'foreign' is also part of a broader conceptual and material pattern.

I spoke with an old Harijan woman, Gendi Bangi, about the changed landscape and the new dominant tree.

> GB: There used to be many cows and buffaloes, and in [*samvat*] 1996 [CE 1940] at the time of the famine,[31] we used to get leaves from the forest and grass, and we could still feed the animals. There were *dhokaṛā* trees on the hills, and now there is only *vilāyatī bambūl*.
>
> AG: Is *vilāyatī bambūl* good or bad?
>
> GB: It's bad.
>
> AG: Why?
>
> GB: Because of the thorns.
>
> AG: But for the cooking hearth ... ?
>
> GB: It's good for burning, but *dhokaṛā* was good for burning too, and it didn't have thorns.

Gendi bluntly states one contrast – salient to women who bear the brunt of firewood collection – between the new and the old dominant tree species. Many people could readily list as many as ten or more trees that were numerous and important in the past, but only one species appeared on everyone's list, and often it was the only one mentioned: *dhokaṛā* (Hindi *dhok*). Forestry books confirm that this species – *Anogeissus pendula* – is indeed the dominant indigenous species for the Banas Basin area where Ghatiyali is located.[32]

Here is Dayal Gujar again, giving a more even-handed account of the good and bad qualities of *vilāyatī*:

> BG: Today the government has planted *vilāyatī bambūl*. Is this harmful?
>
> DG: No, it's a very good thing because we have firewood, and without that no tree would remain at all ... It's good for burning, but it's bad for animals. If we get splinters, it's bad. And beneath it, in its shade, no grass or crops will grow. There is poison in its shade. It is very bad for the fields.
>
> BG: Where does it come from?
>
> DG: It comes from a foreign land (*vilāyat*) and that's why its called foreign (*vilāyatī*).
>
> BG: Which foreign land?
>
> DG: I don't know. First we heard there was such a tree, but we hadn't seen it. It was planted in Devli [a nearby market town and military base], and then little by little it came in this direction. First it was only around our fields; then the Forest Department planted it everywhere. It didn't exist during the time of the *rājā mahārājā*; there were only those other trees like *dhokaṛā, pīlavān, sālarā, mīṭhā khaḍū* and so forth.[33]

Lalu Regar, an untouchable leather worker, contrasts *vilāyatī* to other trees in the specific sense that it fails to 'pull' the rain.

> LR: Before there was jungle, and so many trees from which we had rain; the trees made a wind that pulled the rain ... But, today there is no jungle at all.
>
> BG: When people know this, why don't they pay any attention?

LR: No, today people pay no attention, and so there are no
trees left, only *vilāyatī bambūl,* nothing else.

Lalu Regar's formulation that nowadays there are 'No trees left,
only *vilāyatī,*' is an exaggeration, of course. But his phrasing
suggests that in some ways *vilāyatī* is truly thought of in a
different fashion from all other tree species.

Even children who have no memories of the old forest share
their elders' differential evaluations of *vilāyatī* versus all other
trees.[34] Thus 13-year-old eighth-grader Satya Narayan distinguishes
vilāyatī from other sources of wood when discussing the moral
dilemmas entailed by tree-cutting. Although prompted by his
teacher, Bhoju, to declare that trees have souls, Satya Narayan
frankly affirms that people need to cut trees, no matter what the
moral consequences. However, he exempts cutting of *vilāyatī* from
sin.

BG: Do you incur sin from cutting trees?

SN: Yes.

BG: Why?

SN: Because we shouldn't cut them.

BG: Are trees and plants living things or non-living things?
[Note that the Hindi terms *jīv* and *nirjīv* for 'living' and
'non-living' could also translate as 'souls' and 'non-souls.']

SN: They are living things.

BG: So when you know that trees and plants are living
things, and that it is sin to cut them, why do you cut them
anyway?

SN: To have wood to burn, that's why.

BG: Are there any trees that it is no sin to cut?

SN: Foreign *bambūl*; it is no sin to cut them, and it is no sin
to kill a poisonous animal.

In terms of the local ecology, this truly is the one tree that it does
the least harm to cut. But in thus isolating foreign *bambūl,* and in
connecting it with poisonous snakes, Satya Narayan identifies
vilāyatī with things that are dangerous to humans.[35]

During my last weeks in the village, a 'plantation scheme' administered by Kan Singh, the much-maligned 'cattle-guard', was underway. The scheme involved local elementary school-teachers, who established a tree nursery in the schoolyard, raised funds for a watering system, and cared for what I was told numbered 20,000 *vilāyatī bambūl* seedlings. After the monsoon broke, these were planted in rows on village 'wasteland' – well beyond homes and farmlands, in the hills towards Sawar. I photographed this project shortly before leaving the village in July 1993. Cheerful groups of women labourers were carefully setting each young tree in the earth, while Kan Singh strutted among them, admonishing them not to be slack. No one to my knowledge opposed this project. Several people told me it was funded by Japanese money designated to improve India's environment.[36]

Several other verbally maligned but pragmatically incorporated elements of modern life in Ghatiyali are, like *vilāyatī,* opposed to *desī* or indigenous, but called 'English' (*angrejī*) rather than 'foreign'. These include chemical fertilizer (*angrejī khād*), Western medicine (*angrejī davāī*), and liquor that is not bootleg homebrew (*angrejī sarāb*). All of these are elements in an ambivalently perceived, mutually constructed transformation of environment and quality of life. People accept and employ them, but speak frequently of the damage they do, contrasting them to those waning traditional, local practices and substances the foreign imports have in varying degrees supplanted.[37] Many with whom we spoke attributed the hot, short tempers of people today to eating grain grown with English fertilizer and spoke of a general dwindling of compassion in human hearts. But such changes are also caused by a shortage of dairy products, which itself is caused by decreased livestock herds (resulting in shortage of manure and need for chemical fertilizer). These factors are in turn attributed to increased population and need for agricultural land, and to fodder shortage resulting from deforestation and the advent of *vilāyatī* whose leaves are inedible. Thus the ugly foreign trees with their unpleasant, poisonous thorns, whose shade affords little comfort, but on whose wood people are dependent, are one element in a complexly configured vision of ecological change in post-colonial times. In this vision local products, knowledge and values are depleted and replaced – but not balanced – by foreign counterparts.

Moral Ecologies for the *Kali Yuga*

> Then property alone will confer rank; wealth will be the only source of *dharma*; passion will be the sole bond of union between the sexes; falsehood will be the only means of success in litigation; and women will be objects merely of sensual gratification. Earth will be venerated but for its mineral treasures ... (*Vishnu Purana* on the *Kali Yuga* in Dayal 1983: 65).

> [T]here is always carelessness, passion, hunger, and fear; the terrible fear of drought pits one against another. Scripture has no authority, and men take to the violation of *dharma* ... (*Linga Purāṇa* on the *Kali Yuga* in O'Flaherty 1988: 71).

> [T]here will be little nature without justice and little justice without nature (Kothari and Parajuli 1993: 237).

In recent decades in central Rajasthan the monsoon rains have often been inadequate. Although terrible famines were known in the past, people say that the good years were better and drought years fewer and more widely spaced.[38] Interviews evoked two pervasive theories about why there is less rain today than there used to be. The most prevalent of these – one we heard from school-children as well as unlettered old men and women – poses a direct causal relationship between deforestation and drought – asserting graphically that the trees now vanished from the hill-tops had formerly 'pulled' the rain clouds to the village. *Vilāyatī* do not grow tall enough to do this job, and are thus further contrasted with indigenous species.

The other theory, less widely held and sometimes offered with a certain hesitation, has to do with the decay of social life, religion and love among human beings – all of which are understood to displease God. Reasons posited for divine anger include lack of compassion, insolence towards elders and caste superiors, the decline of community life – including disrespect for common property, and an increasing indifference towards the proper celebration of collective rituals.[39] Obviously, the tree theory and the sin theory are not fully separable, for – as the preceding material suggests – the destruction of the trees is part and parcel of current degenerate moralities.[40]

We heard the straightforward 'less trees less rain' theory many times from persons of all ages and castes. It goes like this, in response to the question 'Why has the rain diminished?' [From Pyarelal Mahajan, one of Ghatiyali's wealthiest merchants:]

PM: Because of the trees not remaining. This is what I think: there are no trees, therefore there is no rain.

[From Hardev Chamar, a poor and unschooled leather worker:]

HC: The trees pulled the rain with the wind; and now there are less trees. The wind pulled the rain. It was the effect of the wind. The trees pulled the wind, but now there are no trees.

Keeping in mind that such statements were both numerous and similar, I turn to the less commonly posed 'God is angry' explanation of climate change. Polu Kumhar, a potter by birth, had attained an economic status beyond most of his caste fellows through a river-bed gardening venture. A reflective, articulate and successful man, Polu spoke thoughtfully of the lessening of rain and affection:

PK: Just as the world's portion has decreased, so God too has become angry.

BG: What do you mean?

PK: We used to greet [hug] each other, we were happy. But today when a person comes, we say, 'No matter, he will have come.' In this way, people's affection is reduced, and in the same way God doesn't love people, and so there is less rain.

Polu thus connects the dwindling of human affection with the dwindling of God's affection for people – a linking he is far from the only one to articulate.

Rup Lal Khati spoke of how people are today richer in material things but poorer in spirit – as consumerism and the jealousy it provokes enter their lives. He connects this with why God no longer hears human prayers for rain.

BG: People used to have less money, but they still had love. But today … ?

RK: Today there is no love at all.

BG: Why?

RK: People are envious of one another. Suppose somebody, like you, earns 2 paisa – whether in sorrow or happiness – and then I see you and I feel envy, and I think, 'Why should he earn money? He ought to stay like me.' There is no progress, just envy.

Like, we see that he washes with soap, he washes his clothes with soap, and we feel envy, and try to do the same. But you have money and I don't, so I get even poorer [from spending money on soap]. So for this reason some farmers are in tight circumstances.

BG: Before, when it did not rain, people used to worship all the gods and do *Indra Puja*.[41]

RK: Yes they used to get the drum and go to worship, and it used to rain even before they got back to the village.

BG: But today they don't do it, why?

RK: Because people's lots have turned bad; and God too has changed towards people (*bhagvān bhī logoṅ se badal gayā*).

Rup Lal very explicitly identifies envy as the source of reduced love, leading in turn to divine displeasure.

Several interviews expressed a completely merged understanding of environmental and moral deterioration. These to me are the most suggestive discussions – and ones that pose a tightly knit moral ecology. Ugma Loda, a farmer in his mid-sixties, offered this complex account.

BG: Why is there less rain?

UL: Because of the trees being cut … Nowadays there are no gardens and no forest.

BG: Why?

UL: Literate people say there is no rain because of the trees.

BG: But what do farmers think about this?

UL: We think the same thing as the rest of the world. I think what you think and accept it. What could I say if I didn't? [He is silent and looks down, then looks up again and resumes.] It is God's manifestation in nature[42] that there is less rain. In the days when God was happy, there was rain and the wells were full, but now God is angry.

BG: Why is God angry? With what things is God angry?

UL: People's behaviour has changed. The biggest thing is that there is no longer compassion in any human vessel (*kisī ke ghaṭ mē koī dayā nahīṅ hai*). Before if someone fell, or was hurt, people would come and take care of them. But nowadays, nothing. … Today nothing is pure; food and drink are bad, and from this our behaviour, compassion, love, have all decreased.

Ugma Loda understands many aspects of the changing world in which he lives to be systemically interconnected.

A very elderly Brahmin, Damodar Sharma Gujarati offered this vivid account of environmental and social history:

DG: In 2004 [CE 1947] all the wells near the village were so full that you could bend over and drink out of them with your hands. That's how much rain there was.

BG: Why isn't there as much rain now?

DG: Because the jungle is destroyed. Because rain comes from trees …

BG: But why?

DG: Farmers say that rain comes from the trees; and there used to be much *dharma*. For example, people used to feed Brahmins, and people used to perform fire oblations for the goddesses and gods, and spread fodder for the cows. But now the Degenerate Age (*Kali Yuga*) has come. It used to be that times were good. Men used to look on women as their sisters and daughters; but today I am a Brahmin and my daughter could marry someone of any caste.

In Damodar's comments we see how fluidly he moves between changes in the environment and changes in religious behaviour, intercaste relationships and sexual morality. Moreover, he uses the traditional Hindu cosmological model of a dark and degenerate age to encompass and account for these changes. Although this was not common, Damodar was not the only one to speak of *Kali Yuga.*

In a conversation with two farmers, Ram Narayan Mali and Shiv Ram Mali, we heard the 'no rain/no trees/no *dharma*' diagnosis debated, and the end of the world authoritatively forecast.[43]

SR: There is less rain and that's why there are no trees and plants.

BG: What is the connection between trees and rain?

RN: The trees pull the clouds, they pull the *pressure.

SR: No, that's not the reason; it is because people have no *dharma.* That's why there is no more rain.

BG: You say that where there are more trees there will be more rain?

RN: From the influence of the trees, the clouds stay.

SR: Everything has its ends. As before there was the rule of the *rājā mahārājā,* that is finished. And as before there were wild animals, but they are finished. And as for the thick woods, its end also came. In the same way, now the end of people is coming and everything will be finished.

Ram Narayan proceeded to sing for us a kind of ballad of the *Kali Yuga,* describing laxness similar to that noted by the elderly Brahmin cited above: immodest women; no respect of high caste by low; no authority of elders in the household.

In *Kali Yuga* lore from Sanskrit texts of over a millennium ago, we hear some remarkably resonant images of selfish, amoral behaviour and ecological disaster. The *Kali Yuga* is said to end in drought, and eventual dissolution (*pralaya*) – a process conveyed in what Kane calls 'harrowing descriptions'. To cite his digest of *Dharmaśāstra::*

There is the absence of rain for a hundred years; the result is that living beings perish and are reduced to earth; the sun's rays become unbearable, and even the ocean is dried up; the earth is burnt by the fierce heat of the sun together with its mountains, forests and continents (Kane 1974: vol. 5, Part 1: 694).

In a sense the *Kali Yuga* texts put the current discourse on environmental and moral degradation in perspective as a cultural construct. But I am also convinced that changes in landscape and in society witnessed by Ghatiyalians (and by much of the subcontinent) over the past fifty years are truly unprecedented. Most people, when asked them point-blank if they were happier twenty years ago or 'today', answered 'today' without equivocation: cash is more plentiful; taxes are far less of a burden; and freedom from personal indignities previously imposed by the absolute rule of the *rājā-mahārājā*s is relished. Yet it is generally acknowledged that the 'quality of life' – indexed by factors such as community solidarity, family harmony and the good taste of food – has diminished. The ecological mood is one of loss, which the barren hills reveal.[44] And, as many old and even not-so-old people put it, including Kalyan Mali, 'Love is less'.

I began this chapter with Kalyan Mali's gripping memories of resistance to power abuse half a century ago – a resistance violently acted out on the symbolically charged but very real bodies of wild pigs. However, the recognized if unnamed heir to the former Court's symbolic status created a different narrative in which the *darbār* held firm in protecting his cherished pigs. This revealed a residual importance for princely identity, even today, lodged in the committed protection of nature. Yet today wild pigs are notable only for their absence, like the old growths of indigenous trees.

I turned then to fragments of an oral history of rapid deforestation and its several causes – a history informed by moral visions of deteriorating times, portraying royalty once again as a force for preservation. Here Vansh Pradip Singh becomes the good king, the tree-planter, in contradistinction to his ruthless successors, who pursue self-interest at the expense of both subjects and nature.

These two parts could appear to hold contradictory lessons to an outsider concerned with environmental wisdom and social justice. For it is difficult not to sympathize with the farmers' cause against the unholy alignment of pigs and kings. However, the voices presented in the second part eloquently express these same farmers' understanding that royal power – however brutal and resented – was genuinely effective in preserving a valued bio-diversity, and a sustainable Commons. Vansh Pradip Singh, the planter of shade trees and punisher of wood theft, appears more of an exemplary ruler than Vansh Pradip Singh who feeds pop-corn to wild pigs; but for him these roles were certainly co-terminous. Next a discourse surrounding disliked, useful, ugly and dangerous foreign trees unfolded as a way of talking about many facets of changing times in the late twentieth century. It led me into still broader themes of decline in moralities, landscape and climate.

For aging villagers, pre-democratic memories and histories are evidently invested with considerable ambivalence – in the word's literal sense of values that shift and move. Tales of the protected jungle are at times tales of *dharma*, at times tales of anger. While all share regrets for the loss of the old trees, no one – except perhaps the royal family – wishes a return to the days when not only pigs but king's agents co-opted a 'lion's share' of the harvest. Indeed, farmers' painful memories of hated power – analogous to the unpredictable ravages of the pigs – were of the *kāmdār* or king's manager arriving on horseback when the crops were ripe, for the tax assessment, and allowing his horse to graze freely on the precious grain while he determined its worth. (In those days most castes paid from one-third to one-half their crops, and this agent determined what the total was before they were allowed to begin reaping.)

Obviously, the landscape and its uses have always been multiply contested. Those in power would have different and often opposing interests from those who laboured in the fields; women from men; herders from farmers, the landless from the landed.[45] In one vivid myth I recorded, a tribal woman wins the boon from Lord Shiva of sending hail to knock the grain from its stalks before harvest: the ultimate disaster for farmers is divine aid to the landless Bhils who laboriously glean food the cultivators con-sider ruined. Nonetheless, it seems to me that Ghatiyali narratives, such as those recorded here, present merged visions of a general human morality with nature's bounty or depletion.

In an eloquent plea for 'cultural and ecological pluralism in India', activist-scholars Smitu Kothari and Pramod Parajuli contend that 'there will be little nature without justice and little justice without nature' (1993: 237). In arguing their point, they draw not only on traditional Hinduism's incorporation of ecological knowledge into its ritual practices, but on evidence from grass-roots movements where communities have mobilized from within to save local environments from various forms of degradation and to save valued traditions rooted in those threatened landscapes.

Current processes may be irreversible, barring a new cycle of *yuga*s. Thus such commonsense understandings as our interviews revealed among most villagers – that selfishness causes drought and that the environment inevitably participates in the fruits of human sin – appear to be important sources of practical and ideological strength infusing India's environmental movements. Kothari and Parajuli thus take their stand – and it is certainly a polemical one – on the real possibility or possible reality of a moral order inscribed in nature. They insist that any environ-mentalism requires a strong component of social justice. Others have noted that it is characteristic of activists in South Asia, as opposed to those in the United States and other Northern nations, to insist on merging environmentalist with human welfare agendas (Guha 1989a). This is based on the conviction that people who work and live close to the land should control natural resources, rather than have conservation imposed on them from above – as it was in the remembered days of Vansh Pradip Singh.

Acknowledgements

Eight months of fieldwork in India in 1992–93 was funded by a CIES Fulbright Scholar Award for Research; I am most grateful for this support, and for the many kinds of assistance extended to me at Fulbright House in New Delhi by the United States Educational Foundation in India. My academic affiliation during this research period was with the Institute for Economic Growth of Delhi University where Professors T.N. Madan and Bina Agarwal offered cordial and generous intellectual inspiration.

Periodic conversations in New Delhi, with Ramachandra Guha were also extremely important to my work in Rajasthan. As ever, I could not have accomplished much there without the help of Bhoju Ram Gujar and his family. I also thank Ugmanathji Natisar Nath and Shambhu Natisar Nath for invaluable help. Many thanks to Daniel Gold, Brian Greenberg, Ronald Herring, Archana Prasad, Vijay Prashad, Gloria Raheja and Uday Shekar for critical readings of earlier drafts; to Pamela Price for inviting me to speak in Oslo; to Sanjeev Prakash for his thoughtful commentary there; and finally, especially, to Stig Toft Madsen both for his meticulous editorial attention and for his patience.

Notes

1. See Comaroff 1985 for one formulation of the dynamics of such a fusion. For explorations linking environment and production with religious and symbolic configurations in specific cultural and ecological settings, see for example, Lansing 1991; Croll and Parkin 1992; Sen 1992; Brightman 1993.

2. In the case of agricultural rituals, for example, farmers directly attribute the decrease in ritual activity to the increasing use of machine power (Gold 1998a).

3. See Jodha 1985; 1990. For deforestation in South Asia, see Agarwal 1986.

4. When using my own words, I say 'forest' for a wooded area. When translating interviews, I use 'forest' if the speaker has said *van*; and 'jungle' if they have said *jangal*. A certain amount of confusion arises from the different meanings of *jangal* and 'jungle' as they have evolved over time in Indian languages and in English. Appadurai notes 'the radical rupture between our modern Western conception of jungle (as a dank, luxuriant, moist place) and the ancient Indian category, which referred to a dry and austere natural setting, which was nevertheless ideal for human subsistence practices' (Appadurai 1988: 206; see Zimmermann 1987). The English implications have, however, slipped back into North India's vernaculars, I believe. For example, the *Rajasthani Sabad Kosh*, a Rajasthani dictionary (Lalas 1962–78, hereafter RSK), offers as definition number 1 for *jangal*: *van* and *araṇya*, which are both terms for forest; definition number 3 is *registān* or desert. For further elucidation of 'jungle' and *jangal* in South Asia, see Dove 1992.

5. Archana Prasad (pers. com.) notes that my rendition of villagers' discourse seems to echo 'colonial stereotypes' of the Indian 'jungle'. I

can only respond that 'dense' (*gaharā*) and frightening (*bhayānak*) were terms frequently used in verbal accounts. When people were trying to impress me with the wild nature of the vanished 'jungle' (rather than its politics) they would speak of *ser* and *bāgh* – terms which Chaturvedi and Tiwari (1975) translate as 'lion' and 'tiger' respectively – more often than of *jangli sūar* ('wild pigs'). I have it on good authority that they cannot mean lions but only tigers, or possibly leopards, as no lions have inhabited Rajasthan in recent centuries. Uday Shekar notes, however, that in certain areas, especially those adjacent to wildlife preserves, pigs remain even at present a serious problem for Rajasthani farmers.

6.   Bhoju Ram Gujar was my research assistant for many years, and more recently has been a co-author. We have worked together since 1979 and it is difficult to disentangle our respective contributions to this research (for his account of our collaborations see Gujar and Gold 1992).

7.   For some recent, varied explorations of emotional and poetic ties between persons and the changing, contested landscapes they inhabit see, for example, Cronon 1983; Roseman 1991; Tsing 1993.

8.   Some works that have influenced my approach here include: on *anthropology and history*, Cohn 1987; Biersack 1991; Roseberry 1989; Comaroff and Comaroff 1992; Dirks 1992; Dube 1992; on *memory and history*, Connerton 1989; Halbwachs 1992; Hutton 1993; on *oral history*, Vansina 1985; Prakash 1991; Tonkin 1992; on *anthropology and memory*, Price 1990; Boyarin 1994.

9.   Three separate works have developed out of these sections: from Part 1, Gold with Gujar 1997; from Part 2, Gold 1995; and from Parts 3 and 4 together, Gold 1998b.

10. While it might be zoologically more proper to use English 'boar' for a non-domesticated pig, I believe it is truer to Rajasthani usage to translate *'jangli sūar'* as 'wild pig'. In spite of a strong distinction made between domestic and wild pigs in terms of their eating habits and their meat's desirability, some significant elements in the semantic domain of piggishness, it seems to me, are shared by both kinds of *sūar*.

11. I am necessarily omitting critical parts of the fragmented history I have thus far learned; for a very brief and still preliminary summary, see Gold and Gujar 1994: 76–78.

12. Sawar was not among the princely states but under British rule as part of the joint district 'Ajmer-Merwara'; see *Imperial Gazetteer* 1989.

13. Four-Armed Vishnu's Temple is the traditional meeting place for the village *panchayat* (Gold 1988: 41–44).

49

14. Although there is no further reference to this fact, this day is even now the occasion of Ghatiyali's largest religious fair. This might explain why a significantly large group could gather thus, spontaneously, without being summoned by the crier as they would be for a regular village council meeting. Four Arms Temple is very close to the Tejaji shrine where the fair takes place and where many men would have gathered anyway for the celebration. This reference also tells us that the event in question took place in the bright half of *Bhādrapad*, well into the rainy season, when the crops would have been growing nicely.

15. Because he is so religious, Vansh Pradip Singh kept a fast, as many high-caste men and women do, on the eleventh of the month.

16. An asterisk preceding a translated word indicates that the English word was used originally.

17. See S. Guha 1995 for nuanced historical research on Maharashtrian kings (1600–1900) and their relationships to trees. See also R. Guha 1989b and Murali 1995 for resistance to government forest policies in other regions of India; and Thompson 1975, Sahlins 1994, and Schulte 1994, for vivid European examples of contest over hunting and other forest rights. For a vivid portrayal of peasant unhappiness under the former princes of Rajputana, see Mukta 1994, especially pp. 84–86.

18. The interpersonal relationships, including status and personalities, involved in interview situations also significantly affect the material I present, as will become clear below. Perhaps most acutely I must recognize that, although I recorded many interviews with women, I found myself selecting mostly male voices in composing these fragmented histories. Men were certainly more ready, especially directed by Bhoju's rather forceful interviewing style, to discourse on political and environmental change. Women, finding me a more pliable listener, often preferred to turn the conversation from broader patterns to personal experience. I blush to acknowledge my collusion in this old 'problem' for anthropology of women (Ardener 1975). Future instalments of this oral history will integrate more fully the richness of women's experiences and expressive modes.

19. See Rudolph and Rudolph 1984 for Rajput history and psychology.

20. In consultation with Bhoju, but bearing sole responsibility, I have decided to risk incurring the current Court's possible displeasure by publishing this story; it does not after all concern his direct forefathers.

21. We encountered yet another less fluently and copiously narrated version of this event, from a Brahman, which has the *darbār* respond: 'Kill them in the fields but not in the jungle; the fields are yours but the jungle is mine.' Vijay Prashad (pers. com.) was struck by the 'spatialization of power' in this formulation, and commented: 'it says that we do

not need to heed the words of the monarch, for a certain section of the land is ours'.

22. The subaltern project is an enterprise designed to locate and listen to the non-elite voices of history – voices that speak against hegemonies both of colonialism and of the indigenous elite. Yet in 'ruling class documents', which constitute the major sources for the historian's craft, often it was not speech but 'silences' that had to be interpreted (Chakrabarty 1988: 179). Chatterjee acknowledges the potential contribution of anthropological materials to an understanding of 'the consciousness of the subaltern classes' (Chatterjee 1989: 169). In oral histories of predemocratic Rajasthan, we hear voices in plenty, speaking loudly, clearly, often with eloquence. See O'Hanlon 1988 and Raheja 1994: 13–17 for critical discussions of theoretical problems inherent in the project of recovering voices, or describing a consciousness, that may be labelled 'subaltern'.

23. See Richards, Haynes and Hagen 1985 for a broader picture of deforestation in North India during this period.

24. I most often retain the original term which has an emphatic potency beyond 'kings'.

25. In the old Indian currency, there were 16 *ānās* in a rupee; today, in spite of the decimal system, people still refer to 25 paise as '4 *ānās*'.

26. Haidar Ali uses Hindu terminology in spite of his Muslim identity. Bhoju interpreted this idiosyncratic usage as meaning: 'No one is responsible for anything; you can use money to pay for sin.'

27. *Bāṛ* means a thorny wall or hedge; Bhoju notes that this proverb may apply to kings as well as forestry guards. In other words, the seeds of exploitation lie within the practice of protection. See Kabir's Sākhī # 106 in Hess and Singh (1983: 101): 'Protect the field with a hedge, the hedge eats up the field. The three worlds whirl in doubt. To whom can I explain?' Thus for the poet-saint Kabir the protector's inherent unreliability is a sign of cosmic doubt. Hess's footnote informs us that hedge translates *bēdā* – 'a barrier of plants that keeps animals out but that also leaches nourishment needed by the crops (1983: 187).' Interestingly enough, this is one of the chief complaints concerning *vilāyatī* – suggesting that indigenous species in previous centuries had similar defects.

28. Bhoju told me, as we translated this interview together, that his own household members had participated in this, stockpiling several years' worth of firewood in their cattle shed. Because women used the cattle-shed as a place to urinate in the daytime, I had often contemplated this massive old woodpile. I had been warned that it might shelter scorpions and knew that it was a hiding place for newborn kittens, but I had never

realized it was a sign of the very sources of deforestation I was researching.

29. In June 1993, economist Bina Agarwal of the Institute for Economic Growth in Delhi, administered survey questionnaires to women in Ghatiyali as part of her multi-regional study of the effects of environmental change on Indian women. She asked older women questions about the time it took them to collect firewood today, as opposed to in the past, and she was surprised that firewood was not a significant problem, despite the evidently severe deforestation, because of the proliferation of *vilāyatī*. In some other parts of India the 'firewood crisis' has had a far more drastic impact upon women's work schedules (see Agarwal 1986).

30. According to Anirudh Krishna (pers. com.) who served from 1991–93 as Director of Watershed Development in Rajasthan, the tree that Rajasthanis call *vilāyatī bambūl* is *Prosopis juliflora*, a kind of mimosa (in spite of the RSK's indication that *bambūl* is *babūl* in Hindi which translates 'acacia'); Robbins 1996 confirms this identification. Bhandari describes *Prosopis juliflora* as originally from Mexico, a 'variable evergreen plant, recently introduced around Jodhpur and Barmer' (arid districts of Western Rajasthan), and 'being introduced elsewhere in the region'. He continues, 'it is a hardy plant, grows fast and is likely to be very useful for afforesting arid land. The ripe pods are greedily eaten by cattle and goats' (Bhandari 1990 [1978]: 137). Amita Bhaviskar informs me (pers. com.) that in the United States we are familiar with *Prosopis juliflora* as 'mesquite'.

Another Rajasthani tree, rather scarce today, is known by contrast to *vilāyatī* as *desī bambūl* or 'local *bambūl*'. To unpractised eyes, it looks much like *vilāyatī*. But while *desī bambūl* has become quite scarce, along with other lamented indigenous species, *vilāyatī* spreads like a weed. According to Krishna, the tree called *desī bambūl* is a true acacia: *Acacia nilotica*. Sharma and Tiagi report of this tree: 'Known as Babool locally and Babbul (Sanskrit), the decoction of the bark and fruits is used medicinally in Ayurveda. Incisions made on the stem yield a gum which carries medicinal value' (Sharma and Tiagi 1979: 105). In the village people often contrasted *desī bambūl* with its multiple uses to *vilāyatī*, which is good 'only for burning'.

31. Kachhawaha 1985 confirms that 1940 was indeed a famine year in Ajmer District.

32. See Shetty and Singh 1987: 22–23. Sharma and Tiagi note important reasons for the depletion of this species beyond cutting it for firewood: 'This tree is worst affected by the goats, overgrazing reduces it to a tuft of green shoots only 6–9 cm high. This dominant species of *Anogeissus* is used for making charcoal' (1979: 155).

33. RSK defines *pīlavaṇ* not as a tree but as a 'thick-stemmed vine which climbs on trees.' For *sālar* it gives 'a special kind of tree … used in Ayurvedic medicine.' *Sālar* is identified by Shetty and Singh (1987: 22) as *Boswellia serrata*, a species associated with the mixed deciduous forests dominated by *Dhokaṛā*. For *mīṭhā khaḍū* or '*sweet khaḍū*,' I have been unable to locate information beyond the RSK's bland definition of *khaḍḍū* as 'a special kind of medium-sized tree'.

34. See Gold and Gujar 1994 for a discussion of Ghatiyali's children's attitudes towards, and knowledge about, the environment.

35. Snakes are beaten to death on sight in Ghatiyali.

36. See SAPROF Team 1991 for a description of this project.

37. I would add synthetic fabric and rubber thong sandals to this list as they are recognized as imports and have replaced traditional products, without being always called 'English' or 'foreign'. These are much in demand and commonly described as bad for health.

38. See Bharara for one study that finds a very close 'correlation between the farmers' recollection of past harvests and the record of actual rainfall in Western Rajasthan' (1982: 352).

39. Wadley 1994 reports on similar perceptions from a different North Indian region with a different local history.

40. Note: the monsoon of 1994 brought, according to letters from Bhoju, the heaviest rains seen in our part of Rajasthan for at least one hundred years. I do not yet have any indication of how this most recent geophysical phenomenon affected the theories reported here.

41. See Gold 1988: 53–58 for a description of *Indra Puja* – a collective ritual in 1980 to entreat the Vedic Rain God, Indra (Rajasthani '*Indar*') who has no temple.

42. This is an intentional but awkward translation of *bhagvān kī kudarat;* it might be more simply rendered as: 'God's nature' or 'God's being'.

43. This was actually a very complex and lengthy argument in which *Kali Yuga* visions combined with a notion perhaps learned from radio or television that the polar caps might melt and flood the earth.

44. See Gold 1995 for other aspects of ambivalence and for further complexities in these perceptions; this history is not simply one of linear degeneration or semi-deluded nostalgia.

45. See S. Guha who writes of the politics of nature in seventeenth- to nineteenth-century Maharashtra: 'a variety of human agencies impacted upon the landscape' (1995).

References

Agarwal, Bina (1986) *Cold Hearths and Barren Slopes: The Woodfuel Crisis in the Third World*, New Delhi: Allied Publishers Private Limited.

Appadurai, Arjun (1988) 'Comments on "The Jungle and the Aroma of Meats: An Ecological Theme in Hindu Medicine"', *Social Science and Medicine*, vol. 27, no. 3, pp. 206–207.

Ardener, Edwin (1975) 'Belief and the Problem of Women', in S. Ardener, (ed.), *Perceiving Women*, New York: Wiley, pp. 1–28.

Banuri, Tariq and Frederique Apffel Marglin (1993) 'A Systems-of-Knowledge Analysis of Deforestation', in Tariq Banuri and Frederique Apffel Marglin (eds), *Who Will Save the Forests? Knowledge, Power and Environmental Destruction*, London: Zed Books, pp. 1–23.

Bhandari, M.M. (1990 [1978]) *Flora of the Indian Desert*, Jodhpur: MPS Repros.

Bharara, L.P. (1982) 'Notes on the Experience of Drought Perception, Recollection and Prediction', in Brian Spooner and H.S. Mann (eds), *Desertification and Development: Dryland Ecology in Social Perspective*, London: Academic Press, pp. 351–61.

Biersack, Aletta (ed.) (1991) *Clio in Oceania: Toward a Historical Anthropology*, Washington, DC: Smithsonian Institution Press.

Boyarin, Jonathan (1994a) 'Space, Time, and the Politics of Memory', in Jonathan Boyarin (ed.), *Remapping Memory: The Politics of TimeSpace*, Minneapolis: University of Minnesota Press, pp. 1–38.

—— (ed.) (1994b) *Remapping Memory: The Politics of TimeSpace*, Minneapolis: University of Minnesota Press.

Brightman, Robert (1993) *Grateful Prey: Rock Cree Human–Animal Relationships*, Berkeley: University of California Press.

Chakrabarty, Dipesh (1988) 'Conditions for Knowledge of Working-Class Conditions', in Ranajit Guha and Gayatri C. Spivak (eds), *Selected Subaltern Studies*, New York: Oxford University Press, pp. 179–230.

Chatterjee, Partha (1989) 'Caste and Subaltern Consciousness', in Ranajit Guha (ed.), *Subaltern Studies VI*, Delhi: Oxford University Press, pp. 169–209.

Chaturvedi, Mahendra and B.N. Tiwari (eds) (1979) *A Practical Hindi–English Dictionary*, New Delhi: National Publishing House.

Cohn, Bernard S. (1987) *An Anthropologist among the Historians and Other Essays*, Delhi: Oxford University Press.

Comaroff, Jean (1985) *Body of Power, Spirit of Resistance: The Culture and History of a South African People*, Chicago: University of Chicago Press.

Comaroff, John and Jean Comaroff (1992) *Ethnography and the Historical Imagination*, Boulder, Col.: Westview Press.

Connerton, P. (1989) *How Societies Remember*, Cambridge: Cambridge University Press.

Croll, Elisabeth and David Parkin (eds) (1992) *Bush Base Forest Farm: Culture, Environment and Development*, London: Routledge.

Cronon, W. (1983) *Changes in the Land: Indians, Colonists, and the Ecology of New England*, New York: Hill & Wang.

Dayal, T.H. (1983) *The Visnu Purana*, Delhi: Sundeep Prakashan.

Dirks, Nicholas B. (1992) 'From Little King to Landlord: Colonial Discourse and Colonial Rule', in Nicholas B. Dirks (ed.), *Colonialism and Culture*, Ann Arbor: University of Michigan Press, pp. 175–208.

Dove, M.R. (1992) 'The Dialectical History of "Jungle" in Pakistan: An Examination of the Relationship between Nature and Culture', *Journal of Anthropological Research* vol. 48, pp. 231–53.

Dube, Saurabh (1992) 'Myths, Symbols and Community: Satnampanth of Chhattisgarh', in Partha Chatterjee and Gyanendra Pandey (eds), *Subaltern Studies VII*, Delhi: Oxford University Press, pp. 121–158.

Gold, Ann Grodzins (1988) *Fruitful Journeys: The Ways of Rajasthani Pilgrims*, Berkeley: University of California Press.

—— (1992) *A Carnival of Parting*, Berkeley: University of California Press.

—— (1995) 'Foreign Trees: Postcolonial Landscapes in Rajasthan'. Paper presented at a Conference on 'Environmental Discourses and Human Welfare', sponsored by the Joint Committees on South and Southeast Asia of the Social Science Research Council and American Council of Learned Societies, Hilo, Hawaii.

—— (1998a) 'Abandoned Rituals: Knowledge, Time, and Rhetorics of Modernity in Rural India', in Rajendra Joshi and N.K. Singhi (eds), *Religion, Ritual and Royalty*, Jaipur: Rawat Publications (in press), pp. 295–308.

—— (1998b) 'Sin and Rain: Moral Ecology in Rural North India', in Lance Nelson (ed.), *Purifying the Earthly Body of God: Religion and Ecology in Hindu India*, Albany: State University of New York Press (in press).

—— and Bhoju Ram Gujar (1994) 'Drawing Pictures in the Dust: Rajasthani Children's Landscapes', *Childhood* no. 2, pp. 73–91.

—— with Bhoju Ram Gujar (1997) 'Wild Pigs and Kings: Remembered Landscapes in Rajasthan', *American Anthropologist* vol. 99, no. 1, pp. 70–84.

Guha, Ramachandra (1989a) 'Radical American Environmentalism and Wilderness Preservation: A Third World Critique,' *Environmental Ethics* no. 2, pp. 71–83.

—— (1989b) *The Unquiet Woods: Ecological Change and Peasant Resistance in the Himalaya*, Delhi: Oxford University Press.

Guha, Ranajit (1983) *Elementary Aspects of Peasant Insurgency in Colonial India*, Delhi: Oxford University Press.

Guha, Sumit (1995) 'Kings, Commoners and the Commons: People and Environments in Western India 1600–1900'. Paper presented at a workshop on 'Science, Technology and Natural Resource Management in a Comparative Global Context', Cornell University, Ithaca, New York.

Gujar, Bhoju Ram and Ann Grodzins Gold (1992) 'From the Research Assistant's Point of View', *Anthropology and Humanism Quarterly* vol. 17 no. 3, pp. 72–84.

Halbwachs, Maurice (1992 [1952]) *On Collective Memory*, Lewis A. Coser (trans), Chicago: University of Chicago Press.

Hess, Linda and Shukdev Singh (1983) *The Bījak of Kabir*, San Francisco: North Point Press.

Hutton, Patrick H. (1993) *History as an Art of Memory*, Hanover, NH: University of Vermont.

Imperial Gazetteer of India (1989 [1908]) *Rajputana*, New Delhi: Usha Rani Jain.

Jodha, N.S. (1985) 'Population Growth and the Decline of Common Property Resources in Rajasthan, India', *Population and Development Review* vol. 11, no. 2, pp. 247–264.

—— (1990) 'Rural Common Property Resources: Contributions and Crisis', *Economic and Political Weekly*, June 30, pp. A65–A78.

Kachhawaha, O.P. (1985) *Famines in Rajasthan: 1900 A.D.–1947 A.D.*, Jodhpur: Hindi Sahitya Mandir.

Kane, P.V. (1974) *History of Dharmasastra*, 2nd edn, Poona: Bhandarkar Oriental Research Institute.

Kothari, Smitu and Pramod Parajuli (1993) 'No Nature without Social Justice: A Plea for Cultural and Ecological Pluralism in India', in

Wolfgang Sachs (ed.), *Global Ecology: A New Arena of Political Conflict*, London: Zed Books, pp. 224–241.

Lalas, Sitaram (1962–78) *Rajasthani Sabad Kos*, 9 vols, Jodhpur: Rajasthani Shodh Sansthan.

Lansing, J.S. (1991) *Priests and Programmers: Technologies of Power in the Engineered Landscape of Bali*, Princeton, NJ: Princeton University Press.

Mathur, Jivanlal (1977) *Brj-Bāvanī*, Sawar: Mani Raj Singh.

Mukta, Parita (1994) *Upholding the Common Life: The Community of Mirabai*, Delhi: Oxford University Press.

Murali, Atluri (1995) 'Whose Trees? Forest Practices and Local Communities in Andhra, 1600–1922', in David Arnold and Ramachandra Guha (eds), *Nature, Culture, Imperialism: Essays on the Environmental History of South Asia*, Delhi: Oxford University Press, pp. 86–122.

O'Flaherty, Wendy Doniger (1988) *Textual Sources for the Study of Hinduism*, Chicago: University of Chicago Press.

O'Hanlon, Rosalind (1988) 'Recovering the Subject: Subaltern Studies and Histories of Resistance in Colonial South Asia', *Modern Asian Studies* vol. 22 no. 1, pp. 189–224.

Prakash, Gyan (1991) 'Becoming a Bhuinya: Oral Traditions and Contested Domination in Eastern India', in D. Haynes & G. Prakash (eds), *Contesting Power: Resistance and Everyday Social Relations in South Asia*, Berkeley: University of California, pp. 145–174.

Price, Richard (1990) *Alabi's World*, Baltimore: Johns Hopkins University Press.

Raheja, Gloria Goodwin (1994) 'Introduction: Gender Representation and the Problem of Language and Resistance in India', in Gloria Goodwin Raheja and Ann Grodzins Gold (eds), *Listen to the Heron's Words*, Berkeley: University of California Press, pp. 1–29.

Richards, John F., Edward S. Haynes and James R. Hagen (1985) 'Changes in the Land and Human Productivity in Northern India', 1870–1970. *Agricultural History*, vol. 59, no. 4, pp. 523–548.

Robbins, Paul (1996) 'Negotiating Ecology: Institutional and Environmental Change in Rajasthan, India'. Ph.D. Dissertation, Graduate School of Geography, Clark University, Worcester, Massachusetts.

Roseberry, W. (1989) *Anthropologies and Histories: Essays in Culture, History, and Political Economy*, New Brunswick: Rutgers University Press.

Roseman, Marina (1991) *Healing Sounds from the Malaysian Rainforest: Temiar Music and Medicine*, Berkeley: University of California Press.

Rudolph, Lloyd I. and Susanne H. Rudolph (1984) *Essays on Rajputana: Reflections on History, Culture, and Administration*, New Delhi: Concept Publishing Company.

Sahlins, Peter (1994) *Forest Rites: The War of the Demoiselles in Nineteenth-Century France*, Cambridge, Mass.: Harvard University Press.

SAPROF Team for the Overseas Economic Cooperation Fund, Japan (1991) 'Final Report on Afforestation Project in Aravalli-Hills State of Rajasthan, India, March 1991', unpublished document, files of the author.

Schulte, R. (1994) *The Village in Court: Arson, Infanticide, and Poaching in the Court Records of Upper Bavaria, 1848–1910*, Barrie Selman (trans.), Cambridge: Cambridge University Press.

Sen, Geeti (ed.) (1992) *Indigenous Vision*, New Delhi: Sage Publications.

Sharma, Shiva and B. Tiagi (1979) *Flora of North-East Rajasthan*, New Delhi: Kalyani Publishers.

Shetty, B.V. and V. Singh (eds) (1987) *Flora of Rajasthan*, Calcutta: Botanical Survey of India.

Thompson, E.P. (1975) *Whigs and Hunters: The Origin of the Black Act*, New York: Pantheon Books.

Tonkin, Elizabeth (1992) *Narrating Our Pasts: The Social Construction of Oral History*, Cambridge: Cambridge University Press.

Tsing, Anna Lowenhaupt (1993) *In the Realm of the Diamond Queen*, Princeton, NJ: Princeton University Press.

Vansina, Jan (1985) *Oral Tradition as History*, Madison: University of Wisconsin Press.

Wadley, Susan S. (1994) *Struggling with Destiny in Karimpur, 1925–1984*, Berkeley: University of California Press.

Zimmermann, F. (1987) *The Jungle and the Aroma of Meats: An Ecological Theme in Hindu Medicine*, Berkeley: University of California Press.

3 | The Use of Metaphor in Himalayan Resource Management

Tor Aase

The Theme

For centuries, the isolated tribes of the Upper Indus have struggled to eke a living out of a harsh environment. The scattered settlements were mostly left unaffected by the outside world until the opening of the Karakorum Highway in 1978 abruptly set off a process of integration into the Pakistani state. Traditional methods of resource management were encountered with externally induced development programmes aiming at the 'general uplift of a backward region'. In their relationship to natural resources, indigenous people are now faced with a new context. Formal administrative routines have been introduced; law and order are maintained by a judicial and police apparatus; and development schemes of various kinds are being implemented. This paper deals with the meeting between traditional society and the modern state. How do local communities adapt to new challenges posed by the state in the management of natural resources?

Recently, this question has been raised in the Sai Valley in the Gilgit District of Northern Pakistan as a consequence of the proposed introduction of a major hydro-electric development scheme. The planned project has given rise to rumours about changes in river flow and availability of new farmland. Administratively, the problem is one of adapting traditional practices of land and water rights to the formal rules of the state. But such an adaptation is not only logistical; in order to accept the new arrangements, villagers must find some *meaning* in practising them. Thus, the

59

adaptation to new circumstances is not only a question of searching for practices that work functionally, but rather, a search for practices that work *meaningfully*. In this way, the challenge of the modern state is also posed at the level of *culture*.

Culturally, the meeting of tradition and modernity can be viewed as the simultaneous articulation of various discourses, each relating to a different system of meaning. A repercussion of such contests between different 'truths' is a reality that emerges as fragmented and discontinuous, and which impedes people in their efforts to live meaningful lives. In such situations, James Fernandez has observed that people try to produce a sensation of wholeness and integrity out of a fragmented and disintegrated culture by the use of *metaphor*. By ascribing meaning from known realms of life to new and unknown modern phenomena, a notion of integrated reality is restored (Fernandez 1986).

My argument is slightly different from that of Fernandez. In adapting to a new context of modern society, local people search their culture and their history for meaning that can be ascribed – transferred, so to speak – to the new arrangements. In this process, not only new practices are assumed, but the practices are loaded with local, quasi-experiential meaning. The cultural change that is usually read into events of modernization is exactly the result of such metaphorization. Through the use of metaphor, cultural innovation produces new practices of resource management that are highly particularistic in their nature, making Sai an idiosyncratic case of modernization, not necessarily to be repeated elsewhere.

Traditional Resource Management

The area in question is locally called Shinaiki – the land of the speakers of the Shina language – and comprises settlements forming a crescent from Tangir Valley in the south along the Indus and Gilgit Rivers up to Yasin in the north (see Map 3.1). Shinaiki can boast of perhaps the most dramatic landscape on earth. Comprising parts of the Himalayas, Karakorum and Hindu Kush, the landscape is literally vertical, relative relief amounting to 6,000 m. The monsoon rains are effectively halted by the Himalayas to the

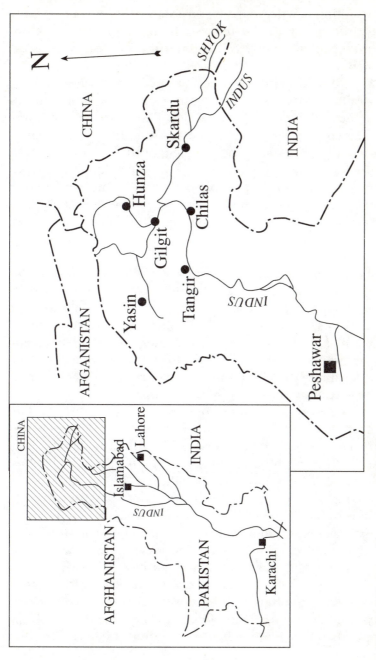

Map 3.1 The northern areas of Pakistan

south, resulting in a dry climate and a semi-arid vegetation. Only in high altitudes, above 3,000 m, are found the remnants of the Western Himalayan coniferous and deciduous forest succeeded by alpine meadows up to the snow-line at 5,500 m.

The hydrology is produced by glacial meltwater. Glacial streams (*nala*) drain the glaciers through narrow sided valleys and gorges into the Indus River in the main valley. The hot season of June–September coincides with the highest flow in the glacial streams, while the highest rainfall occurs in the months of April and May. Thus, the water flow is conditioned by variations in temperature rather than by variations in precipitation which, in the low altitudes, is a mere 125 mm annually. The correlation between water discharge and temperature is high ($r=0.74$), while that between water discharge and precipitation is low ($r=0.07$).

For centuries, people have eked out a living by diverting water from the glacial streams, and irrigating alluvial deposits and moraines in the valley sides. Glacial water is plentiful in the region, and so is cultivable land: the problem is to combine the two. At present, extension of the cultivated area implies construction of long channels in the steep mountain sides, which is technically difficult as well as expensive. The Indus River in the main valley is not accessible with the traditional gravity irrigation technology; thus, the glacial streams are vital to farming.

Farming is by far the most important productive pursuit. The staple crops are winter wheat and summer maize. Wheat is sown in early February and harvested in June. Immediately after harvest, the land is prepared for maize which ripens in October. In addition, some vegetables and alfalfa (fodder) are grown.

To varying degrees, animal husbandry is also practised in combination with farming. Goats, sheep and cattle are kept for milk and meat. During summer, animals are taken far up to the alpine meadows (*nirel*) where they are herded by family members or left in the custody of Gujar semi-nomads. During the winter, the herds must be stable-fed, since no pastures are available. For this, grass is cut from the hillsides and stored, maize stalks and other biomass residues are used, and foliage is taken from trees. Trees are stripped of foliage every three years, after which they are permitted to regenerate. Various coniferous trees are used, like willow and poplar. Even fruit trees like mulberry are used for fodder in this way.

Like Himalayan farming systems in general, the Shinaiki version consists of four integral components: terraced farmland; domesticated animals; lowland forest; and summer pastures in the high mountains. The components are mutually interdependent in a systematic way. Farmland is needed in order to supply winter fodder for animals, and animals are necessary in order to supply manure to the otherwise sterile soils. The survival of animals is dependent upon summer pastures in the high mountains, and on winter fodder, which is partly supplied from the fields (alfalfa and residues) and partly from the forest (foliage). Diminution of one of these four niches implies that the whole system suffers and becomes less productive.

Although variations of this type of farming system are practised in the whole Himalayan region – from Assam and Bhutan in the east to Afghanistan and the Sulaiman mountains in the west – semi-arid areas like those of Northern Pakistan are in a special position. There, the coniferous forest in the valleys are man-made, established by artificial irrigation. Since forest foliage is a necessity for animal husbandry as well as for building materials and for cooking, it follows that the expansion of the population and of settlement is accompanied by expansion of valley forests.

Population increase implies a concomitant demand for more farmland. Historically, this has been supplied by extending existing irrigation channels to uncultivated land (*das*), or by constructing new channels upstream or downstream to existing settlements. However, in order to cultivate new land, manure is needed, thus increasing the demand for animals. Animals can only survive by being stall-fed during winter, in turn necessitating more irrigated forest which is needed for foliage. Thus, population increase is directly related to the expansion of the green areas in the otherwise dusty, semi-arid valley bottoms.

This situation is quite different from that in Nepal, where human and animal population increases are reported by some authors to result in decrease of the *natural* forests in lower altitudes,

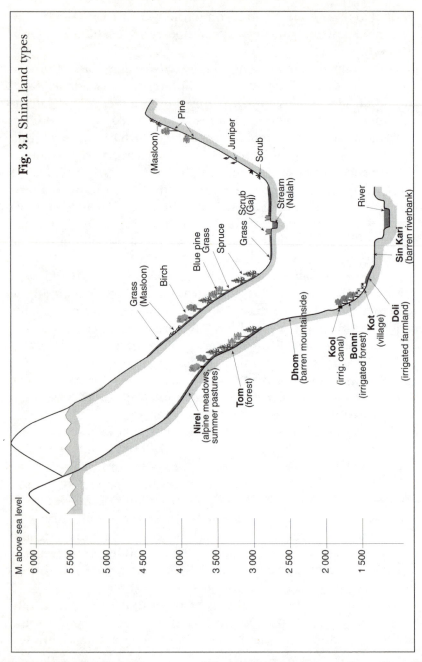

Fig. 3.1 Shina land types

thus generating an inverse relationship between forest and population (Joshi 1986; Myers 1986).

Another way of adapting to farmland shortage has been through raiding. Oral history is full of vivid accounts of families and villages raiding one another for land. Even raiding outside Shinaiki used to take place. In the early twentieth century, people of Shinaiki raided settlements in Kohistan and settled there (Zarin and Smith 1984). This way of coping with land shortage must be seen in relation to the specific type of political organization prevalent in historical Shinaiki.

Politically, Shinaiki belongs to the acephalous area of Pakistan which also includes Kohistan and Swat to the south. Acephalous societies are characterized by the absence of centralized political authority. The only institutionalized political body is the *jirga* – a village council performing the role of mediation. If the verdict reached by the *jirga* is not accepted by the parties to a dispute, open hostility may break out, sometimes resulting in blood feuds (*mar dushmani*) that last for years. Encountering success in the *jirga* or in a blood feud is conditioned by the potential physical power of the contestants. In this way, local power relations are determined by the relative strength of strategic alliances between autonomous kinship groups. Thus, access to water and owner-ship of land have traditionally been conditioned by the number of guns a farmer has been able to mobilize. Indeed, Shinaiki was part of the area formerly labelled Yagistan – 'the unruled land'. This basis of political organization is, however, in a process of change.

The Arrival of Modernity

Geographically, until recently, Shinaiki has only been accessible at certain times and with much difficulty. For five months during the summer, a jeep road used to connect the land to down-country Pakistan via the 4,200 metre Babusar Pass. In addition, a highly irregular airflight occasionally showed up in Gilgit. The modern era commenced when the Karakorum Highway along the Indus River was opened up to Gilgit in 1978 and extended to Xinjiang in China in 1986. This started a process of political, economic and cultural integration in Shinaiki, which is still going on today. The region became part of the Pakistani administrative structure, with elected district councils, formal registration of land ownership, and a police force. Pax Pakistan is also enforced by the presence of substantial military forces, keeping a watchful eye on events in nearby Kashmir. Land and water rights are no longer dependent upon the local power balance. Now access to the vital resources have to be managed in the formal administrative context of the Pakistani state.

Modernity has also arrived in the form of development programmes. Of these, the construction of hydro-electric power plants has in particular affected the management of natural resources, since it competes with agriculture for water. The technology used is similar to that practised in agriculture: water is diverted from glacial streams and conducted in 2–3 km channels in the mountain side, at the end of which a penstock leads the water to a small turbine producing 0.2–1 MW electricity for local consumption. Below the power plant, the water flows back into the river. Thus, part of the river water flow is just borrowed for a few kilometres. The small scale of the schemes produces only negligible environmental impacts.

However, modernity has brought an increasing demand for electricity in the regional headquarters of Gilgit town, which cannot be met by the small plants presently in operation. Gilgit has a population of approximately 60,000 and is expanding rapidly. Small manufacturing industries are being established; the number of tourists demanding hotels and bazaar shops is increasing; and there has been a growth in the construction of public offices of various kinds and schools are added to previous ones. In order to supply the town with energy, the Pakistan Water and Power Development Agency (WAPDA) has turned its attention to Sai River some 40 km to the south of Gilgit (see Map 3.2).

Sai is a bigger hydropower project, estimated to produce 16 MW. Such a scale of production implies that water is channelled out of Sai catchment area to Pari Das, where the topography permits a fall of 700 m. This change of hydrology has two repercussions on local resources: First, new land at Pari Das can be irrigated

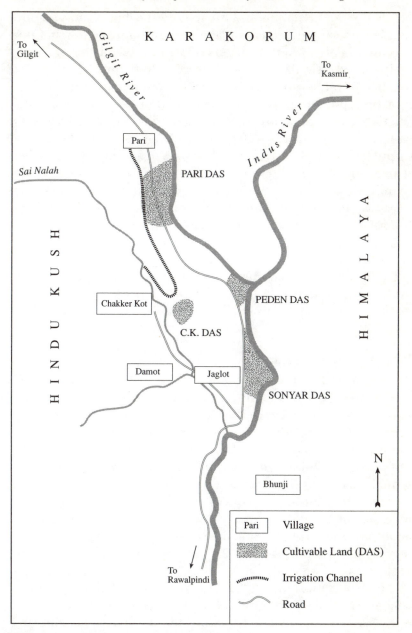

Map 3.2 Sai catchment area

below the power station and turned into farmland; and second, the downstream settlement of Jaglot will be deprived of water now flowing to Pari. How do villagers relate to these changes?

Previously, similar problems were solved through the local balance of physical power. Tribal wars, raiding and family feuds have been the rule rather than the exception in historical Shinaiki. But now, Pakistani enforcement of law and order does not tolerate violence – or the threat of violence – as a means of solving local disputes. Villagers have to find new ways of adapting to spatial re-structuring of natural resources – ways that invoke *legitimacy* rather than sheer power. The gun has to be replaced with argument, persuasion and consensus. This is a new situation in Shinaiki, and forms the focus of our attention here: How is consensus reached – or sought – when traditional ways no longer apply?

Concretely, two questions arise: (1) Which of the neighbouring villages claim legitimate property rights to the new land coming under irrigation at Pari Das? (2) How do people upstream and downstream Sai argue in relation to the diversion of water out of the catchment?

Village Claims to Land

Throughout the history of the Northern Areas, uncultivated *das* land has been converted into farmland by artificial gravity irrigation and by adding manure to the barren soils. Unirrigated *das* land is perceived to be common, the meagre scrub being utilized by semi-nomads and occasionally by local herders for winter pasture. Only when *das* land is converted into farmland (*doli*) do individual farmers establish private property rights. The process of converting *das* into agricultural land goes on continuously as the population increases, making *das* land a scarce resource. Thus, the rumours about the power channel and the concomitant prospects of supplying irrigation water to Pari Das immediately raised the question of who should own it.

My expectation was that Pari Das naturally belonged to Pari village. The old village of Pari has given its name to the *das*, and it is situated in immediate proximity to the village farmland. The settlements along Sai are divided from Pari Das by a high mountain

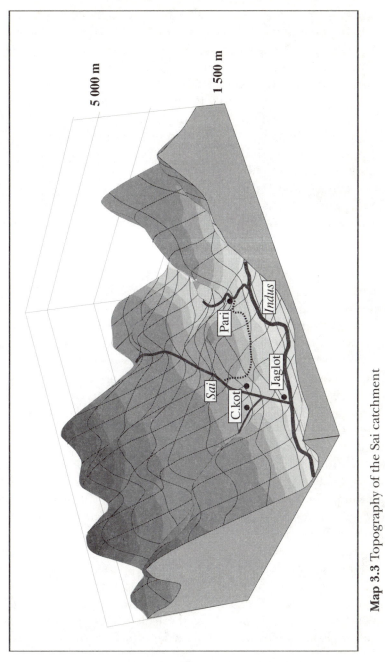

Map 3.3 Topography of the Sai catchment

5 000 m

1 500 m

Pari

Indus

Sai

Jaglot

C.kot

ridge running between the two river systems, making them im-
probable claimants to Pari Das (see Map 3.3). However, to my
astonishment, Chakker Kot upstream Sai emerged as the winner of
the new land. To my even greater surprise, Chakker Kot's ownership
claim was even accepted by Pari!

During the winter of 1994, some time after the hydropower
plans had become known, land division (*taqsim*) was held in Pari
Das. The whole *das* was subdivided by low stone fences, in some
cases demarcating individual plots, and in others indicating
family land awaiting further subdivision. All claimants to the land
belonged to Chakker Kot. Ruling out the old tradition of power
threats, how was that consensus reached? Which arguments had
been applied to establish legitimacy to the land claims? It turns out
that people looked to their recent history, and found a credible
solution there.

During the period from the mid-nineteenth century until the
partition of India in 1947, Shinaiki was ruled by the Kashmiri
ruler – the Dogra – with the blessing and support of the British
colonial administration. In the 1880s, a major Kashmiri garrison
was established at Gilgit. In those days there were no proper roads,
and ammunition and supplies to the garrison had to be carried.
The garrison was quite substantial, since that was the time when
the British feared the south-eastward expansion of Tsarist Russia
(Keay 1990). The main route from the Kashmiri capital of Srinagar
led to Gilgit via the Astor Valley, reaching the Indus at Bhunji.
Another route went from Rawalpindi to Gilgit via the Kaghan
Valley and the Babusar Pass, crossing the Indus above Chilas (see
Map 3.1). The Dogra solved the supplies issue by imposing portering duties on the villages along the route. Each village was allotted
a certain distance of porterage duty, after which the next village
on the route took over. Most settlements were then located up in
the side valleys, while the transport route went on uninhabited
das land along the Indus.

In the area in question, Jaglot and Damot villages were responsible for portering supplies from the neighbouring village
downstream up to Peden Das; there, loads were taken over by
Chakker Kot, which organized carriage to Pari village; Pari took

them on to the next village on the Gilgit road, and so on up to the garrison (see Map 3.2). At Peden Das, Chakker Kot also had to take over loads from Bhunji, coming from Srinagar on the Astor route.

This historical episode, which lasted some sixty years and ended fifty years ago, was used to solve the Pari Das question. Chakker Kot argued that Pari Das belonged to its area since Pari Das was located within its area of the Dogra portering duty, and finally this argument was accepted by neighbouring villages. Most probably other arguments have been used by the contesting villages, but the outcome of the dispute was that the Dogra portering episode established precedence in solving the Pari Das issue.

Only one *das* is disputed. Jaglot claims proprietorship of Peden Das at the Indus–Gilgit River junction, since this was the destination of its transport duties. This claim is not accepted by Chakker Kot, which started its carrying from the same Peden Das. Also, Chakker Kot argued that most goods were carried up to Peden Das by Bhunji people on the Srinagar route, who may also have a legitimate claim to it. The fact that Peden Das is still contested testifies to the argument of historical precedence of the Dogra portering.

But still we may ask: Why did this particular episode invoke legitimacy of village property rights? Is the selection of the Dogra transport duty just a coincidence, or can it be related to some deeper meaning embedded in local culture? The significant thing to notice here is the fact that Pari village accepted the legitimacy of the Dogra episode in allotting Pari Das to Chakker Kot. As cultivable *das* land is an obvious asset to local farmers, it should be expected that Pari village would want the new land for themselves. Since Pari actually accepted the Dogra precedence, albeit grudgingly, it is reasonable to assume that the historical episode touched some chords of common meaning in the affected villages. Somehow, the episode must have been related to another field of experience, where a similar constellation of meaning is accepted and practised. What might that field be? Looking at the way individual farmers are allotted rights to land and water, we find a parallel to Chakker Kot's claim to Pari Das. My argument is that the claim to village property rights is a metaphorization of individual farmers' land rights.

Inside the village, the irrigation channel head is labelled *shishalo* in the Shina language, and the irrigated terrace adjoining the head is called *shishalo dish*. The rule is such that the owner of the *shishalo dish* has the duty to maintain the area of the channel running along his land, irrespective of how many other farmers, who also receive water from the same outlet, are situated below him. In return, he is accorded first priority to receive water. This principle was probably the argument employed to establish legitimacy in the Dogra episode. The innovation of applying this rule to village claims of *das* land implies two extensions to the basic idea. First, the claim to legitimacy was extended from individual households to villages. Second, a conceptual parallel was established between farmers maintaining the channel along their *shishalo dish*, and villages maintaining stretches of the transport route adjacent to their village lands. Channel and road are functional equivalents as means of transportation – of water and supplies respectively.

The metaphorization was made according to the scheme set out in Table 3.1.

Table 3.1: Metaphorization of land allocation

Village	Basic idea	Individual farmer
Road/path	Transportation	Channel
Das land	Proximity	*Shishalo dish*
Dogra portering	Duty	Channel maintenance
Das cultivation	Right	Water priority

The basic principle of the *shishalo dish* arrangement was an institutionalized link between the three ideas of (1) access to water rights, (2) immediate adjacency of land and channel, and (3) maintenance duties. Being highly meaningful to Shina people, the application of this old principle to the new claims on *das* land – hitherto owned by nobody – made those claims legitimate.

By searching their history, villagers found an event – the Dogra portering – that was useful in establishing *precedence* for the solution of the present problem of village rights to the new land. The precedence of this particular event was accepted because of its metaphorical resemblance to traditional channel maintenance arrangements. Metaphorization of the well-known *shishalo dish* practice to the Dogra portering period made sense of Chakker Kot's claim to Pari Das. Thus, the land question was solved.

The Pakistani government is flexible and understanding in matters like this. All privately owned land must be registered with the official land register officer (*patwari*), but the bureaucracy delays registration until local consensus is reached, thus leaving the decisions and procedures to the people involved.

The land division on Pari Das was undertaken on the assumption that the planned hydropower project will supply irrigation water to the land. The realization of the project will, however, generate a classical upstream–downstream water problem in the Sai catchment area. In such a situation, it is to be expected that the downstream settlements will oppose the plan of diverting water out of the catchment upstream. How do villagers relate to the expected hydrological changes, and how do they argue their cases?

Dispute over Sai Water Rights

In a semi-arid area like Shinaiki, water is the very basis for existence, and is thus the scarce resource *par excellence*. In the villages of Bhunji and Pari, water has become so scarce that shares of water rights are commodified for market exchange. In Bhunji, the army has the option for all water for 12 hours a day, while villagers are allowed to share the remaining 12 hours. The present arrangement of water distribution has become very complex through purchases and sales of shares. A permanent, individual share of one-hour weekly water from a one-eighth share of the total channel flow costs presently Rs 30,000 (approximately US$1,000). A subsistence farmer needs several such shares in order for the farm to be viable. In Bhunji and Pari, land is cheap and water is expensive.

In the Sai catchment, on the other hand, water is still free of charge. Once a farmer has obtained some land, he is also entitled to irrigation water on condition that he participate in communal maintenance of channels outside the cultivated area. However, some water rights have been formally divided in Jaglot, proving that the water situation is becoming more difficult downstream Sai.

In Damot village, all land is irrigated from the minor Damot Nala, a tributary to Sai (see Map 3.2). In April, only a small brooklet reaches Sai, hardly sufficient for the women to wash clothes; nearly all the water is used for irrigation. Water scarcity is not felt in Sai at present, but people are well aware that this may happen in the future. Scarcity is especially foreseen during the spring, before summer temperatures have risen sufficiently to melt the snow in the high mountains. This period of low river flow is also a particularly sensitive period for the winter wheat, which starts to germinate in mid-February. Also, a substantial part of the present river discharge is needed in October, when the summer crop of maize ripens.

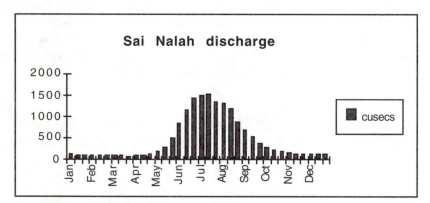

Fig. 3.2 Water discharge (cu ft/sec.) in Sai Nalah
Source: WAPDA 1992

Several conflicts over water are emerging in the catchment area, accelerated by the planned hydropower project. Chakker Kot, which has gained ownership of Pari Das, is eagerly supporting the power scheme, looking forward to expanding its cultivated area. But Damot and Jaglot downstream, on the other hand, strongly oppose it. In the discourse, the upstream and downstream settlements appeal to differing systems of meaning: i.e. to tradition and to religion.

The first settlements in the valley were those of Damot and Chakker Kot. Both claim to be the original one in good-humoured local rivalry, but archaeological findings suggest that there have been at least 700 years of settlement in Damot. Probably, population increase in the original settlement of Damot led some families to move upstream and construct channels at Chakker Kot. Later, they were joined by immigrants from upstream Indus, all belonging to the Shina-speaking clans (*kaom*) of Shin and Yashkun. The uppermost settlers were Shia Muslims, probably originating in Haramosh to the north. All other inhabitants of the valley belonged to the Sunni faith. The original settlers of Damot and Chakker Kot diverted water from Damot and Sai Nala respectively.

Later, but still several hundred years ago, Kohistanis settled beyond the areas used by the Shina population. Their farming technology was adapted to animal husbandry in high altitudes, thus not interfering with the original settlers. Simultaneously, Gujar semi-pastoralists came from Swat in the south, escaping from oppression by the majority Pathans there. They settled in the uppermost part of the valley. All the settlers living in Damot and further upstream, are perceived to be *holoshah* – meaning original settlers in the Sai valley.

Around the turn of the century, when the Kashmiri Dogra ruled the Gilgit Agency, the Shia settlements of the upstream Indus were plagued by frequent raiding by a Sunni Kohistani warlord. On the way to their victims, the Kohistani raiders had to cross Sai Nala at Jaglot, which was then uninhabited. An influential man in Bhunji on the other side of the Indus, Hadul, was promised land in Jaglot by the Kashmiri ruler if he could take control of the passage and prevent the Kohistani raiders from reaching northwards. Hadul succeeded in killing the Kohistani chief, so people say, and settled in Jaglot. He was soon joined by more Bhunji households who settled there to escape water scarcity. After Independence, many Kashmiri refugees settled in Jaglot, as did some newcomers from Kohistan. All inhabitants of Jaglot are perceived to be *operah* (newcomers or recent immigrants) as opposed to *holoshah* (original settlers).

In the time of the Dogras – probably around the turn of the century – a minor irrigation channel was constructed from Sai up to Pari village. Some people from upper Sai settled at Pari, and some of them diverted water to Chakker Kot Das on the hill between Chakker Kot and the Indus, and settled there. These are all *holoshah* people. Later, after Independence, Jaglot *operah* people extended their area of cultivation by constructing a new irrigation channel from Sai Nala. After the opening of Karakorum Highway in 1978, the market of Sonyar at the roadside developed, diverting more water from Sai.

Chakker Kot, in their support of the hydropower scheme, argue from the viewpoint of the *holoshah–operah* (indigenous–newcomer) dichotomy that only farmers belonging to the *holoshah* category have legitimate rights to the commonly held resources of water, high altitude forests and pastures. Thus, all the *operah* immigrants of Bhunjis, Kashmiris and Kohistanis in Jaglot, as well as an agricultural research station located there, and traders and café owners along the Karakorum Highway, are excluded from legitimate claims to water. Besides, Jaglot has extended its cultivated area considerably during the last twenty years without Chakker Kot protesting. It is only to be expected that Jaglot now accepts that some water is diverted to Pari Das, according to the upstream argument.

When it comes to the *holoshah* population of Damot, they have traditionally held rights to water in the Damot tributary, while Sai Nala has belonged to Chakker Kot. Thus, the people of Chakker Kot perceive it as their legitimate right to do whatever they like with the Sai water.

Lower Sai, and especially the *operah* settlers in Jaglot, argue otherwise. They claim it is illegal according to Islamic law (*Shariat*) to deprive downstream settlers of access to water. *Shariat*, in its turn, refers to highly legitimate perceptions of the global hydrological cycle as described in the Holy Quran. The morality is that man should not change the fundamental and divine order of nature, for example by diverting water out of its original catchment. By invoking this divine authority, lower Sai people try to render the *operah–holoshah* dicotomy invalid, and instead refer to the modern Pakistani discourse on Islamization that has recently reached Shinaiki through the activities of various rural religious organizations.

The Jaglot argument is that all people presently using water from the Sai should be able to continue to do so in the future. They have legitimate rights to water *qua* inhabitants of the catchment, irrespective of *holoshah* or *operah* status. Besides, the downstream settlements refer to a *jirga* (local assembly) decision dating back several years, according to which land rights by implication entitle a farmer to water rights providing only that he participate in communal channel maintenance. This *jirga* verdict is now considered invalid by upstream villagers, since it was reached before the advent of the hydropower scheme.

These disputes over water and land rights are recent. People are getting ready to react if changes in the present hydrology are undertaken, and if their perceived legitimate claims to land and water are violated. In discussing the issue, people sometimes resort to the threat of using force, estimating the respective strength of upper versus lower Sai. The traditional acephalous politics is obviously not dead yet.

Acknowleging these potential conflicts, the parties involved in the Sai hydropower project have changed their plans. The Northern Areas Public Works Department (NAPWD), the Water and Power Development Agency (WAPDA) and the Norwegian Agency for Development Cooperation (NORAD) have turned their attention to a smaller power plant in the Sai catchment, which will reduce estimated production from 16 to 10 MW.

Modernization and Local Particularism

The Sai method of coping with natural resource allocation reveals two aspects of the modernization process. First, modernization is not just an assimilation of traditional society into a universalistic state; rather, it is a highly innovative process. Local people – the resource managers – do not adapt to new arrangements imposed by the state in a casual manner. Adaptation is not just an instrumental process, aimed at coordinating local practice within a modern context. People try to make sense of the changes by searching for meaning in tradition (settlement history, Dogra portering), in religion (*Shariat*), and in present practices (channel maintenance). By combining ideas from various fields of meaning through metaphorization, ways are found to solve newly emerging problems of land and water rights. In some instances consensus is reached (land rights), but in others disputes arise about the validity of the various fields of meaning (water rights). Out of this innovative cultural process, new practices emerge, combining historical precedence with the challenges of modernity.

Second, the present case demonstrates the idiosyncratic nature of the innovation process. In Sai, modernization is dealt with by combining general ideas about the *holoshah–operah* (aboriginal–newcomer) dichotomy and rights and duties related to irrigation channels, with the local historical event of Dogra portering. Only the settlements along the Dogra transport routes from Rawalpindi and Srinagar to Gilgit are endowed with that option. Villages that were not included in the Dogra transport scheme must resolve their disputes over land and water in other ways.

References

Fernandez, J. (1986) *Persuasions and Performances. The Play of Tropes in Culture*, Bloomington: Indiana University Press.

Joshi, S.C. (ed.) (1986) *Nepal Himalaya: Geo-Ecological Perspectives*, Nainital: Nainital University Press.

Keay, J. (1990) *The Gilgit Game. Explorers of the Western Himalayas 1865–95*. Oxford: Oxford University Press.

Myers, N. (1986) 'Environmental Repercussions of Deforestation in the Himalayas', *Journal of World Forest Resource Management*, no. 2: 63–72.

Water and Power Development Agency (WAPDA) (1992) *Feasibility Study of Sai Nalah Hydro-electric Project*, Lahore: WAPDA.

Zarin, M.M. and Schmidt, R.L. (1984) *Discussions with Hariq. Land Tenure and Transhumance in Indus Kohistan*, Islamabad: Lok Virsa.

4 | A Community Management Plan: The *Van Gujjars* and the Rajaji National Park

Pernille Gooch

The real pressure on the forests has come not from development nor even timber extraction, except in localized pockets.
The inexorable pressure of population, including tribal population and livestock, has placed a fuel and fodder burden on the
forests that is considerably in excess of their carrying capacity.
The FSI [Forest Survey of India] estimates that some 99 million
tonnes of firewood were illicitly felled from the forests during
1987, such pilferage constituting a cut in excess of the silver-
culturally permissible limit. In the period since 1953, some
1,645 million m^3 of firewood are believed to have been illicitly
removed from the forests, resulting in the total destruction of 3
million hectares and the depletion of over 27 million hectares
(Lal 1989: viii).

There is a common belief that tribals and other vulnerable
sections of the community living in the forest regions are
uncultivated and uncivilized ... But this is a myth and an
illusion; there is so much traditional wisdom amongst these
people, accumulated over the centuries, that they are able to
live in harmony with nature. ... Our plan for forest management must, therefore, take into account the human beings who
live in the forests and nothing should be done which would
affect their daily existence or their means of subsistence (P.N.
Bhagwati, Former Chief Justice of India & Vice Chairman, UN
Human Rights Committee, in the Foreword to *Community Forest
Management in Protected Areas: Van Gujjar Proposal for the Rajaji
Area*, RLEK 1997).

Two contradictory lines of thought dominated discussions of the
Himalayan environment during the 1970s and 1980s, and their
repercussions are still clearly discernible today. One is 'The

Theory of Himalayan Environmental Degradation', depicted as the prediction that the Himalayan region is inevitably drifting into a situation of environmental supercrisis and collapse caused by the alleged population explosion among the mountain people (Ives and Messerli 1989: xvii). As more and more people (and their cattle) are utilizing the same common resources of forests and pastures for survival as well as for individual gains, a 'tragedy of the commons' would seem inevitable. The only viable solution to such a scenario would be a strong centralized state controlling the natural environment and its use through state institutions. This approach became very popular during the 1970s and 1980s and has its most memorable expression through Indira Gandhi's utterance at the Stockholm Conference for the environment in 1972: 'Poverty is the worst pollutant.'

The other approach sees both nature and the mountain subsistence peasant as victimized by 'modern development' and this line of thought was actualized in the Chipko movement. This has developed into a generalized concept with repercussions far beyond the Himalayan scenario, through what we may call the assumption of the 'ecosystem people' (see Gadgil and Guha 1995).

Both approaches see an 'environment in crisis' but they differ in their identification of the culprit. A narrativization with its own myths and utopias – or dystopias – has occurred within both agendas; moreover both have been used as rallying points for political action over the use of natural resources. In one approach 'people' are seen as external to the ecosystem and the harbingers of environmental dystopia, while in the other 'people' have been included in the natural processes and are seen as the providers of hope for a future utopia where both human and non-human elements of nature will live in a state of balance. The arguments contained in those theoretical approaches may also be discerned in discussions concerning environmental management and in the conservation debate. The adherents of the first line of thought tend to see villagers and forest dwellers as a threat to nature; they advocate 'pure conservation' without people in a forest managed by a state authority (like the Forest Department). The second approach sees people as the stewards of nature – or even part of nature – and argues for the involvement of local people in the management of national parks and sanctuaries.

Such changing views of the place of humans in the 'natural world' have been a recurrent theme in (Western) scientific and philosophical traditions:

> The ecological reinsertion of human beings into the world of natural processes is ... quite a recent feature of thought. From 1720 well into the 20th century, most philosophers and natural scientists continued to defend, in one way or another, their investment in keeping Humanity apart from Nature – 'in a world by itself' (Toulmin1990: 143).

During the last decade a change of attitude may be perceived from the strict conservation-without-people approach to one involving local people in the management of protected areas to varying degrees. In this article I shall discuss the changing views on the relations between people and protected areas, using as an example the (proposed) Rajaji National Park in the Shiwalik foothills in Uttar Pradesh and the forest-dwelling *Van* Gujjar pastoralists.

Here it should be stressed that I stayed with pastoral nomadic *Van* Gujjars during fieldwork. They shared their homes with me, discussed their situation with me, and confided their worries about the future. This means than my interpretation of the situation in the forest is to a large degree shaped by my position in the forest as 'being with the *Van* Gujjars'. This is an embodied knowledge and it is from that knowledge that the situation is interpreted. It was a position that I found muted when I first arrived and which then needed representation. There are, of course, countless other perspectives, other positions, from which the situation and the conflicts round the environment and forests in the region may be understood, and I have looked at other perspectives by interviewing differently positioned people. However, a discussion of the complexity of forest and people in western Uttar Pradesh would require far more space than is available here. Still, while the *Van* Gujjar situation in Rajaji is unique in many ways, it is also to a large extent representative of the situation of many other forest dwellers not only in India but all over the world.

The conflict that has evolved round the establishment of Rajaji has been extensively covered in the Indian media and it has mainly been exemplified in the case of the nomadic pastoral *Van* (forest) Gujjars and their struggle for a continued life in the forest. In 1992 the *Van* Gujjars – who have their camps within the park area during the winter – were threatened with eviction as they were conceived by both forest and wildlife authorities and by local 'nature lovers' as the most serious threat to the delicate ecological balance of the park as well as to its wildlife. The *Van* Gujjars answered by mobilizing themselves with the help of a local NGO, and they have actively resisted all efforts to settle them outside the forest. As the controversy round Rajaji intensified and was highlighted in the national media, the forest authorities were forced to allow the *Van* Gujjars to remain in the forest but only on an ad hoc basis. The conflict that followed showed the actors advocating the *Van* Gujjar case that a workable alternative plan had to be produced and presented in order to counteract the proposal for Rajaji as a 'conventional' wildlife sanctuary from which traditional forest dwellers would be banned. The state's policies – embodied in the Forest Department's management of India's forests – were criticized as anti-people. This made it necessary to come up with a powerful counter-image that would embody a pro-people approach to forest management. Through this approach, biodiversity was to be fused with cultural diversity and provide a picture of indigenous people as the last vanguard of nature protection.

The plan was to concretize ideas about forest management put forward by the community (e.g. the *Van* Gujjars themselves) and link these to contemporary discourses round the issue of nature conservation and people. The result was presented at a workshop in Dehra Dun in February 1996 (arranged by the local NGO, Rural Litigation and Entitlement Kendra, RLEK) as a plan for 'Community Forest Management in Protected Areas' (CFM-PA) subtitled 'We will turn this forest into a diamond: A *Van* Gujjar proposal for the Rajaji Area' (RLEK 1997). Here it is suggested that the *Van* Gujjars take over the guardianship of the park. This plan actualizes more theoretical discussions around local involvement in 'resource management' through a *de facto* case and has been seen as a concrete presentation of a utopia. It takes up a critique of prevalent forest legislation and its practical implementations as well as showing a possible way forward. As it proposes that the *Van* Gujjars be the main managers of the park area, with the Forest Department acting solely in a monitoring and supportive capacity, it is much more radical in its solution than the suggestions for eco-development through 'Joint Forest Management'[1] which are now increasingly seen as a way out of the people–conservation quagmire (cf. Saxena 1995).

The *Van* Gujjars' plan for Rajaji has already gained considerable attention as well as 'ardent support' (*Down to Earth*, 15 August 1993: 14). The Foreword to the plan was written by P. N. Bhagwati, former Chief Justice of India and presently Vice-Chairperson for the UN Committee for Human Rights. Bhagwati sees the uniqueness of the plan in the fact that it has been 'prepared with the effective participation of the people who are going to be [its] beneficiaries'. It has been discussed in Parliament (June 1996) and has gained interest in both the Ministry for Environment and Forest and in the Prime Minister's office. Representatives of the World Bank called a delegation of *Van* Gujjars and RLEK activists (September 1996) to discuss the plan and have acknowledged its importance for future policies related to people and nature conservation (A. Kaushal, pers. com.).

The *Van* Gujjars

The *Van*[2] (forest) Gujjars are transhumant buffalo herders, earning their livelihood from the sale of milk. Being one of the few Muslim 'tribal' groups in India, they are outside the caste system and their social organization is based on (relative) equality between interacting *deras* (camps) and lineages. Traditionally, moving from the subtropical foothills, where they stay in winter, to spruce forests and alpine meadows during summer, they practise a combination of forest pastoralism and transhumance. Being pure pastoralists, their whole lifestyle is completely dependent on access to the state forests. This means that they have no formal property rights to land and their use of the local ecosystem is dependent on the readings of customary rights and concession by the force that controls the resources (i.e. the state through its Forest Department).

The relationship between the *Van* Gujjars and the state was never an easy one, and the forest has been an arena for acts of 'hidden resistance' from the side of the *Van* Gujjars in response to state interventions in their forest utilization since the colonial times and the commencement of forest legislation (Gooch 1992). These problems have been intensified by the arbitrary readings of forest codes by forest officials and high demands for bribes now amounting to approximately a third of a family's yearly income. But although circumscribed and regulated, a life in the forest was still possible until the plan for Rajaji National Park forced what was previously a local forest debate out into the the national arena. This also necessarily led to the involvement of new sets of actors in the conflict, as NGOs with their social and environmental activists, politicians and the crucial media people sided with the *Van* Gujjars. For the *Van* Gujjars, the involvement of RLEK has been of the utmost importance. Avdesh Khaushal, the Chairperson of RLEK, already had a number of spectacular victories as a social and enviromental activist behind him when he took up the *Van* Gujjar case. He has been the master strategist behind the very successful fight to gain recognition for the *Van* Gujjars' claim to management over the park. Moreover he has been responsible for lobbying their case among top politicians, administrators and journalists.

Under the prevailing circumstances it would have been very difficult for the *Van* Gujjars to have fought the battle alone. As a nomadic people, they lacked a spokesperson from among their own community: someone with a formal education and sufficient knowledge about the life outside the forest to bring their case to national attention. RLEK became the bridge between the *Van* Gujjars and the outside world. However, the words that emerged from the forest came from the mouths of the *Van* Gujjars themselves and that was what gave them their strength. Now, as the whole issue of forest utilization by people is being questioned through the conservation debate, the *Van* Gujjars are being forced to 'leave the egg' (i.e. the world of the forest), to step outside of it and contemplate their own role in its (ecological) processes.[3] Only by doing that may they be allowed to remain. This means that ecological knowledge that was immanent has to be transcended and made explicit. That is what they were doing at the workshop by presenting themselves to the journalists and academics present as an integral part of the forest. What was advocated was the framework of a 'green ethos': simplicity, peacefulness and non-violence against other creatures. It has also been important to stress that the *Van* Gujjars are vegetarians and do not hunt. One of the main aims of the *Van* Gujjar movement has been to demonstrate that forest dwellers are an integral part of their environment; that they are the best guardians of the forests and can protect and regenerate their habitat while using it.

That the *Van* Gujjars are considered people with close ties to the forest is nothing new; they have long characterized themselves as *Jangli log* (forest people).What is new is that their life in the forest has become a national issue, as part of a new media interest in human–environment relations, where the catchword is 'ecological lifestyle' or 'living in harmony with the forest'. This also connects with wider intellectual debates in India (going back to the time of Mahatma Gandhi and his dream of an India consisting of self-sufficient village republics) which criticize the dark sides of Western development while celebrating the 'simple people' of the Indian countryside. By defying the state and holding on to a lifestyle embedded in Indian tradition and further seen as eco-friendly, the *Van* Gujjars have come to embody the very 'essence' of such considerations.

The 'Ecosystem People'

At the juncture between modernity and 'tradition', so-called traditional lifestyles are often seen as obstructions to development. This has surfaced in frequent debates over dams, conservation, commercial use of forest resources, and quarrying for natural resources. In response to such clashes of interests, local groups often stress identities and practices as embedded in local tradi-tions of sustainable behaviour when they feel threatened by new development projects. The villagers involved in the Chipko movement exemplify this trend. Here, the dominated and disadvantaged peoples, dependent on 'nature' for survival, can identify with an exploited and wounded 'Mother Earth' and through taking her side in the fight against the dominating forces – whether those are a diffusely expressed 'modern development' or more tangible representatives of local industries and local elites – they seek to retain control over local natural resources.[4] Borrowing an expression from Gadgil and Guha (1995: 98), this attitude to environmental problems may be characterized as the 'environmentalism of the poor'.

These grass-roots tendencies have been supported by a number of activists and intellectuals involved in theorizing the human–environment relation in the Indian context. In response to what is perceived as a rapid degradation of the Indian environment – by this group mainly seen as caused by a dangerous and flawed modernization process – demands are being voiced for alternative management solutions for the control over the natural resource base. The state has failed, so it is claimed, to safeguard the environment, so now it is time to try out alternative methods of resource management. And here the future is seen to lie in the hands of the people.

The Delhi-based Centre for Science and Environment (CSE) has been the most influential source for this way of thinking. It issued the 'Citizens' Reports on the State of India's Environment' at the beginning of the 1980s (CSE 1982; 1985). These books are now 'green' classics and were crucial in launching the environmental debate in India. What is depicted in the reports is the clash between India's poor – who are directly dependent on the natural environment – on the one hand, and an alien westernized development model – which furthers the destruction not only of people but also of 'everything natural' – on the other. It is consequently symptomatic that representatives of the CSE were among the first to support the *Van* Gujjar claim for the management of Rajaji. In a book on 'green villages' for a sustainable future, Agarwal and Narain (1989) found that the majority of the Indian people still survive within a biomass-based subsistence economy. The demands of this sector on the products of the land will increase with population growth and as the land area is not going to expand, the land must be made to produce more. This should be done within a 'framework for ecosystem specific develop-ment' and necessitates the management of local resources (the commons) by local communities, because only in that way can they be regenerated. The idea is that the usufructuary rights as well as the management should be given to the users of the natural environment in question. The rationale, then, is simple: to each village (or community in the case of nomads) their own local ecosystem to nurture and protect.

Anil Agarwal[5] made it clear in a discussion about the *Van* Gujjars and Rajaji National Park (pers. com., February 1994) that he included forests in the commons that would be best managed by local communities. Here he tells of two approaches to managing the resources of the forest, but the description also gives an all-round introduction to the theories behind 'resource-management by local communities':

> It is a question of managing that resource in such a way that it improves the ecological conditions as well as meeting the needs of the people. Now there are two ways of managing the resource. One is managing it in the Forest Department's style, which is excluding the people, which in turn will lead to more tensions around the resource and whenever the Forest Department is politically weak, it will lead to the degradation of the resource because the people will become increasingly alienated from the resource. On the other hand there is another possibility, where the people themselves manage the resource. Therefore they have a stake and an interest in that resource and they will have a vested interest in its sustainable management. ...

> What I basically feel is that the only way you can deal with national parks and sanctuaries and protect them properly is by involving people in the management. Which means that they should be the beneficiaries of the resource. Not the world, not the nation, not some great environmentalist or anything of the kind: it has to be the local people. They have to be the primary and most important beneficiaries. ... It is the local communities, if they are saved, that will save the world, not the other way round. ... It is the local people who are crucial. ...

I do not see this as a problem of protection. I see it as a problem of regeneration. That is the big difference. Forest Department and conservationists see that as a problem of protection. I see it as a problem of regeneration. Large proportions of the resource have been degraded and that degradation process continues. That process has to be reversed. ... So to me it seems that there is a clear problem in perspectives in their mindset. When I look at the thing, I look at it as a degraded piece of land which with people's management can be revived. While what they see is something the people are doing to destroy their environment and therefore they need to be thrown out. They see it in protection terms and exclusion terms. Protection in environmental terms and exclusion in social terms. I see it as regeneration in environmental terms and inclusion in social terms. Because I have seen these projects being successful all over the country I am confident it can be done. It is possible to get increased productivity in grass and in leaf fodder. ... The ecology is definitely capable of producing more. Regeneration is very fast in India (Anil Agarwal, pers. com., 1994).

Gadgil and Guha express similar ideas in their book on *Ecology and Equity*. According to them, it is the vast population of Indian rurals who are supposed to take care of nature because if nature is not protected, biomass will not be produced and consequently the rural poor will destroy the very base for their own survival. The ideology behind this is that 'the only route to a proper regime of restraint in resource use is therefore to pass on control to social groups who themselves reap the benefits of prudent use. Today these are by and large India's ecosystem people' (Gadgil and Guha 1995: 119).

Gadgil and Guha borrowed the notion of 'ecosystem people' from Dasman (1988), who makes a distinction between what he terms 'ecosystem peoples' (indigenous subsistence peoples) and 'biosphere peoples'. While the former are completely dependent on a localized ecosystem for their survival and will perish if it is destroyed, the latter depend on the global biosphere and may simply shift to a new location if the ecosystem in which they live deteriorates. Dasman agues that ecosystem peoples will look at their ecosystems as a *home* which must be nurtured and cared for, while biosphere peoples will create national parks in order to conserve nature.

Ecosystem people should be given far greater access to and control over the natural resource base of their own localities. Ecosystem people should also be given an important role in a new, largely decentralized system of governance …Thus the key Gandhian prescriptions that make perfect sense are that ecosystem people must be empowered (Gadgil and Guha 1995: 118–19).

In the introduction I discussed two approaches to environmental protection. One advocates a strong centralized state power to pass environmental laws and ensure their enforcement, using coercion if necessary. The other approach is the one supporting decentralization: that local populations themselves assume responsibility for the protection of their own environmental space. This latter proposition involves a sense of wholeness between environment and people, and has been characteristic of political environmentalism from its beginnings in the late nineteenth century (Bramwell 1989). I took up the utopian aspects of such notions in the introduction to this chapter. The dream behind such ideas is a world in balance where we will all be 'ecosystem people'. In such a scenario existing ecosystem people become the vanguard of the new world order.

What we have in the arguments presented may be synthesized down to something along the following lines: if people are dependent on a local environment (in the form of a common) and its production of biomass for their survival, they will use it because they have to. The 'state' may erect higher and higher fences, impose greater and greater fines, and use any other means of coercion they see fit, but it will not help much. What will happen is just that people will become increasingly alienated and the land more and more degraded. The only thing that may stop people from degrading local commons is to create institutional forms of management that make them responsible and give them usufructuary rights. The premise is that the 'users', in order to survive, will find ways to preserve the environment and enhance the biomass produced. If they fail to do so, they will be the first to perish.

Rajaji: A Forest Context of Trees, Wildlife *and* People

Rajaji National Park[6] is seen as a representative part of the ecosystem of the Shiwalik foothills (see Map 4.1) and is the Northwest limit

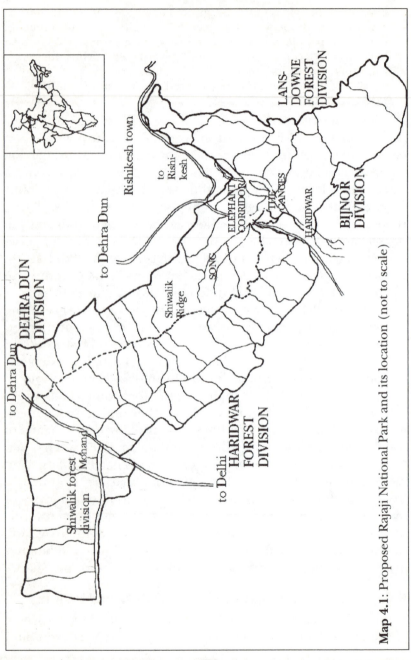

Map 4.1: Proposed Rajaji National Park and its location (not to scale)

of elephant and tiger populations in India. It covers an area of 831 km^2 and it will be the largest national park in the state. It was a favourite hunting ground for the Moguls and later also for the British. Situated between the Himalayas and the Gangetic plains, it is still an area rich in biodiversity and it is considered to be one of the better preserved parts of the Shiwaliks. It is also an extremely fragile system shaped by easily eroded sandstone hills intercepted by deep ravines and broad *raos* (riverbeds that only fill during the monsoons). During monsoons these *raos* become raging torrents carrying vegetation and heavy boulders on their way.

The vegetation consists mainly of *sal* (*Shorea robusta*) or mixed deciduous forests. Grasses and leaves grow rapidly after the monsoons and they keep their greenery through the winter helped by the winter rains. In February the water shortage starts to become evident and the forests begin to dry up. The process accelerates; by April there will be an acute shortage of both water and green fodder, and the forest will look dry and dead. Aerial photos of crown density for 1981 show that approximately half of the forest has 60 per cent or more of crown cover, a third of the area has 20–60 per cent crown cover and the rest less than 20 per cent crown cover (Kumar 1995: 33). When the British forester and nature lover, F. W. Champion, walked or rode through these rugged foot-hills in the 1920s they were still clad in dense forest and abundant with wildlife – a 'naturalist's and sportsman's paradise' (Champion n.d. [*ca.* 1930]: 184). This part of the Shiwalik forests was also at that time the home of the Gujjar pastoralists, characterized by Champion as the 'jungle herdsmen', whose ways were known by the tigers through a long relationship (Ibid.: 126).

The *Van* Gujjars see the forest – their *jungle* – as an inter-dependent system to include *Van* Gujjars and buffaloes. Here it is of importance that the *Van* Gujjars also characterize their buffaloes as *jangli* – and include them in the category of 'wildlife', i.e. life that is integral to the forest. As transhumant pastoralists, they utilize ecosystems at different altitudes according to the avail-ability of fodder and water. In winter they stay in the Shiwaliks and use leaf fodder for their buffaloes. It is only specific kinds of trees, so-called fodder trees, that can be used and these trees are lopped, usually once every other season. In summers they migrate to the pine and spruce forests in the mountains and the buffaloes are left to graze in the alpine meadows. In this way the whole region is seen as a large connected system where in summer the force of life itself moves from the dried-out forest in the foothills up into the new fresh pastures in the mountains. After summer, life moves in the other direction back into the lowland where everything will be fresh and new after the monsoon while life in the alpine meadows will die covered in snow. In this system the *Van* Gujjars and their buffaloes follow the cycle of life on its annual movements. This is the miracle of *qudrat* and the name *qudrat* is used simultaneously for nature and for God. So it is the miracle of the God who is also nature that there is always life in the form of green fodder somewhere in the larger system. In this way the *Van* Gujjars survive by following the natural changes. This is described very eloquently by Noor Jamal from Timli Range:

> When we come down after the summer we find everything looking [as if it were all] one, all is green and you will not find a single tree that is cut. When we leave [the foothills in late spring] then the forest is dry and pale. The hot wind (*lu*) will fire from this side – from that side – blow, blow. There will be life in the hills. That will live and this will die. That will be *qudrat*'s miracle. Then afterwards that will die and this will live [indicating the transfer of life from the mountains up there to the forest down here]. When we go down the leaves will keep drying in the hills. There it will snow and leaves and grass will become buried.

[What happens to the wild animals when the forest dries up?]

> It is like this, the light summer rains will give life to jungle grass [he shows strands of green grass growing at the edge of the *rau*] and on that the animals will live. *Qudrat* provides only grass enough for the [wild] animals to live on, not for Gujjars. For Gujjars it will be in the hills.

The Gujjars claim that they are integral to the world of the forest: 'Forest is a veil behind which we live'. That they are '*jangli log*' – literally forest people or forest dwellers – is what the *Van* Gujjars tell me again and again when they try either to clarify what distinguishes them from surrounding populations or to stake their claims to the forest. They assert that the forest belongs to them and their buffaloes in the same self-evident way in which it belongs to the wildlife. 'See for yourself', they say, 'here, the buffaloes and the deer share the leaves at night beneath the trees.' What they stress is that the natural ties between them and their forest environment are those signifying a people still living *within* the world of nature; they contrast their own 'simple' way of life in the forest with the lives of *gaon log*, village people, or *shahar log*, town people. The two latter groups, according to the *Van* Gujjars, penetrate the forest from the outside, always coming and leaving but not making the forest into a home, unlike the *Van* Gujjars. In public – and I shall exemplify this below with speeches made at the workshop – the *Van* Gujjars use sentences like 'the forest is our mother', 'we are part of forest', 'we have always lived in harmony with the wildlife', 'we are the guardians of the forest', etc. In daily talk in the forest their language will be much more specific and they will show an intimate knowledge of their environment. For the *Van* Gujjars the environment is 'internalized'. It is part of *habitus*,[7] a knowledge gained through childhood practice based on a community's direct actual practice of survival in its natural environment.

But if we consider people living in a direct relationship with their environment through practice we understand that such a relationship must by necessity be environment-specific. This discussion may be broadened by considering two quite different ways of looking at nature. One is the *cosmopolitan* – representative for the 'biosphere people' discussed earlier – where 'love of nature' might mean any piece of nature, as in ecotourism where you might climb Kilimanjaro this year and photograph penguins in Antarctica the next; or, to draw an example closer to the topic of this article, visit Corbett National Park today to spot a tiger and Rajaji Park next weekend for a glimpse of an elephant. Against this perspective may be posited that of the *agriculturist or forest dweller*, people dependent on subsistence in a localized environment. They are situated in a specific environment through a direct human–environment relation and for them nature is not interchangeable. It means all the difference for the *Van* Gujjars if they are in Corbett National Park or in Rajaji Park. *Van* Gujjars are still rooted in place. As old Faqa said when threatened with re-settlement to a place about 50 km away, 'Pathri – the new settlement – is not my country. It is another country where I cannot live.'

With the above discussion in mind, we may look again at the notion of the 'ecosystem people'. In the discussion by Gadgil and Guha they are the people who would be motivated to use a certain locality in a sustainable way because their livelihood depended on it (Gadgil and Guha 1995: 137). And as we have seen above, the *Van* Gujjars show that they have a contextualized relationship with their environment which they know intimately through generations of interaction.

This would mean seeing Rajaji as an ecosystem[8] where trees, animals – both wild and domesticated – *and* people make an eco-logical loop circulating nutrients and energy through the system. Here, the role of the system's human participants would be re-generative, i.e. enhancing the amount of biomass produced for all wildlife (*jangli janwar*), including buffaloes. If we link this to the discussion by Agarwal, quoted above, it would only be through involving local communities directly in the management of forests that this increase in the biomass productivity of the forest could be brought about. Agarwal also provides a model for how biodiversity could be maintained under *Van* Gujjar management of the park:

> Now what I recommended to the government is that they should have a management agreement with the Gujjars. The management agreement should specify the setting up of a committee to identify the biological indicators of regeneration. Let the government say that these are the time-bound biological indicators we expect and it should set up a monitoring committee to look into that. It should be based on scientific indicators and not whims and fancies. And the Gujjars should agree to these biological indicators. ... And if the government feels they are degrading the environment, then it can cancel the management agreement (Anil Agarwal, pers. com., 1994).

Rajaji: A Contested Environment

If we leave the more theoretical discussion over future models and return to the reality that is Rajaji in the 1990s, we shall find a forest that is very different from the 'naturalist's paradise' of the 1920s admired by Champion. The *Van* Gujjars will tell similar stories of a forest that was earlier dense with a wide diversification of trees, with tall grass and teeming with wild animals.

The forest divisions that now constitute Rajaji National Park were taken over by the Forest Department in 1868. After forty years of excessive fellings at the beginning of colonial rule[9] it was declared a reserved forest in 1879. So the area has a history of forest management of more than a century (Kumar 1995a: 73–74). The 'official' management plan for Rajaji compiled by its Director, Diwakar Kumar, gives a depressing review of the first sixty to seventy years of forest management:

> A overview of the past history of management of the area clearly indicates that the initial 60 to 70 years of Management History Conservation and Protection of Wild Animals was not the priority of Forest Managers. More emphasis was [placed] on the exploitation of forests and Shaker [hunting]. Most of the prescriptions and creation of working circles in the management plan were aimed at more exploitation, better yield of forest produce[,] creation of more and more shooting blocks and obtaining more and more revenue out of the forest wealth. Some of the presumptions like removal of Mallets trees, suppression of grasses, planting of eucalyptus in grassy blanks inside the forest area, were contrary to Wild Life Conservation and contributed [to] habitat destruction. Exploitation of timber and NFTP by forest contractors was another major cause of habitat destruction (Kumar 1995a: 191).

Kumar further states that it was not until the 1970s that the importance of conservation and wildlife protection was taken into consideration in the working plans for the area. But in reality the new policies were not implemented and the status quo was maintained. It is only now after the creation of the proposed park that 'regular efforts are being made for protection and conservation of wildlife in the area' (ibid.: 192).

Like other national parks in India, Rajaji has a large human population both within the park area and in towns and villages on the periphery. Modern development has also made major encroachments on the park. Among the more significant are: a large army ammunition dump; an electricity power-plant with an adjoining township; a chemical plant; a railway line; a railway station; and several major roads. The population pressure (from others, not the *Van* Gujjars) in and around the park is immense. Within the park there are twelve revenue villages and a number of settlements, and just outside its boundaries about eighty villages are dependent on the resources of the park for firewood and fodder. Close by are also a number of towns including Dehra Dun, with a district population approaching one million.

Wildlife has been severely affected by these circumstances. For example, the construction of a canal for power generation in the 1970s made it impossible for the elephants to migrate and trapped them in the western part of the park. Wildlife is further disturbed by an army shooting range in the forest just west of Rajaji. Apart from this, the area has been part of forest development schemes where indigenous species, providing food for the wild animals, have been cut down and replaced with plantations of commercially valuable trees.

In their evaluation of what it is that contributes to forest deterioration and threatens to the wildlife the state (i.e. the park authorities) and local communities blame each other. According to the park authorities, the main pressures exist in the form of threats from local people through overgrazing, overlopping, firewood collection, etc. (Kumar 1995a: 197). Representatives of the *Van* Gujjars as well as other local communities, however, see the impact of 'destructive management practices' by the Forest Department as the main threat to maintaining Rajaji in a state of ecological balance. They claim that a century of malpractice in managing the park is now showing in a deteriorating environment. 'The legacy of past practices remains evident' (RLEK 1997: 51; cf. Kumar 1995a: 197–98). All sides agree that malpractice in the forms of poaching and illicit felling of timber by professional gangs constitutes a serious threat to the ecology of the park. But these activities are mainly organized by 'outside' urbanized forces, not by local communities. In the plan compiled by Kumar, the *Van* Gujjars are mentioned as one of the main threats to the park. 'The wildlife authorities and researchers feel that the Gujjars *while they were originally in harmony with nature,* are now causing irreversible ecological damage' (Kumar 1995a: 198, my emphasis). Two main reasons are given. First, they have stopped migrating,[10] which means that the forest is not given a period of rest and regeneration during the summer and monsoon period. Second, they have grown substantial in number and are now competing unfavourably with the wildlife for a diminishing resource base of fodder and water. So what the authorities see in the *Van* Gujjars is a 'fall from grace' because 'originally they were living in harmony with nature'; or in other words a sustainable way of life has changed into an acute state of unsustainability.

What the Forest Department advocates in its management plan for Rajaji is a two-zone system:

- a core zone which will be maintained free of all biotic interference (including prohibition to entry by unauthorized persons) and where all rights and concessions of local people will cease to apply (this is an area which with minor alterations is equal to the present proposed park).

- a buffer zone where rights and concessions will be allowed to meet the needs of the local people (this area is now mainly lying outside the park but will be included in the park administration with the implementation of the plan) (Kumar 1995b: 11).

The buffer zone will be the area where eco-development projects are to be carried out. By doing this it is felt that the incentives of the 1988 National Forest Policy will have been implemented through the 'involvement of local population in the protection and development of the forests and recognizing their rights on the forest produce ... and assuring benefits and rights to usufruct by developing viable partnerships with the village communities' (ibid.: 68–69).

There are about 5,500 *Van* Gujjars living in the park area with approximately 12,000 buffaloes.[11] For them the official plan suggests '[r]elocation of the Gujjars outside the park through a viable package of rehabilitation and fodder farming measures, which consists of stall-feeding buffaloes, giving up of transhumance and receiving efficient marketing support' (ibid.: 69). But the plan also states: 'Any overnight change in their life style is not possible. In fact *any forced attempt* [to 'rehabilitate' them outside the present park area] will lead to serious problems for the park management' (ibid.: 3, my emphasis). The 'serious problems' mentioned here stem from the enormous support given to the *Van* Gujjars' side of the controversy by outside agencies, especially the national media, which has portrayed the *Van* Gujjars as 'the victims of conservation' in countless newspaper articles as well as in television broadcasts. The events that took place in 1992, when the *Van* Gujjars on their return to the foothills in autumn were denied entrance back into the proposed park, have not been forgotten by the forest authorities. It was on that occasion that the plight of the *Van* Gujjars started hitting the headlines of the national media and after a couple of weeks of escalating conflict, the park authorities were forced to let the *Van* Gujjars and their buffaloes back into the park (Gooch 1994; 1997a).

So at the moment the situation is that any relocation of the *Van* Gujjars would have to be voluntary. However, as a voluntary move from the forest is very unlikely for all but a few *Van* Gujjars, the future of Rajaji is at a standstill, which gives the *Van* Gujjars a very strong position at the negotiating table. In this connection it was a significant accomplishment that the Chief Conservator of the Forest (Uttar Pradesh) as well as the regional Conservator of the Forest and a local DFO (Divisional Forest Office) were all present at the national workshop for the presentation and discussion of the preliminary draft of the *Van* Gujjar Management Plan. For the *Van* Gujjar leaders, active in the workshop discussions, this was extremely important and showed them that their case was being taken seriously in the body that had always had the final say in their affairs (and whose representatives were seen as 'minor gods' as well as 'worst enemies'), namely the Forest Department.

A solution could have been JFM (Joint Forest Management), and this is what has been offered by the park administration in accordance with the guidelines given above. But that idea was turned down by the *Van* Gujjars because it was seen as just an extension of current policies. According to this model, the Forest Department and local people should cooperate in managing the forests, in this way forests would be protected and the needs of the people in terms of forest resources would be met. However, to change age-old power relations of exploitation between forest dwellers and forest officials overnight was considered an impossibility. Second, Uttar Pradesh Forest Department's guidelines for JFM do not consider people like the *Van* Gujjars who actually *live* within the forest; the plans involving local people are made exclusively for the buffer zones, while the core areas are left out to be managed entirely by the Forest Department. This was also demonstrated by the official plan for Rajaji presented above. So in order to benefit from JFM, the *Van* Gujjars would have to leave their forest home and settle somewhere on the outskirts, which is exactly what they are struggling to avoid.

Presentation of the Community Management Plan for Protected Areas

The workshop presenting the *Van* Gujjar Management Plan for Rajaji National Park was held at the National Petroleum Institute and the inauguration ceremony took place in the large central hall with room for more than 400 people. Around 11 o'clock the hall started filling up with people, but these were not the usual conference delegates: the people pouring in were bearded men in *loongi* and *kurta* with rough blankets in soft red colours thrown over their shoulders, and a smaller number of women, who were also wrapped in homespun blankets. Several hundred *Van* Gujjars had come out of the forests and, fully aware of their importance at this occasion, they started filling the hall by occupying the front rows first. Quite obviously they had come with a feeling of hope and a new confidence.

The workshop was presented as an event that went beyond the ordinary. D. Bandhyopadya, Chairman, Indian Institute of Management, Calcutta, started his inauguration speech by saying:

> This is a historic moment: many seminars are being conducted around the world these days but very few are meaningful as the people most affected have never been included in them. This management plan will be made with the *Van* Gujjars' and other people's help and in that it will be unique. This is a forest that belongs to the people of the state but the government overlooks the rights of the people and itself starts assuming those inherent rights.

This again links to the discussion with which I started this article: should we opt for centralized State control or decentralized community management of natural resources? *To whom do the forests belong?* And who are the wiser and more ecologically oriented managers of forests – the Forest Department or the forest dwellers? A point that was taken up by speaker after speaker was the fact that everybody wants to preserve the forest; the question is simply how this objective may best be attained. Although the *Van* Gujjars were the actual community involved, it was clear that they were exemplifying much broader discussions about forests and people in India in general.

While the plan synthesizes ideas and suggestions made by the *Van* Gujjars themselves the information was collected and formalized by an independent research team initiated by RLEK, the Dehra-Dun-based NGO which is actively supporting the empowerment of the *Van* Gujjar community through various projects. If we turn now to the actual plan, we see that it proposes an integral view of the forest ecosystem and the people who live within it. Here the concept of people 'as a part of forests' has taken form and been incorporated in the structure of the plan.

Community Forest Management in Protected Areas (CFM-PA) is a set of organizational structures and processes for defining and managing protected areas. According to this framework, the local people who have the traditional rights to inhabit and/or use the area become the leaders in managing the resource while government departments and other stakeholders assume a monitoring and supportive role. The overall objective is to protect and administer in a sustainable manner the ecosystem, its wildlife and the traditional rights and lifestyles *of the local peoples who are integral to it* (National Consultation Workshop, RLEK 1996: 13 (my emphasis)).

In the existing spatial distribution of habitation in the park, the *Van* Gujjars have their camps (*deras*), spread out in the core area, while the villagers traditionally utilize the resources of the border areas. The *Van* Gujjars are already organized spatially in *khols*, i.e. families living along each of the main *raos*. These will form the base for decentralized management equivalent to the village level in the ecosystem specific management structure discussed above. Within each of these *khols*, it is proposed that a *khol* committee should be formed with participation from all *deras*. Women have a strong role traditionally among the *Van* Gujjars, hence gender equity should be taken into consideration.[12] Representatives for the villagers should be members of *khol* committees in relation to their level of use of resources in individual *khols*.[13] The *khol* committee should work on such issues as carrying capacity – e.g. the number of buffaloes allowed within a specific area – and regeneration of forest. They should also be responsible for recording any illegal activities in their area to the appropriate authorities. Here the *Van* Gujjars have suggested that a number of young Gujjars be trained as forest guards and provided with radio communication to perform the supervisory function. The idea behind this is that while the forest officials only patrol the forest in the daytime, the *Van* Gujjars stay in the forest 24 hours a day and will be able to provide the forest with eyes that see without being seen.

Other institutions for decentralized management are committees of villagers for the extraction of the resources traditionally used by them. These will be area-specific and they will be cooperating with the *khol* committees in areas used by both parts. Range *panchayats* will be appointed at a higher level in the structure for mediation and conflict resolution. Those will be similar to the customary *panchayats* (local councils) already functioning among the *Van* Gujjars for the resolution of conflicts. A regional committee will be responsible for the overall policy framework and will act as a monitoring and advisory body. It will also act as a mediator between the community and the government. It should be appointed by the Chief Conservator of the Forest, Uttar Pradesh, and include among its members representatives of the Van Gujjars and the villagers, the NGO involved in the project, as well as authorities from the park, the Forest Department, the police and the Wildlife Institute of India. It should also have three members (one of whom should be a lawyer) with no vested interests in the Rajaji area.

What I presented above is the *Van* Gujjars' proposal translated into academic language. But most of the *Van* Gujjars are illiterate and so far they have no academics among their number to present their case and suggestions directly in written form. It is therefore important to include their own oral representation in the presentation of their case. Leaders of the *Van* Gujjars as well as village representatives sat at the workshop negotiation table with representatives of the Forest Department, activists, lawyers, intellectuals, environmentalists and journalists. And while the intellectuals argued among themselves about the viability of the plan and the journalists took an active part in the proceedings in defence of the *Van* Gujjars, the latter spoke eloquently about how they would be the best managers of the forest. Their words speak for themselves but they also link directly to the discussion about 'ecosystem people' presented above. This is further a discursive use of identity as a political means. These are voices that have usually been subdued but that are now able to represent their community as a part – though still not an equal part – of the environmental discourse. They are speaking on the side of nature and it is only from this 'privileged' position that they are able to gain an audience.[14] This is an expression of the 'environmentalism of the poor and marginalized' which I discussed above. It is further expressing the ecological knowledge of a community in a symbolic language that also makes sense to people outside of that community. An extraordinary situation creates new needs; one of those being the need for a leadership consisting of people who could express such tacit knowledge. Moreover this had to be done in such a way that the community as a whole could identify it as *their* knowledge; it had to be recognized as 'the way of the Gujjars'. Mustooq Lambardar – an illiterate elderly man who had previously been one of many minor leaders – emerged early during the conflict as a master of rhetoric and became the leading representative of his people. He was the one to express this implicit knowledge of the *Van* Gujjars in a language that other *Van* Gujjars recognized 'as the way things are' as well as 'the way we really are'. The strategy used by him has been to establish the *Van* (forest) Gujjars as 'natural ecologists'. Below I shall present extracts from Mustooq's representation as well as that of another leader, Gulam Nabi.

Mustooq Lambardar: I am a *Van* Gujjar and I am here to tell you from where the *Van* Gujjars came; what they do for a living; and what their ideology is. I congratulate all of them [the *Van* Gujjars] because you have given us an opportunity to show everybody what the *Van* Gujjars are. I thank you for your concern. There are many Gujjars in India but I am only speaking for the *Van* Gujjars. Those are the Gujjars who have looked after the forest over the years, who have sustained a symbiotic relationship with the forest and who have continued to stay in the forest. The *Van* Gujjars are my brothers and sisters. Their relationship with the forest is not a new one, it has taken centuries for this relationship to become established and it is characterized by looking after the trees and looking after the buffaloes.

All the *Van* Gujjars share this feeling that if someone harms the forest, they would want to fight that enemy. This power is not with us, it is actually with the Forest Department. The Forest Department is making this forest into a national park which includes the trees and the animals but nobody thought of including the Van Gujjars. The forest division is being given money by the government to protect the forest, but when the weaker animals such as the deer are being threatened by the stronger animals, it is the *Van* Gujjars and their children who protect the animals.

While living in the forest we do not fear the wild animals. When there is so much love between the wild animals and the Gujjars, why then does the government want to exclude the *Van* Gujjars from the forest? Instead of taking us out of the jungle, why don't they ask *us* to be the caretakers of the forest? We should be given the task of protecting the forest instead of throwing us out. So much money is given as taxes to the government by the Gujjars but this money never comes back to us. That money should be used for the betterment of the forest and the *Van* Gujjars. This money should be used for growing more trees and for educating the *Van* Gujjar children. Even on his deathbed the *Van* Gujjar desires to be in the forest in the next life as well. ... The *Van* Gujjars do not have any doors in their houses, and that shows they are not afraid of the wild animals. That is actually how we live together. Even the animals know about the *Van* Gujjars living in the forest: that is why the carnivorous animals do not enter their *deras*. Even the animals accept them as part of the jungle. We often hear that in big cities and towns thieves break in, but nothing of this sort is heard of in our part of the jungle. The *Van* Gujjars only start to fight when they have to protect the trees or the lives of the wild animals. The leaves of the jungle, the soil of the jungle and the water of the jungle are the life, the blood and the living and dying of the *Van* Gujjars.

Gulam Nabi: Ever since the forest began the Van Gujjars have been living in it, and as the world has progressed, other people have risen into lucrative positions but the Gujjars are still where they were, in the jungle. And now if the Van Gujjars are asked to leave the forest and adopt some other livelihood, it is the most difficult thing to do. We do not know any other job and our future generations if they can learn some other activity while living in the forest ,then it may be possible for them but otherwise not. If we are turned out of the forest we will be destroyed and the lives of our wives and children will be destroyed. ...

We pay taxes twice a year. If the *zamindar*, cultivator, pays taxes then he would become the owner after a few years, this I have heard. We have stayed in the jungle for hundreds of years but we have yet not become the owners. When the national park was made, nobody consulted us: when Pathri [a colony made outside the forest for resettlement of the *Van* Gujjars from the park] was made, nobody consulted us. If now a new place is made, it is quite possible that they will say that we came just yesterday [to the forest] and this does not belong to us. We are a very simple people and in order to make one's way in the outside world, one needs an education to survive, but we know only how to look after buffaloes, their fodder and the jungle. It is now that Mr Kaushal [Chairman of RLEK] has given us a chance to speak – earlier we have always been afraid of speaking in front of the outside world in case we should say something wrong.

In speech after speech the *Van* Gujjars were using the workshop as an arena for stating their claim to the forest. The voice from the otherwise downtrodden and marginalized was now delivering a message that as part of the environmental discourse was being given new meanings and a new audience. The tribal, commonly perceived to be 'uncultivated and uncivilized', was speaking with the mouth of 'traditional wisdom... accumulated over the centuries' about how to live 'in harmony with nature' (Bhagwati in the quotations used as an epitaph for this article). Situated now in a new context, the *Van* Gujjars also speak with a newly-found sense of confidence. As Gulam Nabi said, 'Now we have been given a chance to speak – earlier we have always been afraid of speaking ... in case we should say something wrong.'

A very important part of the message is the establishment of a special *Van* Gujjar identity close to nature: 'There are many Gujjars in India [but we are] the *Van* Gujjars. [The] Gujjars who have looked after the forest ... have lived in harmony with it' (Mustooq). 'As long as forests have existed, the *Van* Gujjars have lived in them and when everybody else left, the *Van* Gujjars stayed back and continued their work of taking care of the forest and the wild animals' (Gulam Nabi). After establishing close links to the forest the *Van* Gujjars can speak from the vantage point of the 'voice of nature itself'. Thus they speak not only for themselves and their own survival but also for the continuance of the trees and the wildlife. What the *Van* Gujjars express here is the notion of a shared environment of trees, animals and people, fused in a relationship of interdependence. What is stressed is that one can-not survive without the other. Or in the words of Mustooq: 'The Forest Department is making this forest into a national park but nobody thought about including the *Van* Gujjars.' Now they do.

Conclusion

What we have discussed here is a degrading forest: a piece of nature which is retaining part of its natural grace and relatively varied flora and fauna (it is, after all, one of the best preserved parts of the Shiwaliks) but a nature that is under a perpetual siege from all sides. It is pressurized by the needs of the people for biomass, necessary for survival, as well as being under a strong and powerful assault from modern development – from shooting ranges for India's modern weaponry to encroachment by industrial plants, highways and railroads; and from illegal felling of timber and rampant poaching. What everybody (exempting perhaps the 'timber and wildlife Mafia') agrees on is that the fragile ecological system of Rajaji must be preserved for the future. Rajaji is now to a great extent dysfunctional. Instead of degrading it further, the process should be reversed and it should again become the rich bio-diversity described by Champion in the 1920s. The problem is just how this miracle may best be realized. This is where people do not agree. The *Van* Gujjars claim that they will be the best and most prudent managers of the park, or, in the words of Mustooq Lambardar when he first came out with the idea, 'Why not give the management to us? We will turn this forest into a diamond' (at a meeting with CSE in Delhi, autumn 1992).

One of the strongest and most persuasive arguments of the *Van* Gujjars is that they are the only ones who know the forest from inside; that they are an integral part of its natural processes and as such they cannot harm it. As long as the *Van* Gujjars are perceived to speak with authenticity – that they are what they claim to be – this becomes a very strong argument which it is difficult for any urbanized person with a belief in the strength of the people (as well as the vices of the state) to oppose. And it is through arguments of this sort that they have gained growing support for their case. Now, when they actually have a workable plan – a 'people's plan', as an alternative to the Forest Department's (or the state's) plan – their position in the negotiations over the management of Rajaji has become very strong. As I stated in the introduction, there is now great political backing for the *Van* Gujjars' case as well as pledges of support from World Bank representatives.

Perhaps surprisingly, the *Van* Gujjars' management plan has also gained strong support from local villagers who use the Rajaji environment. The plan has been discussed with local village leaders and their suggestions have been included. It seems that also they prefer an alternative to the present 'rule' by the Forest Department. The Forest Department's plan for JFM has not been seen as convincing. On the basis of people's earlier experiences with the arbitrary rule of forest officials, the suggestion that the same officials should start to consider the needs of local villagers and sit down and share power with them is mainly seen as the 'tears of the crocodile'. Nobody believes that the Forest Department will really reliquish part of its power to the users of the forest. As positions stand at the moment, the main resistance to CFM-PA (Community Forest Management of Protected Areas) comes from the Forest Department and the Wildlife Institute, which is natural as they are the ones who will have to yield power in order to let in the *Van* Gujjars. Giving the management to the *Van* Gujjars and other local people in Rajaji will be like opening Pandora's Box because behind them, in the wings, countless other forest-dwelling groups in India (and beyond)[15] who are watching and waiting. Nobody knows if the *Van* Gujjar management will be successful or if they can manage to withstand all the pressures on the park area; but the plan has come from the *Van* Gujjars themselves and a number of safety valves have been built into it. The concept of people as the best managers of natural resources also needs to be concretized. How successful the *Van* Gujjars have been in persuading representatives for the Forest Department is clearly demonstrated by a commitment made by the Conservator of Forest from Meerut at the last session of the workshop – and I will let him have the concluding remark:

> Gujjars are part of the ecology of the forest. That is most important. And they have to stay in the forest. They can't go outside. It is my personal form of commitment. While protecting the forest all facilities must be given to the Gujjars.

Acknowledgements

The author is grateful to Avdesh Kaushal and his family in Dehra Dun for their hospitality and friendship during fieldwork. I also want to thank Praveen Kaushal for assistance and for all discussions we have had about the *Van* Gujjars and their situation in the forest. Thanks also go to Anil Agarwal, RLEK staff and to participants in the workshop on community forest management in Dehra Dun. I further want to thank Staffan Lindberg, Göran Djurfeldt and Stig Toft Madsen for critical comments. Most of all my thanks go to the *Van* Gujjars in the forests, who shared their life experiences and worries with with me, and especially to the *Van* Gujjar leaders Mustooq Lambardar from Chilla Range and Gulam Nabi from Kaluwalla. My research project on the Gujjars is financed by the Swedish Agency for Research Cooperation with Developing Countries (SAREC).

Notes

1. Forwarded by agencies such as the World Bank.

2. Adding the suffix *Van* (forest) to the common Gujjar name has been a strategy used to delineate the pastoral nomadic Gujjars using the Uttar Pradesh foothills for their winter quarters from the countless other Gujjar groups in Northern India. As the conflict intensified into a fight for the rights of this group of Gujjars, the identity of the community to benefit from the struggle had to be made crystal-clear.

3. There is here a similarity to Zygmunt Bauman's (1991: 5) discussion of the onset of modernity. 'We can think of modernity as a time when order – of the world, of the human habitat … *is reflected upon*; a matter of thought, of concern, of *a practice that is aware of itself* … ' (my second emphasis).

4. The argument is that by liberating nature they are liberating themselves, as it is seen to be the same power that enslaves nature and dominates men and women. Similar arguments are put forward by ecofeminists (cf. Plumwood 1986; Warren 1994).

5. As Director of the Delhi-based organization CSE (Centre for Science and Environment) and editor of the magazine, *Down to Earth*, Anil Agarwal has been very influential in the environmental debate in India.

6. Intentional notification for the creation of the park was made in 1983 but local claims and rights have not yet been settled in accordance with the Wildlife Act, which is why final notification for the park has not been issued.

7. In the sense used by Bourdieu (1990:10–11).

8.   There are, of course, a number of ontological problems involved in seeing people simply as part of ecosystems, but this discussion warrants an article of its own and I am purposely simplifying here to press a point.

9.   In a report from the area by Dietrich Brandis, Inspector General of Forests (1882), it was stated, 'The *sal* forests did not contain many large trees due to past excessive fellings ... (Kumar 1995a: 75–76).

10.   This is a matter of controversy, and in fact some people may stay back for different reasons, but most buffaloes have to migrate because it is practically impossible to get the animals to produce milk in a sustainable way in the dried-out forest of the Shiwaliks during the summer months.

11.   There have been discrepancies regarding the number of *Van* Gujjars and their buffaloes living within the park area. The official number is 512 families, or the number of official permit holders according to the last census made back in 1937. Forest Department estimates have been pending (cf. Kumar 1995; RLEK 1997). The numbers given here are according to the census made by RLEK in 1992–93 for a literacy project and should be reasonably accurate.

12.   While a suggestion was made for 50-per-cent representation of women in the *khols* committees, the *Van* Gujjars women themselves opted for one-third as the minimum. The logic behind this was that husbands formed one part, sons another and wives a third. As *Van* Gujjars practise patrilocality, daughters will move to their husbands' *khol* and do not need representation in their native *khol*! It is also in accordance with the suggestions for the *panchayat raj* (local democracy) structure, where women are guaranteed one third of seats in local governance.

13.   For the villagers the most important resource collected from the forest core area is *bhabar* grass, an important minor forest produce. *Bhabar* grass is not gathered by the *Van* Gujjars.

14.   The moment the *Van* Gujjars' voice loses its authenticity as an expression of nature (and the exotic), they would also lose their privileged position and be like 'any other' nondescript rural community in India. In this sense, their position is simultaneously a strength and a weakness. The hegemonic relationship between the 'tribals' and representatives of the wider society has not ceased to exist.

15.   The *Van* Gujjar case has been supported and mediated out to global audiences by organizations such as IWGIA (International Work Group for International Affairs).

References

Agarwal, Anil and Sunita Narain (1989) *Towards Green Villages*, New Delhi: Centre for Science and Development.

Arnold, David and Ramachandra Guha (eds) (1995) *Nature, Culture, Imperialism: Essays on the Environmental History of South Asia*, Delhi: Oxford University Press.

Bauman, Zygmunt (1991) *Modernity and Ambivalence*, Cambridge: Polity Press.

Berkmuller, K.L. (1986) *Pressure and Dependency by Local People on the Resources of Rajaji*, Dehra Dun: Wildlife Institute of India. Mimeo.

Bhasin, C.L. 1979, *A Study of the Problem of Gujars and Their Rehabilitation*, (Hindi) Uttar Pradesh Government Publication.

Bourdieu, Pierre (1990) *In Other Words: Essays towards a Reflexive Sociology*. Cambridge: Polity Press.

Bramwell, Anna (1989) *Ecology in the 20th Century. A History*, New Haven: Yale University.

Champion, F.W. (n.d. *ca.* 1930) *The Jungle in Sunlight and Shadow*. London: Chatto and Windus.

Cherail, Koshy (1993) 'Time to Change. Wildlife Conservation Strategy', *Down to Earth*, 30 November, pp. 5–9.

Choudhury, Ashok (1993) 'Rajaji: Another View', *Sanctuary Asia*, vol. XIII, no. 4, pp. 21–25.

Chopra, Kanchan, Gopal K. Kadekodi and M.N. Murty (1990) *Participatory Development. People and Common Property Resources*, New Delhi: Sage.

Clark, A., H. Sewil and R. Watts (1986) *Habitat Utilisation by Gujar Pastoralists in Rajaji Wildlife Sanctuary*, Dehra Dun: Wildlife Institute of India. Mimeo.

CSE (Centre for Science and Environment) (1982) *The State of India's Environment 1982: The First Citizens' Report*, New Delhi: Centre for Science and Environment.

—— (1985) *The State of India's Environment 1984–85: The Second Citizens' Report*, New Delhi: Centre for Science and Environment.

Dalal, Nergis (1993) 'The Gujjar Problem in Rajaji National Park', *The Himachal Times*, 23 May.

Dang, Himraj (1991) *Human Conflicts in Conservation: Protected Areas, The Indian Experience*, Delhi: Har-Anand Publications.

—— (1986) *Conservation and Development in Apparent Conflict: A Preliminary Case-Study of the Proposed Rajaji National Park in the Siwalik Hills of*

India and the Local Pastoral Gujjar Population. Dehra Dun: Wildlife Institute of India. Mimeo.

—— (1991) *Human Conflicts in Conservation. Protected Areas: The Indian Experience,* Delhi: Har-Anand Publications.

Dasman, R.F. (1988) 'Towards a Biosphere Consciousness', in D. Worster (ed.) *The Ends of the Earth: Perspectives on Modern Environmental History.* Cambridge: Cambridge University Press.

Dogra, Bharat (1993) 'Parks and People – Report on a Workshop', in *Sanctuary Asia,* vol. XIII, no. 6, pp. 59–65.

Down to Earth (1993) 'Unique Opportunity for Kamal Nath', *Down to Earth,* 31 January.

—— (1995) 'Forests for Whom?' *Down to Earth,* 31 December, PP:?.

Gadgil, Madhav and Ramachandra Guha (1992) *This Fissured Land. An Ecological History of India,* Delhi: Oxford University Press.

—— (1995) *Ecology and Equity. The Use and Abuse of Nature in Contemporary India,* London and New York: Routledge.

Gooch, Pernille (1992) 'Transhumant Pastoralism in Northern India: The Gujar Case', *Nomadic Peoples,* no. 30, pp. 84–86.

—— (1994) 'Nomadic *Van* Gujjars Fight to Maintain Their Life in the Forest', *Indigenous Affairs,* no. 3, pp. 4–16.

—— (1995) 'When the Land Shouts', *Down to Earth,* 15 February, pp. 46–47.

—— (1997a) 'Conservation for Whom?'. In Staffan Lindberg and Arni Sverrisson (eds) *Social Movements in the South. Dilemmas of Globalization and Democratization,* London: Macmillan.

—— (1997b) 'The World of the *Van* Gujjars: Indigenous People and the Natural World', RLEK *Community Forest Management of Protected Areas: Van Gujjar Proposal for the Rajaji Area.* Dehra Dun: Natraj Publishers.

Guha, Ramachandra (1991) *The Unquiet Woods: Ecological Change and Peasant Resistance in the Himalayas,* New Delhi: Oxford University Press.

Hassan, Amir (1986) *A Tribe in Turmoil,* New Delhi: Uppal Publishing House.

Ives, Jack D. and Bruno Messerli (1989) *The Himalayan Dilemma: Reconciling Development and Conservation,* London and New York: Routledge.

Indira (1992), 'Conservation at Human Cost: Case of Rajaji National Park' in *Economic and Political Weekly,* 1–18 August, pp. 1647–50.

Jena, Nalni R. (1993) 'A Critical Analysis of the Legal Provisions of Sanctuaries and National Parks in India.' Paper prepared for the 'National Workshop on Declining Access to and Control over National Resources in National Parks and Sanctuaries', Dehra Dun, 28–30 October.

Kathi, D.S. (1993) 'Problems in Paradise'. In *Sanctuary Asia,* (EDS?) vol. XIII, no. 4, pp.16–21.

Kothari, Ashis (1993) 'Wildlife and Tribal Rights: Is a Resolution Possible?' Paper presented at the National Workshop on 'Human Rights, Environment and the Law', Bangalore.

Kumar, D. (1995) *Management Plan of Rajaji National Park*, Dehra Dun: Rajaji National Park.

Lal, J.B. (1992) *India's Forests: Myth and Reality.* Dehra Dun: Natraj Publishers.

Plumwood, Val (1993) *Feminism and the Mastery of Nature*, London and New York: Routledge.

RLEK (Rural Litigation and Entitlement Kendra) (1997) *Community Forest Management in Protected Areas: Van Gujjar Proposal for the Rajaji Area*, Dehra Dun: Natraj Publishers.

Society for Participatory Research in Asia and Rural Litigation and Entitlement Kendra (1993) 'Report on *National Workshop on Declining Access to and Control over National Resources in National Parks and Sanctuaries*', Dehra Dun, 28–30 October.

Toulmin, Stephen (1990) *Cosmopolis: The Hidden Agenda of Modernity*, New York: The Free Press.

Tucker, Richard P. (1991) 'Resident Peoples and Wildlife Reserves in India: The Prehistory of a Strategy.' In Patrick C. West and Steven R. Brechin (eds), *Resident Peoples and National Parks: Social Dilemmas and Strategies in International Conservation*, Tucson: University of Arizona Press.

Warren, Karen J. (ed.) (1994) *Ecological Feminism*, London: Routledge.

5 | The Role of Voluntary Organizations in Environmental Service Provision: The Case of Madras

Håkan Tropp

Urban Expansion – New Institutional Challenges

A common feature in most developing countries is an unprecedented urban expansion. Apart from dynamic demographic and socio-economic changes, this expansion has a number of physical and environmental consequences, locally as well as on a larger scale. These include a sizeable infringement into previously rural lands in the vicinity of the burgeoning urban conglomerations as well as a growing effective competition for natural resources on a national scale. Perhaps most obvious, though, is a degradation of the living environment within many cities. It is not only in sites with pockets of poverty that we find this threat; it is equally significant in booming parts of expanding urban areas. Moreover, it is important to note that resource and environmental consequences are increasingly felt outside slum areas, 'economic hotspots' and even outside the city itself. Areas located in downstream positions are a particularly noticeable case in point. As a result of the rapid urban expansion, the 'carrying capacity' in many agglomerations, especially large cities, has reached its limits regarding proper functioning of physical infrastructure (e.g. water supply, sewerage systems and transportation).

A dramatic change in the rural–urban demography with significant environmental consequences, among others, is to be expected in developing countries during the next decades. If we take Asia and the Pacific as an example, it is projected that by 2010, the urban population will equal the rural population. After 2010, the urbanites will most probably outweigh the ruralites. For India, it is estimated that the urban population at the turn of the century will compose one-third of the total population of one billion (World Development Report 1992).

In India, the rapid pace of urbanization goes hand in hand with industrialization, which is a part of the development process, although not linked to an equivalent and much needed expansion of infrastructure and basic services. This process of unbalanced modernization has its price in the form of an increased pressure on natural resources, through inefficient and wasteful utilization, leading to depletion and an inadequate supply of natural resources to sectors of society.

In addition, environmental degradation is taking place, i.e. water and air are becoming highly polluted. Not only will ecological life and systems suffer, but there will be direct and indirect impacts on society such as increased health hazards, decreased economic productivity and a loss of amenities (ibid.). Organizations that are responsible for environmental management will face new challenges. Action must be taken to prevent pollution; moreover the development of distribution systems and improved management of scarce and vulnerable natural resources will become even more crucial.

A pertinent question is to what extent the public sector is capable of handling the situation of increased pressure on natural resources and environmental degradation. A debate that has been going on in many developing countries is that due to weak public sector performance, the management of some public services might be transferred to other entities, with better accountability and responsibility. It is often argued that entities located in civil society are more responsive to people's need and therefore they can deliver the required services more efficiently than the public sector. The entities in mind are often referred to as Voluntary Organizations (VOs) including Non-Governmental Organizations (NGOs) and Community-Based Organizations (CBOs).[1] These organizations are supposed to play a vital role not only as providers of various services but also as a crucial force for democratization, poverty alleviation, sustainable development and efficiency enhancement (Farrington and Lewis 1993: 6).

It will be argued that VOs located within civil society can be a complement to state involvement in the area of environmental service delivery and distribution. The purpose is not to eradicate the role of the state in the process of development. The attempt is merely to suggest that actors within civil society can organize participation through collective action around common interests and goals.

This study mainly emphasizes VOs as problem-solvers; but the role of VOs in political and social transformation is equally important. If some service provision is transferred to VOs it can be a political change in itself, since political decisions are decentralized and the role of state authorities can be altered. This means that decentralization cannot be seen solely as the passing over of state responsibilities, it should be viewed in a wider perspective. Lindberg points out:

> further democratization in the Indian context would mean a broadening and deepening of popular participation in political decision-making, as well as a gradual extension of popular control over those aspects of the economy which deal with issues of poverty and the distribution of goods and services among various sections of the population (Lindberg 1992: 202–3).

It can be added that this is not only valid in the Indian case, it can also be applied in many other developing countries. However, there is no assurance that VOs will be better able to cope with environmental problems or induce political and social change at a macro level (Garain 1994: 337). But one cannot deny that they can have a profound impact on the local scene both in terms of problem-solving and transformation of political and social processes.

In the following section there will be a short discussion about the state. Furthermore, some analytical concepts will be introduced, which suggest a possible approach to the role of VOs. The last section is a case of citizens' initiatives in the area of garbage collection in Madras.

Shortcomings of the State

In many developing countries the state has been or is still viewed as the main vehicle for transforming society and the economy.

One *raison d'être* for the state, according to its proponents, is the belief that the state can cope with market failures and the 'tragedy of the commons'. It is also argued that public goods and services require governmental control and regulation if the objectives of efficiency and equity are to be reached.[2] In effect, the state will control the use of natural resources and take charge of the distribution and provision of public services.

Some of the main arguments that have been used to champion the state as provider and distributor of public goods and services are found in Garrett Hardin's *The Tragedy of the Commons* (1968) and Mancur Olson's *Logic of Collective Action* (1965). These two approaches are commonly illustrated with the *Prisoners' Dilemma Game* (see Axelrod 1984). Hardin and Olson essentially explain the difficulty of getting individuals to pursue a joint welfare, with the underlying assumption that individuals are not capable of cooperating. As a result, it is concluded that if individuals are to cooperate around common resources or interests, an external coercive power is needed. In other words, a sovereign institution (i.e. the state) is required to impose collective action upon people, whether they want it or not.

During the 1970s the state was particularly criticized by neo-liberals. The market and local-level initiatives (collective action) were considered to be realistic and proper alternatives to a larger extent. Some of the criticism is based on a lack of accountability, transparency, responsiveness and the fact that state involvement in many cases fosters inefficiency (see MacIntosh 1992; Ostrom 1993). An alternative approach is to decentralize decision-making as well as implementation to bodies that are supposed to be more responsive and that also have the capacity and ability to empower people at the local level. As a result, the state's role in economy and social life would change and assume more of a coordinating and enabling function.

During the last two decades the empowerment of civil society has become a deliberate and targeted activity of international donor and aid organizations. The donor strategy is to activate or reactivate parts of civil society that claim to represent various social groups. In essence this means that they have a public interest and purpose. As a result a lot of interest and resources have been invested in different kinds of VOs. The rationale behind this not only rests on the shortcomings of the state, but also on the assumption that VOs provide a more innovative, flexible and dynamic institutional framework than the bureaucratic state apparatus (see for instance Harbeson et al. 1994; Fowler 1991). This has created immense expectations of the voluntary sector as a salvager in the development process.

Compliance, Participation, Legitimation and Autonomy

Migdal (1988: 9) maintains that the mode of the state in today's developing countries is characterized by a duality. While the state's capacity to penetrate society is strong, its potential to make citizens do what the policy-makers want them to do is weak (cf. Kothari 1988; Kohli 1991). This means that the role of the state to mobilize collective action is limited, and, as a result, implementation of socio-economic-political changes has to a large extent been disappointing. Migdal argues convincingly that the core issue in state–civil society relations is the power to make rules. The question is: Who has the right and ability to make rules? The rules are in turn tied to *social control*, which is the basic objective: the rules are not an end in themselves but a means to exert social control and regulation over the use of assets and resources. The way to measure social control is reflected in three interrelated indicators (Migdal 1988: 32–33): *compliance* (obedience to rules), *participation* (the ability to organize collective action) and *legitimation* (the degree of acceptance of the rules of the game and social control). The essential message is that the more compliance, participation and legitimation there are, the greater the social control and control of the use of assets and resources. These indicators can be used not only to understand the state–civil society nexus, but also relations within civil society. A concrete example is the relation between NGOs and CBOs, where NGOs are supposed to play a supportive role to CBOs. Migdal argues that 'many other social organizations in an environment of conflict have not shared the belief that the state should be predominant in the entire society, and they, too, have desperately sought social control' (ibid.: 33).

As a result the voluntary sector comprises disparate organizations and networks with different means and ends. This makes it difficult or even impossible to view the voluntary sector as a homogeneous entity; rather it can be characterized by heterogeneity or pluralism with regard to means, ends and strategies. Omvedt argues that Indian movements are confronting not only the state, but also *exploitative* fractions within civil society (Omvedt 1993: 40). In the case of environmental movements this is obvious, since their targets, apart from the state, are polluting industries, farmers' organizations demanding subsidized irrigation, and contractors who deforest large areas.

Compliance refers to the use of force and to the ability to control the distribution of a variety of resources and services, which are considered to determine the degree to which compliance can be demanded.

Participation (or collective action) by the people for various reasons is used to gain strength to reach certain goals. Participation is a prerequisite for the power of the voluntary sector. Obstacles to effective participation are not only the result of inequitable distribution of resources and assets and resistance by the elite. It is also to be found within civil society such as exploitative interests, conflictive and heterogeneous interests and goals. Moreover, Marsden argues that in a patron–client relation, which is routinized and accepted, 'participation is little more than co-optation' (Marsden 1991: 29). It should be evident that in the Indian context factionalism and patron–client relations can be a major hindrance to bottom-up participation.

The third indicator, *legitimation*, is an important factor in analysing the state and VOs. Legitimation is broadly understood as acceptance of the rules of the game. In effect, this means that the role of the state or VOs is understood, known and valid. To facilitate legitimacy, those in power must be accountable to the people and the political process must be characterized by transparency (Fowler 1991: 60–61).

A fourth component that can be added is *autonomy*. Autonomy in this case is linked to relations within the voluntary sector, and how the state reacts to voluntary sector initiatives. The three principal strategies used by the state are:

* repression
* cooptation
* division

The best-known response is repression. Through force or threat of force, the state can demand compliance by the people. It is assumed that if the state is too strong in its repression of citizens, it will impede or even suffocate local initiatives.

A more subtle way to intervene in the voluntary sector is cooptation. The state in India is characterized as interventionist, thus cooptation of organizations operating outside the state is imminent (see for instance Kothari 1988; Wiguaraja 1993). This strategy is not unique for the Indian corporatist state, it has successfully been used in many other developing and developed countries. The implication of cooptation is that there is an imminent risk that VOs become static and bureaucratized, which in turn can lead to a decline of, in Migdal's vocabulary, social control. What complicates the situation is that some VOs deliberately adopt the strategy of cooperating with state authorities. In effect, cooperative and joint efforts with the state can be a difficult balancing act between autonomy and cooptation. Additionally, there has been a lot of debate among Indian VOs as to the extent to which cooperation with the state is desirable.[3]

The third strategy is division, which means that the state supports some VOs and not others. The objective in doing this is to segment the voluntary sector and marginalize some VOs, while others will be favoured and legitimized by the state. Finally, as a corollary to this, there are also attempts from the state to set up their own VOs, the so-called GONGOs (Government Organized Non-Governmental Organizations). The purpose for doing this is mainly to get access to otherwise inaccessible resources, such as international donor funds (Fowler 1991: 81).

The Environment and Voluntary Initiatives in Madras City
Salient features of the Madras environmental situation
The Madras Metropolitan Area (MMA) which includes the city, semi-urban and rural areas, has a population of 5.4 million and the largest share, about 70 per cent, is concentrated in the city.

Many of the environmental problems that have become visible in Madras can be ascribed to the rapid growth of population in already dense areas, and spontaneous expansion of urbanization into the rural fringe. Two noticeable interconnected features of the Madras Metropolitan Area are a shortage of water and the pollution of water, air and habitat in general. Generally, the disposal and treatment of waste water is afforded far less attention than the question of the supply of fresh water.

An overall degradation of the urban environment is a noticeable trend in other metropolitan and urban areas in India. In environmental terms, these urban agglomerations are inherently unsustainable. Not only are the urbanites affected, but so are adjacent rural areas. As cities grow, the urban dwellers will require more natural resources and disseminate their waste over larger areas.

Water resources that were previously used for irrigation are now being claimed for urban purposes. In the fringe of the MMA, a large number of water tanks (reservoirs), which were originally constructed for rural purposes and to facilitate rainwater storage and infiltration have now been converted to meet the needs of urban expansion.

The gradual exhaustion of tanks in and around the city, together with the increasing withdrawal of groundwater has serious implications. Saltwater intrusion into groundwater is a fairly widespread phenomenon. Wells formerly used for domestic purposes are now yielding non-potable water. Groundwater levels have been lowered throughout the MMA, since withdrawals exceed replenishment. To alleviate the water shortage in the MMA, two major water diversion projects have been planned (Madras Metropolitan Development Authority 1991). The hope is primarily vested in diversion of water from the River Krishna (located in the neighbouring state of Andhra Pradesh) and through the Veeranam project, where water will be brought some 150 km from the River Cauvery.

Nearly 50 per cent of the population within the city do not have access to the piped water-supply system. The lack of clean water, both for drinking and industrial uses, has reached critical proportions. Poor sanitation is a continuous environmental and health hazard. Furthermore, the three major waterways crossing Madras are highly polluted, due to inadequate capacity of the sewerage system and discharges of untreated effluents. The worst affected are slum dwellers, who constitute one-third of the city's population. The slums are, to a large extent, scattered along the river banks crossing Madras, and those living there are marginalized with very limited access to waste disposal, potable water, sanitation and other public services. As a result, the rivers are used as dumps.

Even under 'normal' conditions, this would be highly undesirable. Considering the fact that the water discharge in the rivers for part of the year is quite low, the waterways turn into stagnant sewers with a host of hazardous and highly unaesthetic implications. In spite of various programmes aimed at eradicating the slum conditions, the problem has grown worse. A recent study points out that the average water supply for slums is 8 litres per capita per day (lpcd), while the average supply of water in Madras is approximately 69 lpcd (Panch 1993: 12). In years of shortages, the availability drops 50 per cent or even more. As a result of poor water distribution and supply, citizens have to buy water from the private water vendors or rely on their own wells, if they have any.

Supply and quality of public services is thus far from satisfactory. This applies to water supply as well as to other important services. In the field of solid waste collection, the responsible authorities are operating at a low level. The inhabitants of Madras City generate approximately 3,000 tons of garbage per day. The per capita contribution is, though, quite low – less than 1 kilo on average (Appasamy and Lundqvist 1993: 445). Recycling of newspapers, glass, metals and plastics is common, and in many places 'waste trade' is taking place. Waste has become lucrative and is seen not as waste, but as an income-generating resource. There is a growing need to view waste as a resource that can be recycled or used in other ways; yet the local authorities have paid little attention to this.

Environmental responsibility, service provision and the development and distribution of natural resources are to a large extent under the public sector umbrella. One result of the poor public sector performance in Madras as well as in many other (similar) contexts is the emergence and actions of various environmentally concerned VOs.

Garbage collection: local state authorities' legitimacy and citizens' compliance and participation

The formal responsibility for the collection and disposal of solid waste in Madras City falls under the jurisdiction of the Madras Corporation (hereafter referred to as the Corporation). Outside the city limits, municipalities and town *panchayat*s take on the same responsibility. Until 1971 the role of the Corporation, which deals exclusively with the city of Madras, was to provide most of the urban infrastructure and different kinds of civic services. As the city has been growing and expanding beyond its limits in a rather uncontrolled manner, this has led, together with the insufficient capacity of the Corporation, to a number of areas being transferred to specialized agencies set up by the government of Tamil Nadu. The main responsibilities of the Corporation are, *inter alia*, maintenance of roads and stormwater drains, solid waste disposal, and health measures like vaccination and epidemic control.

People complain regularly to local state authorities about the environmental situation, insufficient services and an inappropriate or lack of response to their grievances. In some streets or neighbourhoods garbage is not collected for several days at a time, and many slums are totally ignored. These conditions naturally create very unhealthy situations. A woman in Thiruvalluvar (southern Madras City) says: 'In the morning the area resembles a beehive with flies swarming into your flats and at night, the mosquitoes are all over the place.' Similar experiences are reported at various locations in Madras. A resident of Peryar Nagar (north-west Madras) relates how 'uncleared garbage is mounting for months at a time, creating a foul smell. Pigs and dogs scatter the garbage all over the area.' Stories like these are very common and there are also numerous examples of the Corporation's failure to respond properly to complaints from the public. This negligence from the local authorities' side is not restricted to garbage collection. Other environmental and public service issues, such as stagnant water due to poor storm-water drainage, insufficient drinking water supply and sanitation, receive their fair share of censure from the public, and negligence from the local authorities.

The Corporation faces many kinds of difficulties in its attempts to keep the city clean, for example traffic jams and a lack of finances. Furthermore, a myopic environmental approach is generally adopted by the local authorities. This last point indicates that there is limited cooperation among different local authorities, as each authority will only look after its own affairs. The lack of proper urban planning must also be emphasized as one of the reasons for the increasing environmental problems. The MMA has definitely not been planned to accomodate 5.4 million people.

However, one of the more fundamental and serious impediments the Corporation faces in local environmental efforts concerns its relationship to the public. Basically, the Corporation finds it very difficult to mobilize and motivate people both at individual and collective levels. The result is non-compliance and non-participation of its citizens. Without participation from the public there will be a low degree of environmental awareness and sense of responsibility. This means that the local authorities exert a limited control over the citizens' environmental behaviour. The ability to influence the citizens and their environmental awareness could be assumed to be just as limited. Thus, the limited compliance and participation make people inclined to throw garbage in water streams, in streets and all over the city.

If we follow the above line of reasoning, there is a great lack of accountability and responsiveness (i.e. a legitimacy problem) concerning the Corporation's activities. Moreover, it is difficult for the citizens to control the Corporation (i.e. a situation of limited transparency). In October 1996 local elections were held in Madras for the first time since 1970.[4] The previous situation of the dormant Corporation, Municipalities and town *panchayats* constituted problems on at least two levels. First, local authorities are responsible for providing a wide range of public services. Second, they are the primary democratic bodies at the grass-roots level. The lack of elections meant that the Corporation, municipalities and *panchayats* were run by bureaucrats and politicians of the government of Tamil Nadu, with very limited inbuilt systems of checks and balances for the public. This implies one set of problems regarding the capacity to implement public services and policies. The other set of problems brings local democracy centre-stage. The public service performance by the local authorities is insufficient and there are very limited democratic ways to check or influence them.

As a result of these circumstances, the role of VOs has become emphasized, both in terms of service delivery and the strengthening of local democracy. In this sense VOs have a potential to fill a political vacuum. They channel discontented citizens' views into the local state authorities and also attempt to disseminate ideas on what is happening inside them. At the same time VOs can complement local authorities in service provision.

Who Is to Blame?

So far, much of the blame for the environmental conditions has been placed squarely at the door of the local authorities. However, the public and the industrial sector must also share the blame for the environmental deterioration. A common viewpoint among citizens is that 'since we have paid tax to the Corporation, we expect them to take care of garbage collection and related environmental problems'. It should be obvious to everyone that unless the public and industries in general are willing to accept responsibility for environmental matters, the task of the authorities to make them comply will indeed be Sisyphean. This lack of responsibility among citizens is here interpreted in two directions. First, responsible authorities have failed to educate citizens and make them aware of the causes of environmental problems, health hazards, depletion of non-renewable resources, etc. Second, citizens have failed to do anything about their own living conditions, i.e. collective action has been too confined. This last point shows some of the limitations within civil society and its capacity to deal effectively with environmental problems.

Environmental irresponsibility is reflected in many households' 'not-in-my-backyard' approach to environmental problems. As long as people do not have the waste and garbage in their immediate vicinity, they do not see a problem. It is simply a question of moving the rubbish out of sight. In effect, the household's own premises will be kept clean, while the pavement outside the premises will be used as a dumping ground.

On a practical level there are many reasons why garbage often ends up in the wrong place. The Corporation bin might be too far away. Some people also throw garbage next to, rather than in, the bin, with the result that other people feel reluctant to walk through the scattered garbage and place their garbage in the proper place. The result is that the Corporation bin will be the cleanest spot in the entire neighbourhood. Although this is true in some areas, a more likely scenario is that people in other areas will put the garbage in its proper place, but the Corporation will neglect to empty the bins on a regular basis. The bins will overflow, which will create unhealthy conditions, a foul smell and unaesthetic surroundings. The situation is aggravated by cows, dogs and pigs who roam around in the filth.

Creating and Alleviating Environmental Problems

The above indicates that both the state and citizens contribute to environmental deterioration. The local authorities' capacity is limited and its relationship with the public is unsatisfactory. Moreover, for various reasons the public does not dispose of its garbage responsibly. This demonstrates that environmental measures need to be taken within the sphere of both civil society and the state. Thus, the state–civil society interface becomes important in order to manage environmental problems.

As observed by Hydén (1983) in the African context, the state-centred approach with its public sector dominance has created a dependency. Instead of solving local problems, people are inclined to await initiatives from the state. This pattern has been observed in many contexts. Environmental movements in India, for instance, have a tendency to expect the state to be the caretaker of environmental problems. Paradoxically, they also accuse the state of being a part of, or causing, environmental problems (Omvedt 1993: 144). One interpretation of this paradox is

that many environmental organizations are attempting to mobilize people to increase the pressure on the state and industry and
not to cope with the problem themselves. The alternative for
mobilized forces is to work directly towards environmental improvement and protection of natural resources, thus bypassing
the state. The paradox may hold on a more general level but
there are cases where people bypass or to some extent cooperate
with the state and create their own environmental institutional
solutions. The garbage collection in Madras is such a case and
there are other examples in Indian cities regarding garbage
collection.

Voicing Environmental Discontent

Environmental, community-based action and initiatives are present
in many forms. People will gather to demonstrate, some will write
to the local newspaper and complain about the civic negligence
of local authorities, while others will go to court. People also get
together to solve day-to-day problems within their neighbourhood and to work for better standards of living regarding health,
sanitation, sufficient water supply, clean air and water, shelter,
etc. Examples of people's protest are given below.

Residents and traders of Madhavaram (a suburb in north
Madras) and neighbouring areas blocked traffic at Moolakkadai
during the morning rush-hour in a desperate move to force the
local authorities to look into their civic and environmental
problems. Later, after much pleading and assurances from the
authorities, they dispersed. A similar attempt shortly after led to
the use of 'mild force' by police, though the police denied that
they violently dispersed the group, which mainly comprised
youths.

In many cases the response from the citizens has been on an
ad hoc basis. A community will gather together for a protest,
alternatively memoranda may be sent to the local authorities.
The local authorities invariably respond by saying that they will
look into the grievances, but this promise may very well be
forgotten the day after. The authorities know it will take some
time for the citizens to mobilize again.

The methods of effecting an improvement in basic amenities are manifold and some attempts are more ingenious than others. One such case was when residents of Mogappair renamed their area Jayalalitha Nagar (Miss Jayalalitha was the former Chief Minister of the Government of Tamil Nadu) in the hope that this would encourage the officials to take concrete action. However, when the residents realized that this renaming had not worked, they resorted once again to more 'direct methods' of protest (blocking the streets, demonstrations, etc.). Despite a 'protracted and often militant struggle', the only achievement was when the authorities removed slum encroachments from the Mogappair Road, improved the central median lighting and also carried out some road construction. The residents, however, feel that these improvements were the result of a visit by the Chief Minister to a corporate hospital in the area, rather than a direct consequence of pressure put on the corporation by the residents. Examples cited are taken from *The Hindu*, 26 January 1996.

Events like those above (which occur frequently) show that the citizens are far from satisfied with the civic and environmental conditions. Further, the response from the local authorities is in many cases inadequate. Nevertheless, concerted efforts by citizens are sometimes manifested in the creation of CBOs, constituted by the affected people and restricted to the immediate vicinity such as a neighbourhood, a village or a street. In Madras City such CBOs have mushroomed. They are called Civic Exnoras (CEs) and deal mainly with garbage clearance.

The Exnora Movements

In the late 1980s Exnora (EXcellent, NOvel, RAdical) International (here referred to as Exnora) was started in Madras by an environmentally concerned citizen. Exnora has an explicit environmental approach both in its objectives and actual activities. At the same time, this environmental approach is combined with a set of more general development objectives. One of the basic objectives of this NGO is to clear the city of garbage. The means to achieve this is to 'generate ideas', create awareness among people, and provide public services through the realization of 'generated ideas'. In other words this means that one of Exnora's purposes is to organize participation through collective action among citizens to reach its objectives. Exnora also acts externally as a pressure group vis-à-vis the state and industry. Other objectives are to bridge the gap between people and state authorities, i.e. a mediating as well as an innovative role to strengthen civil society and cope with environmental problems.

Strategies and methods applied by Exnora

The strategy from both Exnora and the CEs is to collaborate with local authorities as much as possible. There is no wish to confront or criticize too much. Their notion is that without local authorities' consent or involvement, very little can be achieved to improve the environmental situation. Two reasons have been identified why the CEs and Exnora seek cooperation. The first has to do with some of the present limitations of the voluntary sector. If we take solid waste management as an example, it is difficult to see how the present capacity of the VOs can go beyond primary collection of household waste. For instance, there is too limited a financial capacity to take care of secondary collection or disposal of garbage. An important point to make is that the Exnora initiative in garbage collection requires local authorities to fulfil their responsibilities. If household waste collected by Exnora were not collected in a secondary stage and transferred to local dumps by local authorities, Exnora's work would be without meaning. The second reason is related to how local authorities respond to voluntary initiatives. Consent and recognition by the local authorities have been identified by Exnora as vital to its efforts. If a VO actively attempts to co-operate, it will reduce the risk of being ignored or of encountering hostility. In some cases support is required in the form of equipment, e.g. brooms for sweeping streets in clean-up campaigns.

Another type of strategy, which is directly geared towards the community, is to be action-oriented. Put very simply this means that if the state is not doing anything about the environment, you should do it yourself. If your house were to catch fire, you would not wait for the fire brigade to come, you would definitely try to put out the fire yourself. This is the way Exnora reasons in the case of the garbage situation in Madras. However, this approach has turned out to be rather controversial; it has received criticism from other VOs in Madras. The content of this criticism is basically that VOs should not carry out services for which the state is responsible. The role of the VOs, so it is argued, is to lobby, exert pressure and advocate, not carry out actual services.

The Civic Exnoras gain momentum

When the CEs started to take shape, it more or less coincided with a new project which was to be implemented by the Corporation. In some parts of Adyar (town district in the southern part of Madras City), the Corporation had set up hydrocons (a type of garbage container with a capacity of 8 tonnes). According to the Corporation the success of these hydrocons very much depended on public participation. If the households did not dump their garbage in these hydrocons, it would be a failure to introduce them. Exnora stepped forward and offered their assistance to the Corporation. The CEs took on the task of collecting garbage directly from the households, and disposing of it in the hydrocons (primary garbage collection). Then it became the responsibility of the Corporation to empty these hydrocons on a regular daily basis (secondary garbage collection). The result of the CE involvement in solid waste management was encouraging and from this initial foray the CEs started to mushroom. In effect, the CEs have mainly evolved and emerged around solid waste management and the main task is to organize primary collection of garbage from the households.

Today approximately 1,000–1,500 CEs operate in Madras City. The size of each CE varies but normally it comprises roughly 75–150 households, located in the same neighbourhood. Thus, CEs are based on community participation and considered as CBOs. Since a CBO normally deals with all kinds of problems that the members and community are facing, the CEs do not limit their parameters to garbage collection: in many CEs there are other environmental and social activities.

Initiatives for the formation of CEs come, to a very large extent, from the residents of each community, who know what kinds of problems they are facing; in many cases they also know how to deal with them. How this is done varies from community to community and depends on the particular needs and circumstances – herein lie the dynamics of the CEs. Many of the communities seek their own solutions: blue-prints are not viable in a longer perspective.

The system of primary garbage collection

The CEs take care of the primary collection of household garbage in various ways. But, primarily two different systems have been distinguished. In the first type of system a garbage collector is employed, a so-called street-beautifier. This person earns a monthly salary of approximately Rs 700–800 but in some areas it could be more. Additional income is generated from recyclable waste, such as paper, plastics, bottles and metals. Initially, one of Exnora's aims was to involve the local rag-pickers; it was considered necessary to have their cooperation to achieve good results. The hiring of rag-pickers would also bring other advantages: it would offer them a secure income and a more respectable status within the society. Thus, rag-pickers are employed to collect household garbage and sweep streets. Sometimes though the garbage collector is not recruited among the rag-pickers, but will come from another low-income group.

The street beautifier will, on a daily basis, collect garbage directly from the households and transport it to Corporation bins. In many cases he will also sweep the streets. The transportation of waste is carried out by means of a 'three-wheeler' (bicycle). Normally, the three-wheelers are privately donated by companies or individual households, although on occasion the CEs have taken out bank loans to purchase these bicycles.

Every household that is a member of the CE must pay a subscription to help cover the CE's expenditures. The monthly household contribution varies from Rs 5–20, depending on income level and number of households. The largest share of the CE's income will go to pay the street beautifier's salary. Besides this, there may be other expenditures for the maintenance of the three-wheelers, repayment of bank loans, etc. If the households pay promptly this system is very easy to operate, and requires a minimal expenditure of effort by each household. This system is primarily found in middle-class and well-to-do areas.

The second type of garbage collection system does not involve any type of monetary contribution from the households in order to pay a garbage collector. In this second system each household is responsible for placing its own garbage in the proper place. If the households are not willing to follow the CE recommendations and rules, volunteers (mainly youths) will remove garbage from the streets on a regular or irregular basis (daily, weekly or whenever necessary). Apart from this, their main task is to persuade the individual households to put their garbage in the Corporation bin.

This is a common system, particularly in low-income areas and slums. The households in these areas have less money to contribute to collective purposes. If the CE activities cost money, there may be small donations from some households; generally, though, the activities cost very little. Thus, in this system garbage collection requires more from each member in terms of time and effort rather than money.

Which one of these systems is adopted depends on the characteristics of the community, in terms of an identification of environmental problems and needs within the community and income levels. In some locations the residents give priority to other environmental problems: an adequate water supply and sanitation may be considered more important goals. In some places the secondary collection of garbage functions quite well, thus, there is no reason to organize primary garbage collection. This is the case in some CEs in Anna Nagar, which generally can be characterized as a well-to-do area (though there are pockets of slums). These CEs have employed street beautifiers, but only to sweep the streets; they are not involved in regular primary garbage collection from the households. The reason for this is that the households do not think it is necessary, since the Corporation is carrying out the secondary garbage collection on a fairly regular basis.

Although CEs are present in all income groups, most of them are to be found in middle- and upper-middle-income groups.

This indicates the difficulty of reaching the low-income groups, especially slums. There can be several reasons for this. There are, for instance, strong political interests operating in the slums, which consider VOs as uninvited competitors.[5] Besides, there is also a low degree of environmental awareness and motivation. Moreover, it shows that it is relatively easier for VOs to reach the middle-class and richer echelons of society.

Generally the efficiency in collecting household garbage is greater in the first type of system. Garbage is collected on a routine basis by salaried street beautifiers, while the second system is entirely dependent on voluntary efforts. However, a common problem occurring in both systems is the irregularity of garbage clearance by the Corporation, which of course has environmental implications. This can also discourage voluntary initiatives and undermine the legitimacy of CEs, as shown in the following case (based on interviews and internal letters).

In Rasi CE Unit One (located in Thiruvanmiyur, south Madras) regular garbage clearance did not take place. The street beautifiers in this area were left with little alternative but to dump garbage near the overflowing bins, which created a nuisance factor for other residents. As a result the street beautifiers were chased by 'hired people' and prevented from dumping garbage. The situation created a tense atmosphere in the area, whereby the affected residents strongly criticized the CEs for creating the problem. In a complaint made in a newspaper (*Indian Express*, 19 Sept. 1995) they said that repeated requests to the Exnora people had had no effect: 'It appears that the Corporation considers Exnora area to be out of bounds to them, leaving garbage disposal entirely to local efforts.' Further, they demanded that the Corporation must stop 'this total autonomy being given without authority to local chieftains'. They concluded that if the Rasi CE could not find other ways to dispose of the garbage, their activities should come to an end and be left to the responsible authorities who are financed by the taxpayers.

The office bearers within the Rasi CE were very worried about the situation. Exnora, which is seen as a symbol for environmental improvements, was now vilified as a 'garbage menace'.

Furthermore, they also realized that the Corporation would not respond to the situation.

> To expect the Corporation authorities to solve the Exnora problem means that we have not understood their limitations. The Corporation has neither the resources nor the management capacity (with a bureaucratic structure at higher levels working under the pressure of VIPs diverting the limited resources to cater to their needs and at lower levels the workers remain in the payrolls of hotels and restaurants) (Internal letter, Rasi CE).

Ultimately, in this case, some people's garbage problems are only solved at the expense of others. Thus, the garbage problem effectively remains while at the same time it creates unexpected social problems. If secondary collection of garbage is not properly carried out, the primary collection from households becomes quite meaningless. This once again stresses the important role of the Corporation: without their cooperation very little can be achieved.

Levels of Participation and the Civic Exnoras

A key concept in the CEs' various functions, activities and ideologies is participation. Participation by the CEs is found at two levels: first, within the organization itself and second, in local political decision-making processes. In both cases of participation, good relations between the state, CEs and Exnora are seen as essential. How CEs relate to the populace also affects their relations and interactions with the state. Whether the state allows the voluntary sector to participate in political processes or to share responsibilities and tasks in providing public services is largely dependent on relations between the two of them.

Chowdry (1989: 12) has divided participation into four distinct areas; decision-making, implementation, benefits and evaluation. Within the CEs, as well as the interface between the CEs and the state, these various types of participation are of concern. The CEs' participation in garbage collection is viewed as rather spontaneous and locally induced within the neighbourhoods. Within the CEs, participation in implementing garbage collection services and thus receiving benefits was identified as relatively high, especially in those areas that employed street beautifiers. The lion's share of households in this system comply with the CEs' rules and pay their subscriptions promptly. Visible environmental improvements are probably an important reason why the bulk of households continues to pay – they receive a high level of service for their money. Thus, as long as the CEs carry out their duties (and the Corporation theirs) people feel willing to contribute financially to this solid waste management system. Those who stay outside the system (free-riders) mainly argue that they have already paid tax once to the Corporation, so why pay twice for a service? Normally, the garbage from those who do not contribute financially to the CE is also collected. A few incidences were reported where garbage had been dumped outside the door of those refusing to pay their subscriptions. In most CEs with street beautifiers, 5 to 10 per cent of the households do not participate. However, this is seen by the CEs as an acceptable level since it does not threaten the viability of the garbage collection system. In the second type of CE – those without financial abilities to employ street beautifiers, participation in both implementation and benefits is much lower.

A slum CE, for example, may consist of around 100 households, while the whole slum area may comprise ten times this number. In this system there are difficulties in the recruitment of volunteers to cover larger areas. To some extent this system requires more from each household in terms of labour (voluntary work) and time. For instance, they have to walk some distance to dispose of their waste or take part in regular collection of garbage from streets. However, members of these CEs often attend the frequent meetings (monthly or fortnightly) of the organization and take part in processes of decision-making and evaluation. The situation in the other type of CE is somewhat different. Although many of them have frequent meetings (monthly), they report that participation in decision-making and evaluation of functions is fairly low. A similar point has been made from a detailed case about solid waste management in some of the oldest residential areas in Madras (MIDS 1995: 38–40). The sample included CEs in middle- and higher-income areas. The result concludes that participation in receiving benefits is high and most of the households contribute financially to the system. However, participation in other types of activities or meetings is fairly low.

A difference between CEs and Exnora is that they do not receive the same type of benefits. Local people involved in CEs directly benefit from their activities. Exnora may never have the satisfaction of direct results, other than that of having mobilized people into action. Possibly their name will also gain further recognition – which in itself would please any NGO.

Motivation of the people living in a neighbourhood is essential, if any viable positive environmental results are to be achieved. The motivation to participate in most CEs is linked to participation in accrued benefits. However, motivation is also sought in bottom-up approaches, by making people accept a higher level of environmental responsibility and by sensitizing them to do something about their environmental situation. Padmanabha Nagar CE expressed this in the following way:

> Each resident must ensure that garbage is not thrown on the streets. Cleanliness must extend beyond one's drawing room to the surrounding area. We must exert social pressure on erring residents and neighbours.[6]

Participation of these CEs in the state machinery's hierarchical structures of decision-making and evaluation hardly exists; there is in fact a great reluctance and resistance by the state apparatus to open the way to participation by these voluntary organizations. In the CEs' *modus operandi* there is participation in the state's implementation of solid waste management system. Garbage from households is transported to collection points where the Corporation workers carry out secondary collection. From this it follows that they also participate in the benefits of garbage collection. It is also reported in many CEs that participation in benefits has increased since the initiation of CEs. Before the existence of the CE, the work of the Corporation was in most areas considered as highly inefficient and irregular. In many cases Corporation workers have to some extent become more responsive to people's complaints.

Flexibility and Autonomy between Exnora and the CEs

The number of CEs is growing rapidly and the Exnora office is lagging behind in keeping an up-to-date register of all the CEs. Administration and intra-organizational work is not prioritized by Exnora. Action and concrete results are the things that matter most. Moreover, the rapid expansion has made it impossible for Exnora to communicate with all the CEs. As the founder of Exnora puts it: 'There has been so much pressure on us to start more and more Civic Exnoras that we have had little time to formulate full guidelines for forming and running [them].' However, lately efforts have been made to formalize some areas of the relations, expectations and responsibilities both within each CE and between Exnora and CEs. Some of these regulations and formalities stipulate that the CEs must register at the Exnora office. Each CE should adopt a standard constitution, to regulate accounts, rights and obligations of the members, the duty and power of office bearers, arbitration procedures, etc. The affiliation fee is currently Rs 100. This is supposed to be an annual subscription, but in many cases it is only paid once as a joining fee. In practice Exnora does not pay much attention to these fees, which are considered to be largely symbolic.

Exnora seeks to regulate and formalize as little as possible, in order to retain a flexible organization that can respond to new demands, needs and situations in an innovative way. Too many formalities would suffocate the voluntary spirit and bureaucratize the whole organization. Thus, in practice the relation between the CEs and Exnora is very informal and loose in its structure. The control of the CEs is limited and there are no regular meetings between each CE and Exnora. The CEs could be involved in all kinds of activities decided by the community. Basically, Exnora is lending its name to each CE, which gives them the goodwill to take up any problem with any local state authority like the Corporation and effectively tackle them, since Exnora is 'popular and widely known'. At the same time, the Exnora movement as a whole has benefited from the formation of CEs, which has increased the bargaining power of Exnora with local state authorities, which in turn would be used by Exnora to help the Civic Exnoras. Thus, the Exnora and CE activities will provide mutual benefits.

When a CE is started, Exnora will usually be present to offer some environmental education, information about the Exnora and some practical suggestions on how best to approach the local state authorities. After this 'start-up package' the CE is supposed to take care of its own problems, and as much as possible to work independently of Exnora. This last point is the policy of Exnora and it is envisaged that the CEs should become autonomous bodies and only in some 'common important' issues be under the control and guidance of Exnora. In this respect Exnora encourages CEs to register as independent bodies with the Tamil Nadu Society Registration Act of 1975, the Tamil Nadu Act no. 27 of 1975, and the Tamil Nadu Societies Registration Rules of 1878. The objectives of giving the CEs autonomy is that this will make it easier for them to tackle specific local environmental and civic problems. A second motive is to encourage and develop local leadership, which in turn will ease the burden on Exnora. However, if CEs run into difficulties, for example in their dealings with the authorities or in local disputes among CEs or individuals within the CE, they can, of course, contact Exnora.

Exnora usually has open-house meetings one evening per week, when anyone can come and discuss their experiences. Informal communications occur frequently between CE members and Exnora. As a result of the contacts Exnora will, in some cases, contact (through letters, personal communication and face-to-face meetings) the responsible local authorities with the intention of putting more pressure on them. In many cases Exnora has personal contacts and relations with civil servants within the local authorities, which can sometimes help to resolve community problems.

Eight CE fora have recently been set up in different areas of Madras City. These bodies are supposed to have a mediating function between Exnora and the CEs, but the practical use of these fora has so far been sporadic and limited. The CEs prefer to contact people at the Exnora office directly, which creates difficulties for Exnora since it cannot properly look after all the problems the CEs run into. The number of staff is limited and there are only a handful of people who have the necessary contacts with the authorities.

The Response from Local State Authorities

Officially the CE initiatives in garbage collection have mostly been welcomed by the Corporation. In the rhetoric they encourage any attempts by the CEs, whereas in practice the situation is more complex. The attitudes from the officials range between encouragement and hostility. There are no guidelines for the Corporation and its civil servants on how to approach the CEs or the voluntary sector as a whole for that matter. To some extent it becomes each civil servant's own attitude that will decide the outcome of the contacts between CEs and the local authority. This type of relation is characterized by arbitrariness and follows the logic of patron–clientelism. The CEs can never be sure of the result, but more often than not the attitude of the local authorities will be that of the cold shoulder or even open hostility. A former secretary of the government who is now working actively within the voluntary sector, explains: '[T]his activist bandwagon, without even knowing the details ... will write all kinds of letters, or protest in the press or even demonstrate. But the government does not really care, because ultimately nothing results from it.' To minimize the arbitrary outcomes in the interaction with the local authorities, VOs adopt a strategy of cultivating access to the right channels. The likelihood of a positive outcome will increase if you know someone within the local state authority who is in a position to help you.[7]

The relation between the CEs and the Corporation is informal. The question of whether it should be formalized or not is debated within Exnora. According to some the CEs will lose in momentum, or even be dissolved, if the Corporation gets involved in the primary collection of garbage. They argue that one of the reasons for the encouraging results at the community level is the absence of local authorities. If the system were to be formalized, e.g. if the Corporation were to finance some parts of the system (the purchase of three-wheelers or part-payment of the garbage collector's wages), this would entail an increased involvement by the Corporation. The danger is that if they were paying, they would also want to control the CEs. If this happened, it is assumed by Exnora that the CEs would be bureaucratized, inflexible and less responsive to the needs of the community (cf. Carroll 1992: 177).

The response from the Corporation has been to reject any attempts to formalize cooperation with the CEs. The Corporation mainly says that they are responsible for garbage collection and legally they do not have to cooperate with any VOs. A further argument used by the Corporation is that if the voluntary CEs fail, one can say it was a pity it did not work out, but if the Corporation fails in a formalized system, its performance will be thoroughly scrutinized. From the Corporation's point of view this would be cooperation on unequal terms: the Corporation would most probably carry the burden of failures.

Environmental participation by the public, as in the CE case, is seen by some civil servants inside the Corporation as an efficient way of improving the solid waste management system. But the Corporation is reluctant to move forward for various reasons, e.g. political and trade union problems (Dhanalakshmi and Sundaram 1994: 58). Moreover, a formal agreement would lead to more demands for transparency. Among state officials there is a great reluctance to open up the local authorities to public control. A zonal officer within the Corporation narrated frankly: 'We cannot come too close to NGOs … NGOs can become a sort of check and balance.' The implication of this is that cooperation is on some level desired by the Corporation, but not too much and not too close. Additionally, it is difficult for the CEs to know how the local authorities will respond. The CEs are to some extent divided. They consider cooperation with the local authorities to be necessary in order to achieve effective results. At the same time there are those who see a danger if the local authorities are too closely involved, whereby the latter might demand control, and thereby suffocate the voluntary spirit and efforts of CEs.

Dynamics of Voluntary Organizations

Initially, it was stated that the voluntary sector can be a comple-ment to the state in providing environmental public services.

The case of Exnora shows that complementarity can be realized at the local neighbourhood level, despite rather reluctant local state authorities. The Exnora achievements in the area of primary garbage collection are due to three main reasons:

- The approach is bottom-up. People are joining the CEs on a voluntary basis; they are not compelled by anyone.

- The system of garbage collection is carried out on a small scale at the community level. This implies that the system is under local supervision and control.

- The garbage collection system is flexible, simple to operate and based on the needs of the community.

These three points show some of the advantages of involving VOs in the provision of public services. However, it should be pointed out that the CEs predominate in middle-class areas and that those in most need of proper garbage collection – slum dwellers – have benefited only to a marginal extent. The middle class is in a far better position than slums to pay for services and often endowed with proper personal linkages to negotiate about benefits flowing from the state.

The environmental difference made by Exnora and CEs has largely been positive, though impossible to quantify. In most CEs it is perceived that the environmental situation in their neighbourhood has improved considerably since the initiation of collective efforts. On an aggregated level, i.e. total quantity of garbage collected in the city, it is uncertain what impact these CBOs have had. Statistics are scant and to judge from Corporation figures any significant aggregated impact on the Madras garbage situation has not been visible. However, Exnora's role in providing services should not be seen in a narrow way. The environmental activities of Exnora demonstrate the ability of VOs to come up with innovative institutional solutions, which are not costly to implement. Moreover, some CEs report that local state authorities have become more accountable and responsive to people's needs, although this should not be exaggerated.

A pertinent question that has to be raised is why the voluntary sector, in this particular case, is achieving more than the state, in terms of influencing people's environmental action and their propensity to participate in common environmental efforts. Interpreted in Migdal's terms, this means that VOs have relatively more social control. Thus, it is easier for VOs to make people do what they want them to do. If we consider the state, it is characterized by a low degree of legitimacy. Legitimation is seen as the acceptance of the rules of the game and a question of enforcement. Even if the role of the state is understood and accepted, enforcement of the rules of the game is necessary to achieve an adequate degree of legitimacy. This becomes obvious if we consider the VOs, since their legitimacy is heavily based on successful results and struggles, i.e. enforcement of objectives. A likely outcome of these successful struggles is that people will be more inclined to participate in communal endeavours.

Compliance with the rules of the game works fairly well in the Exnora case. The small-scale approach makes it easier to exercise social control. There will always be the free-riders in the system, but with effective local social control, this problem has been minimized.

The autonomy of Exnora and CEs and the sustainability of their efforts in the provision of services cannot be overlooked. Generally, there is a tendency from the Indian state to intervene in the voluntary sector. However, such indications have not been visible in the case of Exnora and CEs. If the strategy of cooptation is used, the long-term implications for the VOs could be that they become rigid and bureaucratized. In turn, the VOs will lose in strength which will adversely affect legitimacy, participation and compliance. Rephrased this means that there will be less social control for the VOs. However, the relation between the state and VOs has here been characterized as arbitrary. This type of relationship has been identified as a hindrance to facilitate voluntarism.

Perhaps one of the most important insights that the Exnora case offers centres on approach: instead of only applying external pressure to the responsible local authorities, initiatives and action *within* the community are being taken with the aim of solving local environmental problems. In this respect one can say that people are capable of managing, in part, their own local environmental problems.

Acknowledgement

The author wishes to thank the Swedish Agency for Research Cooperation with Developing Countries (SAREC) for financial support.

Author's Note

This article is an extract from a project about the role of VOs (voluntary organizations) in Madras. The case of Madras derives from interviews and other primary data collected mainly from September 1995 to February 1996. In 1996 Madras officially changed its name to Chennai. However, locally as well as nationally, Madras is still the most used name.

Notes

1. In this paper the term VOs will be used. In turn, VOs are divided into NGOs and CBOs. CBOs are considered to be operating at the community level and are therefore micro actors within civil society. NGOs are operating in a wider setting nationally, regionally and/or locally and support CBOs. NGOs are considered to be macro actors within civil society. Some characteristics can be distinguished for VOs (Fowler 1991: 78–79; Butler and Wilson 1990: 6–9). VOs must not be political in the sense of supporting political parties or fractions. But, in another sense, VOs are political, as they try to redistribute political power and influence political outcomes. A second feature is that they operate from non-profit motives. Further, there should be an indication of 'public good'; a number of people should benefit through their activities, not just a selected few.

2. See, for instance, Ostrom 1993. Ostrom does not take this position herself; instead, she argues that local self-management of common pool resources can be successful.

3. In 1986, the Code of Conduct was proposed by the central government to involve NGOs in implementing anti-poverty programmes in rural areas. This proposal was strongly opposed by urban NGOs, which saw a clear threat to the autonomy of the voluntary sector and the likelihood of bureaucratization. The proponents argued, *inter alia*, that the Code of Conduct was a platform for sorting out differences between the state and VOs. However, with strong opposition from some NGO sectors, the question has disappeared from the agenda (see Kothari 1988; Garain 1994 for a more thorough discussion of the Code of Conduct).

4. In 1993, the 74th Amendment was added to the Indian constitution. This amendment makes it compulsory to have local elections. The constitution gives the corporations (only existing in major urban areas), municipalities and the village or town *panchayat*s a greater role in the process of development. Article 243-W regarding the powers, authority and responsibilities of municipalities states that locally elected bodies (both in rural and urban areas) shall 'function as institutions for self-government'. This means a decentralization of power and responsibilities with respect to 'the preparation of plans for economic development and social justice' and 'the performance of functions and implementation of schemes'. In other words the urban local bodies are requested by the 74th Amendment to widen their developmental role in addition to the service provision role they already fulfil.

5. See de Wit (1993) about politics and patron–client linkages in the slums of Madras.

6. Internal circular to members of the Padmanabha Nagar CE.

7. See Blomkvist (1988) for a thorough discussion about patronage and the Indian state.

References

Appasamy, P. and J. Lundqvist (1993) 'Water Supply and Waste Disposal Strategies for Madras', *Ambio*, vol. 22, no. 7, pp.442–48.

Axelrod, R. (1984) *The Evolution of Cooperation*, New York: Basic Books.

Blomkvist, H. (1988) *The Soft State: Housing Reform and State Capacity in Urban India*, Uppsala: Uppsala University Press.

Butler, R. and D. Wilson (1990) *Managing Voluntary and Non-Profit Organizations*, London: Routledge.

Dhanalakshmi, R. and S. Sundaram (1994) *Approaches to Urban Solid Waste Management: Linkages between Formal and Informal Systems of Source Separation and Recycling*, Madras: Nayudamma Memorial Science Foundation.

Carroll, T.F. (1992) *Intermediary NGOs: The Supporting Link in Grassroots Development*, West Hartford, Conn.: Kumarian Press.

Chowdry, A.N. (1989) *Let Grassroots Speak: People's Participation, Self-Help Groups and NGOs in Bangladesh*, Dhaka: Dhaka University Press.

Edwards, M. and D. Hulme (eds) (1992) *Making a Difference – NGOs and Development in a Changing World*, London: Earthscan.

Farrington, J. and D. Lewis (eds) (1993) *Non-Governmental Organizations and the State in Asia – Rethinking Roles in Sustainable Agricultural Development*, London and New York: Routledge.

Fowler, A. (1991) 'The Role of NGOs in Changing State–Society Relations', *Development Policy Review*, vol. 9, no. 1, pp. 53–84.

Garain, S. (1994) 'Government – NGO Interface in India: An Overview', *The Indian Journal of Social Work*, vol. LV, no. 3, pp. 337–46.

Harbeson, J. *et al.* (eds) (1994) *Civil Society and the State in Africa*, London: Lynne Rienner Publishers.

Hardin, G. (1968) 'The Tragedy of the Commons', *Science*, vol. 162.

Hydén, G. (1983) *No Shortcuts to Progress*, London: Heinemann.

Khator, R. (1991) *Environment, Development and Politics in India*, Lanham: University Press of America.

Kohli, A. (1991) *Democracy and Discontent – India's Growing Crisis of Governability*, Cambridge: Cambridge University Press.

Kothari, R. (1988) *State against Democracy: In Search of Humane Governance*, Delhi: Ajanta Publications.

Lindberg, S. (1992) 'Peasants for Democracy? Farmers' Agitation and the State in India', in L. Rudebeck, (ed.), *When Democracy Makes Sense*, AKUT – Working Group for the Study of Development Strategies, Uppsala University.

MacIntosh, M. (1992) 'Questioning the State', in M. Wuyts, *et al.* (eds), *Development Policy and Public Action*, Oxford: Oxford University Press.

Madras Environmental Project (1992) 'Sustainable Cities Programme', First Revised Draft MEP/5–1992, Madras.

Madras Metropolitan Development Authority (1991) *Madras 2011 – Policy Imperatives – An Agenda for Action*, Madras: MMDA.

Marsden, D. (1991) 'What is Community Participation?', in R.C. Crook and A.F. Jerve (eds), *Government and Participation: Institutional Development, Decentralisation and Democracy in the Third World*, Report 1991: 1, Bergen: Chr. Michelsen Institute.

MIDS (1995) *Solid Waste Management in Madras: A Socio-Economic Survey of Households and Commercial Establishments*. Report prepared for ERM and MMDA, Madras.

Migdal, J. (1988) *Strong Societies and Weak States: State – Society Relations and State Capabilities in the Third World*, Princeton, NJ: Princeton University Press.

Olson, M. (1965) *The Logic of Collective Action: Public Goods and the Theory of Groups*, Cambridge, Mass.: Harvard University Press.

Omvedt, G. (1993) *Reinventing Revolution – New Social Movements and the Socialist Tradition in India*, New York and London: M.E. Sharpe.

Ostrom, E. (1993) *Governing the Commons – The Evolution of Institutions for Collective Action,* Cambridge: Cambridge University Press.

Panch, J. (1993) *Urban Water Supply: An Exploratory Study on Water Supply Systems in Madras,* Ahmedabad: Centre for Environmental Planning and Technology.

Wiguaraja, P. (ed.) (1993) *New Social Movements in the South – Empowering the People,* New Delhi: Vistaar Publications.

Wit, J. de (1993) 'Poverty, Policy and Politics in Madras Slums: Dynamics of Survival, Gender and Leadership', unpublished dissertation, Amsterdam.

World Development Report (1992) *Development and the Environment,* New York: Oxford University Press.

6 | International Production of Pesticides: Case Study of Gujarat, India

Petter Lindstad

Introduction

My main hypothesis is that a global shift in the world-wide production of polluting chemical industries has taken place, whereby the developing countries (South) are getting a growing share.[1] This is the result of a number of factors, the principal ones being stricter environmental regulations and enforcement in the developed countries (North); a lack of enforcement of such regulations in the South; and the possibility in the South of utilizing obsolete technology which cannot be sold in markets in the North. Obsolete technologies are often more pollution-intensive compared to new technology (Bergstø and Endresen 1992). The shift is partly based on an increasing involvement of transnational corporations (TNCs), and may take place either as a part of the global strategies of TNCs or through growing international competition in domestic markets in the South.

By using India as a case study, I shall show that within the industry, a global shift is taking place in the part that produces pesticides of the organophosphorous compound. In this sector, an increase in the pollution level may be caused by reduced demand for organophosphorous pesticides in the North, and the use of obsolete technology and increased competition between large and small firms in the South. In India, the pesticide industry is structurally composed of two different branches: (a) the manufacture of technical-grade *material* and (b) the formulation industry. The production of technical-grade material is dominated by

TNCs and large Indian firms, while the formulation industry consists of TNCs and both large and small Indian firms. The formulation industry purchases technical-grade material from large Indian firms and TNCs, and is licensed to manufacture formulations from these firms. However, competition between firms producing technical-grade material and firms manufacturing formulations may cause a marginalization within the formulation industry. One reason for this is that while many firms producing technical-grade material also engage in the manufacture of formulations, firms in the formulation industry engage in formulations only. Firms in the formulation industry have neither the knowledge nor the production technology to compete with the low cost of production and effective advertisement strategies of larger firms producing technical-grade material. An alternative to closing down may be to increase the production or marketing of environmentally dangerous organophosphorous formulations.

Since most people are not familiar with the context in which international production of pesticides occur, I shall begin with a brief outline of structural relations in the pesticide industry. In the second part I shall highlight some findings in the material collected in Gujarat. However, as I am in the preliminary stage of my analysis, complete answers to the questions implied by my hypothesis should not be expected.

Pesticides

Pesticides are defined as any substance or mixture of substances intended for preventing, destroying or controlling any pest, including vectors of human or animal diseases, unwanted species of plants or animals causing harm during, or otherwise interfering with, the production, processing, storage, transport or marketing of food, agricultural commodities, wood and wood products or animal feedstuffs, or which may be administered to animals for the control of insects, arachnids or other pests in or on their bodies (FAO 1986).

The term generally includes substances used as a plant-growth regulator, defoliant or fruit-thinning agent or agent for preventing the premature fall of fruit; additionally it covers substances applied to crops either before or after harvest to protect the commodity from deterioration during storage and transport. Although selective toxicity is desirable, it is never absolute. Most pesticides are toxic, to a greater or lesser extent, to non-target organisms, including humans. By the very nature of their use they tend to be common contaminants of water, air and food. One may say that they pollute the environment by definition (Hodgson *et al.* 1988, UNIDO 1988), and that the manufacture of pesticides involves highly hazardous chemical processes (Chandalia and Rajagopal 1993).[2]

Hazards Connected with Organophosphorous Pesticides

In the manufacture of organophosphates, a main hazard is the use of toxic basic chemicals and intermediates with the ability to form a large number of secondary toxic substances. The problem with the secondary substances is their reactive ability, that is, their ability to form other toxic substances (Stenersen 1994).[3] The main environmental hazards connected with the use of organo-phosphorous compounds is, first, their general-purpose activity. They have to be applied in large amounts and are used against a large number of pests on a wide range of crops, in which a large number of organisms are affected. Second, being related to nerve gases by chemical structure, they affect the nervous system and are considered to be highly toxic when in contact with the skin; in particular, the body enzyme cholinesterase at the nerve endings is attacked (Hassall 1990). Cholinesterase is necessary for proper nerve function and is destroyed or damaged by organic phosphates when taken into the body through any path of entry (UNIDO 1988).

Health hazards associated with pesticide use are mostly due to the indiscriminate and improper application of the poisonous substances. In the South, most labourers working as sprayers in the field ignore the necessary precautions associated with the handling of pesticides (Mencher 1991). This also applies to Indian farmers (Rao and Kumar 1994). According to WHO, 220,000 people die and 700,000 are poisoned yearly due to exposure to pesticides. According to Rosenstock, 99 per cent of the deaths occur in developing countries (Rosenstock 1992; WHO 1992).

Since 1979 scientists have conducted approximately twenty-five major studies investigating possible indirect effects of cholinesterase-inhibiting pesticides on wildlife. Some of the secondary poisoning studies suggest or confirm a hazard in the field. Exposure to organophosphates has resulted in changes in, for example, behaviour, hormones, cold tolerance, growth and embryonic development (Hall 1987). There is also evidence from West Africa that the use of organophosphore in agriculture is implicated in some instances of the pesticide resistance in mosquito vectors of malaria. It seems that resistance to one organophosphorous pesticide promotes resistance to others (Adams 1990).

The International Production of Pesticides

The pesticide industry

The pesticide industry encompasses both the small, unregistered, backyard production unit in Asia and Africa (manufacturing for the tiny roadside stall, where a farmer can easily purchase a small unlabelled packet of pesticides) and some of the largest TNCs, handling pesticides from research and development through production, to final marketing and disposal of industrial wastes. The major global producers of pesticides include TNCs like Ciba Geigy, ICI, Bayer, Dupont, Dow Chemical Co., Monsanto, American Cyanamide Co., BASF, Hoechst and Shell Chemical Co. These companies are also heavily involved in related industries, such as the production of basic chemicals, pharmaceuticals, dyestuffs, plastics, fertilizers and agricultural machines (Norris 1982; Wheelwright 1985; Chemical Business 1993).

The manufacture of technical-grade pesticides is done in different stages, from treatment of the initial basic chemicals to the production of the finished technical-grade material. However, while the manufacture of technical-grade material is a typical fine chemical industry, involving production of basic chemicals in bulk, the production of formulations is a processing activity in which technical-grade pesticides in high concentrations are mixed with water and solvents. The final product in the formulation process is the pesticide ready for use by the farmer.

The Indian pesticide industry

Until the 1960s, indigenous production of pesticides in India was mostly based on imported technology or production by foreign-owned companies. However, a small indigenous production of pesticides began in 1952–53 with the establishment of an organo-chlorine plant producing DDT and BHC. Today 75 per cent of local pesticide consumption is covered by indigenous production (Central Pollution Control Board 1994) and India features as a larger manufacturer of basic pesticides than any South Asian, East Asian or African country, with the exception of Japan (Ministry of Industry 1989).

At present, the production of technical-grade material is carried out by fifty-seven firms in the large-scale sector, while formulations are manufactured by about approximatly 675 firms (Central Pollution Control Board 1994). The majority of the formulation firms are in the small-scale sector. Among the fifty-seven firms producing technical-grade material there are both TNCs and large public and private Indian companies.

Pesticide production in Gujarat

With twenty firms producing technical-grade material (Central Pollution Control Board 1994), Gujarat occupies a key position in the pesticide industry in India.[4] According to *Pestology Annual* (1994), there are 151 firms in the formulating industry in Gujarat. The production of technical-grade material is mainly concentrated in Ankleshwar and Vapi, while the formulation units are located in Ahmedabad, Baroda and Kheda.

In Gujarat 85 per cent of the industrial activity is located in industrial estates. A characteristic of the Gujarat industry's approach to pollution control is that the effluent control arrangements are not well organized and are not subject to systematic control measures, either on an individual or a collective basis. This also applies to the pesticide industry. One main environmental problem connected with pesticide production is the lack of up-to-date waste management systems for safe treatment of air pollution and disposal of solid and fluid toxic materials (UNIDO 1990).

The local state authorities in Gujarat are known for their active policy of setting up a supporting network of institutions, for instance, the Gujarat Industrial Development Corporation, the Gujarat State Financial Corporation, the Gujarat Industrial Investment Corporation and the Gujarat Small Industries Corporation (Dholakia 1991). The state is also renowned for its active promotion of international participation in production (*Economic Times* 1991).

Global differences in the demand for pesticides

In global terms, the industrialized countries constitute the largest market for pesticides. Approximately 70 per cent of the pesticides used in the world are applied in the developed countries, the remaining 30 per cent in the developing countries (Dhaliwal and Pathak 1993). While the pesticide market seems to have reached a slow but continuously growing maturity stage in the industrialized regions using advanced agricultural technology, the demand in the South, particularly in the countries dependent on exports of primary products, is in the exponential growth stage of the market life-cycle curve (UNIDO 1988).

The differences in demand between the North and the South may indicate both a North/South dimension in the market for manufactured pesticide products, and a structural difference between the North and the South in the technology employed in the manufacture of pesticides. In the case of countries in the South, the structural difference may be a sign of an industrial development that includes an increase in the amount of pollution-intensive technologies. There may be several reasons for such a development. First, there may be a demand in the South for products manufactured with pollution-intensive technologies. Second, there has been a change in demand in the North. Third, the pesticides preferred in the South utilize a simple technology which increases their accessibility to the farmer. This may also affect demand.

The South: a haven for pollution-intensive technologies?

Within several industrial sectors there seems to be a market in the South for goods containing certain substances or intermediates that are either banned, severely restricted or being replaced by new or qualitatively superior products in the North. Products containing these substances appear to have a limited future market internationally. As controls on the use of pesticides tighten in the North, markets in the South are thus increasingly attractive to producers, particularly when pesticides banned at home can be exported to countries where environmental controls are more lax (Norris 1982; Adams 1990). According to Leonard (1988), more and more substitutes for highly toxic pesticides are being introduced in the North, while simultaneously there has been a comprehensive export to the South of pesticides that are either banned or severely restricted in the North (Aalstad 1991).

The opportunity to manufacture products with banned or heavily restricted substances in the South may not be the sole reason for a firm to relocate production from North to South. Other factors include a shrinking market in the North; cheap labour in the South; also a lack of enforcement of environmental laws and regulations in the South. This applies in particular to industries where the costs connected with stricter environmental standards are particularly high, and where competitiveness is determined more by direct production and shipping costs than by possession of technological advantages. Instead of modernizing technology, finding substitute products, or installing expensive pollution controls in the North, a relocation of production to the South may make up for the lack of efficiency and/or the lack of competitiveness in the North. In industries that manufacture products for which consumption is declining in the North, the location of production units closer to expanding markets in the South may extend the profitable life of both pesticides and production processes. Furthermore, relocation to the South may be a way to increase production in this industry.

Measured by tonnage, approximately 70 per cent of all pesticides used on Indian farms are banned or severely restricted in the North, and identified by the WHO as extremely toxic or hazardous (Iyer 1993). There are several examples of TNCs including pesticides in their agrochemical product lines that have been banned or severely restricted by their home governments (FIL 1995). They may continue to sell these pesticides in the largely unregulated markets of the South.

A change in demand in the North

In the North a growing awareness of the dangers of pesticides has resulted in an increased demand for alternatives with less harmful side-effects on humans and wildlife. This has contributed to the production of new generations of technology-intensive and more expensive pesticides with a greater specificity against target pests: these can be used in much smaller quantities than the older types. Another feature of some of these new pesticides are that they are biodegradable and therefore ecologically less damaging.

Forty years of pesticide development have thus witnessed a move from broad-spectrum pesticides affecting a large number of organisms (including humans) to a variety of more selective pesticides affecting the targeted organism only, or to a combination of products that more closely fits a given situation. For instance, some modern weedkillers are applied at one-twentieth the amount per hectare compared to their predecessors. Also, by the early 1980s, commodity surpluses were occurring in many countries in the North. This resulted in decreasing farm incomes and in millions of hectares being taken out of food production world-wide. Simultaneously, market penetration in the North has, for certain crops, approached an upper limit. In consequence, the tonnage used in the markets in the North is no longer increasing at the rate of earlier years, even though there is still scope for an increase of the financial value of the products on the world market (Hassall 1990).

The demand in the South

With less demand in the North for pesticides developed in the 1950s and early 1960s, markets in the South are viewed by large producers in the pesticide industry with increased interest. In the South, the demand for pesticides is dominated by what are often classified as the first and second generations of pesticides. These are often patent-expired, established product, for example, pesticides of the organophosphorous compound.[5] Organophosphore is derived from phosphorous acid. With regard to classification of pesticides, as a hazard to man, organophosphorous rates as the most toxic. Organophosphorous pesticides were developed in response to the dangers of organochlorides (of which DDT is the most notorious), and are today the largest group of pesticides in the market, whether the criterion of usage is tonnage produced or wholesale value (Ware 1975, 1978; Hassall 1990).

What makes organophosphore pesticides of special relevance to the farmer in the South is that they are manufactured with standardized product specifications and simple technology. Developed in the 1950s, organophosphorous pesticides are an example of a mature product having reached a high degree of market saturation in the North. They are thus low in price and require little technical knowledge. This makes them both attractive and accessible in markets with little purchasing power. In countries with poorly developed infrastructure and a high degree of manual labour in the primary industries, the market will be limited to a few first- or second-generation pesticides (WHO 1990). From the farmers' point of view, it usually implies a cheap and effective way of achieving an immediate reduction in the pest population (Hammond *et al.* 1978).

The Fieldwork in Gujarat

In Gujarat representatives from nine firms producing organophosphorous technical-grade material were interviewed. Six of these firms also manufactured their own formulations. In the formulation industry, I interviewed representatives from six firms.

The firms producing technical-grade materials were located in one of Asia's largest industrial estates, Ankleshwar Industrial Estate, which is situated halfway between Bombay and Ahmedabad. In Ankleshwar Industrial Estate over 1,400 industrial units provide employment for more than 100,000 people.[6] Approximately 1,000 small-, medium- and large-scale chemical units, from a wide variety of chemical branches, produce 15 per cent of India's bulk drugs, 10 per cent of dyes and pigments and 19 per cent of pesticides.[7] Every year about 10,000 tonnes of various classes of insecticides are manufactured at Ankleshwar, of which 50 per cent are of the organophosphorous class (Golwala *et al.* 1995).

I spent eight days and nights in Ankleshwar. The air in the estate was thick with the smell of chemical gases and every night

I had a headache and felt dizzy from breathing the air. Chemical waste was spread almost everywhere. In the vicinity of many firms, labourers and their families were living in sheds made out of throw-away materials and garbage. The water in the open gutters was red, blue or yellow from the waste-water of dyestuffs and colour production.

The formulation firms were located in Naroda Industrial Estate and Vatva Industrial Estate, just outside Ahmedabad. My impressions after visiting these resembled that of Ankleshwar.

Field observations

• *Localization of firms*

The Indian industrial location policy prior to 1990 emphasized the development of infrastructure in backward areas of the country. The New Industrial Policy, which was announced in 1991, made far-reaching changes in the location policy along with a general liberalization of the economy. Together with the large-scale delicensing of industry, most location restrictions have been lifted.

The central government's new economic policy may result in increased competition between states to attract new investments. On the question of the localization of firms, representatives from firms producing technical-grade material and from formulation firms pointed to backward area subsidies, cheap production facilities and good infrastructure (access to buildings, machinery, water and electricity) provided by the local government as important locational factors. A chemical-producing milieu, good communications with Bombay (road, train, plane, ports) and a well-disciplined and cheap labour supply were also deemed very important.

One result of the increased competition between states to attract new investments may be seen in the cheap production facilities supplied by local governments. In this process a strict enforcement of existing environmental legislation may sometimes be sacrificed.

• *Ownership structure*

The formulation firms were all independent companies. Except for one firm, they had either sister units or ownership in other (small) firms, either on the production or marketing side. The firms producing technical-grade material were production units of large chemical companies. These companies had production units in other parts of India in a variety of branches within the chemical industry. All firms were wholly Indian except for one, which was a production unit of a large German chemical TNC, with a 51-per-cent German and 49-per-cent Indian equity share. Many of the firms had licensing agreements or other collaborative arrangements with the TNCs, usually in the field of know-how and/or marketing. From annual reports it was evident that several of the firms had offices and/or production units in many countries (including Europe and the USA), and that they were owned by or had ownership in other Indian chemical firms through equity share arrangements.

This shows that there are connections between TNCs and large Indian companies in the pesticide industry. In a given situation of increased demand for pesticides in India, such connections may be employed to transfer from the North the production of hazardous pesticides with decreasing demand in the industrialized countries.

• *Products, markets, and purchase of raw materials and intermediates to the production*
In five out of six firms in the formulation industry there had been a change in the composition of products over time, from pesticides of the organochlorine compound to pesticides of the organophosphorous compound. Today, all firms manufactured a wide range of organophosphorous formulations, in addition to other classes of pesticides. All the company representatives interviewed saw the market for organophosphorous pesticides as a growing one.

It was also pointed out that in the peak season, from mid-May to mid-October, many formulation firms had difficulties purchasing enough raw materials and intermediates for production in the local market. The local market comprises both Indian and foreign-owned firms producing technical-grade material. Two formulation firms did not, however, have this problem. These were associated formulators, that is, subcontracting firms for large producers of technical-grade material. It is common for firms in the formulation industry to be approached by firms in the technical-grade pesticide industry. Associated formulation firms have their raw materials supplied by the technical-grade material manufacturers, and thus are assured a steady supply even in the peak season. In one formulation firm I was told that they subcontracted the formulation of the (organophosphorous) pesticide phorate to another formulation firm. They did this simply because they regarded the manufacture of phorate as too dangerous to carry out themselves. On a list of insecticides approved for registration in India together with their toxicity ratings, phorate is classified as both extremely toxic and extremely hazardous, and rates as the second most dangerous (Shah 1990).

The product range in the firms manufacturing technical-grade material resembled that of the small firms. All firm representatives whom I interviewed emphasized the growing market for organophosphorous pesticides. Basic chemicals and intermediates used in the production of organophosphorous technical pesticides were purchased from a variety of large Indian and local foreign-owned chemical firms. In three firms some of the raw materials or intermediates were imported from abroad. On the question of markets for technical-grade material, representatives confirmed that their products were sold to a number of different formulators. In one firm the market was constituted by approximately 100 different formulation firms spread all over India.

Several of the firms also exported organophosphorous pesticides to other countries in the South. In firms that manufactured their own formulations, capacity problems in the peak season were solved by subcontracting parts of the manufacture of formulations to firms in the formulation industry. Before starting formulation of a new (to the firm) organophosphorous pesticide, in two firms the production was subcontracted to small formulation firms. This was a way of testing the market and the firm thereby reduced the economic risks connected with market failure. If the new product sold well, the large firm would take over the production the following season.

The cooperation between firms in the formulation industry and firms producing technical-grade material may support the assumption that the former needs to engage in collaborations with the latter in order to survive, and that there may be a market for firms in the formulation industry willing to manufacture hazardous products. It may also indicate that there is an export market for pollution-intensive products in the South, and that India may be used by TNCs and large local firms as a base for the export of hazardous products.

- *Production technology*

Except for one firm, in which the production technology was five years old, the age of the production equipment in the formulation firms ranged from ten to thirty years. There was no labour union membership among the workers. The number of employees in the non-managerial position varied from fifteen to seventy-five, with an 8-hour working day and two shifts a day. Two firms were running three shifts in the peak season. Most firms took on extra labourers when demand was high. One firm with seventy employees in non-managerial positions took on approximately a hundred extra contract workers in the peak season. Contract workers employed on a daily basis were paid Rs 38 per day (*c.* US$1.23).

This may indicate that the possibility of employing large amounts of cheap labour may be preventing the utilization of more efficient technology; and that the use of obsolete technologies may be a factor in the increased pollution level within the pesticide industry. The production process in the Indian pesticide industry is mostly of the batch-process type, which was confirmed by firm representatives during the interviews. To be able to handle high demand in the peak season, speed in the production lines is increased. The result of this is a greater spill of chemicals.

In all the formulation firms visited, I was invited to see the production lines. In some of the firms production had not yet started for the season. I was assured by all the managers that workers in the production line wore adequate protective clothing, i.e., gloves, caps, boots, glasses and mouth-cover. However, in at least one firm, where pesticide dust was clearly visible, labourers worked in shorts and sandals and with their bare hands. Everything inside the production hall was covered with a layer of dust. The air was thick with dust from the production, and the only protection used by the workers was filthy cloths to cover their mouths.

- *Occupational health and safety*

According to company representatives, the formulation industry's production process leaves no by-products, and thus does not pollute. However, a main pollution problem in the formulation industry is the drainage of chemical-contaminated water from the cleaning of production tanks and barrels into the public drainage system. Another problem is the selling of empty barrels in which basic chemicals and technical-grade material have been packed and stored during transport. By law, firms are required to destroy barrels or return them to the supplier after use. However, in Gujarat, there is a local market for these empty barrels, which are bought and sold by industrial companies. At least five formulation firms sold empty barrels in the local market; in one firm I was told that they could not manage without this revenue. This may indicate that the selling of empty barrels may be a part of a survival strategy for hard-pressed firms.

While visiting firms manufacturing technical grade material, I was not invited to see the production lines. I was only shown the pollution treatment systems, and these were located in the outskirts of the firms premises. By law, all large-scale firms are required to have the necessary pollution treatment systems. The technical-grade manufacturing firms I visited all had waste-water treatment systems, that is, solar evaporation systems and biological treatment systems. Most firms also had an incinerator, while some also had scrubbers in which gases are neutralized. However, according to several representatives as well as various other people, firms in the pesticide industry are reluctant to upgrade the pollution control system in line with the expansion of production. This is said to be a question of finance. Also, it is said to be common practice to operate the pollution treatment system only when inspectors from Gujarat Pollution Control Board (GPCB) visit the factory.

In all firms I was told about a system of bribes being paid by the firms to the inspectors. One manager told me that they had to comply with this system, as otherwise 'they [the GPCB-inspectors] will make trouble for us'. Studies by Pandya (1988, 1992) about risks and hazards in chemical plants in Gujarat, report difficult working conditions for the inspectors and a questionable framework laid down by the public authorities for this kind of work. In a report from the government of Gujarat the GPCB inspectors are described as engaging in 'harassment'. In the report it is suggested that the number of inspectors are reduced drastically 'so that an entrepreneur can concentrate on the production and related issues' (Government of Gujarat 1993:30). According to *The Times of India* (1992), there seems to be a lack of effort by national authorities in India to relate policies of economic growth to environmental policies.

This information may support the assertion that there is a general lack of enforcement of environmental regulations in the South. It also reinforces the premise that the combination of cheap labour, the opportunity to produce with obsolete technology, an increased market demand, and a lack of enforcement of environmental laws in the South, lies behind the relocation of hazardous production from the North to the South.

Concluding Remarks

A main objective of the fieldwork carried out in Gujarat was to identify signs of a global shift in the production of organophosphorous pesticides. A main difficulty is to connect the decrease in the market for organophosphorous pesticides in the North with an increase in demand in India. However, with the help of statistics from OECD countries, and a combination of primary and secondary data collected in Gujarat, I believe a shift will be identified.

Notes

1.   This is a preliminary analysis of data collected during my fieldwork in Gujarat from January to April 1995.

2.   Pesticides may be classified according to group (insecticides, fungicides, rodenticides, herbicides and fumigants), chemical identity (organic and inorganic) or 'generations' of pesticides (i.e. according to when they were introduced in the market) (UNIDO 1988; Aalstad 1993). In this paper I use the term 'generations' of pesticides. The term

is closely related to the expressions 'family' or 'classes' of pesticides (Doyle 1985; Wheelwright 1985; Goldenman and Rengam 1988; Goldenman and Rengam 1989; Adams 1990; Gips 1990; Hassall 1990).

3. Interview in October 1994 with Professor Jørgen Stenersen, Department of Biology, University of Oslo.

4. Compared with fourteen firms in Maharashtra and four in Andhra Pradesh.

5. Lead arsenate pesticides and copper sulphate pesticides are classified by some (Kohn 1987; Stenersen (interview, October 1994)) as first-generation pesticides, while those of the organochloride and organophosphorous compounds are classified as second-generation. Nimmo et al. (1987) classify organochloride pesticides as first-generation pesticides, while organophosphates and carbamates are classified as second-generation. Hassall (1990) however, classifies the insecticidal organophosphorous compounds developed during the Second World War as belonging to the first generation and organo-phosphates developed in the 1950s and 1960s as second-generation. Third-generation pesticides are usually understood as sterilants, pyrethroids, pheromones and chitin inhibitors (Nimmo et al. 1987).

6. Final draft for 1995 information brochure, Ankleshwar Industrial Association.

7. Interview with A. T. Buch, Ankleshwar Industrial Association. Numbers relate to 1992.

References

Aalstad, R. (1991) 'Industriforurensning i u-land: Et spørsmål om teknologi?' [Industrial pollution in developing countries: a question of technology?]. In M.R. Midtgard *et al.* (eds) *Samfunnsgeografi Hovedfagsårbok 1991* [Social Geography Yearbook 1991], Oslo University: Faculty of Social Geography, IKS.

—— (1993) 'Forurensningsintensiv Industri i et Nord–Sør Perspektiv. Handelsrestriksjoner som miljøpolitisk virkemiddel' [Pollution-intensive industry in a North–South perspective: trade restrictions as a lever in environmental politics], Oslo University, thesis in social geography.

Adams, W.M. (1990) *Green Development. Environment and Sustainability in The Third World*, London and New York: Routledge.

Bergstø, B. and S.B. Endresen (1992) 'From North to South: A Location Shift in Industrial Pollution?', *Norsk Geografisk Tidsskrift*, vol. 46, no. 4. Scandinavian University Press, Oslo, pp. 175–182.

Central Pollution Control Board (1994) *Wastewater Management in Pesticides Industry. COINDS/47/1993–1994*, New Dehli: CPCB.

Chandalia, S.B. and R. Rajagopal (1993) *Environmental Perspectives of Chemical Industry*, Bombay: Sevak Publications.

Chemical Business (1993) 'Organophosphorous Pesticides. The Future', vol. 6, no. 11, June.

Dhaliwal, G.S. and M.D. Pathak (1993) 'Pesticides in the Developing World: A Boon in Bane', in G.S. Dhaliwal and B. Singh (eds), *Pesticides. Their Ecological Impact in Developing Countries*, New Dehli: Commonwealth Publishers.

Dholakia, J.R. (1991) 'Gujarat: Saga of Industrial Opportunities'. *Sunday Observer*, 13 January.

Doyle, J. (1985) *Altered Harvest*, Harmondsworth: Penguin.

Economic Times (1991) 'Gujarat's Giant Leap in Industrial Sector', 5 March.

FAO (1986) *International Code of Conduct on the Distribution and Use of Pesticides*, Rome: Food and Agriculture Organization of the United Nations.

FIL (Forurensende Industri-Lokalisering) (1995) Database of the Department of Human Geography, University of Oslo.

Gips, T. (1990) *Breaking the Pesticide Habits. Alternatives to 12 Hazardous Pesticides*, Penang: International Organization of Consumers Union.

Goldenman, G. and S. Rengam (1988) *Problem Pesticides, Pesticide Problems. A Citizens Action Guide to the International Code of Conduct on the Distribution and Use of Pesticides*, Penang: International Organization of Consumers Unions and Pesticide Action Network.

—— 1989. *The Pesticide Code Monitor. A Resource Book for Trainers.* International Organization of Consumers Unions and Pesticide Action Network, Penang.

Golwala, D.S., N.G. Shah, A.K. Patel and A.L. Choumal (1995) 'Management of Organophosphate Pesticide Poisoning and Its Clinical Effects'. Unpublished report.

Government of Gujarat (1993) *Report of Sub-Committee on Pesticides*, Gandhinagar: Industries Commission.

Hall, R.J. (1987) Impact of Pesticides on Bird Populations', in G.J. Marco *et al.* (eds), *Silent Spring Revisited*, Washington DC: American Chemical Society.

Hammond, K.A., G. Macinko, and W.B. Fairchild (1978) *Sourcebook on the Environment. A Guide to the Literature.* The Association of American

Geographers, Chicago and London: The University of Chicago Press.

Hassall, K.A. (1990) *The Biochemistry and the Use of Pesticides. Structure, Metabolism, Mode of Action and Uses in Crop Protection*, London: Macmillan.

Hodgson, E., R.B. Mailman and J.E. Chambers (1988) *Macmillan Dictionary of Toxicology*, London: Macmillan.

Indian Pesticides Directory. Third Edition (1992) Bombay: Scienta Publications Pvt. Ltd.

Iyer, R. (1993) *The Chemical Industry in India. Occupational Hazards and Pollution.* Occasional Paper, series B, no. 1/93: Development Studies. Oslo: Centre for Development and the Environment, University of Oslo.

Kohn, G.K. (1987) 'Agriculture, Pesticides, and the American Chemical Industry,' in G.J. Marco *et al.* (eds) *Silent Spring Revisited.* Washington DC: American Chemical Society, pp. 159–74.

Leonard, H.J. (1988) *Pollution and the Struggle for the World Product: Multinational Corporations, Environment, and International Comparative Advantage*, Cambridge: Cambridge University Press.

Mencher, J.P. (1991) 'Agricultural Labour and Pesticides in Rice Regions in India. Some Health Considerations.' *Economic and Political Weekly*, September 28, Bombay, pp. 2263–68.

Ministry of Industry (1989) *Perspective Plan for Chemical Industry (up to Year 2000 A.D.). Report of the Sub-Group on Pesticides.* Government of India.

Nandini Chemical Journal (1994) 'Organophosphorous Pesticides Complex', February, pp. 43–49.

Nimmo, D.R., D.L. Coppage, Q.H. Pickering and D. J. Hansen (1987) 'Assessing the Toxicity of Pesticides to Aquatic Organisms', in G.J. Marco *et al.* (eds) *Silent Spring Revisited*, Washington DC: American Chemical Society, pp. 49–69.

Norris, R. (1982) *Pills, Pesticides and Profits. The International Trade in Toxic Substances*, New York: North River Press Inc.

Pandya, C.G. (1988) *Hazards in Chemical Units.* Gandhi Labour Institute, Ahmedabad. Oxford and New Dehli: IBH Publishing Co.

—— (1992) *Risks in Chemical Units.* Gandhi Labour Institute, Ahmedabad. Oxford and New Dehli: IBH Publishing Co.

Pestology Annual (1994) Bombay: Scienta Publications Pvt. Ltd.

Rao, B.B. and S.S. Kumar (1994) 'Protective Wear for Safe Handling of Agrochemicals'. *Indian Farming*, vol. 44, no. 5, pp. 26–27.

Rosenstock, L. (1992) 'Chemical Hazards.' In M.L. Meyers *et al.*, *Papers and Proceedings of the Surgeon General's Conference on Agricultural Safety and Health, April 30–May 3, 1991, Des Moines, Iowa.* Cincinnati: US Department of Health and Human Services, Ohio. Publication no. 91–105.

Shah, M.P. (1990) *Directory and Handbook of Pesticides Industry*, Ahmedabad: Gujarat Pesticides Formulators' Association.

The Times of India. (1992) 22 June.

UNIDO (1988) 'Global Overview of the Pesticide Industry Sub-Sector', Sectoral working paper. Vienna: United Nations.

—— (1990) *Pollution Control in Dyestuffs and Pesticides Industries.* Technical report: Findings and recommendations. Vienna: United Nations.

Ware, G.W. (1975) *Pesticides. An Auto-Tutorial Approach*, San Francisco: W.H. Freeman and Co.

—— (1978) *The Pesticide Book*, San Francisco: W.H. Freeman and Co.

Wheelwright, T. (1985) 'The Worldwide Pesticide Industry', in T. Wheelwright (ed.), *Consumers, Transnational Corporations and Development*, Transnational Corporations Research Project, Sydney: University of Sydney, pp. 127–42.

WHO (World Health Organization) (1990) *Public Health Impact of Pesticides Used in Agriculture*, Geneva: WHO.

—— (1992) *Our Planet, Our Health. Report on the WHO Commission on Health and Environments*, Geneva: WHO.

7 | Linkages between Income Distribution and Environmental Degradation in Rural India

Rabindra Nath Chakraborty

Introduction

In the literature on environment and development, it is usually claimed that the poor are forced to destroy their natural environments in order to satisfy their basic needs (Leonard *et al.* 1989). This relationship, however, offers only a partial insight into the interaction between income distribution and environmental degradation, for in many cases such a situation arises as a result of prior deprivation of the poor. Furthermore, the role of the rural rich has been neglected in the analysis of environmental degradation.

The purpose of this paper is to identify general causal relationships between income distribution and environmental degradation with reference to rural India. The analysis will focus on the incentives that poor and rich households face with regard to natural resource use.

The central hypothesis is that a two-fold linkage between environmental degradation and income distribution exists. First, processes of environmental degradation affect the poor more than the rich and in that sense have an impact on income distribution. Second, an increase in rural income inequality (with aggregate income held constant) can accelerate environmental degradation. This possibility arises not only because the poor need to use a minimum quantity of natural resources for subsistence, but also because the rich are exposed to a broader range of opportunities for the generation of profits.

To keep the analysis tractable, linkages to population growth and intergenerational equity will not be dealt with in this paper. Gender issues will not be taken up here for the same reason.

This essay is organized as follows: After a description of the approach to environmental degradation which underlies this analysis, linkages between income distribution and environmental degradation are discussed in the following section within the wider framework of interrelations between the allocation and distribution of economic resources. As income distribution is linked to environmental degradation not only through differences in income but also through other correlated variables, the next section gives an overview on structural differences between the rural rich and poor. The next section describes the effects of environmental degradation on income distribution while the final section discusses the impact of income distribution on the level of environmental degradation.

The Value Dimension of Environmental Degradation

Environmental degradation can be characterized by a physical and a value dimension. The former can be identified from the fact that nature undergoes changes whenever the natural environment is degraded. The concept of environmental degradation implies that these changes are detrimental. This means that a value judgement is made on the types of environmental change observed, which constitutes the value dimension of environmental degradation.

Different approaches to environmental degradation vary in the ways these value judgements are made. One way is to place an intrinsic value on nature, which is considered as independent from the value placed upon it by humans. From this perspective, nature is seen as being valuable in itself or of having value conferred upon it by God through the act of creation or by transcendental universal law (Sylvan 1985).

Another approach focuses on the value that humans place on nature. These values belong to distinct categories, which encompass a broad spectrum.

• *immediate use value* refers to individual natural resources as objects of human consumption, raw materials for production, and (in the case of ecosystems) sinks for waste.

- *indirect value* is represented by the amenity services provided by environmental systems. These include life-support processes like the hydrological cycle and the stability of the local and global climate.

- *option value* (Pearce and Turner 1990): an environmental system may be considered valuable because it may provide services for hitherto unknown operations in the future. For example, certain species in a forest may be found to provide the basis for important medications in the future.

- *aesthetic value*: humans typically value nature not only for its actual or potential services as an input to material production and consumption but also because they find it beautiful and enjoyable.

- *existence value*: finally, humans place value on ecosystems because of their very existence. This category comes very close to the view that nature has intrinsic value.

Whatever the basis for the assignment of value to the environment, environmental degradation is identified by comparison of the actual with a desired state of nature. If the observed state is considered inferior to the desired state, the environment is considered degraded. If the value gap between the actual and the desired state has widened over time, it is concluded that environmental degradation has taken place. Environmental degradation can in principle be caused by humans and by nature itself. The following analysis, however, limits itself to anthropogenic environmental change.

The desired state can be defined in two ways: First, it may be identified with a *historical state* of nature. This is often the case when an ecological equilibrium prior to human intervention is envisaged as a state of reference. However, nature changes in the course of time, which makes the selection of any historical point of time as a point of reference somewhat arbitrary. Second, the state of reference may be defined as a *theoretical optimum*, which has not necessarily been observed so far. Again there are two possibilities, as it can be defined either in absolute or in relative terms. An absolute optimum does not depend on circumstances that change over time. In contrast, a relative optimum is conditional on a given set of historical circumstances.

If nature is viewed as being intrinsically valuable, an obvious state of reference is a historical state of nature as it was before human intervention occurred. Another solution would be to choose an absolute optimum. However, neither of these methods of valuation enable us to determine socially desirable levels of the use of nature when there is a conflict between the value of nature and human needs, especially the need for survival. The remaining option is to define a relative optimum subject to a set of conditions which may change over time.

This is the approach pursued by neo-classical environmental and resource economics. The state of reference is determined as a relative optimum, which takes into account both the value of nature and the value of the goods produced by humans with the help of natural resources. The value of the environment is deemed to be human-based. It can, however, encompass all categories described above, ranging from direct use value to existence value. The comparison across different categories is based on a generalized measure of welfare which is typically expressed in terms of utility.[1] It is then concluded that environmental degradation has taken place if total welfare in the actual state of nature including human production is less than in the state of reference. From this point of view, the clearfelling of a forest in itself is not an act of environmental degradation unless it leads to a suboptimal level of total welfare.

The assessment of environmental change as welfare enhancing or welfare decreasing is very sensitive to the categories of values included in the analysis. Moreover, there are direct and indirect, local and national, private and public benefits of environmental change. Net welfare will be different depending on the range of costs and benefits taken into account.

Allocation and Distribution of Economic Resources

The following considerations are based on the neo-classical view of environmental degradation as a state of nature, which entails a welfare loss compared to a theoretically feasible optimal state.

This view can be reformulated in terms of allocation theory: instead of assigning different categories of value to nature, it is possible to distinguish different *uses* of nature. Each use corresponds to one category of values. Nature is then 'used' to produce a particular value, ranging from direct use to existence value. Viewed from this perspective, nature is an economic resource which can be allocated among competing uses just like any other economic resource. Obvious qualitative differences between nature and other economic goods (for example, human-made capital) would be incorporated into the costs and benefits of alternative uses of nature.

An optimum allocation of nature is an allocation of natural and other economic resources which maximizes welfare. Conversely, the environment is considered degraded if the allocation considered produces less than the maximum possible amount of welfare.

Two problems are related to this perspective. First, the contributions of alternative uses of nature to welfare have to be assessed in terms of a single unit of measurement. Typically, utility is chosen as a category of evaluation. Second, the collective entity (village, nation, global society) whose welfare is evaluated cannot be considered homogeneous. The perception of use values of nature can be expected to differ significantly among individuals. If individual utilities are not comparable, they cannot be aggregated into a measure of social welfare: an allocation which maximizes aggregate welfare simply cannot be identified in this case.

However, there is a criterion for assessing the relative welfare position of two different allocations. One allocation may be considered superior to another if it increases the welfare of at least one individual without decreasing the welfare of anybody else (Pareto-superiority:[2] see Dasgupta and Heal 1979: 32). An allocation for which a Pareto-superior allocation *cannot* be found is called (Pareto-)efficient, because it is not possible to improve anybody's welfare without making somebody else worse off. Conversely, an allocation for which a Pareto-superior allocation *can* be found is called (Pareto-)inefficient. In neo-classical environmental economics, the concept of an efficient allocation of nature serves as a proxy for a socially optimal state of nature. It is analysed whether a given allocation of nature among competing uses can be transformed into a Pareto-superior allocation. If this is possible, the environment is considered degraded. If not, the environment is not considered degraded from an economic point of view because adverse changes in environmental quality (e.g. pollution) are exactly offset by benefits from the production of goods and services. In other words, the concept of environmental degradation implies that the existing allocation of nature is Pareto-inefficient.

A weaker formulation of this definition takes into account the possibility of compensation: if a new allocation increases the welfare of some individuals while decreasing the welfare of others, it is superior to the initial allocation if the (gross) winners can compensate the (gross) losers and still achieve a net gain.

The suitability of the Pareto criterion for policy recommendations is severely limited by the fact that it treats the distribution of individual resource endowments at the time of the welfare analysis as given. If a group of actors has deprived others of their resources before the time of evaluation, the straightforward application of the Pareto criterion would allow them to keep their prey forever. As an alternative, the efficient allocation at the point of time in question could be calculated on the basis of a previous distribution of resource endowments. In this case, it is necessary to choose a historical point of reference, which may be considered arbitrary.

Irrespective of historical arguments, the distribution of resource endowments on which an efficient allocation is based may be viewed as inequitable from an ethical standpoint (Hahn 1981: 74). As allocation determines the distribution of income, this argument carries over to income distribution.

For a variety of reasons further discussed in the fourth section – on the effects of historical patterns of natural resource use on income distribution – an economy can move from an efficient to an inefficient allocation of natural and other economic resources. As a result, somebody will inevitably be worse off. It will be argued that in many historical settings in rural India, it was the poor who had to bear the loss, which led to increased income inequality.

The reverse is true for the transition from an inefficient to an efficient allocation: Somebody has to experience a net gain. But are there forces in society that guarantee that efficient allocations are attained at least in the long run? If this were the case, environmental degradation problems would eventually solve themselves.

Markets are an obvious candidate for such a force. However, general equilibrium theory has shown that markets produce efficient allocations only under restrictive conditions which are not fulfilled in practice (Hahn 1991). In the real world, economic externalities abound. Some of them can in principle be internalized by negotiations. Negotiations, however, involve transaction costs while the pervasiveness of uncertainty with regard to natural processes makes actors doubt whether an efficiency gain can be achieved at all. In this essay, I shall emphasize impediments to the realization of efficiency gains which result from the skewedness of income distribution. It will be argued that under conditions relevant to today's rural India, income inequality and the incidence of absolute poverty can make it more difficult for a community to move from an inefficient to an efficient allocation of natural resources, that is, to reduce environmental degradation. The reasons can be traced to structural differences in the alternatives for economic action between the rich and the poor. To bring out these differences more clearly, the following section will look into structural asymmetries between the two groups.

Structural Asymmetries between the Rural Rich and Poor

The size distribution of income has an impact on patterns of natural resource use because differences in income are related to differences in economic opportunities among households. These differences can be identified with respect to a wide range of social, economic and political criteria. As they concern unequal opportunities for action, they are termed *structural asymmetries*. The causes of structural asymmetries are complex: while some can be traced directly to income inequality, others have to be viewed together with income inequality as joint effects of a common cause.

Agrarian society in India displays a wide spectrum of both incomes and economic opportunities across households and indi-

viduals. Economic opportunities may differ even among households with identical incomes. For the extreme ends of the income
distribution, however, there is a set of socioeconomic characteristics
which is related unambiguously to income.

In order to identify linkages between income distribution and
environmental degradation on a general level, the following analysis
concentrates on the two extreme ends of the rural income
distribution. Households at the lower end are termed 'poor':
they comprise all households whose income is below the Indian
poverty line for rural areas (i.e. Rs 49.09 per capita per month at
1973–74 prices).[3] The households at the upper end are termed
'rich'. In principle, they could be identified empirically by a
'wealth line' defined in analogy to the poverty line. Viewed from
an institutional perspective, it is the big landowners (> 4 ha),
moneylenders and large traders who constitute this group. Absentee
landlords who reside in the cities are considered members of the
rural rich.

There is always a problem in broad generalizations about the
poor. It has been warned that these generalizations reflect rather
the prejudices of researchers and development agencies than
the true situation of the poor (Chambers, *et al.* 1989; Chambers
1994). In the analysis that follows in the next section, these
generalizations will be used as abstractions which enable us to
analytically describe some mechanisms of environmental degradation considered typical for India.

Table 7.1 contains a typology of the relevant structural asymmetries between the rich and the poor. The criteria of comparison
have been grouped into four classes which comprise resource
endowments, positions in markets, political economy variables and
derived variables.

As far as *resource endowments* are concerned, it is well known
that poor households are endowed with less land, natural resources
and capital than the rich (Chambers, *et al.* 1989). Furthermore, the
productivity of their assets is lower at a given level of labour input:
the poor own less productive soils and capital. Closely related to
this is the fact that the resources owned by the poor are more
vulnerable to ecological degradation. The poor settle and practise

Table 7.1: Structural asymmetries between rural rich and poor

	Criterion	Poor	Rich
Resource endowments	Endowment with productive assets: land, capital, natural resources (productivity/quantity)	Low	High
	Ecological vulnerability	High	Low
	Changes in endowments with natural resources prior to degradation	Deprivation	Enrichment
Position in markets	Access to credit, information and technology	Low	High
	Access to output markets (transport and information costs)	Low	High
	Monopolistic market structures (factor, goods and credit markets; interlinked markets)	Weak side	Strong side
Political economy variables	Capacity for collective action (transaction costs)	Low	High
	Influence on state action (policy design and implementation)	Low	High
	Insecurity of property rights	High	Low
Derived variables	Economic alternatives	Few	Many
	Dependence on local natural resources for survival	High	Low
	Ability to appropriate common property resources	Low	High
	Ability of protection against detrimental effects of environmental degradation	Low	High

agriculture on steep slopes that are prone to erosion, or they live in low-lying areas close to rivers which are subject to floods. In times of drought, their wells dry up earlier than those of the rich.

Environmental degradation processes have often been preceded by the deprivation of a social group of its natural resource base, as will be shown in the next section. An example is the decline of the forest area available to tribal peoples in India since the nineteenth century (Fürer-Haimendorf 1982), which has made the formerly efficient practice of shifting cultivation inefficient. The poor have been more affected by these processes of deprivation than the rich, who at times have appropriated natural resources at the expense of the poor. People have become impoverished by these deprivation processes in many cases.

Another class of structural asymmetries between the rich and the poor is their relative *position in markets*. It has been widely recognized that the access of the poor to credit, information and technology (including modern agricultural inputs) is comparatively deficient. In addition to this, the access of the poor to output (goods) markets is constrained by high transport and information costs. It has to be emphasized that information is distributed very unequally in rural areas (Dasgupta and Mäler 1993). Moreover, the poor have to face adverse market structures: they often negotiate in monopsonistic factor markets as suppliers of labour and face monopolistic conditions when demanding credit and goods. As a result, prices are higher and wages are lower compared to a setting where perfect competition prevails. A special problem is posed by interlinked markets, where the landlord supplies goods and credit while demanding labour from the tenant at the same time. Being on the strong side of each market, the landlord is in a position to accumulate rents (Rao 1986: 63) and further decrease the tenant's utility.[4] The impact of both factors is reinforced by the geographic fragmentation of markets, which makes access for the poor to non-local markets costlier and favours the emergence of local monopolies.

A third class of asymmetries relates to *political economy* variables. In a democratic society, the prospects of a social group to influence political decision-making in its favour depends crucially on the ability of its members to organize themselves in order to achieve common goals. As there are significantly more poor individuals than rich ones, higher transaction costs will exist for the poor to organize themselves (Olson 1965). This refers both to the cost of transport and to the cost of communication over distances. Given the highly unequal distribution of information, a lack of communication will impose high costs on the poor.

Another impediment to communication is illiteracy, which limits communications to oral processes including audio media. For the rich, in contrast, it is less costly to organize themselves. This also makes it easier for them to exert pressure on state officials and governments to design and implement policies in their favour. Members of rich families enter politics or government service, which helps to build up networks of influence. As a result, the rich are often able to appropriate a disproportionate fraction of the benefits of government programmes targeted at rural society.

A combined effect of both forces is the insecurity of property rights for the poor. At the local level, property rights to a natural resource are guaranteed either by the state or by mutual agreement within a local group (community). As the rich can exert stronger pressure on the state to change local rules than the poor and at the same time dominate decision-making within the community, the property rights of the poor can be expected to be comparatively fragile.

The last group of structural differences contains characteristics which can be *derived* from the other classes but are particularly relevant for the analysis of problems of natural resource use. As a result of their resource endowments and market positions, the rich can choose from a wider range of income-generating activities than the poor. It involves lower transaction costs for them to exploit new economic opportunities that arise in the course of economic growth. Therefore, their dependence on local natural resources for survival is lower. As they harvest considerably more than they require for survival, a small decline in the regenerative capacity of the resource threatens the satisfaction of their basic needs much less than it threatens that of the poor.

This relationship is even stronger for resources managed under common property regimes. With regard to a region in Uttara Kannada, South India, Nadkarni *et al.* (1989: 166) found that the rich derive a higher absolute imputed income in terms of harvested forest produce valued at local prices from common property resources than the poor. On the other hand, imputed income from common property forests represents a higher percentage of total imputed income of the poor than of the rich.[5] Jodha's (1986: 1173) results show that in several dry regions of India the proportion of animal unit grazing days spent on common property pastures as compared to private grazing lands is higher both absolutely and as a relative share for the animals owned by the poor than for those of the rich.

Apart from this, consumption patterns differ between both groups. While the consumption behaviour of the poor is dominated by the necessity to satisfy basic needs, the rich are able to imitate urban lifestyles, which entails high levels of natural resource use. Moreover, the rich are in a position to appropriate common property resources. Their political and economic power and easier access to resource extraction technologies enable them to seize control of a part of the resource system in violation of the common property management rules (Jodha 1990: 16).

Finally, the rich have more options to protect themselves from the damages caused by environmental degradation. Given their resource endowments, they are able to undertake investments to secure the availability of a shrinking resource stock, e.g. to sink deep wells in areas with declining water tables. In many cases, this works to the detriment of the poor (Bhatia 1992: 35). As access to markets is easier for the rich, they can rely on non-local supplies to procure a locally scarce resource, e.g. firewood (Shiva 1991).

The structural asymmetries presented above can be categorized into two classes: First, the rich can choose among a wider range of alternative activities than the poor. These alternatives include both income-generating activities in a direct sense and options to alter the restrictions to these activities, e.g. to exert influence on public policy or on local processes of institutional change. The second class of asymmetries refers to the set of activities that are feasible for both groups. Here, the amount of benefits the poor can generate is limited by their endowment with economic resources. This restriction has a supply-side and a demand-side dimension. On the supply side, the low-resource endowment of the poor results in low output, both on the whole and (in many cases) relative to the resources employed. As far as the demand side is concerned, the necessity to consume a certain amount of output in order to satisfy basic needs is a binding constraint to the economic behaviour of the poor but not to that of the rich. As a result, time profiles of consumption tend to be shifted to the present, leading to consumption paths which would be inefficient in the absence of a minimum consumption requirement. Savings and investment may, therefore, be inefficiently low while natural resource extraction rates may be excessively high.

The Effects of Historical Patterns of Natural Resource Use on Income Distribution

Based on a brief account of the history of patterns of natural resource use in India, the effects of environmental degradation on income distribution will be analysed in this section. The analysis proceeds on a theoretical level within the framework developed in the previous sections. It will concentrate on forests, grazing lands, ground-water and soil. As a prerequisite, the causes of environmental degradation will also be analysed, which will serve as an input to the final section. The natural environment is considered degraded if nature has been allocated in an inefficient manner. The uses to which nature may be allocated comprise its direct use value, its amenity value and its option, aesthetic and existence values.

Apart from irrational behaviour, the causes of environmental degradation can be described in terms of institutional failures. Two important classes of institutional failures are market failure (in the sense of environmental externalities) and government failure. Dasgupta and Mäler (1993: 32) define a market as 'an institution that makes available to interested parties the opportunity to negotiate courses of action'. This definition goes beyond the description of markets as arrangements that facilitate the exchange of goods against money. Market failure can emerge in very different forms: one is 'reciprocal externalities' (ibid.), where the members of a group of actors inflict structurally identical externalities on one another.

Reciprocal externalities occur whenever a resource is used jointly by a number of users (see, for example, Dasgupta and Heal 1979: Ch. 3). As the productivity of the resource is negatively related to the quantity harvested, each user inflicts a negative externality on all other users per unit of the resource he or she harvests. With positive harvesting costs, there exists an optimum level of harvest for all users as a group, which is characterized by the equality of the marginal cost to marginal productivity of harvesting effort. As an individual, however, each user can increase his or her profit by increasing harvesting effort until the marginal cost of harvesting equals average productivity. As a result, rents are reduced. Moreover, if the harvest rate continuously exceeds the regeneration rate of the resource in absolute terms, the existence of the resource is threatened. In this situation, each user could be made better off by restricting harvest collectively. This could be achieved by a set of rules, which could be imposed by an external agent (e.g. the state) or agreed upon by the users themselves.

Another class of market failures can be described as 'unidirectional externalities' (Dasgupta and Mäler 1993). Here some actors inflict an externality upon other actors, while the latter are unable to reciprocate by imposing an identical externality upon the former. This occurs for example if some users of a resource recognize its amenity value in planning their resource use levels while others do not. In other cases the users of a particular resource plan their resource use levels while ignoring ecological linkages to other natural resources, which, however, generate benefits for other user groups. If the regeneration rate of resource B positively depends on the stock of resource A and the users of A do not take this linkage into account when they determine harvesting strategies for A, the resource B may be underproduced. An example is the extraction of timber from forests: as trees are logged, the availability of non-timber forest products such as food or medicinal plants is reduced to inefficient levels.

Government failure occurs whenever a government takes economic policy measures which lead to resource use inefficiency. A well-known example is the distortion of price controls. Furthermore, restrictions on the harvesting rate of a resource can be a source of inefficiency, if the permissible harvesting rate is too high or too low. Another source of government failure is the conversion of land to alternative uses for development projects such as dams, factories or roads. In case the government does not recognize the amenity and other values of the land, it may convert inefficiently much land to alternative uses.

Forests

Forests perform a variety of functions (Lyska 1991; Shiva 1991): they are sources of firewood, fodder, construction materials, medicine and food. Moreover, they produce amenity services: they help to arrest soil erosion and have a favourable impact on the microclimate. As they are capable of storing water immediately after the rainy season, they also stabilize the flow of surface waters, thus making many rivers perennial. Forests also conserve biodiversity, which is considered a major source of option value.

Before the colonial period, forests in India were managed as common property resources by local communities and, to some extent, regional authorities (Guha 1989). The exploitation of forest products was regulated by a set of rules which allocated forest resources to users. This system was sustainable in the sense that a significant forest cover could be maintained over centuries. There is, therefore, some reason to assume that it was efficient with respect to the value categories mentioned above or that the welfare loss compared to an efficient state was lower than it was in later periods. Furthermore, the existence of sacred groves, as pointed out by Gadgil and Vartak (1994), shows that something like existence value was recognized. The role of forests in ancient arts and philosophy reveals the historical importance of its aesthetic value too (Bahuguna 1988: 4–5; Shiva 1991: 74–75).

There is no reason to romanticize the past. The very necessity to establish elaborate systems of (harsh) sanctions against forest offences (as documented by Guha 1989: 29–34) reveals that access to forests was a permanent source of social conflict. Besides, the availability of forest products to the local population was unequal (Shiva 1991). The segmentation of natural resource use by caste (Gadgil 1987, 1991) was no less questionable from an ethical perspective.

In disregard of traditional management regimes, the colonial rulers seized control of the forests. They denied the local population access to a substantial part of them and overexploited the areas reserved for themselves. The government of independent India continued this policy *mutatis mutandis* (Chopra 1989: 340). The appropriation of forests by the state amounted to a redistribution of natural resource endowments to the detriment of the local communities. As the same number of local users had to share a smaller resource base, the existing CPR management regimes came under severe pressure. One option for the local communities was to change the rules in such a way that harvest rates of forest products were reduced to efficient levels. Wherever this happened, resource use inequality tended to increase, for it was to be expected that the rich would use their strong position *vis-à-vis* the poor to force a disproportionate reduction of harvesting levels upon them.

Another outcome has been the gradual erosion of common property resource management regimes, which has occurred in many parts of India. Historical management regimes based on the principle of regulated access to forests were transformed into regimes that displayed more and more characteristics of open-access regimes, e.g. weak or even absent monitoring mechanisms or, more generally, the incomplete specification of rights and duties of each user. As a result, environmental degradation has been accelerated.

This process was amplified by an incentive structure which favoured the conversion of forests into agricultural land. As the taxation system introduced by the British required land taxes to be paid in cash (and not in kind), there was a tendency to increase market-oriented agricultural production by the conversion of forests (Richards and McAlpin 1983: 84). The impact on income distribution has been disadvantageous to the poor. Given their access to technology, information, wage labour and transport, the rich are able to exploit forests faster than the poor in an open-access situation.

The second source of institutional failure is forest use by the state itself. Even if the state aims at the efficient (that is, non-depleting) utilization of forests, there is a collective action problem with regard to the amenity function of forests. As the latter is a public good to both the state and the local communities, each party may try to avoid the opportunity costs of keeping the harvest at a lower level. Forest management by the state may then be efficient with regard to its direct use value but inefficient with regard to amenity and other values. The problem of amenity value is complicated by the importance of the spatial distribution of forest area for its amenity functions.

There are strong indications that the state has run down the forest stock under its control in India. The wood harvested has been sold either to urban markets as firewood or to wood-processing industries as raw material at subsidized rates (Fernandes 1990: 41; Gadgil 1992: 133). This could be efficient for the following reasons. First, the large-scale supply of firewood to urban centres may keep the cost of fuel and hence wages for industrial labourers low. Moreover, raw material costs are reduced for industry. As a result, industrial expansion may be accelerated, which in turn may generate higher employment and per-capita income. On the other hand, the weak Pareto criterion is violated because there is no adequate mechanism to compensate the rural communities (especially the rural poor). Furthermore, the amenity value of Indian forests as a whole can be considered high. It is quite unlikely that the decrease of forest area experienced since 1972 can be termed efficient once the amenity value of forests is taken into account. The behaviour of the state can be better explained by the power of vested interests.

As forest use by the state was unsustainable, there was an inherent tendency in state action to enlarge the area of reserved forests over time. As a consequence, the pressure on community forests increased, with adverse effects for the poor, as outlined above.

As a result of state intervention, the position of the poor deteriorates for two reasons. First, the redistribution of endowments considerably narrows the range of economic opportunities available to the poor. In this context, it has to be emphasized that the poor typically rely on forests not only as a source of fuel, but also for the non-timber forest products mentioned above (CSE 1985). Second, the poor are more affected than the rich by the inefficiency of forest use which results from redistribution.

Another reason for forest degradation is the emergence of new economic opportunities in the process of growth. The regional integration of markets has made non-local demand a significant component of total demand for firewood. In quantity (that is, in weight) terms, firewood purchased in urban areas accounted for 56 per cent of total firewood purchases in (rural and urban) India during 1978–79. However, a large proportion of the firewood consumed is not purchased but collected. Firewood purchased in urban areas therefore amounted to only 35 per cent of total consumption (that is, firewood purchased *and* collected) during the same period (Natarajan 1985: 30).

As access to urban firewood markets is easier for the rich than for the poor, the former can be expected to supply a higher share to the urban markets. Moreover, new fields of income-generating activities open up in the course of economic growth. Examples are rural non-farm production, commerce and manufacturing in the urban private sector (both formal and informal). Finally, the integration of the banking system enables savers to invest in a wide range of financial assets. As a result, there are incentives for the rich to overuse forest resources: urban firewood demand enables them to convert forest produce into money (disregarding the amenity and other values of forests), while the factors described above create opportunities for investment which are not accessible to the poor.

These incentives operate independently of the effects of state intervention described above. Of course, both processes can act upon each other cumulatively: if the rich perceive their property rights to be insecure because of the state's tendency to expand control over forests, accelerated logging may result. On the other hand, the state may anticipate encroachment by the rural rich and, therefore, head for a cooperative solution, allocating concessions freely to them.

Finally, regional market integration makes the rich less dependent on the local poor as suppliers of labour and buyers of goods

(Shiva 1991). This may foster individualistic values and accelerate the erosion of traditional rights embodied in common property regimes.

A third class of reasons for forest degradation is formed by ecological linkages between forests and other resources. The degradation of grazing lands, for example, aggravates the shortage of fodder prevalent in many parts of rural India (CSE 1985). As a result, the poor take their cattle into the forests where they contribute to forest degradation.

Grazing lands

With regard to grazing lands, state intervention has taken a different form: as a part of welfare programmes, a share of the common lands has been redistributed to individual households. The objective of this privatization was to give land to the poor. However, a considerable proportion of this land was appropriated by the non-poor. Furthermore, the poor subsequently sold or leased out to the non-poor a substantial part of the land they had received. As a result, pressure on the remaining common property resources increased (Jodha 1986: 1178). Besides, the shrinkage of forests as a source of fodder has aggravated the pressure on open pastures. The processes of erosion of common property regimes for pasture lands can be expected to be similar to those described in the preceding section.

As far as new economic opportunities are concerned, urban demand for meat and milk plays a similar role in the overexploitation of pastures as firewood demand does with regard to forests (Jodha 1987). Furthermore, government programmes that made subsidized credit available to the poor for buying livestock without simultaneously expanding the fodder base (CSE 1985) have contributed to growing pressure on grazing lands. The same is true of government programmes aimed at the regional integration of markets for milk ('operation flood').

Another problem has been the shrinkage of grazing lands accessible to nomadic peoples, which has led to fierce conflicts among nomads and settled agriculturalists, as traditional systems of cooperation have broken down (CSE 1985).

Groundwater

Increasing groundwater scarcity is reported in many locations in India. For example, the groundwater table has declined by 0.5 to 4.0 m in parts of eight of the twelve districts of Punjab during 1978–86 (Singh 1992: 105). In Mehsana district (Gujarat), long-term data are available for eighty-six traditional wells. While all wells supplied water in May 1973, 43 per cent of them had run dry by May 1990. There is similar evidence from other districts in Gujarat (Moench 1992b: A–172).

Dhawan (1995) presents data collected by the Central Groundwater Board on the exploitation rates of groundwater at district and block levels. The exploitation rate is calculated as the quantity of groundwater used for irrigation divided by the quantity of the annual groundwater recharge earmarked for irrigation purposes by groundwater planning agencies. The exploitation rate exceeds 100 per cent in eleven districts, which are situated in Punjab (6), Haryana (3) and Rajasthan (2). In Tamil Nadu, 11 per cent of all Development Blocks have exploitation rates above 85 per cent. In Andhra Pradesh, the corresponding figure is 9 per cent, while it is 10 per cent for all *talukas*[6] in Gujarat.

The reasons for increasing groundwater scarcity are related to a long-term increase in the use of energized pumpsets. The number of electrical and diesel pumpsets in India increased from 87,000 in 1950 to 12.6 million in 1990, which amounts to an annual growth rate of 12 per cent (Moench 1992a: A–7). This shows that it became technically feasible to extract larger quantities of groundwater than could be harvested with the help of traditional water extraction mechanisms. The increase in the number of pumpsets itself need not result in declining groundwater tables, if the operators restrict water extraction to sustainable levels. The reasons why this has not occurred can be found in the presence of reciprocal externalities and state intervention.

Groundwater resources within an aquifer are connected by sub-surface flows. By extracting groundwater, each groundwater user reduces the total quantity of groundwater available not only for his or her own use but also for all other users. As he or she does not take the cost inflicted on others into account when determining the level of groundwater extraction, the user inflicts a negative externality on all other users. As all groundwater users behave identically in this respect, a reciprocal externality results. The resulting level of water extraction is inefficient even if only its direct use value is considered. In many localities, extraction exceeds recharge, which leads to declining water tables. If extraction is not reduced, wells run dry.

A second reason for the problem of water scarcity is government subsidies. For example, rural electricity prices have been heavily subsidized. According to calculations made by the National Council of Power Utilities, the average cost of Rs 0.772 per kWh incurred by the State Electricity Boards is only partially recovered from rural water users, as the average revenue is Rs 0.14 per kWh (Chandrakanth and Romm 1990: 495). The Tamil Nadu government decided in 1989 to supply farmers with electricity free of charge following an agitation by the farmers' association Tamilaga Vyvasayigal Sangam (see Staffan Lindberg's chapter in this volume). Moreover, several state governments switched from a pro-rata tariff to flat-rate pricing of electricity during the 1980s. As a result, the marginal cost of electricity becomes zero, which leads to increased water extraction.

Another type of subsidy pertains to credit for the installation of modern water extraction mechanisms. The National Bank for Agriculture and Rural Development (NABARD) has provided subsidized credit for agricultural water users. Although there exist restrictions on the provision of subsidized credit in Development Blocks where the exploitation rate exceeds 65 per cent, it is easy for wealthy farmers to circumvent these obstacles (Bhatia 1992; Moench 1992a: A–8).

Declining water tables raise the cost of groundwater irrigation, as more energy has to be used to transport the same quantity of water to the well head. These costs are not necessarily borne by the water users because energy prices are heavily subsidized. However, traditional wells and shallow modern (i.e. energized) wells will dry up first. As the rural rich own a disproportionately higher share of modern water extraction mechanisms compared to marginal farmers,[7] they are less affected. Moreover, owing to their comparatively easy access to credit, they are in a better position to sink deep wells in order to reach declining water tables.

This often directly works to the detriment of the poor, as the installation of deep modern tubewells in the vicinity of traditional wells can cause the latter to dry up. Bhatia (1992: 35) reports cases where this has led to substantial economic losses to poor owners of traditional wells. These losses can be mitigated by water markets. Farmers whose wells run dry can buy water from the owners of functioning wells. If water markets are competitive, an efficient allocation will ensue. Many water markets, however, are characterized by monopolistic structures, which enable the rich (as owners of modern wells) to extract monopoly rents from the poor (as water buyers; see Shah 1993).

In many areas (e.g. in Andhra Pradesh, Rajasthan, Maharashtra, Karnataka and Tamil Nadu), there has been an erosion of traditional common property regimes which were in operation before the colonial period. These systems involved the construction and maintenance of tanks and canals. The destruction of traditional systems of authority in combination with a self-interested colonial (and post-colonial) administration has led to the decay of these systems without the emergence of adequate substitutes (Chandrakanth and Romm 1990; Shiva 1991). As a result, farmers relied increasingly on groundwater irrigation. While the rich have been able to install modern water extraction mechanisms, the poor have witnessed the groundwater table fall in traditional wells.

As far as ecological linkages are concerned, deforestation tends to increase water scarcity, for both total surface water run-off and the variability of water supply increase, as was sketched in the section on forests.

Soil

In contrast to the other resources described above, soil is managed privately. State intervention has been relevant to soil management insofar as input prices have been subsidized, especially in the areas where the Green Revolution has spread. This has often led to agricultural practices which threaten the long-term productivity of the soil. Soil salinity and waterlogging, for example, have been caused by the excessive use of subsidized water. The reclamation of salinized soils involves high costs both in terms of cropping area (in the case of surface drainage) or capital requirements (for subsurface drainage).

For drainage to be effective, a compact minimum area has to be covered, which usually comprises fields belonging to different owners. It is therefore necessary for a group of farmers to invest jointly in drainage. In addition to this, drainage creates positive externalities, as the water table declines not only in the area covered by drainage works but also below the adjacent fields. Joshi *et al.* (1987: 205) found that in the village Kailanakhas in Haryana the yields on agricultural lands adjacent to the drainage area increased from 600 kg/ha to 1,600 kg/ha. Therefore, there are strong incentives for an individual farmer to act as a free rider, that is, not to participate in the provision of drainage. As a result, drainage is 'underproduced' in many areas (Datta and Joshi 1991).

With regard to salinization, it is not clear whether the poor are more severely affected than the rich. If access to water is more difficult for the poor, they can be expected to apply less water to their crops, which tends to reduce the incidence of soil salinity or waterlogging. However, poor farmers are less able to bear the costs of soil reclamation than the rich.

One field of soil degradation where the bias against the poor persists is soil erosion. As pointed out in section 3, the poor are often forced to settle on steep slopes prone to erosion. Owing to labour scarcity and limited access to credit they are less able to undertake investments in soil conservation, e.g. terracing or bunding.

New economic opportunities created by non-local demand for agricultural goods and changes in agricultural technology (Green Revolution) set incentives to intensify soil use. As a result of the structural asymmetries outlined in Table 7.1, the rich are more capable of responding to these incentives than are the poor. Soil erosion and salinization often occur as unanticipated effects, which are perceived only after a considerable time-lag. Deforestation can accelerate soil erosion.

As far as the effects of environmental degradation on income distribution are concerned, the poor have to bear higher relative income losses than the rich. The poor are endowed with ecologically more vulnerable resources and are less able to protect themselves from the detrimental effects of environmental degradation. If the environment is degraded above a certain level, the reduced productivity of nature can entail a survival threat to the poor.

Table 7.2 summarizes the principal factors which lead to natural resource degradation. The left column is structured according to the system in which the basic types of causes considered (state intervention, emergence of new economic opportunities, and ecological linkages between resources) originate. Compared with the terminology of Dasgupta and Mäler (1993), 'state intervention' corresponds to government failure, whereas 'economic growth' roughly corresponds to market failure. More precisely, the entries in this row show the factors that determine the scale of welfare losses caused by environmental externalities. The reasons why efficient institutions are not created (that is, why the externalities are not internalized) will be discussed in the following section with reference to income distribution. While the redistribution of endowments is a central force underlying the degradation of forests and grazing lands, explanations of soil degradation and water resource depletion have to focus on price distortions and technological change in agriculture. Obviously, this is a simplified picture: timber is sold at subsidized rates by the state while a redistribution of endowments with irrigation infrastructure has occurred under colonialism (CSE 1985; Shiva 1991).

As far as ecological linkages are concerned, the degradation of grazing lands leads to increased fodder scarcity. The decline in forest area causes increases in grazing pressure (as a major source of fodder is lost), water scarcity (as the hydrological cycle is disrupted), and soil erosion.

The Impact of Income Distribution on Environmental Degradation

In the environmental economics literature (e.g. Dasgupta and Heal 1979), the analysis of the causes of environmental degradation

Table 7.2: Mechanisms of environmental degradation

System	Forest	Grazing land	Water	Soil
Political (state intervention)	redistrib'n of endowments		price policy	
	reservation and exploitation of forests	reservation of forests; land redistribution	energy price subsidies; promotion of technological change	input price subsidies
Economic (growth)	non-local demand			
	firewood	meat, milk	water-intensive crops	agric. goods
	investment in other sectors	land use; promotion of cattle-rearing by the state	technological change	
Ecological (linkages)	degradation of grazing lands	decline in forest area		
	fodder scarcity	grazing pressure	water scarcity	soil erosion

centres around externalities, which as such do not depend on income distribution. This perspective corresponds to the strict separation of distribution and allocative efficiency in the general theory of allocation: with perfect markets, income inequality does not have an impact on allocative efficiency. If markets are imperfect, however, the interaction of market imperfections can lead to inefficient outcomes. In the case of environmental degradation, environmental externalities are one type of relevant imperfections. Another is the set of imperfections that are related to the structural asymmetries between the rich and the poor, e.g. unequal access to information and credit or monopolistic market structures.

There are three reasons why income distribution can have an effect on allocative efficiency with regard to natural resources. First, the deprivation of the poor of income-generating environmental assets can be a source of environmental degradation. Second, income distribution determines the scale of welfare losses incurred as a result of environmental externalities. Third, an increase in rural income inequality can make the provision of efficient CPR management regimes at the local level less likely.

It has been stated that the redistribution of forest endowments by the state has resulted in a greater loss in the availability of forest products to the poor than to the rich. As forest resources are income-generating assets, this has led to an increase in income inequality at the local level. As their resource endowment shrinks, it becomes increasingly difficult for the poor to derive sufficient income from the exploitation of the resource to satisfy their minimum consumption requirement. Hence, their interest in the continuity and stability of the traditional common-property resource allocation rules decreases. The resulting resource use pattern is unsustainable and leads to environmental degradation because a redistribution of income would relax the minimum consumption constraint to the poor and, hence, enable them to reduce their harvesting rate. An example is the poor who sell firewood to urban centres as self-employed 'headloaders' (CSE 1985: 189–92). Clearly, this phenomenon is an indirect result of prior deprivation. Another example is the decline in the productivity of grazing lands.

In the course of economic growth, new opportunities for income generation open up as a result of the regional integration of markets and technological change (see central row in Table 7.2). Many of these opportunities are accessible to the rural rich but not (or only to a small extent) to the poor. Once they are exploited, levels of resource use change. In many instances, the gap between the social and the private cost of natural resource use increases with rising extraction rates. That is, the social marginal cost of resource use rises faster than the private marginal cost.

For example, the regenerative capacity of many renewable resources is exhausted if the resource stock shrinks below a threshold level. Increases in the extraction rate of a resource (e.g. timber) which is part of a system of ecologically interlinked resources (e.g. forest) may lead to the disintegration of the resource system. With regard to groundwater depletion, the cost of lifting water to the field level increases with a falling water table. If the water table continues to fall, more and more wells dry up, which imposes an additional cost for the deepening of old and the sinking of new wells. In all three cases, disproportionate collective effort is needed to regenerate the resource. At the same time, the benefits of regeneration become more uncertain as resource stocks decline, which makes the design of institutions for efficient resource use more difficult.

If income or wealth is redistributed from the poor to the rich, structural asymmetries between the two groups are accentuated. When increasing economic opportunities exist, the rich as a group will be better able to make use of them, thus amplifying the scale of already existing environmental externalities both in terms of a decline in resource stocks and in terms of welfare losses. Inefficiencies caused by the difference between private and social costs are enhanced as the set of feasible activities expands for one group of actors.

In reality, pure redistribution (with aggregate income held constant) seldom occurs. Distributional changes usually take place in conjunction with changes in aggregate income. An increase in aggregate income makes it easier for all members of a community to exploit new economic opportunities, whereas a decline lessens this equality of opportunity.

One example is colonial forest policy in India. The establishment of a state monopoly over forests in general and of reserved forests in particular reduced the resource base (and, hence, income) for all members of rural society. However, the privileged treatment of the resource needs of the rich *vis-à-vis* those of the poor by the state effectively redistributed income from the poor to the rich. The latter were able to respond much more positively to the evolution of non-local firewood demand than were the former, thus accentuating already existing externalities. A similar outcome can be observed with regard to grazing lands.

As far as groundwater use is concerned, technological change in combination with the emergence of non-local demand for agricultural products presented the new opportunity to be exploited. While market demand raised irrigation needs, technological advances enabled farmers to increase groundwater extraction to unprecedented levels.

It has been demonstrated in section 4 that one reason for environmental degradation has been the erosion of traditional CPR management regimes without the creation of adequate substitutes. As a Pareto improvement can be attained by moving from an inefficient to an efficient allocation, one would expect self-interested individuals to take appropriate steps. However, two problems have to be solved if a set of rules for sustainable management of a resource is to be adopted by a user group. First, agreement has to be reached on the distribution of the efficiency gain in question. Second, the users have to make a credible commitment to the rules agreed upon. This is true both for private and common property systems.

It has been recognized that conflicts over the distribution of the efficiency gain achievable by the CPR regime in question can make the provision of the regime more difficult and, hence, less likely (Libecap 1989a: 7–8). These difficulties increase the more skewed the distribution of benefits under the proposed regime becomes (Libecap 1989b: 24). What is less clear is the impact of the status quo distribution of income among resource users on the prospects of provisioning a CPR regime. If the behaviour of individuals is guided exclusively by self-interest and rationality, no commitment will be considered as credible by the group. For there is always an incentive for each party to desist from co-operation as long as the others cooperate. Monitoring and enforcement mechanisms only translate the credibility problem to a different level: the commitment to monitor behaviour and enforce rules itself has to be made credible.

How does cooperation, then, come about in the real world? One possible reason is the existence of shared norms among the users. Shared norms are norms that are not only internalized by individuals but also socially accepted. They derive their sanctioning power both from internal sources (such as the feeling of guilt) and from the disapproval of the violator's behaviour by other group members (Ostrom 1990: 206). According to Ostrom, shared norms are more likely to evolve when resource users live near the CPR and interact with one another on numerous occasions.

One class of shared norms particularly relevant to income distribution is the notion of fairness. An institution that is considered fair by all users is more likely to be accepted than an institution that is perceived as unfair by some. Among other factors, the perception of an institution as fair or unfair depends on the distribution of the efficiency gain and the relative economic position of the users within the status quo. A given distribution of gains will be considered unfair by more members the higher the degree of income inequality (with aggregate income held constant). As the rich perceive their bargaining strength to increase, they expect their 'justified' share to be higher than before. On the other hand, the poor increasingly feel that their share is 'inequitably' low, as the rich raise their demands and their shrinking share comes closer to their minimum consumption requirement.

A third impact of income inequality on the provision of efficient natural resource management regimes is related to monitoring and enforcement costs. In a variety of settings, these costs are not equal for all members of the user group but depend on the alternatives for action available to each member. Given the structural asymmetries between rich and poor actors, monitoring and enforcement costs can be expected to differ between the two groups. As far as forest use is concerned, the rich are able to carry large quantities of wood away with the help of trucks, whereas the carrying capacity of the poor is limited to headloads or animal-driven carts. Hence, it is more difficult to detect the extent of the violation of wood extraction rules by the rich than non-compliance by the poor.

There are cases where it is more difficult to detect the rich as violators of rules. As a result of their easier access to non-local markets, they can extract wood faster than the poor can. If they employ wage labour for cutting the wood, the labourers appear to be the violators while it may be difficult to find out their employer's name. They may even employ people from a different region who do not know the local languages.

Enforcement is necessary once a user has been detected as infringing a resource extraction rule. One recourse is to apply sanctions to the violator: for example, his (or her) behaviour may be disapproved of socially. Alternatively, he or she may be required to pay a fine or be excluded from further resource use. It is easier for the rich than for the poor to avoid (or resist) these sanctions because their larger scope of (economic and non-economic) action enables them to retaliate against the rest of the community. A rich violator may, for example, refuse outright to pay a fine. In this case, a concerted effort by all the other members of the community is required to enforce the rule. The success of this effort depends on the prevailing constellation of power. Even in the case of success, the cost of enforcement is higher than it would be *vis-à-vis* a poor violator with more limited means to retaliate. As a result, an increase in income inequality in the status quo increases monitoring and enforcement costs to the poor while at the same time reducing their capacity to bear these costs. As the poor anticipate this outcome, they may prefer an open-access regime over a regulated-access regime which would prove excessively costly to them.

Conclusion

There are strong indications that the use of natural resources in rural India has become more inefficient in recent times. This seems to be true even if the values assigned to nature are restricted to its immediate use value. Moreover, there are many cases in which environmental degradation has had a polarizing effect on income distribution.

There is no simple causality between income distribution and environmental degradation. Instead, the rural rich and poor have different incentives to degrade the environment. While the high dependence of the poor on local natural resources for their survival can lead to overexploitation, it has to be recognized that this situation has arisen in the case of forests and grazing lands as a result of the prior deprivation of natural resource endowments.

The rich, in contrast, degrade their environment because of the emergence of alternative opportunities of income generation in the process of economic growth. State intervention often creates incentives for both groups to overuse resources.

There are, of course, intervening factors not dealt with in this paper. For example, population growth may relieve or aggravate environmental degradation while increased productivity in agriculture and the emergence of new rural non-farm employment opportunities for the poor may mitigate its effects on income distribution. Anyway, the policy implication is that restricting access to natural resources either by price or quantity-oriented instruments may reduce environmental degradation by the rich but will not achieve the same end with the poor. If the poor are to be enabled to use natural resources efficiently, environmental policy has to be integrated into a policy of poverty alleviation.

Acknowledgements

The author wishes to thank Heiko Körner, Gisela Kubon-Gilke, Detlef Radke and Frank Weilemr for constructive comments on an earlier draft.

Notes

1.   This description is true only for a society that consists of identical individuals. The case of differences between individual utilities will be taken up in section 2.

2.   The terms 'Pareto-efficiency' and 'Pareto-superiority' have been named after the welfare economist Vilfredo Pareto (1848–1923), who was the first to use these concepts in a generalized way.

3.   Government of India (1993: 8).

4.   Bardhan (1989: 240–41) emphasizes that the interlinkage of markets can lead to a Pareto improvement for both landlord and tenant when market imperfections prevail and the tenant's utility in the case of separate markets has already been reduced to a minimum below which the tenant will not enter into any transaction with the landlord (reservation utility). If the tenant attains a utility level above his or her reservation utility in the case of separate markets, interlinkage may make the tenant worse off.

5. Imputed income is the sum of the income earned through exchange against cash in markets and non-cash income derived from collection for self-use.

6. In India, the lowest level of spatial administrative units is called a Development Block. *Talukas* are regional administrative units just below the district level. One *taluka* contains a number of Development Blocks.

7. Marginal farmers are farmers whose operational landholding covers a hectare or less. A sample survey by Pant (1992) shows the distribution of pumpsets across operational holdings. The results of Bhatia's (1992) sample survey based on the distribution of ownership across castes points in the same direction.

References

Bahuguna, Sunderlal (1988) 'Chipko: "The People's Movement with a Hope for the Survival of Mankind"', *ifda dossier*, vol. 63, Jan./Feb., pp. 3–14.

Bardhan, Pranab (1989) 'A Note on Interlinked Rural Economic Arrangements', in Pranab Bardhan (ed.), *The Economic Theory of Agrarian Institutions*, Oxford: Clarendon Press, pp. 237–42.

Bhatia, Bela (1992) *Lush Fields and Parched Throats: The Political Economy of Groundwater in Gujarat*, Helsinki: World Institute for Development Economics Research (WIDER), Working Paper no. 100.

Chambers, Robert (1994) *The Poor and the Environment: Whose Reality Counts?*, Brighton: Institute of Development Studies Working Paper no. 3.

——, N.C. Saxena and Tushaar Shah (1989) *To the Hands of the Poor. Water and Trees*, London: Intermediate technology Publications.

Chandrakanth, M.G. and Jeff Romm (1990) 'Groundwater Depletion in India – Institutional Management Regimes', *Natural Resources Journal*, vol. 30, no. 3, pp. 485–501.

Chopra, Kanchan (1989) 'Forty Years of Resource Management: The Gainers and the Losers', *Social Action*, vol. 39, no. 4, pp. 333–44.

CSE (1985) *The State of India's Environment 1984–85*. The Second Citizens' Report, New Delhi: Centre for Science and Environment.

Dasgupta, Partha and Geoffrey Heal (1979) *Economic Theory and Exhaustible Resources*, Cambridge: Cambridge University Press.

—— and Karl-Göran Mäler (1993) *Poverty, Institutions, and the Environmental Resource Base*, Beijer International Institute of Ecological Economics Discussion Paper no. 27, Stockholm.

Datta, K.K. and P.K. Joshi (1991) *Cost and Benefits of Sub-Surface Drainage for the Control of Soil Salinity and Water-Logging*, Karnal, Haryana: Central Soil Salinity Research Institute.

Dhawan, B.D. (1995) 'Magnitude of Groundwater Exploitation', *Economic and Political Weekly*, vol. 30, no. 14, pp. 769–75.

Fernandes, Walter (1990) 'Forest Policy: A Solution to Tribal Deprivation?', *Indian Journal of Social Work*, vol. 51, no. 1, pp. 35–56.

Fürer-Haimendorf, Christoph von (1982) *The Tribes of India: The Struggle for Survival*, Berkeley/Los Angeles/London: University of California Press.

Gadgil, Madhav (1987) 'Social Restraints on Exploiting Nature: The Indian Experience', *Development*, no. 1, pp. 26–30

—— (1991) 'Ecological Organization of the Indian Society', *ICSSR Newsletter*, vol. 21, no. 4, pp. 1–9.

—— (1992) 'State Subsidies and Resource Use in a Dual Society'. In Anil Agarwal (ed.), *The Price of Forests*, New Delhi: CSE, pp. 132–37.

—— and V.D. Vartak (1994) 'The Sacred Uses of Nature'. In Ramachandra Guha (ed.), *Social Ecology*, Delhi: Oxford University Press, pp. 82–89.

Government of India (1993) *Report of the Expert Group on Estimation of Proportion and Number of Poor*, New Delhi: Perspective Planning Division, Planning Commission, Government of India.

Guha, Ramachandra (1989) *The Unquiet Woods*, Delhi: Oxford University Press.

Hahn, Frank (1981) 'General Equilibrium Theory'. In D. Bell, and I. Kristol (eds), *The Crisis in Economic Theory*, New York: Basic Books. Reprinted in F. Hahn, *Equilibrium and Macroeconomics*, Oxford: Basil Blackwell, 1984, pp. 72–87.

—— (1991) 'The Welfare Economics of Market Economies'. In David Vines and Andrew A. Stevenson (eds), *Information, Strategy, and Public Policy*, Oxford/Cambridge: Basil Blackwell, pp. 51–70.

Jodha, N.S. (1986) 'Common Property Resources and Rural Poor in Dry Regions of India', *Economic and Political Weekly*, 5 July, pp. 1169–1181.

—— (1987) 'A Case Study of the Degradation of Common Property Resources in India', in Piers Blaikie and Harold Brookfield (eds), *Land Degradation and Society*, London/New York: Methuen, pp. 196–207.

—— (1990) 'Rural Common Property Resources: Contributions and Crisis', Foundation Day Lecture, Society for Promotion of

Wastelands Development, Supplement to *Wastelands News*, vol. 5, no. 4, New Delhi.

Joshi, P.K., O.P. Singh, K.V.G.K. Rao and K.N. Singh (1987) 'Sub-surface Drainage for Salinity Control: An Economic Analysis', *Indian Journal of Agricultural Economics*, vol. 42, no. 2, pp. 198–206.

Leonard, H. Jeffrey, M. Yudelman, J.D. Stryker, J.O. Browder, A.J. De Boer, T. Campbell, and A. Jolly (1989) *Environment and the Poor: Development Strategies for a Common Agenda*, New Brunswick/Oxford: Transaction Books.

Libecap, Gary D. (1989a) 'Distributional Issues in Contracting for Property Rights', *Journal of Institutional and Theoretical Economics*, vol. 145, pp. 6–24.

—— (1989b) *Contracting for Property Rights*, Cambridge: Cambridge University Press.

Lyska, Brigitte (1991) *Umweltpolitik in Indien*, Aachen: Alano, Ed. Herodot.

Moench, Marcus (1992a) 'Drawing down the Buffer. Science and Politics of Groundwater Management in India', *Economic and Political Weekly*, vol. 27, no. 13, pp. A-7–A-14.

—— (1992b) 'Chasing the watertable. Equity and Sustainability in Groundwater Management', *Economic and Political Weekly*, vol. 27, no. 51, pp. A-171–A-177.

Nadkarni, M.V., Syed Ajmal Pasha and L.S. Prabhakar (1989) *The Political Economy of Forest Use and Management*, New Delhi/Newbury Park/London: Sage Publications.

Natarajan, I. (1985) *Domestic Fuel Survey With Special Reference to Kerosene*, vol. 2, New Delhi: National Council for Applied Economic Research.

Olson, Mancur (1965) *The Logic of Collective Action*, Cambridge, Mass.: Harvard University Press.

Ostrom, Elinor (1990) *Governing the Commons*, Cambridge: Cambridge University Press.

Pant, Niranjan (1992) *New Trend in Indian Irrigation*, New Delhi: Ashish Publishing House.

Pearce, David W. and R. Kerry Turner (1990) *Economics of Natural Resources and the Environment*, Baltimore: John Hopkins University Press.

Rao, J. Mohan (1986) 'Agriculture in Recent Development Theory', *Journal of Development Economics*, vol. 22, pp. 41–86.

Richards, J.F. and Michelle B. McAlpin (1983) 'Cotton Cultivating and Land Clearing in the Bombay Deccan and Karnatak: 1818–1920', in Richard P. Tucker, and J.F. Richards (eds), *Global Deforestation and the Nineteenth-Century World Economy*. Duke Press Policy Studies, Durham, NC: Duke Press, pp. 188–93.

Shah, Tushaar (1993) *Groundwater Markets and Irrigation Development*, Bombay: Oxford University Press.

Shiva, Vandana (1991) *Ecology and the Politics of Survival*, New Delhi: Sage Publications.

Singh, Baldev (1992) 'Groundwater Resources and Agricultural Development Strategy: Punjab Experience', *Indian Journal of Agricultural Economics*, vol. 47, no. 1, pp. 105–13

Sylvan, Richard (1985) 'A Critique of Deep Ecology', *Radical Philosophy*, Nos. 40, pp2–12 and 41, pp. 10–22.

8 | Deforestation and Entrepreneurship in the North-West Frontier Province, Pakistan

Are J. Knudsen

Introduction

This chapter analyses the social and institutional factors behind the high logging pressure and deforestation in the North-West Frontier Province (NWFP) of Pakistan (see Map 8.1). Forest management may at first appear as a dull subject, one best left to specialists such as foresters and, possibly, historians. Over the past decades, however, there has been a shift from viewing forestry as primarily a technical exercise, to emphasize the social context of forestry as well as its embeddedness in institutional and political fields of larger scale. People who live in and near the forests hold the key to their conservation, but as this chapter should demonstrate, the conservation of forests is not only dependent on local management practices but also influenced by forest policies, various stakeholders and market demand.

The NWFP holds about 30 per cent of Pakistan's remaining 5 per cent of forest cover (NCS 1992: 175; Jan 1993: 2). Most of the coniferous forests in the province are found in the Malakand and Hazara Divisions.[1] About 85 per cent of the forests that are commercially exploited in the NWFP come under some form of private ownership. It has been estimated that if the present rate of deforestation continues, the remaining forest will disappear within the next thirty years. Hence, gaining a better understanding of the dynamics of deforestation in private forests is urgent and holds the key to understanding deforestation in the province as a whole.

Map 8.1: North-West Frontier Province, Pakistan.

While the prime focus is here on the causes of contemporary deforestation,[2] it is evident that present-day practices are embedded in the environmental history of the South Asian continent. As such the 'major factors in the depletion of the Himalayan forests [are] ... essentially a historical question' (Tucker 1987: 328). In order to comprehend the process of deforestation in the NWFP, there is a need to combine an understanding of current management practices with a diachronic view of the underlying factors that have shaped them. The rationale behind current management practices must be sought in the interface between the economic payoffs to different stakeholders and the legal and institutional framework of forest management. This chapter argues that shifting forest policies, bureaucratic reforms, market demand for timber and rural poverty exposed the private forests in the NWFP to damaging logging pressure. Central actors in this process were the local middlemen, i.e. the forest contractors (*tekhedars*), who took advantage of the unplanned implications of federal forest policies. In order to understand how this process unfolded we have to return – quite appropriately – to its roots, namely British colonial forest policies in the nineteenth century.

Forest Management in British India

Deforestation is a problem throughout the hilly and mountainous areas of South Asia and its origins can be traced to early colonial forestry policies affecting most of the Western Himalayas (Tucker 1982). Early nineteenth-century forest exploitation in British India focused on 'hardwoods', in particular sal (*Shorea robusta*). Later when the hardwoods became depleted, the interest turned to 'softwoods', primarily Himalayan cedar (*Cedrus deodara*) which was used for railway sleepers. The commercial exploitation under British administration was already in the 1850s so high that doubts were raised about its sustainability (ibid.: 116) and the period 1850–60 has been termed 'the first period of massive deforestation in the Himalayas' (Tucker 1987: 329). The first forest laws were promulgated in 1878, and the Indian Forest Law introduced two main legal categories: 'Reserved Forests' and 'Protected Forests' (Tucker 1982: 117). Reserved forests were set aside to be managed by the newly created Forest Department. The protected forest category was instituted to give temporary shelter to forests until management plans could be worked out. The prime motive for demarcating the reserved forests was to safeguard valuable timber, especially Himalayan cedar, for the needs of the state. Thus, 'the Forest Department spent the next half century demarcating the Reserved Forests in which they worked with private contractors to harvest timber for distant markets' (Tucker 1987: 329). After the state had demarcated the reserved forests, selected areas were set aside to fulfil the subsistence needs of local communities. Originally known as 'public wastelands', they were later termed *Guzara* [meaning private or community-owned] forests (Azhar 1989, 1993). Demarcation of the first *Guzara* forests began in 1882 and involved curtailing local privileges such as grazing rights and the right to collect firewood and grass. Due to strong local protests, demarcation had to be suspended and some of the initial restrictions relaxed but felling of timber remained a state prerogative (Schickhoff 1995a: 12). The combination of high pressure and commercial exploitation in the *Guzara* forests continued well into the 1930s (Azhar 1993: 120). In 1938 a commission reviewing the management of the *Guzara* forests advised that management should be transferred to provincial forest departments and involve local users in management.

Not only the delimitation of *Guzara* forests was problematic. The demarcation of reserved forests in Kumaon (Uttar Pradesh, UP) met with very strong protest and coincided with a nationwide outcry against British colonial oppression. In 1921 thousands of acres of forest were set ablaze in Kumaon and massive forest fires raged for more than a month (ibid.: 118). Investigating the incident, a fact-finding commission – the Wyndham Commission – concluded that the UP Forest Department should devolve control of the new forest reserves to local villagers. In 1923 the new forestry plan adopted the Wyndham Commission's recommendations, and granted local villagers ('concessionaries') more control of the use of forest. According to the new plan, villagers were now entitled to a percentage of the revenues from commercial felling of forest. Instead of saving the trees, this increased the logging pressure. Since the Forest Department lacked the manpower resources to carry out logging, the department 'auctioned the right to harvest marked trees in preannounced tracts each year. The winning bidders sent their own crews into the hills to cut the purchased trees' (Tucker 1984: 344). Since competition was intense, 'winning bidders became determined to squeeze maximum profits from their coupes [areas delineated for commercial forestry]' (Tucker 1982: 119). Despite local protests, this 'forester-contractor coalition' continued well into the 1930s (Tucker 1984: 350).

The Second World War and the transition to independence for Pakistan and India in 1947 marked a 'second great wave of deforestation' (Tucker 1988: 91). High demand for timber during the war meant that prices rocketed. By taking advantage of favourable market conditions, 'private contractors could make fortunes in one season by dealing directly with individual owners, often bypassing the Forest Department entirely' (Tucker 1984: 350). The forest policies of British India had to a large degree 'saved' the reserved forests but there was a heavy toll on the *Guzara* forests after independence. In the late 1950s, the NWFP forest department undertook heavy felling in the *Guzara* forests (Azhar 1993: 122).

Forest Laws and Classification in Pakistan

The colonial legacy of forest management is evident in present-day Pakistan; the forest legislation which was instituted before partition has to a large degree remained unchanged.[3] A legacy of its colonial past, the state of Pakistan inherited a bundle of different legal categories of forest (Khattak 1976a, 1976b). As already described, the major work of classifying forest was undertaken through region-by-region land settlement in the nineteenth century. To document which rights ('concessions') had been granted to local people, their rights and privileges were specified in a document known as the *Wajib-ul-Arz* ('Land Obligations' – a village register of rights and duties) (Jan 1993: 17). These rights included firewood collection, grazing rights and the right to timber for house construction.

Forestry management in Pakistan is regulated by the Forest Act of 1927, and for the Hazara Division especially, the Hazara

Forest Act of 1936. While the Forest Act of 1927 has been amended several times, there have not been any changes concerning the penalties prescribed for offenders. As an example, the maximum penalty under the Forest Act is still either a fine of Rs 500 or six months in jail, penalties which are no longer adequate to discourage offenders.[4] Ownership of forest in Pakistan is complex, with a number of legal categories where ownership and use rights are shared between the state, the communities and in some instances, individuals (NCS 1992: 174). The Forest Act distinguishes between state-owned and private (i.e., non-state) forest (see Table 8.1). Among state-owned forests, the two most important tenure classes are the reserved and protected forests. In reserved forests local people have no rights at all and even firewood collection is prohibited. Moreover, all types of use by human beings, including the grazing of their livestock, are prohibited, unless specifically permitted by the government (Jan 1993: 3). In protected forests this principle is reversed and with the exception of commercial timber harvesting, both grazing and firewood collection are allowed unless explicitly banned by the government. The protected forest category is often used in cases where ownership is disputed, but is not meant to be a category where forest shall remain indefinitely (Khattak 1994: 1).

The 'private forest' category is the most problematic in Pakistan's forestry and reflects the historical struggle between state and local communities for control of the forest. The two most important tenure classes are *Guzara* and communal forests (see Table 8.1). *Guzara* forests proper are only found in the Hazara Division and regulated by the Hazara Forest Act of 1936. Communal forests are a subcategory of *Guzara* forests and are mostly found outside settled areas.

Although both *Guzara* and communal forests are classified as 'private' (see Table 8.1), they are only nominally controlled by local communities and management is, in most instances, a state prerogative. In general, these forests are the joint or communal property of local shareholders, who are entitled to proceeds from the sales of timber ('royalties'). The size of the royalties ranges from 60 to 80 per cent of the revenues, with the remainder going

Table 8.1: Legal classification of forests in Pakistan*

Type	Category	Ownership	Management	NWFP (km²)	Pakistan (km²)
State	Reserved Forests	State	State	940	16,820
	Protected Forests	State	State	40	9,940
	Other	State	State	1,470	2,510
Private	*Guzara* Forests	Communal	State/Communal‡	5,850	6,220
	Commu-nal Forests	Communal	Communal	8,090	8,780
	Other	Private	State	420	510
	Total			16,810	45,780

Notes:
* Present data on forest cover in the NWFP are unreliable. New estimates based on remote sensed data (Landsat™) will be available shortly.
‡ Communal management by Forest Cooperative Societies.

Source: Jan (1993: 7)

to the provincial government. The present management system in private forests lacks credibility in the eyes of local communities and leaves the forests prone to over-exploitation. In order to understand why, there is a need to look more closely at the system of forest management and harvesting.

Forest Management and Harvesting

Most of the remaining coniferous forests in the NWFP are found in a narrow altitudinal belt ranging from 1,500 to 3,000 m above sea level. The conifers that are commercially exploited are Himalayan cedar (*Cedrus deodara*, 'deodar'), spruce (*Picea smithiana*), silver fir (*Abies pindrow*), blue pine (*Pinus excelsa* or *wallichiana*, 'kail') and chir pine (*Pinus longifolia*). Owing to its high market value, Himalayan cedar is the most intensely logged species; moreover as a result of its climatic requirements, it is the conifer with the least spatial extension (Schickhoff 1995b: 74ff.).

Forest planning in Pakistan has traditionally focused on timber harvesting rather than forest regeneration. Forests in the NWFP are logged in accordance with a harvesting plan, known as a 'working plan' (ibid.). Areas suited for commercial forestry are delineated into sections known as 'compartments' where a prescribed harvesting volume ('prescribed yield') is fixed for the compartment as well as the 'felling cycle', that is the period from one harvesting to the next. A major problem with current working plans is that they prescribe a harvesting volume which is too high and do not provide funds for regeneration (Khattak 1994). Despite official statistics showing massive tree-planting efforts in the NWFP (PFI 1992: 7), regeneration of coniferous forests is low. The reasons for this seem to be a combination of improper care and lack of technical expertise in forest nurseries, free grazing of animals and land-use change.

The total volume to be logged from a compartment is known as the 'standing volume'. The marked trees, which together constitute the compartment's standing volume, are cut, the bark is removed and the logs transported to the nearest road. From the perspective of sustainable use, it would have been preferable to transport the timber as round logs, which entails only 10–20 per cent volume loss. Most of the timber which is logged in the NWFP is, however, converted into scantlings ('scants', 'sleepers'), which averages more than 50 per cent volume loss (Swati and Cheema 1991). Conversion into scants is a wasteful harvesting method but preferred due to the lack of negotiable roads. The scants are transported down the steep mountain slopes to the nearest road or stream on custom-made slides (*pathru*) built by skilled lumberjacks. A recent technical innovation is the use of skyline cranes (*zanga*) which make it possible to transport round logs over great distances. Due to higher initial purchasing costs, skyline cranes are not yet in common use (Usui 1994: 38).[5] Whereas local technology (such as timber slides and skyline cranes) has made it possible to harvest timber on steep slopes and in distant valleys, the construction of new roads simplifies transport and increases logging pressure. A recent study of fifteen field sites (primarily in the Northern Areas) confirms the strong correlation between accessibility and deforestation (Schickhoff 1993a).[6]

The impact of timber logging is aggravated by crude felling methods which cause collateral damage to timber stands. Instead of directional felling, trees fall downhill, thereby damaging standing trees and undergrowth (Guha 1989: 166). There is also a tendency not to spare seed trees with mature cones which are vital to the natural regeneration of the species. Natural regeneration is also hampered by a very high grazing pressure, especially in *Guzara* forests where people have rights to livestock grazing (Schickhoff 1995a: 14). There is also a substantial piecemeal logging of single trees by subsistence users, who need timber for firewood and as a building material. The most extensive forest loss is, however, due to deliberate over-cutting and violation of working plans in the commercial forestry sector. To understand the underlying causes, it is necessary to consider the changes in the harvesting system and forest policies which began in the 1970s.

Implications of Changing Forest Policies

Forest administration in Pakistan is divided among the federal and the provincial authorities, but implementing forest policies is a provincial responsibility. Until 1977 the NWFP Forest Department (FD) was in charge of both felling and marketing operations. This organizational set-up was problematic because it was not open to public scrutiny. Moreover, the FD was reliant upon private timber merchants, 'forest contractors', for carrying out the actual timber harvesting. Until 1973 forest contractors could bid for standing trees and, once they got the tender, took charge of felling and marketing operations. Thus, forest contractors under minimal FD supervision logged the trees and later sold them. Known as the 'contract' or 'permit system', this led to widespread over-harvesting. When the contract system was abolished in 1973, no alternative had been prepared to replace it. In order to strengthen the FD as well as to find an alternative to harvesting by contractors, the Forest Development Cooperation (FDC) was established as a semi-autonomous organization in 1977 (Jan 1990: 28).[7] The intention was to let the FDC replace contractors and handle both harvesting and marketing. In reality, the FDC continued to sublease harvesting to contractors (Treacy 1994: 7). However, as long as contractors only logged the trees (i.e. they were labour contractors) they had no vested interest in over-cutting but earned money from working efficiently. Initially, the FDC only worked in government-controlled reserved forests in Hazara. The rates for felled timber were determined by calculating backwards from the market price to the standing trees ('stumpage rate'). In reserved forests people have no share in the revenues, therefore the stumpage rate was only a means to calculate the government revenue as well as the FDC's administrative charges.

This changed when the FDC began timber harvesting in Hazara's *Guzara* forests, where the local owners are entitled to proceeds from the sale of timber. The *Guzara* forest owners refused to be paid in accordance with the stumpage rate. They argued that the FDC's charges were too high, and because of the long time-gap from when harvesting began until it was completed, the initial market price set did not reflect rising timber prices. To solve the problem a commission was formed in 1977 to find an alternative to the stumpage rate. In 1981 the commission reached an agree-ment for a new system termed the 'net-sale system' which would bring the value of timber closer to the market price. The net-sale system was similar to the stumpage rate but the FDC's pre-calculated profit was fixed at 20 per cent. Moreover, owners had to give their written consent to the award of contracts, and royalties to owners were to be paid in instalments. The net-sale system's advantage was that it gave forest owners a say in the award of contracts and had in-built provisions for rising labour charges as well as timber prices. Under the net-sale system, the harvested timber is auctioned at official timber markets and sold to the highest bidder. When the extraction costs (including taxes) are deducted, the net revenue from the sales is divided between the state and the local concession-aries. The net-sale system was gradually implemented from 1983–84. Originally the net-sale system was designed for use in the *Guzara* forests in the Hazara Division but in 1981 the FDC tried to extend it to the Malakand Division.

In order to explain the events that followed we have to consider the increase in timber royalties from the mid-1970s. Initially, royalties were only paid to concessionaries in *Guzara* forests in the Hazara Division. The Hazara Forest Act granted shareholders 80 per cent of the royalties while the state was entitled to the remaining 20 per cent as administrative charges. Local communities in the Malakand Division did not have such rights, because they were not provided for in the Forest Act of 1927 and forest royalties were either very small or absent. The reason for this is to be found in the recent history of the area.

What is today known as the Malakand Division was formerly ruled by three feudal principalities governing Swat, Dir and Chitral (Barth 1985). In 1954 parts of the Swat principality were declared a tribal area and all forests were claimed as the property of the state. The locals were accorded 10 per cent of the revenue. After abolition of the Swat principality in 1969, the FD took charge of forest administration and fixed the royalties at 5 per cent. After massive complaints, the royalties rose to an average 15 per cent in 1972. Later the same year the government declared that all forests in the former Swat principality would become the property of the government (KIDP 1988). In 1974 the Forest Act of 1927 was extended to Swat, Dir and Chitral and all forests were declared protected forests. A year later, in 1975, they were reclassified as reserved forests, which was the strictest tenure class in the forest legislation. In 1976 the dissatisfaction with the government's forest policy in general and the royalties in particular sparked a revolt in Dir District (Malakand Division). The strength of this protest forced the government to concede that whereas the reserved forest classification would remain in place, in practice they would be managed as *Guzara* forests, and royalties ranging from 60 to 80 per cent would be paid to the local concessionaries (Mumtaz 1989:15ff.). In the following years this settlement was extended to all the three districts (Swat, Dir and Chitral) of the Malakand Division (Masud-ul-Mulk 1994: 52).

This was the situation in 1981 when the FDC tried to reach an agreement with the forest concessionaries in the Malakand Division. To the FDC this deal was very important because the organization was obliged to deliver logs at fixed concessionary rates to a newly built wood-processing plant in Chakdarra. Though agreeing in principle to let the FDC begin harvesting, the forest owners in Malakand did not agree to be paid according to the net-sale system. They feared that they would be paid not the real worth of the timber on the open market, but the low concessionary rates of the Chakdarra processing plant. They therefore demanded pre-fixed rates for their timber. To resolve the issue a commission used the same method that was utilized for calculating the stumpage rate; they calculated backwards from the market price to the value of the standing trees. The new pre-fixed rates per cubic foot (cu ft) were: cedar (Rs 51), blue pine (Rs 37) and fir/spruce (Rs 22). The new pre-fixed rates did not take into account factors such as problems connected to logging and distance from the road, nor that the rates had already become outdated due to increased market prices. Thus, despite the fact that the net-sale system was now in place, forest owners in the Malakand Division were paid according to what came to be known as the 'fixed-price system'.

When the Chakdarra factory was forced to close down in 1987, timber could freely be auctioned on the open market. During the period 1981–87 the market rate of timber had surpassed the initial fixed-price rate. It was now suddenly in the FDC's interest to keep the fixed-price system (in Malakand) because the organization now took advantage of the price hike. In view of the fact that the pre-fixed rates were no longer in their favour, the locals demanded higher prices for their timber. The FDC, on its side, feared a lengthy battle over new rates and advocated the virtues of the net-sale system with timber being auctioned on the open market. By the end of the 1980s, two modes of royalty payment were in place; a system of pre-fixed rates ('fixed-price system') and the net-sale system. The significance of this development became even more crucial as the timber prices escalated.[8] As the gap between the pre-fixed rates and the market price of timber continued to widen, the incentive for pocketing this price difference rose, and forest contractors were quick to take advantage.

Economic Strategies of Forest Contractors

Despite its virtues, the net-sale system never became popular among concessionaries. The main reason was that after being sold in the marketplace, the refunds from the sales passed through a slow bureaucratic treadmill before being forwarded to the local owners. Both the delay and risk of pilfering that this caused limited the net-sale system's popularity. The key to take advantage of the net-sale system was to short-cut the payback process by offering to buy royalty rights directly from forest owners.[9] This was a variant of the pre-1973 'contract system' where contractors took charge of harvesting and marketing and bought standing trees directly from forest owners. Instead of waiting for the FDC to tender the work of logging a forest coupe, contractors approached local owners of compartments which were to be harvested shortly.

The contractor could find out this by consulting the working plan, which is an official document listing when compartments are to be logged and how much is to be extracted. In those areas where official land titling has been completed (for example, most of District Swat), the ownership of a forest is fixed in an official record (*kataoni*) maintained by the local revenue officer (*patwari*) with the name of every owner and their shares (*bach*) in the forest. From this document it is possible to glean the number and identity of the shareholders. To the contractor such detailed information about ownership makes it possible to assess the risk of royalty rights acquisition. Moreover, land settlement in itself reduces the risk of royalty rights purchase because it minimizes ownership disputes. Usually, the contractor negotiates a royalty rights purchase with representatives of the owners. For the owners the main advantage is getting paid in advance, instead of having to wait until the compartment is logged.

In areas where official land titling has been resisted (for example, District Kohistan), there is no official record of ownership. In general, all villagers – male and female – have shares (*hissa*) in the forest.[10] Ownership is often contested and may cause bitter fights among villages and tribes. This makes royalty rights purchase more risky and, because all the shareholders must agree to sell, the process becomes time-consuming and difficult. Due to such problems, harvesting falls far behind that planned under working plans and the harvested volume is, in exceptional cases, less than 5 per cent of what has been prescribed (Mushtaq 1989). However, in some areas forest ownership has been usurped by powerful leaders (*maliks, khans*) who sell royalty rights at their own discretion. Where features of social organization allow it, contractors can there-fore negotiate directly with local power-holders. This, it seems, makes it easier to close deals and allows harvesting to proceed in accordance with working plans.

For the contractor it is crucial for making a profit that villagers agree to sell their royalty rights. Without acquiring these rights he is only paid for felling the timber and bringing it to the road-side depot ('labour contractor'). This is a type of work which does not generate substantial profits. In general, contractors offer to pay slightly more than the FDC's pre-fixed rates. For example, the contractor may offer to pay Rs 60 per cu ft for cedar, compared to the FDC's fixed rates of Rs 51. Should the owners still decline to sell their royalty rights, the contractor may try to enlist the support of influential elders, the 'white beards' (*spin giris*) and powerful members of local assemblies (*jirga*) by secretly offering them better than average terms. Thus, the contractor takes ad-vantage of his knowledge of the social organization and village politics. Another asset is the contractor's knowledge of forest operations and market conditions. When the compartment comes up for tender, the contractor enters the bidding round. Having already purchased the royalty rights, he can undercut the price of all other bidders. The FDC, for its part, is obliged to award the tender to the lowest bidder.[11] When the contractor is awarded the tender, he is in reality entering as contractor for the same forest coupe which he has bought through the royalty rights purchase. It is therefore in the contractor's interest to cut more trees than have been marked. As the owner of the royalty rights, his gross profit will be proportional to the amount of timber being auctioned at the timber market.

After being awarded the tender by the FDC, the contractor (or his associates) hires skilled lumberjacks who fell the trees and handle the transport to roadside depots. When the timber has reached the depot, the harvested volume is controlled and verified by the FD. If found to be in order, the FD issues a 'transit pass', which enables the FDC to move the logs to the timber market where it is sold according to the 'net-sale system'.[12] The revenues from the sales (less the costs of extraction) are divided between the government and the local owners. However, because the contractor has already purchased the royalty rights, the proceeds will be transferred to him directly or through a middleman.

The gross profit to the contractor is therefore the difference between the costs of purchasing the royalty rights based on the negotiated fixed price and the sum transferred to him after the timber has been sold according to the net-sale system. Neither the government's profit nor the FDC's pre-calculated profit are affected by the royalty rights purchase. The community members, however, earn much less than they could have gained had they not sold their royalty rights and had in lieu opted for the net-sale system directly. Instead, it is the contractor who profits from the price difference between the negotiated rate and the market price. To understand the reasons why rural communities accept such deals and are willing to sell their timber below its market value, it is necessary to look more closely at the factors which locals must consider when deciding whether to sell or not.

Economic Rationality, Risk and Decision-making

Despite the financial clout and ingenuity of forest contractors, it remains a puzzle why villagers who may be illiterate, but certainly know basic arithmetic, agree to sell their timber far below its current market value. In order to understand why local forest owners prefer to sell to forest contractors, one has to consider the poverty that characterizes much of Pakistan's countryside. In general, people lack opportunities for paid work and timber is therefore the only commodity that has the potential to contribute substantially to household earnings. In isolated villages where the lack of roads hinders the marketing of agricultural products,

214

income from forest royalties can be critical to a person's livelihood (*News*, 14 Dec. 1992). The villagers' primary economic assets are therefore their rights to timber royalties. They generally lack the specialized skills and equipment needed for commercial felling of timber. Moreover, they lack crucial information about market mechanisms and have an immediate need for cash income. As an example, the average annual cash income in parts of District Kohistan is only Rs 4,000, which underlines the importance of timber royalties to household viability (Usui 1994: 9).[13]

To an outsider the advantages of the net-sale system seem obvious. Instead of agreeing to low pre-fixed rates, the villagers are entitled to 60 or 80 per cent of the much higher market value. However, villagers tend to distrust government officials and are suspicious of the net-sale system. In addition there are a number of other reasons why it is rational for villagers to sell their royalty rights to contractors. They can be summarized as follows (Khattak 1994):

- Villagers lack information about the felling schedule, hence do not know when their forest(s) are to be logged.
- Even when villagers have secure information about felling schedules, they know that felling schedules can be changed or manipulated.
- Villagers are under the impression that only by agreeing to contractors' offer will their forests be logged according to the felling schedule.
- As a result of the poverty which is typical of the countryside, villagers must look to immediate needs and not to future benefits; in other words, they have a high 'discount rate'.

The reasons for selling royalty rights to forest contractors seem to be a combination of poverty (high discount rate), the uncertainty which afflicts logging operations, combined with the risks associated with future compensation. If the locals were to comply with FDC's harvesting regulations, they would neither be paid in advance nor assured of being paid later.[14] From this perspective it becomes understandable why accepting the contractor's offer of immediate cash payment is so attractive, even though in purely economic terms it gives them much less than the timber's market value.

Villagers' previous encounters with the state and its representatives have made them aware of risks associated with timber logging. Moreover, locals fear that future market prices may prove to be financially disadvantageous (Treacy 1994: 5).[15]

Despite the overall profitability of royalty rights purchase, contractors face various economic risks which can either diminish revenues or cause heavy financial losses. In particular, there is concern over factors that hinder logging of compartments according to the felling schedule, meaning that money invested in royalty rights purchase cannot be recovered. Examples of potential hazards from the perspective of contractors are:

- owners feel cheated and ask for more money;
- influential villagers change their minds about the deal;
- roadside timber depots are set on fire to protest against unjust deals or in response to ownership disputes;
- the FD stops the transport of timber due to irregularities (over-cutting);
- local disputes over forest ownership delay or block logging/transport operations;
- higher costs than assumed (higher transport cost, less output volume);
- natural calamities or interventions (flash floods, timber logging ban).

It is common for large contractors to sublease part of the total logging work to subcontractors ('petty contractors'). Generally, felling and conversion into scants and transportation to roadside depots are subleased to petty contractors. This is a practical way of handling large felling operations and also helps to spread the economic risk. Moreover, contractors tend to cover risks on investment by extensive over-cutting (HJP 1993a). A case study from District Kohistan shows that two compartments were over-cut by close to 300 per cent in the case of cedar and 180 per cent in the case of blue pine, the two most valuable tree species (Usui 1994: 28–29).

Despite the economic limitations that contractors face, it is their central role in the rural credit market and their ability to extend credit in advance of logging operations, which allow them to control the timber logging business. This in particular is the case in District Kohistan, where the local population did not permit the FDC to take charge of forest harvesting.[16] Conceding to the demands, the government has since 1981 allowed local shareholders to take control of harvesting through the creation of forest harvesting societies. Regulations require harvesting societies to pay harvesting costs in advance of market sale – money which they typically lack. To underwrite such expenditures, harvesting societies could seek to obtain a bank loan. However, because Islam condemns bank loans with interest, they instead prefer to accept advance payments from contractors who purchase forest royalties and take control over harvesting operations (HJP 1993b). Thus, vesting management responsibility with local communities did not decrease contractors' economic leverage. While the locals in Kohistan were only granted the right to harvest their forests, *Guzara* owners in the Hazara Division were allowed to take charge of both harvesting and management. The reform quickly became a battleground for various vested interests and a test case for institutional reform in the forestry sector.

Forest Cooperative Societies and the Timber Ban

Forest management in the Hazara Division is regulated by the Hazara Forest Act of 1936. In order to promote conservation and give local communities more control of their forests, the government amended the Hazara Forest Act in 1981. The amendment allowed *Guzara* forests to be managed by communities organized as Forest Cooperative Societies (FCS) where local stakeholders are members. Most importantly, the reform allowed cooperative societies to take charge of felling and marketing operations in *Guzara* forests under their control. Between 1981 and 1992 perhaps thirty-three forest cooperatives were formed (Cernea 1989: 62–63). Since their inception, the forest cooperatives have generated a lot of controversy and been accused of promoting uncontrolled felling. An evaluation report concluded that all the cooperative societies, in clear violation ... [of rules] ... have sold standing trees or converted timber through forest contractors, thereby undermining the concept of cooperative working. After purchasing trees, the contractors are felling trees and extracting timber (Jan 1990: 92).

The report also argued that the cooperatives had been hijacked by influential individuals with a vested interest in over-cutting, thus

small owners are not accepted in the societies unless they agree to sell standing trees or converted timber to the big owners or forest contractors selected by them at the terms and rates dictated by the big owners (ibid.).

Forest loss in parts of the Hazara Division is staggering. By using remote sensing data it has been estimated that the reduction of the forest cover in the *Guzara* forests in District Mansehra is close to 55 per cent in just nine years (see Table 8.2).[17] Contrary to popular opinion, forest loss during the period 1979–88 is lower in *Guzara* forests managed by forest cooperative societies than in the other legal forest classes. One of the reasons for this can be that cooperative societies in charge of *Guzara* forests ban non-members from collecting firewood. To fill their need for firewood they have to exploit surrounding forests in the other forest classes (Khattak 1994).

Table 8.2: Reduction in forest cover (District Mansehra, Hazara Division)

Legal status	1979	1988	per cent loss
Reserved forest	10,950	5,903	46
Protected forests	4,648	2,370	49
FCS forests*	11,098	7,907	29
Other *Guzara* forests	4,170	1,936	54
Total demarcated area	30,866	18,116	41

*Note: *Guzara* forests managed by Forest Cooperative Societies

Source: SDPI (1995: 32)

Probably, there would have been little national attention paid to the controversy over forest cooperatives in Hazara had it not been for an unexpected event. In the beginning of September 1992, Northern Pakistan was struck by torrential rains which developed into a devastating flood. Among the hardest-hit areas was Hazara Division. In the aftermath of the disaster, extensive over-cutting of the forests was identified as one of the major causes of the destruction (Ilyas 1992). The removal of the forest cover, it was argued, had allowed water to be discharged directly into the swelling rivers, thereby contributing to the extensive flood damage.[18] In addition to the flood water, much of the damage to bridges and houses was caused by huge amounts of logs and scants awaiting transport from forest and roadside depots. Propelled by the flood these logs crushed everything in their path.

Officially, the rampant deforestation in Hazara was blamed on the timber harvesting carried out by FCSs. To end the heavy toll on the forest in Hazara, the government sought to suspend them but legal entanglements made this difficult. As a last resort to curb the cooperative societies, the caretaker government chose to impose a general ban on logging in the whole of Pakistan, including the nominal 'free state' of Azad Jammu and Kashmir. On a direct order from the Prime Minister, the thirty-three co-operative societies in the Hazara Division were suspended and a two-year nationwide moratorium on timber harvesting was imposed in the autumn of 1992 (Prime Minister's Directive 1993). There was widespread criticism of this decision and demands that the ban should be lifted because timber was 'the only source of income for locals in Kohistan and other northern areas' (*Frontier Post* 16 Dec. 1992). Moreover, the former provincial minister for forests in the NWFP argued that the FDC and not the cooperative societies should be blamed for the rapid deforestation in Hazara's *Guzara* forests:

> [The minister] said that the FDC's officials right from the top to the bottom are involved in corruption and nobody could be absolved from charges of corruption and negligence. ... He also accused the FDC for doing nothing in the development of forest in the province. He said that the provincial government was not

taken into confidence by the federal government before announcing a ban on Forest Cooperative Societies (ibid.).

Similar points were raised by speakers in the NWFP provincial assembly, who argued that unilaterally 'blaming the cooperative societies for the whole affair was not correct as most of the cutting was being done under the supervision of the FDC' (*News*, 16 Dec. 1992). The press, too, claimed that the FDC had 'merely replaced the private contractors as irresponsible exploiters of forest resources' (Ilyas 1992: 26), while others claimed that the FDC had collaborated with 'large forest owners and assist[ed] contractors in cutting trees illegally from the reserved forests' (SDPI 1995: 43). The FCS were charged with illegal activities too, such as keeping fake records of timber auctions, cartel formation, and appropriation of money to be set aside for afforestation (ibid.: 40ff.). The FD also was criticized because working plans prepared by the department allowed commercial harvesting at unsustainable levels (ibid.: 43). The FD, for its part, blamed high grazing pressure, itinerant livestock herdsmen (*gujars*) and low survival rate of planted trees (*News*, 1 Nov. 1994). In short, all sides in this conflict have been charged with responsibility for the disaster.[19]

To complicate the matter, the Hazara Division is an ethnic hotchpotch where some groups (Swatis and Syeeds) have traditionally been political patrons and landowners (Ahmed 1986: 115; SDPI 1995: 38). Some members of these groups have been able to gain control of large parts of the *Guzara* forests, which in turn has enabled them to disregard working plans and make huge personal fortunes. SUNGI Development Foundation, a local NGO, has been a vocal critic of the forest policies in Hazara (*News*, 1 Nov. 1994). By siding with the villagers against the powerful landlords and *Guzara* owners, SUNGI's staff have put themselves at risk by exposing the extent of illegal timber harvesting (SUNGI 1995). The controversy over forest cooperative societies has been a stark reminder of the problems facing sustainable forestry not only in Hazara but in the NWFP in general. In addition to immediate effects on the domestic forestry sector, the moratorium on logging turned out to have implications for timber harvesting in a neighbouring country – Afghanistan.

Cross-border Timber Trade

The trade in timber from Eastern and Central Afghanistan to British India dates back to the second half of the nineteenth century (Fischer 1970: 81ff.). Timber was initially transported on the rivers; later over land, using camels. Most of this early export of timber was used for extending the railway network to cities such as Peshawar (1882) and later to strategic border posts such as the Khyber Pass (1912). In the early twentieth century much of the timber was needed for the growing domestic consumption. Improvement of the road network in the 1950s eased the transport of timber inside Afghanistan. While the Afghan timber market was in balance, Pakistan experienced a net deficit of timber (ibid.: 129). Market conditions favoured timber export to Pakistan, which expanded rapidly during the 1960s (Rathjens 1974: 303ff.). In the 1970s, timber sold in Pakistan commanded prices three to four times higher than those achievable in markets in Kabul (Fischer 1970: 100).

The limited scale of the mixed mountain agriculture practised by Pashtuns in Eastern Afghanistan made additional income vital (ibid.: 127). This is one explanation why the modern commercial trade in timber was handled almost exclusively by Pashtuns, who employed camel-herding nomads for transporting timber across the border to Pakistan. The profitability of this trade also enticed sedentary farmers to take up timber transport and buy their own camels. For the nomadic pastoralists, the timber trade could be integrated with their seasonal migration to winter pastures in Pakistan (Rathjens 1974: 305). Moreover, immigrant Pashtuns who settled in Pakistan took an active part in the Pakistani timber trade and expanded into Kohistani areas of Northern Pakistan (Fischer 1970: 118).

Due to the outbreak of the war in Afghanistan in 1978, little is known about the cross-border timber trade in the period 1975–90. Nevertheless, the imposition of the timber ban in Pakistan in 1992 made cross-border timber trade more profitable. Despite the fact that the timber ban has not been strictly enforced, it is likely that, to some degree, the moratorium forced a relocation of logging activities from Pakistan to Afghanistan. It has been argued that Pashtun timber merchants were earlier unable to expand their timber trade beyond the linguistic boundary presented by the non-Pashtun (Nuristani) speaking areas of Eastern Afghanistan (Fischer 1970: 127). This no longer seems to be the case. Much of the present logging activity now takes place in Nuristan (Nuristani 1994: 30). In response to the timber ban, Pakistani timber merchants acting in collusion with local contractors in Kunar – colloquially known as 'quick [rich] Khans' (*Samdasti Khans*) – intensified their logging activity. The timber was later stockpiled along the Pakistan–Afghan border (ibid.: 31). During a three-month period in 1993, Pakistani authorities lifted the import ban, which allowed the timber merchants to transport an estimated 3,000 truck-loads of timber across the border (Ismael 1994: 21).[20] Information provided by MADERA, a French NGO working in Afghanistan, estimated that 300,000 cu m of timber had been sold annually to Pakistan (*Jungle* 1993). This information was confirmed in an eye-witness account by the Danish anthropologist, Asger Christensen:

> [The] few remaining forests in Paktia and Kunar are being cut down at an alarming rate and exported to Pakistan. Although there is a high demand for timber for reconstruction in Afghanistan, the purchasing power is higher in Pakistan and the timber goes there. ... The often desperately poor communities, who hold the traditional rights to the forests, sell these to Afghan timber merchants, some of whom are *mujahidin* commanders who act in collusion with Pakistani traders. Pakistan maintains a ban on the import of timber but occasionally this ban is lifted for a certain period. What then could be observed during 1993 was the build-up of a huge stock of timber on the Afghan side of the border, the lifting of the Pakistani import ban for a few weeks, and the rapid transport by hundreds of trucks of these stocks to Pakistan. (Christensen 1995: 83)

The civil war in Afghanistan has precluded an effective control of timber exports; in addition it has increased the need for cash income among the resident population and, particularly, the local warlords. The current export of timber has its roots in the nineteenth-century timber trade; the driving force behind the trade is, then as now, the much higher price of timber in Pakistan. Timber is a commodity whose origin is hard to trace and the difference between 'legal' and 'illegal' timber is blurred. After taxes and penalty fees have been paid, timber is technically legal and can freely be moved to Pakistani timber markets. On a more general level, the cross-border timber trade shows that a strictly 'local' perspective on the dynamics of deforestation in the NWFP is inadequate and that forest contractors maintain networks that go beyond the confines of the locality.

Forest Contractors as Rural Entrepreneurs

Forest contractors have been an integral part of the commercial exploitation of forest since the mid-nineteenth century and were also at that time accused of 'cutting more trees than they had legally purchased' (Tucker 1982: 119). The public image of forest contractors continues to be very poor. Popular opinion conceives of contractors as 'forest thieves' (*jangal chor*) (Ahmed 1986: 115) and blames them for all that is wrong in Pakistan's forest management. In particular, the collusion between political and economic interests, which in the press is often described as a 'timber mafia' (Ilyas 1992: 36; Yusufzai 1992; Nasar 1995: 7) permits politicians, large contractors and bureaucrats to develop informal networks which give them immunity from forest laws and a *carte blanche* to undertake forest operations at their own discretion. In my opinion, some of the complaints against contractors are misplaced. It is the loopholes in the forest legislation combined with weaknesses in the organization of forest harvesting which have enabled contractors to prosper.

This would not have been possible without the cooperation of local FD and FDC staff. The payment of bribes (*bakhshish, sifarish*) is common in Pakistan, and is naturally also frequent in a setting where a valuable commodity is involved. This fact is acknowledged both in the higher echelons of the FD and FDC, as well as among forest contractors. Pakistan's forest policies allow forest contractors to establish themselves as brokers between the provincial bureaucracy and rural communities. They have detailed information about the harvesting procedures, timber prices and regulations governing timber logging. Moreover, as natives of the area, they know the sentiments, needs and demands of local people.[21] By combining such insights, forest contractors turn their middleman position into commercial profit. Another asset is their central position in the rural credit market and ability to underwrite harvesting costs prior to logging operations (HJP 1993b).

Forest contractors are not, however, a uniform group. They range from small businessmen to wealthy patrons ('timber barons') with the financial clout to undertake large felling operations by using mechanized equipment and their own workforce of skilled lumberjacks. From the perspective of forest owners, collaborating with forest contractors is at present their best option for getting a share of their forests' worth. From the perspective of the forest administration, forest contractors are – due to their ability to work in a hostile tribal setting – a vital link to the local forest owners, thereby making logging possible.

Analytically, forest contractors can be characterized as rural entrepreneurs (Barth 1972: 6). Etymologically, the word entrepreneur stems from the French verb *entreprendre* which means 'to undertake'. Entrepreneurs are profit motivated, innovate new avenues of transaction and are willing to take risks (ibid.: 8). Forest contractors exploit discrepancies between economic spheres and tend to position themselves in such a way that they reap profits from bridging spheres. As Barth has noted 'entrepreneurs will explore various possible implications of *de facto* situations, and where it seems to their advantage, choose to exploit any one or several of the unplanned or even undesired implications of governmental action' (ibid.: 17). In this case, forest contractors took advantage of the fact that whereas the fixed-price system had been replaced by the net-sale system, the former system persisted – albeit informally – as a simple and generally accepted mode of royalty payment. By combining the two modes of royalty payment, forest contractors were able to make a profit from short-cutting the payback process.

Conclusion

Environmental problems are complex, involve many conflicting interests and often become politicized. Thus, 'deforestation' becomes entangled in social, economic and political webs which are not only difficult to come to grips with, but often outright impossible. The heterogeneous causes of deforestation in Pakistan illustrate this complexity and represent a challenge to sustainable forest management. This does not mean that Pakistani authorities are not interested in promoting sustainable forestry. They are, but the odds against their succeeding are great. To understand the problems affecting Pakistan's forestry sector one has to consider a number of factors: the role of the state and the bureaucracy ('*institutions*'), the costs involved in changing the present organization of forestry ('*transaction costs*'); short-term returns against long-term profitability ('*discounting*'); and the motivation of the individual against the interests of the collective (*the problem of* '*collective action*').

As long as poverty, population growth and limited cultivatable land are characteristics of the countryside, the problem of creating incentives for conserving forest remains. The economic value of forest in a context of rural poverty should be the baseline for any investigation into the causes of deforestation in Pakistan. The key to understanding the willingness to sell forest royalty rights lies in rural poverty and urgent need for cash (high discount rate). Alas, rural forest-owning communities are paid only a fraction of the timber's market value while the lion's share of the profit is pocketed by forest contractors, the FDC and the provincial treasury. The importance of market forces for deforestation is also evident in the cross-border trade with Afghanistan. Since the 1960s, forest contractors have taken advantage of the fact that low-priced timber from Afghanistan can be sold at much higher prices in Pakistan.

Property rights to forest are also at stake. Behind the private forest category lies a long-standing struggle between the state and local communities for control of the forests. The historical resistance to state control makes local owners feel justified in managing their forests as they see fit. Seen from this perspective, selling forest royalty rights (alienation) becomes the ultimate manifestation of this ownership. This strategy is reinforced by the uncertainty which afflicts logging operations as well as the economic needs faced by local owners. In the private forests, people have joint property rights, i.e., they are shareholders in a common property forest resource. It may be tempting to attribute the failure of forest management to the 'the tragedy of the commons' (Hardin 1968). There is no indication, however, that collective ownership in itself promotes deforestation. On the contrary, tentative evidence suggests that collective ownership of the forest makes it more difficult for contractors to settle deals with the many owners (high transaction costs). If a contractor suspects that there are unresolved forest ownership disputes among the shareholders, he might decide not to proceed with royalty rights purchase since he risks not recovering his money as long as the compartment cannot be logged. In comparison, privatization of forest ownership by local power-holders eases the purchase of royalty rights and allows logging to progress in accordance with working plans.

Entrepreneurship is deeply ingrained in the environmental history of South Asian forestry and there is a historical continuity from the role contractors played in pre-partition India to present-day Pakistan. The study of entrepreneurship adds to the under-standing of deforestation by providing a framework for analysing how concurrent processes prepared the ground for the entrench-ment of forest contractors after 1987. First, the unintentional implementation of a dual-price system enabled contractors to buy forest royalties directly from the owners and sell timber at a huge profit at timber markets. Second, conceding to local demands for better payment and higher forest royalties, more of the funds from logging were earmarked for local communities. This should, in theory, have benefited the owners but instead increased the economic payoff to contractors. At the same time, rising timber prices boosted the incentive to manipulate the payback process. The creation of the FDC and separation of management from harvesting were meant to prevent forest contractors from becoming part of harvesting operations, but neither improved the FDC's relations with forest owners, nor did they reduce the contractors' leverage on the countryside.

Turning to the sustainability of the forestry sector, the current harvesting system and management practices have failed. Violation of harvesting plans and over-logging are common and threaten the biodiversity of Northern Pakistan (Duke 1994). This problem is aggravated by inadequate attention to forest regeneration and tree planting. Remaining forests should neither be viewed as a source of provincial revenue nor wasted by outdated harvesting methods. Whereas forest contractors tend to be blamed for everything that is wrong in Pakistan's forestry sector, it is the FD and the FDC which should bear the brunt of responsibility for the failure of the current management and harvesting practices. Forest management is suffering from unclear objectives and bureaucratic ineptitude in a context of high urban demand for timber. If the bureaucrats and the field staff had enforced forest legislation to the letter of the law, the scale of illegal activity would have been significantly reduced. The extensive over-logging, mismanagement and malpractice found in the forestry sector are unimaginable unless custodians either turn a blind eye or accept bribes.

Are the problems in Pakistan's forestry sector an argument for vesting management with local communities or is the interest of conservation better served by state management? Without the state actively promoting sustainable forestry, little can be done to salvage Pakistan's remaining forests. The case of forest cooperative societies in Hazara shows that devolving management responsibility is, in itself, not enough to create a vested interest in conservation. Instead this allowed the seizure of power by large shareholders, reflecting rural power imbalances and surviving patron–client relationships.

Dixon and Perry have argued that 'most of the effects of environmental mismanagement observed in [Northern] Pakistan are rooted in the environmental illiteracy of the population' (Dixon and Perry 1986: 304). This is a distortion of the facts and based on a superficial understanding of the situation facing rural people. It also perpetuates the myth that people are not interested in the conservation of natural resources. The problem is not to convince forest-dependent communities that they have a stake in the protection of forests – they know this very well. The problem resides in the structures and institutions which prevent them from playing any meaningful part in the management of the forest.

This does not mean that local people are necessarily motivated by an 'environmental ethic'. It does mean, however, that they would protect their forest better if they were assured of enjoying the future benefits. This is a conclusion borne out of the last ten years of research on common pool regimes (McCay and Acheson 1987; Berkes 1989).

The International Union for the Conservation of Nature and Natural Resources has declared that the 'institutional problems facing forestry in Pakistan include outdated forest policies and laws' (IUCN 1993: 73). There is at the moment a commitment both at the federal and the provincial level not only to amend the forest legislation in the NWFP but to implement a new legal and institutional framework concerned with forest management and conservation. This will be a crucial test of whether the federal government can come to grips with the problems affecting the forestry sector. The timber-logging ban which was imposed in 1992 has recently been extended indefinitely. This has given the government a breathing space in which to reconsider its forestry policies. The opportunity should not be wasted.

Acknowledgements

My fieldwork in 1994 was supported by a grant from the Norwegian Ministry of Foreign Affairs' 'North–South Research Programme'. A follow-up study in 1996 was funded by travel grants from the Nordic Institute of Asian Studies and the Institute for Comparative Studies in Human Culture. I am grateful to Arild Angelsen, Fikret Berkes, Eyolf Jul-Larsen, Richard Moorsom, Adam Nayyar, Narve Rio and Mohammad Yusuf for comments on previous drafts. For help in the field I am indebted to Mark Treacy, Mohammad Yusuf and Manzar Zarin. Any errors are the author's responsibility.

Notes

1. The Federally Administered Tribal Areas (FATA), which make up about one-third of the NWFP, have substantial forest resources but are not considered due to lack of adequate data (but see Khan *et al.* 1993).

2. It is a problem that 'the generic term "deforestation" is used so ambiguously that it is virtually meaningless as a description of land-use change' (Hamilton 1988: 8).

3.   However, Pakistan is currently undertaking a major revision of its environmental legislation (Knudsen 1995). The most important planning documents are the 'National Conservation Strategy' (NCS 1992), the 'Forestry Sector Master Plan' (FSMP 1992) and the 'Sarhad Provincial Conservation Strategy' (SPCS 1996).

4.   In practice, no one has been sentenced to jail for violating the forestry laws. In general the offenders are only asked to pay for the excess volume of timber. The value of Pakistan rupees is approximately Rs 41 to US$ 1 (September 1997).

5.   For a more detailed comparison of the costs of various harvesting methods, see Ayaz and Stöhr (1988).

6.   Moreover, the study estimates that 45 per cent of the forest cover has vanished, primarily during the last twenty years. This coincides with the completion of the Karakoram Highway through the region in the late 1960s and is a further proof of the link between accessibility and deforestation. The link between roads and deforestation is also documented by Khan *et al.* (1993: 14) using remote sensing data from the Khurram Agency (FATA).

7.   The effectiveness of this organizational change has been questioned, and both the FD and FDC have repeatedly been accused of bribery and corruption (*Frontier Post* 16 Dec. 1992; *News* 16 Dec. 1992).

8.   In 1984 cedar logs fetched Rs 137 per cu ft on the open market (PFI 1992: 15). During the period 1990–95 the price went up from Rs 199 to Rs 400.

9.   It is important to note that whereas over-cutting is illegal, buying forest royalties is not. Although undesirable from the point of sustainable forestry, forest royalties can be traded.

10.   For a discussion of joint property rights in forest, see McKean and Ostrom (1995).

11.   Even if the FDC suspects that royalty purchase is involved, it is bound by the law to accept the lowest bid. However, in order to block tender bids which grossly underestimate the costs of logging, the FDC has begun to fix a minimum price which is quoted in the tender notice.

12.   Due to the ban on timber harvesting (imposed in late 1992), the market price ('net-sale') of timber has continued to rise. Unofficially, the price of cedar now ranges from Rs 600 to 800 per cu ft (1997).

13.   Keiser (1991: 69) reports that in 1983 annual forest royalty payments to each family in a Dir Kohistan village amounted to Rs 15,000.

14.   The FDC is obliged to pay 10–20 per cent of the net revenue as advance payment to concessionaires. However, it is likely that payments, in reality, are either much less or withheld by the FDC.

15. The willingness to forgo a future benefit suggests that 'risk discounting' is a significant factor and promotes short-term decisions (Angelsen 1994).

16. Instead of timber logging being based on open tenders, deals are settled directly between forest owners and contractors. Essentially, the only task left to the local FD is to ensure that the timber has been cut in accordance with working plans and collect the government revenue (20 per cent).

17. This should be considered a worst-case scenario and is primarily based on data from the Siran Valley. A recent study from the Kaghan Valley (District Mansehra) shows that the major part of the forest loss took place in the nineteenth century. Population pressure in the twentieth century has, in comparison, not had significant impact on the forest cover (Schickhoff 1993b: 176ff., 1995a: 14ff.).

18. Despite the uncertainty of such a claim, it underlines that the environment in Hazara is under stress and that there is an inability to address the problem (cf. Minissale 1991). For an analysis of the link between loss of forest cover and floods, see Hamilton (1992: 17ff.).

19. Afghan refugees who were settled in the Hazara Division may also have been implicated in the rapid deforestation (Allan 1987).

20. Another source estimates that 13,000 truck-loads of timber crossed the border to Pakistan (Nuristani 1994: 31).

21. Forest contractors tend to begin their career in their areas of origin, but as they gain more wealth and experience, expand their operations to new areas.

References

Ahmed, Akbar S. (1986) *Pakistan Society: Islam, Ethnicity and Leadership in South Asia*, Karachi: Oxford University Press.

Allan, Nigel J.R. (1987) 'Impact of Afgan Refugees on the Vegetation Resources of Pakistan's Hindu-Kush Himalayas', *Mountain Research and Development*, vol. 7, no. 3, pp. 200–04.

Angelsen, Arild (1994) 'Shifting Cultivation, Expansion and Intensity of Production: The Open Economy Case', CMI Working Paper, no. 3.

Ayaz, Mohammad and Gerhard Stöhr (1988) 'Comparison of Timber Harvesting Systems in the Forest Areas of Hazara Civil Division, NWFP', *Pakistan Journal of Forestry*, vol. 38, no. 4, pp. 261–74.

Azhar, Rauf A. (1989) 'Communal Property Rights and Depletion of Forests in Northern Pakistan', *Pakistan Development Review*, vol. 28, no. 4, pp. 643–51.

—— (1993) 'Commons, Regulation, and Rent-seeking Behavior: The Dilemma of Pakistan's *Guzara* Forests', *Economic Development and Cultural Change*, vol. 42, no. 1, pp. 115–29.

Barth, Fredrik (ed.) (1972) *The Role of the Entrepreneur in Social Change in Northern Norway*, Oslo: Universitetsforlaget.

—— (1985) *The Last Wali of Swat*, Oslo: Universitetsforlaget.

Berkes, Fikret (ed.) (1989) *Common Property Resources: Ecology and Community-Based Sustainable Development*, London: Belhaven Press.

Cernea, Michael M. (1989) *User Groups as Producers in Participatory Afforestation Strategies*, Washington DC: World Bank Discussion Papers, no. 70.

Christensen, Asger (1995) *Aiding Afghanistan: The Background and Prospects for Reconstruction in a Fragmented Society*, Copenhagen: Nordic Institute of Asian Studies (NIAS), NIAS report no. 26.

Dixon, R.K. and J.A. Perry (1986) 'Natural Resource Management in Rural Areas of Northern Pakistan', *Ambio*, vol. 15, pp. 301–05.

Duke, Guy (1994) 'A Participatory Approach to Conservation Safeguarding the Himalayan Forests of the Palas Valley, District Kohistan'. In Asian Study Group, *The Destruction of the Forests and Wooden Architecture of Eastern Afghanistan and Northern Pakistan: Nuristan to Baltistan*, Islamabad: Asian Study Group, pp. 40–48.

Fischer, Dieter (1970) *Waldverbreitung, bäuerliche Waldwirtschaft und kommerzielle Waldnutzung im östlichen Afghanistan*, Afghanische Studien, Band 2. Meisenheim: Verlag Anton Hain.

The Frontier Post (1992) 'NWFP PA Body to Probe Smuggling of Timber', December 16.

FSMP (1992) *Forestry Sector Master Plan: Executive Summary*, prepared by UNDP and the Asian Development Bank in collaboration with Ministry of Food, Agriculture and Cooperatives, December.

Guha, Ramachandra (1989) *The Unquiet Woods: Ecological Change and Peasant Resistance in the Himalayas*, Berkeley: University of California Press.

Hamilton, Lawrence S. (1988) 'Semantics, Definitions and Deforestation', *IUCN Special Report Bulletin*, vol. 18, no. 4–6, pp. 8–9.

—— (1992) 'The Protective Role of Mountain Forests', *GeoJournal*, vol. 27, no. 1, pp. 13–22.

Hardin, Garrett (1968) 'The Tragedy of the Commons', *Science*, vol. 162, pp. 1243–48.

HJP (Himalayan Jungle Project) (1993a) 'Forest Management Planning', Islamabad: Himalayan Jungle Project (mimeo).

—— (1993b) 'Forestry and Conservation in the Palas Valley' (Biodiversity importance of Palas), Islamabad: Himalayan Jungle Project (mimeo).

—— (n.d.) 'Natural Resource Management (Annex 3)'. Islamabad, Himalayan Jungle Project (mimeo).

Ilyas, Mohammad (1992) 'The Root Cause', *Herald*, (October), pp. 35–36.

Ismael, Mohammad (1994) 'Afghan Forestry'. In Asian Study Group, *The Destruction of the Forests and Wooden Architecture of Eastern Afghanistan and Northern Pakistan: Nuristan to Baltistan*, Islamabad: Asian Study Group, pp. 16–22.

IUCN (1993) *The Way Ahead: IUCN's Programme in Pakistan for the Triennium 1994–96*, Karachi: The World Conservation Union.

Jan, Abeed Ulla (1990) 'A Case Study of Forest Harvesting Systems in Mountain Forests of Pakistan', Islamabad, unpublished report.

—— (1993) *Forest Policy: Administration and Management in Pakistan*, Islamabad: Winrock International Institute for Agricultural Development and GOP-USAID Forestry Planning and Development Project.

Jungle (1993) 'Forest and Wooden Architecture: The Trail of Destruction from Nooristan to Baltistan', *Jungle – Forestry Extension Network Newsletter*, vol. 1, no. 2.

Keiser, Lincoln (1991) *Friend by Day, Enemy by Night. Organized Vengeance in a Kohistani Community*, Fort Worth: Holt, Rinehart & Winston, Inc.

Khan, Amir, D.A. Garner, and C.M. Conner (1993) 'Feasibility of GIS as a Regional Planning Tool for Sustainable Development: A Case Study of Kurram and Orakzai Agencies of Federally Administered Tribal Areas (FATA)', *Pakistan Journal of Geography*, vol. III (June–December), pp. 1–18.

Khattak, Ghaus M. (1976a) 'History of Forest Management (I)', *Pakistan Journal of Forestry*, April, pp. 105–16.

—— (1976b) 'History of Forest Management in Pakistan (II): Temperate and Coniferous Forests', *Pakistan Journal of Forestry*, July, pp. 163–70.

—— (1994) 'Strategy for Sustainable Development of Forestry in NWFP', Peshawar: IUCN-SPCS (Draft), 42 pp.

KIDP (Kalam Integrated Development Project) (1988) 'Background Information on Kalam Tehsil, Malakand Division, NWFP, Pakistan', Kalam and Zürich: Geographisches Institut, Universität Zürich and Kalam Integrated Development Project.

Knudsen, Are J. (1995) 'Forestry Management in Pakistan: Failed Policies or Local Mismanagement?', Bergen: Report to the Norwegian Ministry of Foreign Affairs's 'North–South Research Programme'.

Masud-ul-Mulk (1994) 'Managing Forests in Chitral'. In Asian Study Group, *The Destruction of the Forests and Wooden Architecture of Eastern Afghanistan and Northern Pakistan: Nuristan to Baltistan*, Islamabad: Asian Study Group, pp. 51–55.

McCay, Bonnie J. and James M. Acheson (eds) (1987) *The Question of the Commons: The Culture and Ecology of Communal Resources*, Tucson, Arizona: The University of Arizona Press.

McKean, Margareth and Elinor Ostrom (1995) 'Common Property Regimes in the Forest: Just a Relic from the Past?', *Unasylva*, vol. 46, no. 180, pp. 3–14.

Minissale, Gregory (1991) 'Plunder in the Hills', *Herald*, February, pp. 81–86.

Mumtaz, Khawar (1989) 'Pakistan's Environment: A Historical Perspective'. In K. Mumtaz and Abidi-Habib (eds), *Pakistan's Environment: A Historical Perspective and Selected Bibliography with Annotations*, Karachi: JRC and IUCN.

Mushtaq, Muhammad (1989) *Revised Working Plan for Palas Forests of Kohistan Forest Division (1988–89 to 2002–03)*, Peshawar: NWFP Forestry Pre-Investment Centre.

Nasar, Anita D. (1995) 'Into the Woodwork', *The Way Ahead – Pakistan's Environment and Development Quarterly*, September, pp. 6–7.

NCS (1992) *The Pakistan National Conservation Strategy*, Karachi: Government of Pakistan, Environment and Urban Division in Collaboration with the IUCN – The World Conservation Union.

The News (1992) 'Tribals Clash over Ownership to Forest', December 14.

—— (1992) 'Heated Debate in NWFP PA on Forest Co-operatives, Deforestation', December 16.

—— (1994) 'Kaghan Valley Rises to Fight Illegal Logging', November 1.

Nuristani, Yusuf (1994) 'Traditional Use of Nuristani Forests'. In Asian Study Group. *The Destruction of the Forests and Wooden Architecture of Eastern Afghanistan and Northern Pakistan: Nuristan to Baltistan*, Islamabad: Asian Study Group, pp. 25–31.

PFI (Pakistan Forest Institute) (1992) *Forestry Statistics of Pakistan*, Peshawar: Pakistan Forest Institute.

Prime Minister's Directive (1993) 'Action Plan regarding Management and Malpractices in Forest Cooperative Societies in Hazara Division and Forests in General in Pakistan', September 30.

Rathjens, Carl (1974) 'Die Wälder von Nuristan and Paktia: Standort-bedingungen und Nutzung der ostafghanischen Waldgebiete', *Geographische Zeitschrift*, vol. 62, pp. 295–311.

Schickhoff, Udo (1993a) 'Interrelations between Ecological and Socio-economic Change: The Case of the High Altitude Forests in the Northern Areas of Pakistan', *Pakistan Journal of Geography*, vol. III (June), pp. 59–70.

—— (1993b) *Das Kaghan-Tal im Westhimalaya (Pakistan)*, Bonner Geographische Abhandlungen, Bonn: F. Dümmlers Verlag.

—— (1995a) 'Himalayan Forest-Cover Changes in Historical Perspective: A Case Study from the Kaghan Valley, Northern Pakistan', *Mountain Research and Development*, vol. 15, no. 1, pp. 3–18.

—— (1995b) 'Verbreitung, Nutzung und Zerstörung der Höhenwälder im Karakorum und in angrenzenden Hochgebirgsräumen Nordpakistans', *Petermanns Geographische Mitteilungen*, vol. 139, no. 2, pp. 67–85.

SDPI (Sustainable Development Policy Institute) (1995) *Nature, Power, People: Citizens' Report on Sustainable Development, 1995*, Islamabad: Sustainable Development Policy Institute.

SPCS (1996) *Sarhad Provincial Conservation Strategy*, Peshawar: IUCN – The World Conservation Union.

SUNGI (1995) *Mit-thay Huay Sayey* [Vanishing Shadows], Abbottabad: Video film produced with support of the Friedrich Naumann Foundation.

Swati, Muhammad K. and Muhammad A. Cheema (1991) 'Outturn Volume of Chir Pine in *Guzara* Forests of District Mansehra', *Pakistan Journal of Forestry*, vol. 41, no. 2, pp. 94–101.

Treacy, Mark (1994) 'The Timber Harvesting Ban and Its Implications: Points for Discussion'. In Asian Study Group, *The Destruction of the Forests and Wooden Architecture of Eastern Afghanistan and Northern Pakistan: Nuristan to Baltistan*, Islamabad: Asian Study Group, pp. 3–10.

Tucker, Richard P. (1982) 'The Forests of the Western Himalayas: The Legacy of British Colonial Administration', *Journal of Forest History*, July, pp. 112–23.

—— (1984) 'The Historical Context of Social Forestry in the Kumaon Himalayas', *Journal of Developing Areas*, vol. 18, no. 3, pp. 341–56.

—— (1987) 'Dimensions of Deforestation in the Himalayas: The Historical Setting', *Mountain Research and Development*, vol. 7, no. 3, pp. 328–31.

—— (1988) 'The British Empire and India's Forest Resources: The Timberlands of Assam and Kumaon, 1914–1950'. In J.F. Richards and R.P. Tucker (eds), *World Deforestation in the Twentieth Century*, Durham: Duke University Press, pp. 91–111.

Usui, Shunji (1994) 'Opportunities for Conservation and Development through Evaluation of Forests: A Case Study in Western Himalayas', MSc. thesis, Edinburgh: Scottish Agricultural College.

Yusufzai, Rahimullah (1992) 'The Timber Mafia', *Newsline*, vol. 4, no. 5, pp. 126–30.

9

The Irrigating Public: The State and Local Management in Colonial Irrigation

David Gilmartin

In recent years, literature on the management and operation of irrigation systems has stressed the importance of organized irrigator input into irrigation management. Though large-scale irrigation works have served as monuments to man's ability to transform the natural environment by bringing water to arid lands, they have long been the focus also of criticism for their massive inefficiencies and lack of attention to local irrigator priorities. Indeed, the problems in running large-scale works without irrigator input impressed themselves on irrigation planners and engineers so forcefully in the 1970s and 1980s that the concern to mobilize irrigator participation in irrigation systems became a centrepiece of irrigation planning.

However, as experience has now shown, attempts to engineer 'grass-roots' participation in irrigation systems have produced a very mixed record. Nirmal Sengupta has noted that 'the euphoria' for farmers' participation in irrigation works has waned. Planners have been increasingly chastened by the difficulties in 'engineering' local-level collective action from above, and this has spurred an increasingly sophisticated literature on the nature of local-level community organization with respect to irrigation management (Uphoff 1986; Sengupta 1991: 13). In order to understand the problems in local-level irrigator organization, social scientists have increasingly analysed indigenous, historical models of local irrigator organization as guides for understanding the elements that have encouraged or discouraged local-level collective action and cooperation in irrigation. This has led to an increasingly nuanced understanding of the cultural, social and ecological variables that shape local irrigator organization.

One of the most interesting recent treatments of these issues relating to South Asia is Robert Wade's book, *Village Republics* (1988), which is an account of the operation of a realm of local, village-level control over irrigation and grazing in South India. In his book Wade provides a masterful analysis of the local ecological constraints, relating primarily to scarcity and risk, that have shaped collective, local-level organization in the management of resources. By examining a number of irrigated villages in South India, Wade delineates local variables that have shaped the emergence of what might be termed a 'public realm' at the village level, a sphere of collective input and decision-making regarding local resource use (Wade 1988: x–xi). Wade's work is extremely useful in suggesting the reasons for marked variation in patterns of local collective action. His work suggests that many of the most powerful determinants of local collective action are rooted in local circumstances not easily 'engineered' from above.

But however useful in underscoring the importance of local environmental variation (and particularly variation in scarcity and risk) in shaping the existence of a local-level 'public realm' in collective resource management, Wade's analysis also highlights problems in defining the meaning of a 'public' voice in irrigation management. Wade's analysis of these forms rests ultimately on an underlying conception of a 'public realm' almost entirely independent of the state, a realm in virtually no significant way shaped by the structure of the state itself. Though Wade suggests that such forms of local collective organization might in limited ways be employed by the state for developmental purposes, his analysis firmly roots these forms of collective local community in a world of relationships and calculations almost entirely independent of and anterior to state authority. Indeed, in analysing the 'public', Wade is not particularly interested in a realm that stands between society and the state, interfacing with both, but rather with a realm of collective, cooperative action defined by principles entirely separate from those shaping the state. In this respect, his local 'public' realm is not a 'public sphere', in the sense developed by analysts such as Jürgen Habermas. It is not a public arena where an irrigator voice emerges that is capable of engaging the state and constraining its actions. It rather defines the potential roots of the village's autonomy.

This is critical to note, because in some respects Wade's analysis replicates the vision of the British state itself with respect to local resource management during the era in which India's great modern irrigation works were first built. Wade's title itself harks back to notions that played a prominent role in shaping colonial thinking about the Indian village as a realm with its own inner logic, but one almost entirely separate from the rational realm of state authority, and thus offering no significant political constraint on the state's own actions.[1] The 'village republic' was, for many colonial administrators, a 'traditional' realm, open to the manipulation of the state but always separate from it.

This paper investigates the roots of the interface between the state and the local community in irrigation in order to understand the meaning that the British ultimately attached to the notion of the 'public' in matters of irrigation. In spite of their construction of large, bureaucratized irrigation works, the British colonial state was hardly oblivious to the role of local community in the operation of works for irrigation. Quite to the contrary, a long series of nineteenth- century British administrators saw local organization as central to the success of virtually all irrigation works. But they also saw local community within a distinctive framework of analysis that had critical implications for the future of irrigation. British ideas about the proper relationship between the local community and the state – ideas that developed in the period before the construction of large-scale irrigation works – had ultimately as profound an impact on shaping and constraining the emergence of a 'public' voice in irrigation as did the local variables that encouraged and constrained collective action and irrigator cooperation in 'village republics' independently of the state.

Water Management and Colonial Rule

This paper focuses on the Indus Basin region of colonial India, particularly the Punjab. British approaches to irrigation in the

Punjab were shaped by the distinctive forms of irrigation that they found when they arrived in the region. When the British annexed Punjab to their empire in the 1830s and 1840s, they found a wide variety of forms of irrigation and irrigation management. Forms of irrigation were in fact as varied as the ecology of the region, ranging from Persian wheels on the plains of central Punjab to small dams that impounded runoff rainwater; from small canals in the hills to the underground *karez* found in the foothills of Baluchistan. Perhaps most central to early British debates about irrigation, however, were the myriad, seasonal inundation canals on the plains, drawing on the Indus and its tributaries that filled in the spring and summer and ran dry during the winter months. Many were little more than small, natural creeks, cleared and maintained by local villagers. Others were far larger and more elaborate channels. Prone to heavy silting during the summer floods, most of these canals required considerable annual mainten-ance to be kept open from year to year. Ongoing silt clearance during the winter months and occasional re-excavation were thus central to the workings of most inundation canal irrigation. Be-cause this required considerable yearly mobilization of labour for canal maintenance and operation (and thus considerable expense), effective operation of these canals depended heavily on the structure of local political and social relationships, and particularly on the relationship of local irrigators both to each other and to the state.

From the beginning, the British thus sought to define an administrative approach to the operation of inundation canals that made sense of this relationship between the state and local communities. In some cases, the British found that irrigator share systems had shaped significantly the operation of inundation canals, regulating both rights of access to water and obligations to provide regular labour for canal maintenance. Though varied in form, the presence of such share systems suggested to many British officials the existence in the Punjab of popular, collective foundations of irrigation management, rooted not in state control but in mutual rights and responsibilities defined both in relation to the provision of water, and in relationship to other structures of local community. But in many inundation canals (including many with share systems), the British also found evidence that earlier states had played critical roles in water management, even in the context of such share systems. Central to early British efforts to make sense of inundation canal management in the Punjab was thus the effort to distinguish various aspects of both state and local, collective control, and to define the relationship between them.

In seeking to understand the operation of such irrigation systems, the British were of course profoundly influenced also by the frameworks that they had developed for understanding the operation of the bonds of local social solidarity in Punjabi society more broadly. Through a series of land settlements in the second half of the nineteenth century (and through the application of developing social evolutionary theory to the study of Punjabi society), the British had produced an elaborate literature on the nature of local, landed communities in the Punjab. They saw these communities as having evolved under the joint influences of 'tribal' kinship, the vicissitudes of state power, and relations to the land. In recording both revenue obligations and property rights in land, the British had defined a set of principles that generally linked landholding to the structure of local communities. Individual property rights were recordable under British law, but were rarely fully separable, in British eyes, from shares in the local community, which might be legally embodied in shares in the village commons or reflected in common village or 'tribal' customs relating to rights of inheritance, rights of pre-emption, or rights in other village resources. As the British developed a structure of law and revenue in the Punjab, they saw themselves not as the creators of these rights, but as their recorders and arbiters, enumerating them at settlement in village registers of rights (*wajib-ul-arz*), and ultimately adjudicating them through a system of customary law (*rivaj-i-am*).

Control over water by no means fit fully into this structure of local community shares (*hissa*) and rights (*haq*), but the village papers prepared by the British at each settlement normally included shares and rights in water as well as land. 'So important are

the rights in wells, usually hereditary, following the same law as
the right in the soil,' noted one Settlement Officer in Ludhiana
District, 'that a complete statement of the sub-division of property
in each well forms part of the settlement record' (Tupper 1881:
III, 179).[2] In addition to this register of village wells, the village
papers normally included also 'customs (*rivaj*) regarding irrigation'
more generally. These entries varied dramatically from village to
village in terms of the specificity of irrigation rights or shares
recorded.

A collection at the Punjab Board of Revenue of translated
samples of irrigation entries in the various village *wajib-ul-arz* of
Jagadhri Tahsil (Ambala District) from the late nineteenth century
illustrates this. For some canal-irrigated villages, the entries merely
noted that, in addition to wells or ponds, villagers also had access
to canal water, which they raised into the fields from small cuts
by means of leather buckets. Often, as one entry stated, 'no
particular system of irrigation by turns is observed'. In other villages,
however, elaborate systems of shares in water were recorded, with
turns to water determined according to holdings and to divisions
within the villages, with shares of water on village watercourses
fixed according to *pahars* (or units of time) for day and night,
and labour obligations *vis-a-vis* cleaning and maintaining channels
enumerated also according to shares. Although water in most of
these villages was taken with official permission from government
canals (in this case, the Western Jumna Canal) and a water-rate
paid, these arrangements were recorded not as official depart-
mental arrangements, but as village customs based on reciprocal
obligations, worked out by the villagers themselves, and varying
markedly from village to village (Punjab Board of Revenue).

Such rights were recorded also for more elaborate systems of
water distribution. A good example concerns the irrigation from
the Degh *Nala*, a tributary of the River Ravi from which upwards of
125 villages were irrigated in the mid-nineteenth century. Though
a natural stream, the irrigation from the Degh depended on the
existence of large numbers of *jhalars*, or wheels, along its banks,
and on the periodic construction and opening of *bands* (or small
dams) to raise the water level for flow irrigation, particularly

during seasonal periods of low flow. According to Leslie Saunders, the Lahore Settlement Officer in the 1860s, equitable use of the stream's waters depended on elaborate mutual agreements about 'the periods and space of time these *bands* are allowed to exist and irrigate each village'. In addition to specifications as to the numbers of *pahars* that each village was allowed to 'monopolize the water' by erecting and breaking small *bands* during times of water scarcity, the agreement also dealt with responsibilities for maintaining and repairing the larger *bands* that divided the stream's waters, and with limitations on rights to put *jhalars* into the stream. As in the case of village records of rights, Saunders ordered that this system should be recorded officially, with mutual rights and responsibilities attested to by the irrigators and embodied in a written agreement (Saunders 1873: 49, Appendix I).

But it was a system, he declared, that had essentially 'been in force without any interference on the part of Government for many years and is thoroughly understood and acted on by the people' (ibid.: 49). Whatever the role of the British in recording this system (and in allowing the courts to adjudicate certain aspects of it), it was, for Saunders, a system of common management quite distinct from one defined by government control, a point that he made forcefully in comparing this system with the system of water distribution on the new Bari Doab Canal, which was managed directly by government. There, he noted, 'no man can take water, even for one field, without satisfying the rapacity of a whole army of [bureaucratic] understrappers' (ibid.: 43). In the case of the Degh, the system was essentially, in his view, one of popular, collective control. Though popular arrangements were officially recorded, for Saunders, and other British officials, the distinction between official and customary arrangements was critical.[3]

Defining this distinction ultimately proved to be difficult, however, not only for natural streams like the Degh, but also, and more importantly in the long run, for the many inundation canals of the region, in whose construction the state itself had played an important role. These dated mostly to the period before British rule. For the British, the historical role of the state in the original construction of productive works provided the most powerful indicator of the state's ongoing rights and responsibilities in irrigation works. But, as the British discovered when they began to investigate the historical operation of inundation canals, the separation of a clear historical realm of state management from a realm of common, collective rights and responsibilities proved a problematic endeavour in the case of many canals – though one that strongly influenced developing British ideas about the nature of irrigation management.

The Shah Nahr

A case in point was the Shah Nahr in Hoshiarpur District, one of the first inundation canals to fall under British supervision after the annexation of the Jullundur Doab in the mid-1840s. According to a Mogul *sanad* produced for the British by a prominent local Muslim *zamindar*, the Shah Nahr was first constructed in the reign of the Mogul Emperor (Muhammad Shah (r. 1719–48)), by Rai Muhammad Murad, zamindar of Tapa Bhangala and Jhandwal, who brought the canal from the Beas River to water his *jagir* in the Hajipur *pargana*.[4] At the time of the earliest mention of the canal in British records, it had silted up, and was only re-constructed in the 1840s, with the permission of the British Deputy Commissioner, by a group of *zamindar*s at their own expense. These zamindars each subscribed capital towards the reconstruction of the canal, and constituted a body of shareholders (*hissadar*), whose proprietary interest in the canal was initially recognized by John Lawrence, the first Commissioner of the trans-Sutlej states, in part, apparently, on the basis of common investment, and in part on the basis of historical precedent.

After the canal was extended in 1847 and 1848 (and additional shareholders added), however, the state intervened repeatedly to define the precise form of the shareholding community. The original *sanad* was, as a later Settlement Officer noted, ambiguous in terms of creating a precedent for the state's role. 'From the wording of the sanad, the canal may have been constructed either as a private concern, or at the direction, and with encouragement, of the State officials.' In those days, he continued, 'no distinction between state and private property as now understood was observed' (Dane 1886). Few British officials of course imagined that no property rights had existed under the Moguls. But defining the exact role of the state in Mogul canal-building was difficult. At stake was less the question of proprietary right under the Moguls than the distinction between the 'private' and 'public' capacities of local Mogul officials, which could not be easily distinguished according to nineteenth-century British terminology.

In 1848, however, the Deputy Commissioner asserted more direct reasons for the British stepping in to regulate the canal's management.

> So long as the canal was confined to the pargana of Hajipur, there was little or no necessity for the intervention of government officers except as advisers; but the growing importance of the canal has rendered some arrangements necessary to secure to the public-spirited and enterprising individuals the profits of their outlay (quoted in Dane 1886).

In fact, the Deputy Commissioner saw the definition of clear, legal shareholder rights in the canal as the surest way to protect the 'public' interest. He thus laid out a *dastur-ul-amal*, or statement of principle, to delimit and secure distinct shareholder rights in the canal. It provided, as the *Hoshiarpur Gazetteer* later put it:

> that those who had co-operated to restore the canal [the shareholders] should get water free; that a water-rate should be levied from other irrigators; that the canal should be managed by a local committee or *panchayat* of the shareholders in the canal; and, finally, that certain powers of revision and control should be reserved for government (*Hoshiarpur District Gazetteer* 1905: 115).

Having 'accepted the principle that the canal was the property of the persons who reconstructed it', and having, accordingly, recorded what amounted to private shareholder rights in the canal, the government thus defined a structure of collective management overseen by the government.[5]

Nevertheless, the nature of the 'public' interest in the canal remained ambiguous. Both changing irrigating conditions and changing social and economic conditions (which opened new possibilities for extending irrigated agriculture and encouraging higher revenue-value commercial crops) dictated an ongoing government interest in the canal that seemed, at times, to transcend the private rights of the shareholders (see, for example, Fagan 1901–02: 5–6). Even while recognizing and maintaining the existence of a legally defined shareholding community, the British re-organized the canal's shareholders in the early 1850s for the purpose of re-excavating and extending the canal. Matched by a Rs 6,000 loan from the government, zamindars along the canal now contributed an additional Rs 6,000, on the basis of which they, in effect, bought into a redistribution of canal shares and a reconstitution of the shareholding community.

As in previous arrangements, shares included the right to take water from the canal without charge, the right in time of scarcity to take water in proportion to their shares, the right to share in the profits of the canal's operation (based on water sold to non-shareholders), and the responsibility (according to their shares) for the maintenance of the canal and repayment of the loan. Sixteen villages along the canal's route and three leading zamindars (who came to comprise the managing committee) took up the shares (which were unequal and in some cases minutely subdivided).[6] The managers (acting in the name of the shareholders but supervised by the government) undertook the responsibility for carrying out the new canal excavations, and for mobilizing labour for annual clearance and maintenance. The re-excavation thus maintained a collective body of shareholders with legal claims distinct from those of the state. But at the same time, it suggested that the state's interest in the canal transcended any privately defined shareholder rights.

The tension that this engendered became clear when the Deputy Commissioner of Hoshiarpur, H. E. Perkins, reviewed the working of the canal in 1870. Perkins now argued that the administration of the canal was fundamentally flawed as it failed to protect the interest of the larger irrigating 'public'. The operation of the reconstituted community of shareholders had created a vested interest, Perkins argued, contrary to 'public' interest defined more generally. The 'so-called shareholders', as he now called them, had failed miserably to make good on the extension of the canal and to secure the full benefit of the canal to the country through which it ran. Problems of distribution had led to water being monopolized by powerful upper irrigators on the channel, whom the managers were both unable and unwilling to control. Several of the zamindars on the committee of management were in any case incompetent in Perkins' view; one was 'a confirmed drunkard' and another 'in the hands of a corrupt agent'. Perkins therefore proposed reconstituting the shareholders once again, with state protection of the public interest, as he saw it, in mind. In December 1870 he gathered all those with an interest in the canal (including both the shareholders and other irrigators) to a mass meeting (attended by some 230 persons) to assent to an agreement for the 'future good government' of the canal. Though the agreement protected the financial rights of the shareholders, Perkins put the management of the canal under a single manager (the most competent of the old managers), to be overseen by the government. He denied the shareholders rights to free irrigation and interference in the canal management (except to examine the manager's accounts and, if necessary, take him to court). They could expect only a continuing return on the profits of the canal once maintenance expenses (and a fixed cut for the manager) had been met. In an attempt to drive home the nature of real proprietary right in the canal, Perkins included in the agreement an assertion that the government also had the right to assume the control and management of the canal 'whenever it pleases', to which the government 'persuaded' the shareholders to assent (Perkins 1871).

Indeed, when the government exercised this option less than twenty years later, it suggested the emerging, if still conflicted, vision of 'public' management that shaped the thinking of the British. Though management of the canal still presented problems (including inequalities in distribution and shortfalls of income), officials admitted that Perkins' system (and the skill of the manager) had in fact improved significantly the management of the canal (Singh, K. 1886). Subsequent correspondence suggested, however, that the legalistic form of the shareholding body increasingly challenged the government's own view of its role as a protector of the local community. For many officials, the chief objection to the role of the shareholders was that they in fact fully represented neither the state nor the irrigators. As the Senior Financial Secretary wrote, 'It is an undoubted evil that there should be this third body of so-called shareholders between the Government and the irrigators, and the sooner it is done away with the better' (Thomson 1885). The Punjab Settlement Commissioner, Major E. G. Wace, put the matter even more clearly: Before 1853, he argued, the shareholders had not had the legal status of a distinct body apart from the combined interest of the irrigators. 'The present system only stands at all,' he wrote, 'because the state has authorised the shareholders to charge occupier's rates [water charges] to the irrigators'. The British aim, he said, should therefore be to return the system to

> its original status, viz., to that of a concern in which the irrigators and the State were the sole parties interested ... A third body unnecessary to its management, and interested mainly in the imposition of unnecessarily high charges on the irrigators, should not be any longer allowed to exist (Wace 1882).

The notion of an intermediate legal interest between the state and the local community of irrigators was, in other words, unacceptable. The key to British policy, as officials saw it, was for the state itself to act, as R. M. Dane put it, 'in the true interest of the majority of the inhabitants of the surrounding country' (Dane 1886).

Underlying the evolving management of the canal was thus the British vision of a binary opposition between two essential forms of interest in the canal. On the one hand, the state defined itself by its own rational interest in efficient administration and orderly agricultural progress. On the other hand, the irrigators possessed an interest in the canal defined largely by popular customary rights and historical irrigation usages. Between these two, as the British increasingly saw it, there was little room for the expression of a rational, public (i.e., direct, irrigator) interest in the administration of the canal, certainly not in the form of a community of legal shareholders. Indeed, it was the state that encompassed, through its rational administration and recording of customs, both these forms of interest.

To this, of course, some of the shareholders objected, suggesting that their position was rooted in a distinctive form of proprietary right, separate and independent of the state, but neither private nor rooted exclusively in custom: 'We ask government to respect our rights', a shareholder petition declared, 'as the canal is common property' (Ram *et al.* 1886). But the British based their takeover of the canal on the assumption that the interest of the inhabitants – that is, of the collective public – could only be embodied by the state as it recorded and protected local irrigation rights and usages within the framework of a rational system of public administration. Indeed, even as the British officially took over the canal, and denied the shareholders any continuing proprietary right, they continued to recognize certain 'old' shareholder rights (such as prior rights to water if the canal should run low), recorded now as legally recognized usages (Douie 1890). The British in fact recorded the customary water claims of irrigators generally under the terms of the Canal Act of 1873, which mandated the recording of 'existing usages' and the protection of 'old, established irrigation', much in the manner that such rights were recorded in the village *wajib-ul-arz*, or in Saunders' recording of irrigation practices on the Degh.

The result, however, was a system with little room for a community of public interest in canal administration defined by voluntary combination and investment (rather than historical custom). If there were a 'public' interest in irrigation, it would now be reflected fully by the colonial state, through a commitment to efficiency and rational administration on the one hand, and through the recording and recognition of customary rights and usages on the other.

The Inundation Canals of Muzaffargarh and Multan

The Shah Nahr's experience was not, of course, universal. Distinct shareholding communities continued to exist on some Punjab inundation canals, and, in some cases, to receive continuing support and encouragement from the British government into the twentieth century. Doubtless, local ecological and social circumstances played an important role in divergent institutional outcomes. But the tensions that were played out in the development of the Shah Nahr were nevertheless illustrative of broader tensions as the British attempted to come to terms with the nineteenth century management of irrigation more broadly. Nowhere was this clearer than in the long official debate of the late nineteenth century on the administration of the inundation canals of south-western Punjab.

To a far greater degree than on the Shah Nahr, inundation canal water was absolutely central to cultivation in arid south-western Punjab. In the years before the opening of the great Punjab canal colonies (beginning in the 1880s), inundation canal operation was critical to the agricultural prosperity of this region, and once again relations between the state and local communities of irrigators occupied a central place in British discussions of irrigation.

Central to canal management in most of the central Indus Basin region was a system of annual silt clearance by unpaid labour known as the *chher* system.[7] In a region in which large-scale silt deposits marked the annual rise and fall of water in the canals, yearly mobilization of labour for silt clearance was essential for most inundation canals to remain in long-term operation. Though the workings of the *chher* system varied within the region, its outlines were suggested by the system that the British found operating in Multan, where the Sikh Governor, Diwan Sawan Mal, had ruled in the 1820s and 1830s. A British Settlement Officer described the system:

> When the time for clearing the canals arrived [usually during the 'slack' agricultural season, from December to February], the *kardar* [a local Sikh official] of each pargannah demanded as many laborers as he considered necessary for the season, according to the state of the canal and the extent of clearance required. The number to be furnished by each village and proprietor was then determined on, some furnishing according to the numbers of their wells or yokes, and others according to the produce of their lands in the past seasons (Morris 1858).

Those taking water from the canal were thus responsible for providing the labour for maintenance. In most cases, zamindars sent their tenants or dependants, though in many instances land-owners (or their family members) performed the work themselves. Clearance operations were supervised by a *darogha* (overseer) and one or more *moharirs* (to record names and keep track of *chher* attendance). The overall operation of the canal was left to the supervision of a *mirab* or *maimar* (variously translated as 'water bailiff' or 'water master'), whose general responsibilities were to look after the canal and deal with the distribution of water. These men usually worked closely with zamindars along the canal in distributing the *chher* demand and in dividing up water. Those who failed to provide their required *chhers* (or whose *chhers* failed to remain for the entire clearance season), were charged a labour commutation fine (called *nagha*), and the fund collected from these fines (*zar-i nagha*) was used, in theory, to pay for hired sub-stitutes and for the canal clearance supervisory staff (Morris 1858).

In outline, this was hardly a system of canal shareholding, such as existed on the Shah Nahr. The system was one in which the role of the state was central, and, indeed, some British officials saw it as a system of state-coerced 'statute labour' (Bombay Government 1856). But most Punjab administrators saw in the system the working of collective irrigator responsibility – responsibility based on the reciprocal exchange of unpaid labour for rights to access to water. The *chher* system for most could not be viewed as a system of coerced state labour, for irrigators were under no obligation to provide labour if they did not take water. At the core of the system was rather the voluntary cooperation of the irrigators, shaped by a system of reciprocal rights and respons-ibilities. It is 'a system', the government declared in 1879, 'whereby the parties who benefit by the canals, under mutual agreement, effect the necessary silt clearances at the proper time of year' (Bernard 1879). As James B. Lyall put it,

> [t]he chher system is a canal irrigator's co-operative clearance system, and each owner of irrigable land (i.e. of land which, accidents excepted, can get water if the owner does his work properly) is by the system bound to do his share in proportion to his holding (Lyall 1888).

It was in Lyall's opinion a system 'solidly founded on custom', which suited 'the habits and circumstances of the people concerned' (ibid.). The role of the state was simply to supervise and systematize its operation.

Defining the proper relationship between the state and the local community thus lay at the heart of the system's operation. To delimit the nature of the rights and obligations involved, Punjab administrators attempted to institute written *chher* rules in various districts, which specified the role of both voluntary association and custom on the one hand, and of the coercive authority of the state on the other. Approaches varied from district to district (in keeping with the British vision of *chher* as an essentially local system). In some districts (such as Muzaffargarh), the organization of the *chher* system was left (at least initially) 'in the hands of the people' themselves, who were overseen by the district revenue authorities. However, in other districts (such as Multan), the operation of the *chher* system was brought directly under the supervision of the provincial Irrigation Department. In both cases, however, the initial key was to develop rules reconciling the maintenance of a system rooted in the reciprocal rights and responsibilities of the irrigators, with a system of state enforcement and supervision.

No element was more important in this than the delineation of the place of local canal *panchayats*, which represented for British officials, the 'voice of the people' (or of the irrigating public) in the organization of canal clearances and rights to water. Canal *panchayats* had existed in various forms under earlier rulers, and the British sought to adapt these to legitimize their continued operation of the *chher* system. According to the *chher* rules promulgated in Multan in the 1850s, for example, representatives for *panchayats* were selected from circles of villages, marked off 'according to their position on the canal', the numbers of members of the *panchayat* varying from three to nine depending on the size of the canal. They were, according to the rules, selected by government, but were intended to 'represent' the interests of irrigators at different positions along the canal.

In Muzaffargarh, such 'representation' was even more direct. There, members of *panchayats* on each canal were elected by the *lambardars* of the villages watered by that canal. They were responsible not only for working with government officers on the administration of the *chher* system, but also for exercising, in the words of one official, a 'general control over the distribution' of water on the canals, looking after their own interests and 'the interests of those they represent' (Garbett 1871: 6). Such 'representatives' were, in the opinion of many officials, critical to adapting existing canal administration to British rule. J. H. Morris wrote at the time of the first settlement in Multan in the 1850s:

> To secure a successful system of canal management, the services of the community must be enlisted, by the appointment on each canal of a panchayet, all of the members of which will have a direct and personal interest in the efficiency of that canal (Morris 1858).

As the Deputy Commissioner of Muzaffargarh put it,

> At present the canal-management is one of local self-government which has sprung up on the spot and would, I think, for that cause alone, commend itself to a race who are strongly attached to their ways and methods, because they are *their* ways (Tremlett 1874).[8]

This was a powerful statement of the system as one structuring a voice for the 'irrigating public' in the management of irrigation.

But the relationship between these *panchayats* and the state was nevertheless a highly ambiguous one. Though canal *panchayats* 'represented' the irrigators on each canal, and distributed the demand for *chher* labour, the boundaries and character of the 'community' of irrigators they represented were extremely difficult to define. Canal supply on most inundation canals varied markedly from year to year, making it often impossible to fix precisely who would (or could) take water each season – a difficulty compounded by the fluidity of property and the shifting character of much cultivation in the arid reaches of western Punjab. Legally speaking, as the Settlement Officer of Muzaffargarh wrote, 'the persons entitled to irrigation cannot be specified, because any person whose land can be reached by water can become an irrigator' (O'Brien 1876). The *chher* system was thus *not* marked by the existence of legally closed and independent communities of water-sharers, such as characterized the Shah Nahr; nor for that matter was it generally marked by bounded cultural communities rooted in common, long-standing relationships to canals. Instead, officials tried simply to record those responsible for supplying *chher*s on each canal on the basis of those who had irrigated the previous season. The community of canal sharers, in these circumstances, though undergirded by cultural norms of reciprocal obligation, was based largely on interest: those who took water were obligated (by implicit contract) to perform (or provide) labour for the canal's annual maintenance.

In one respect, of course, this helped precisely to address the dilemma that had shaped the British reaction to the share system on the Shah Nahr. Since shares were not permanently and legally fixed, the system had little tendency to define a body of legal shareholders in the canal distinct from the actual irrigators on the canal. It was the interests of the actual irrigators that *panchayat*s theoretically represented, thus defining in principle a fluidity of representation critical to the emergence of a 'public voice' in irrigation. But the nature of the represented community nevertheless remained ambiguous. Delimitation of the boundaries of the interested 'public' on many major canals fell largely to the state itself, however much officials argued that public interest on these canals was rooted in voluntary association. Though government officials in most cases maintained rolls (on the basis of recorded irrigation) indicating who was responsible each season for the provision of *chher*s, these could easily be manipulated by officials for their own purposes. As the Settlement Officer of Muzaffargarh admitted, it was usually easier to get into a local community of irrigators on an inundation canal than to get out of it: 'It was easy enough to get brought on the roll of irrigators,' he wrote, 'but almost impossible to get removed from it, and, consequently, from the obligation to supply labour' (O'Brien 1882: 100–104). Officials, after all, had their own reasons for maximizing the labour potentially available for maintenance of the canals.

Far more serious, however, in terms of British attempts to work the system as one of voluntary community regulated by state supervision and direction, was the problem of dealing with conflict among the members of each canal community. Whether selected by government appointment or by election, *panchayat* members and heads (*sarpanches*) were selected within a milieu of ongoing competition over water among the irrigators. Conflict over water distribution was particularly acute on inundation canals during periods of low flow in the spring and autumn. Access to adequate water often depended during these times on rights to put dams into channels to raise levels; head and tail enders naturally had sharply divergent interests at these times. Such conflicts were particularly acute in areas of cash-cropping, where the success of crops often depended critically on an adequate supply of water at the beginning and end of the growing season. Just whose voice, in such circumstances, were the *panchayats* to represent?

In theory, of course, *panchayats* might have been viewed as an arena (demarcated by the state) within which various interests could contest to define a public voice in irrigation. *Panchayat* members (whether appointed or elected) were, after all, men with local cultural, economic or tribal influence, often unconnected to the control of water. British *chher* rules reinforced their local influence by conferring on them a status as privileged irrigators within the irrigation system, granting them a reduced demand for the provision of *chher* labour. The control exerted by *sarpanches* over *mirabs* and other local water officials derived however not only from their positions on *panchayats*, but also from the more generalized cultural and economic influence they wielded. It was, as one official noted, not state policy, but the tradition of 'community' payment of *mirabs* in kind, a system based on reciprocal exchange, that placed water distribution to an important degree under the influence of the men recognized by the British as 'leading irrigators'. For *mirabs*, good relations with powerful local men was critical to their remuneration. 'A good deal of the *mirab*'s time is taken up in collecting his grain', a Multan official wrote. 'Being a servant of the irrigators, [the *mirab*] is not likely to report breaches of the rules on their part.' Nor was he likely to ignore the wealth and influence of the most powerful irrigators (and their clients) in matters of water distribution (Stevens 1882).

Influence and privilege were thus an inseparable part, in this context, of a structure of community relations – a structure rooted not in equality (or even clarity) of legal rights, but rather in patterns of local political power and influence constrained by local cultural expectations and patronage. The establishment of a controlled structure for the play of inequality on legally constituted canal *panchayats* was, it could be argued, critical in these circumstances to the very definition of an irrigating 'public'.

Still, the acceptance of privileged irrigator influence within the framework of *chher* rules created increasing tension as the system developed, much as it did on the Shah Nahr. Though the operation of influence within the *chher* system potentially bridged the divide between rational state administration and local community, it unsettled many administrators for this very reason. Some state officials, in fact, complained pointedly at times about this influence, which threatened to undermine the legitimacy of the entire system. 'Muharrirs and Mirabs do not see that every person supplies his quota of labor,' wrote one canal overseer bitterly, 'and they wrongly charge the poor with fines, while the rich escape both fines and having to supply the full amount of laborers.' Local *mirabs* often looked the other way when influential zamindars made special cuts in canals to assure themselves of adequate water during low supply, or erected dams or put *jhalars* in channels to maintain their supply in difficult times (Gholam Murtaza 1874).

This was particularly unsettling to canal engineers. Fundamental to irrigation, in their view, was the clear separation of rational, public administration from a reliance on community control of canals, whether in terms of assessment or mobilization of labour. The confusions in the *chher* system, as some argued, tended not only to undermine efficient canal clearance, but also to tie the hands of engineers interested in 'rationalizing' canal operation according to principles of 'scientific' design and management. One leading engineer put it thus:

> That the system, at least as worked under the British administration, leads to oppression on the part of the headmen of villages, and that it is unsatisfactory to the Engineers, whose object is to maintain the canals in an efficient state, are facts not denied by any one who has had experience in the matter (Crofton 1875).

Indeed, for many engineers, the system encroached on the preeminence of technical knowledge. Efficiency of operation was for engineers far more important than irrigator input in defining principles for the 'public' operation of canals. It was for many precisely the rejection of special influence and the denial of privilege that underscored the state's claim to speak with a public voice.

British administrators in fact found it increasingly difficult to fit the *chher* system into a framework of administrative thinking that demanded a clear, conceptual demarcation between the realms of rational state administration on the one hand and the customary organization of society on the other. As James Lyall (a strong proponent of the *chher* system) recognized, it was the mingling of local influence with state direction in the operation of the *chher* system which raised the most serious problems. Irrigator influence that was unobjectionable when exercised entirely independently of state control, could nevertheless become problematic when drawn into a system recognized and enforced by the state. By the very process of regulating canal committees, Lyall observed, the danger arose that the government would fix and regulate privilege. Lyall's answer was that the state needed to provide its own counterweight: as it recognized *panchayats*, government had a concomitant obligation, Lyall wrote, to provide 'some officer of Government above them, with very strong powers of interference, to whom complaints can be easily and cheaply preferred' (Lyall 1882). But administrators chafed increasingly at their inability in these circumstances to define clear boundaries between what was the province of the state and what was to be left to the operation of the local irrigating community.[9] The meaning of the public, in these circumstances, became increasingly problematic.

Indeed, uncertainty about the clear conceptual definition of state and community roles led to bitter debate about the entire structure of the *chher* system in the last decades of the nineteenth century. When the revision of the Muzaffargarh settlement in the late 1870s suggested that canal operation had deteriorated since the arrival of the British, some officials suggested that the underlying confusion in the *chher* system about the roles and responsibilities of the state and the local community lay at the heart of the problem. Viewing the *chher* system as essentially 'voluntary' – and the canals as essentially reciprocal zamindari operations – had, in the analysis of some, tempted many officials to downplay the role of the state and to put undue reliance on popular, co-operative community in running the canals, with the result that canal clearances had not been adequately executed. The outcome was a decline in irrigation, the Settlement Officer wrote, a product (at least in part) of a misplaced faith in the 'people' collectively to manage their own affairs. Looking to the public had only caused confusion in canal administration. 'The zamindars are entirely without sufficient combination to carry out the annual clearances or any other large work,' he declared (O'Brien 1882: 3; 1874: 15). 'There are so many confuting interests', wrote another official, 'that they cannot combine, and never have combined without State aid' (Garbett 1871: 21). By relying too heavily on the collective initiative of the irrigators, some now argued, the British had mis-interpreted the underlying nature of the *chher* system itself.

But to suggest that the system could be worked wholly and unambiguously as one of state management raised the equally unsettling spectre that the system amounted to little more than a structure of 'statute labour'. This was a position that most British officials were unwilling to entertain. On what basis could the state rely on involuntary mobilization of labour? It was little surprise, therefore, that by the end of the nineteenth century the challenge to the continuation of the *chher* system became sufficiently strong that the system was abolished.

One of the main arguments put forward for the abolition of the *chher* system was that its continuation would undermine the clear separation of state administration from traditionally organized local communities. Though customary irrigation rights were still recorded, as on the Shah Nahr, the management of main canals (and the recording and enforcement of rights) increasingly became the exclusive prerogative of the state. Private and village watercourses remained, of course, in the hands of zamindars or village communities, but 'public' control of irrigation in the region came essentially to mean state control. The separation of state and customary realms was once again confirmed, with customary rights recorded in British papers, but with the 'public' interest resting clearly on the state side of the ledger.

Conclusion

This conflation of 'public' control over irrigation with state control became all the more marked in the succeeding decades. Beginning in the 1880s, the British built a system of perennial canals in the Indus Basin that superseded the region's inundation canals, and as they did so they moved ever more forcefully towards a system that separated state control from local community influence in irrigation management. While local communities continued to influence irrigation at the village level, large-scale, extra-village canal management came to be an almost exclusive prerogative of the colonial state. All forms of local community organization were (in legal theory) rigidly excluded from the operation of the large, new water delivery systems that shaped the new Indus Basin 'canal colonies'. The canal colonies came, in fact, to be monuments to the 'public' power of the colonial state, dramatically increasing state revenues in the region, and opening up vast new areas for agricultural settlement (Ali 1988).

This was a far cry from a notion of an 'irrigating public' as an organized popular voice in irrigation management. But as the story of the Shah Nahr and of the inundation canals of south-western Punjab suggests, this came about not because the British were oblivious to the potential importance of local community in the structuring of irrigation, but rather because the state increasingly defined its own power in stark opposition to the realm of the local community. Indeed, the evidence suggests that the British made serious efforts in the nineteenth century to define structures of management that would reconcile local control with state supervision and management. Nonetheless, their efforts were fraught with contradictions, not least because the definition of a clear conceptual separation between state authority and local community was central to the principles on which the British conceptualized and developed their rule. Even as they sought to define mechanisms by which the state could mobilize local community in the interest of effective administration, the British saw their state as operating in a world that was fundamentally distinct from that of village society.

British administration was, in their eyes, rooted in principles of rational, bureaucratic organization. Local society was rooted in a world of customary community. Though many officials saw both as important to effective canal management, few ever doubted that these worlds were fundamentally separate, and that the structural maintenance of this separation was critical to the definition and continuance of the state's power and to the efficient functioning of irrigation. While customary community could be embodied in 'customary rights' recorded and enforced by the state, the public realm of canal administration came to be almost wholly dominated by the state.

In establishing, ultimately, an irrigation system dominated by state-managed perennial canals, the British thus moved to put in place a structure of irrigation management that clarified the confusions marking earlier canal development, and that has influenced irrigation up to the present day. The new structures of canal administration that emerged with the expansion of perennial canals defined a conceptual bifurcation between the state and the village more starkly than ever before. Along the new perennial canals of the Indus Basin, the outlet itself became a *physical* divider of two worlds. On the one side of the outlet was the world of rational canal administration, managed wholly by the colonial state. On the other side was a world of local communities, the essential containers, as the British saw it, of indigenous society in the region. Having struggled in the nineteenth century to make sense of the relations between the state and society in the management of irrigation, the British ultimately constructed a massive structure of irrigation works in the Indus Basin which, in important ways, hinged between the state and the village at the canal outlet, which physically linked but conceptually separated these two worlds. In constructing their great irrigation works, the British came to rely on a structure of irrigation in which the outlet, separating the main canals from the villages, also came to separate, in a conceptual sense, colonial state and society.

Modern critics (and many colonial engineers themselves) of course pointed out the productive and social costs of the colonial structuring of irrigation. Viewed from above the outlet, the benefits of large-scale irrigation sometimes appeared to be compromised by wastage of water and inefficient management below the outlet. Whatever the conceptual separation between the state and the village, engineers could never be totally oblivious to the vicissitudes of irrigation below the outlet, for it inevitably impinged on larger system efficiency. But for most of the British era and beyond, the administrative separation of the main system from the world of the village remained a basic principle of administrative (and political) irrigation doctrine.

More recently, both foreign experts and governments have with increasing urgency directed attention to the problems inherent in this structure. In the 1970s and 1980s, South Asian governments attempted to organize local users' associations and to increase grass-roots involvement in the management of irrigation as a key to effective local-level water use. This led to an increasingly sophisticated understanding of the variables shaping village-level water management and community. The world below the outlet jumped to the centre of irrigation planning.

But scholars have only begun to analyse the political and conceptual framework within which relations between state and community historically developed. As Robert Chambers has pointed out, scholars of irrigation have themselves often been divided on the basis of whether their focus is on the world above the outlet or below. While irrigation engineers have tended to focus on the needs of physical structure above the outlet, social scientists have focused largely on the requirements of community organization and mobilization below the outlet (Chambers 1988: 68–85). In important respects, the differing fields of knowledge defined by engineers and social scientists continue to reflect the dichotomy between a state realm of rational administration on the one hand and a distinctive societal world of community organization and conflict on the other. Though few irrigation specialists now deny that an integrated approach encompassing both sides of the outlet is necessary to effective irrigation reform, few have studied the conceptual roots of the colonial separation between state and society as a separate and important element. Yet this is a story that has historically had a profound impact on modern Indus Basin irrigation systems. Indeed, in searching for historical precedents for popular control of irrigation apart from the state, irrigation reformers have at times themselves replicated the structures of thinking that shaped the colonial development of irrigation. In this sense, a fuller history of the colonial state's relations with local irrigating communities may provide an important perspective on the modern search for an irrigating public.

Notes

1.   In emphasizing the variety in forms of village organization, Wade explicitly attacks the notion of a single, essentialized model of village organization. But he nevertheless loosely identifies his notion of a 'public realm' in the village with the classic model of village community associated with the writings of Sir Henry Maine. For a discussion of the notion of 'village republics' within colonial thinking, see Inden 1990.

2.   This is not to say that rights in wells always followed identically rights in the land, but rather that the same notions of shares governed each. The significance of shares in wells is suggested in a comment by the Settlement Officer of Lahore District: 'It is my experience among natives that in the fair and equitable division of a share they are unequalled by any nationality. ... In the thousands of wells which are studded all over the country there are innumerable and minute shares existing in almost every well, that oblige each owner's bullocks to be yoked and unyoked at certain stated times of the night and day, to take the place of or to make room for the cattle of another shareholder ... Disputes or quarrels in such minutiae seldom or ever come into our courts' (Saunders 1873: 45).

3.   Such systems of popular management with rules reduced to writing at the time of settlement were found elsewhere as well, for example on the *kuhls* of Kangra. There, as the *Gazetteer* noted, 'the management rests entirely with the people, who receive no assistance from the Government. They maintain an organized staff of officers called *kohlis*, every village supplying its respresentatives who patrol the water-courses to prevent theft, to stop leakages and to distribute the water. Every village has its own code of rules, which was reduced to writing during the 1868 Settlement' (*Kangra District Gazetteer* 1926: 280).

4.   This Shah Nahr was distinct from the older and larger Shah Nahr (or Badshahi Nahr) in Gurdaspur District, a canal which took off from

the River Ravi and dated back to the reign of Shah Jahan (Singh, C. 1991: 100, 126).

5. This was the general view, though there was, from the beginning, ongoing debate about the nature of proprietary right in the canal (Dane 1886).

6. In some cases, the shares were held jointly by villages, who apparently divided their rights to water (and the return on their capital) according to their internal shares in the village land, usually as measured by their shares in the commons (Perkins 1870).

7. The labourers furnished by the irrigators for canal work were known as *chher*s, and it was for this reason that these systems were known as *chher* systems, though they differed in detail from locality to locality. Similar systems were also known by other names in the Indus Basin, as, for example, the *tinga* system in Isa Khel.

8. Emphasis in original. 'Besides these sentimental considerations,' he continued, 'the people are in favor of this plan of each canal being managed by the persons who use it, because they fear that were the State to take the matter into its hands, their own immediate interests would often be sacrificed to considerations of general interest and improvement' (Tremlett 1874).

9. The inability to define such boundaries led to a long search by some for principles to determine the 'ownership' of each canal. The hope, of course, was that 'ownership' (determined usually, as in the case of the Shah Nahr, by reference to the original construction of the canal) could guide whether primary responsibility for the administration of particular canals should fall to the state or the local community. In practice, attempts to determine 'ownership' of particular canals usually produced little result. In most cases, the state and irrigators were both implicated in canal construction (and periodic reconstruction) in ways that made a historical determination of primary state or irrigator responsibility impossible. See O'Brien (1876).

References

Ali, Imran (1988) *The Punjab under Imperialism, 1885– 1947*, Princeton: Princeton University Press.

Bernard, C. (1879) Officiating Secretary to Government of India, Home, Revenue & Agriculture, to Secretary to Government, Punjab, 19 August 1879. Punjab Revenue, Agriculture & Commerce, A procs, September 1879, no. 3. India Office Records, London.

Bombay Government (1856) 'Official Correspondence on the Abolition of Statute or Forced Labour in Sind'. Selections from the Records of the Bombay Government, no. XXXIV – New Series.

Chambers, Robert (1988) *Managing Canal Irrigation: Practical Analysis from South Asia*, Cambridge: Cambridge University Press.

Crofton, Col. J. (1875) Joint-Secretary to Government to Secretary to Government, Punjab, 9 March 1875. Punjab Revenue, Agriculture & Commerce, A procs., September 1875, no. 8. India Office Records, London.

Dane, R.M. (1886) Settlement Officer, Gurdaspur to Commissioner and Superintendent, Jullundur Division, 6 May 1886. Punjab Revenue & Agriculture, Irrigation, A Procs., May 1889, no. 3. India Office Records, London.

Douie, J.M. (1890) Senior Secretary to Financial Commissioner to Junior Secretary to Government, Punjab, 3 June 1890, with Deed of Transfer to Government of Shareholders' Rights in the Shah Nahr Canal, 21 July 1890. Punjab Revenue & Agriculture, Irrigation, A Procs, August 1890, nos 8–9. India Office Records, London.

Fagan, P.J. (1901–02) Memorandum II on the Shah Nahr Canal, Hoshiarpur District. *Indian Irrigation Commission*, Minutes of Evidence (Punjab).

Garbett, H. (1871) *Report on Canal Irrigation in the Muzaffargarh District*, 12 April 1871. Punjab Archives, Lahore.

Gholam Murtaza (1874) Report by Superintendent of Alipur (trans. by E. O'Brien), in 'Management of the Inundation Canals in the Muzaffargarh District.' Appendix to Punjab Revenue, Agriculture & Commerce, 1876 (IOL marking P/867). India Office Records, London.

Hoshiarpur District Gazetteer, 1904 (1905) Lahore: Punjab Government Press.

Inden, Ronald (1990) *Imagining India*, London: Basil Blackwell.

Kangra District Gazetteer, 1924–25 (1926) Lahore: Punjab Government Printing.

Lyall, J. B. (1882) Memo by the Financial Commissioner, Punjab, 2 August 1882. Punjab Revenue and Agriculture, Irrigation, A procs, November 1882, no. 1. India Office Records, London.

—— (1888) Demi-official letter from Junior Secretary to Government, Punjab to Senior Secretary to Financial Commissioner, 8 June 1887. Punjab Revenue and Agriculture, Irrigation, A procs, November 1888, nos 1–4. Punjab Archives, Lahore.

Morris, J.H. (1858) 'Report on the Inundation Canals of the Multan District,' 18 September 1858. Punjab Revenue, 11 December 1858, Procs 9–14. Punjab Archives, Lahore.

O'Brien, Edward (1874) Settlement Officer, Muzaffargarh to Settlement Commissioner, Punjab, 4 July 1874, in 'Management of Inundation Canals in the Muzaffargarh District.' Appendix to Punjab Revenue, Agriculture & Commerce, 1876 (IOL marking P/ 867). India Office Records, London.

—— (1876) Settlement Officer, Muzaffargarh to Settlement Commissioner, Multan and Derajat, 30 June 1876, in 'Management of the Inundation Canals in the Muzaffargarh District.' Appendix to Punjab Revenue, Agriculture & Commerce, 1876 (IOL marking P/ 867). India Office Records, London.

—— (1882) *Report of the Land Revenue Settlement of the Muzaffargarh District of the Punjab, 1873–1880*, Lahore: Central Jail Press.

Perkins, H.E. (1870) Memo by the Deputy Commissioner, Hoshiarpur, 14 December 1870. Punjab Revenue & Agriculture, Irrigation, June 1885, no. 5. India Office Records, London.

—— (1871) Deputy Commissioner, Hoshiarpur to Commissioner and Superintendent, Jullundur, 4 March 1871. Punjab Revenue & Agriculture, Irrigation, June 1885, no. 5. India Office Records, London.

Punjab Board of Revenue, Lahore. File no. 251/17 KW.

Ram, Hari, *et al.* (1886) Statement of Hari Ram and 20 other Lambardars representing the 15 villages holding a 40-pie share in the Shah Nahr, recorded at Mukerian, 28 April 1886. Punjab Revenue & Agriculture, Irrigation, A procs, May 1889, no. 3. India Office Records, London.

Saunders, Leslie S. (1873) *Report on the Revised Land Revenue Settlement of the Lahore District in the Lahore Division*, Lahore: Central Jail Press.

Sengupta, Nirmal (1991) *Managing Common Property: Irrigation in India and the Philippines*, New Delhi: Sage.

Singh, Chetan (1991) *Religion and Empire: Panjab in the Seventeenth Century*, Delhi: Oxford University Press.

Singh, Kharak (1886) Statement, recorded at Mukerian, 28 April 1886. Punjab Revenue and Agriculture, Irrigation, May 1889, no. 3. India Office Records, London.

Stevens, W. (1882) Executive Engineer, Lower Sutlej and Chenab Division, to Deputy Commissioner, Multan, 25 May 1882. Punjab Revenue and Agriculture, Irrigation, A procs, September 1882, no. 4. India Office Records, London.

Thomson, R.G. (1885) Senior Secretary to Financial Commissioner to Junior Secretary to Government, Punjab, 6 March 1885. Punjab

Revenue & Agriculture, Irrigation, A procs, June 1885, no. 5. India Office Records, London.

Tremlett, J.D. (1874) Officiating Deputy Commissioner to Settlement Officer, Muzaffargarh, 7 April 1874, in 'Management of the Inundation Canals in the Muzaffargarh District.' Appendix to Punjab Revenue, Agriculture & Commerce, 1876 (IOL marking P/867). India Office Records, London.

Tupper, C.L. (1881) *Punjab Customary Law,* 3 vols, Calcutta: Government Printing.

Uphoff, Norman (1986) *Improving International Irrigation Management with Farmer Participation: Getting the Process Right,* Boulder, Col.: Westview.

Wace, Maj. E.G. (1882) Commissioner of Settlements and Agriculture to Senior Secretary to Financial Commissioners, 24 November 1882. Punjab Revenue & Agriculture, Irrigation, A procs, June 1885, no. 5. India Office Records, London.

Wade, Robert (1988) *Village Republics: Economic Conditions for Collective Action in South India,* Cambridge: Cambridge University Press.

10 When the Wells Ran Dry: The Tragedy of Collective Action among Farmers in South India

Staffan Lindberg

> Ruin is the destination towards which all men rush, each pursuing his own best interest in a society that believes in the freedom of the commons. Freedom in a commons brings ruin to all (Garret Hardin, *The Tragedy of the Commons*, 1968: 1244).

In the contemporary world economy, the use of ever-increasing powerful machines, unless politically controlled, often leads to over-exploitation of natural resources. In particular this pertains to economic settings where individual (or sectional) rationality conflicts with overall collective rationality,[1] which makes it difficult to manage natural resources in a sustainable manner. The situation may become even worse if such individual rationality is pushed through collective action to represent sectional interest in a democratically organized political system. Unless the political system has mechanisms for controlling this contradiction, the situation may easily get out of control.

The following case study illustrates this dilemma in a powerful way. In Tamil Nadu a new and pioneering farmers' movement in the early 1970s mobilized farmers and peasants in dry areas of the state, who rely mainly on well irrigation for the cultivation of their land. The movement fought for lower electricity tariffs and remission of loans contracted for the construction of wells and purchase of pumpsets. It initially achieved some success, but was crushed in the 1980s by political manoeuvring and state repression. In this defeat there was, however, a paradoxical outcome: it appears that successive Tamil Nadu governments believed that only by giving free electricity to all farmers for well irrigation could they neutralize the demands created by the farmers' movement. This type of politics has been labelled 'competitive populism', and was 'produced' by the Tamil nationalist politicians coming to power after 1967. It has contributed to an ecological crisis in the dry areas of the state. With over a million energized wells, about 20 per cent of all energized pumpsets in India, Tamil Nadu is suffering from a sinking groundwater level in the dry areas, and farmers are over-exploiting the groundwater resource to such an extent that agricultural output is suffering. Lack of rules and coordination as well as low electricity prices have all reinforced this situation.

The present paper will describe the background to this development, the growth of a state-sponsored well irrigation economy as the starting point for a producer-oriented farmers' movement – the Tamilaga Vyvasayigal Sangam (VS), or the Tamil Nadu Agriculturists' Association (TNAA) as they call themselves in English.[2] It was to be the first of the new producer-oriented farmers' movements in India emerging after the advent of the Green Revolution.[3] It will then trace the trajectory of collective actions and state reactions and the specific political opportunity structures within which these took place. In the process, class differences among the peasants and farmers involved in the movement also seem to have played an important role.

The Setting: Dry, Rain-Fed Areas with Well Irrigation and Electric Pumpsets

It was not the Green Revolution as such that sparked off a new farmers' movement in India, it was the 'pumpset revolution'! This 'revolution' happened in the dry areas of Tamil Nadu, beginning in Coimbatore District.

After Independence, wells became the leading source of irrigation in Tamil Nadu. Like elsewhere, in the Deccan cultivation is predicated upon a sustainable use of groundwater available in a particular area, recharged periodically from rainfall. The use of groundwater is, however, fraught with complexities: ecological, economic, political and cultural. The basic predicament is that wells, unlike surface irrigation which is mostly publicly owned and maintained, 'are often privately owned and operated, although the underground aquifers on which they draw are part of the commons' (MIDS 1988: 180). This contradiction has sharpened with the tremendous growth of well irrigation in Tamil Nadu after Independence. Large areas were electrified. Institutional loans were extended to farmers through banks and cooperatives to construct or deepen wells and purchase electric pumpsets.

The number of wells nearly doubled from about 6.3 lakhs (630,000) at the beginning of the 1950s to 11.9 lakhs at the end of the 1960s, and went up by a further 4.4 lakhs to over 16 lakhs by the late 1970s. Between 1950 and 1970, the net area irrigated by wells rose from 12.5 to 19.4 lakhs, i.e. by about 7 lakh acres; and, in the 1970s alone, there was a further increase of 8.6 lakh acres, reaching a total of about 28 lakh acres in 1978–79. Electrification of wells has also proceeded at an impressive pace. Prior to Independence, only a meagre 4,300 wells were connected. The figure rose to about 1 lakh at the end of the 1950s, went up to 6 lakhs by 1971–72, and over 9 lakh pumpsets had been electrified by 1980–81 (ibid.: 181).

Up to the end of the 1960s this development seemed unproblematic. Farmers could intensify cultivation and were able to repay their loans, as indicated by the fact that the cooperative societies in Tamil Nadu had only about 10 per cent of arrears on repayments in the beginning of the 1970s.[4] The financial position of the Tamil Nadu Electricity Board (TNEB) was fairly stable (ibid.: 245). Reportedly, many areas seemed to prosper after the advent of the pumpset revolution, increasing output and intensity of cropping of a number of remunerative commercial crops. Employment opportunities increased in agriculture as well as in complementary occupations, such as pump operators, mechanics, etc. (ibid.).

In the beginning of the 1970s, however, problems started to appear. Madduma Bandara (1977: 337) reports from North Arcot:

> On the basis of the foregoing analysis it is possible to diagnose that the hydro-ecological balance in North Arcot District is under strain, if not becoming rapidly upset. This is evidenced

both by lowering water-table conditions, even within a period as short as three years, and by decreasing yields of natural streams in relation to the rainfall of the area ... It is argued that the overriding reason for these changes is the over-extraction of sub-surface water resources which in turn is a concomitant of the recent agrarian changes. ... In view of this situation, further expansion of lift irrigation may lead in the near future to unwelcome hydrological consequences such as lowering of water-tables and dwindling of surface water resources, unless suitable preventive measures are introduced in time.

The period 1965–76 was one of near-continuous droughts in large parts of Tamil Nadu, and many farmers depending on well irrigation started to feel the pinch. It was at this moment that the state government and the TNEB decided to increase the electricity tariff for agricultural producers from 8 to 10 Np (new paise) per kWh (100 Np = Rs 1). Whatever the motivation, this proved to be an inopportune moment since the move gave rise to a widespread farmers' movement with consequences that nobody could foresee.

First Wave: 'One Paisa Agitation'

Until the late 1960s peasant movements had been dominated by landless labourers, small tenants, and poor peasants, who fought for land reforms, rent reduction, etc. However, the new farmers' movement in Tamil Nadu sprang out of a small regional organiza-tion, 'The Northern Coimbatore *Taluk*[5] Farmers' Association', formed in 1966 by farmers in two *panchayat* unions north of Coimbatore, an area with a long tradition of commercial cropping and one highly dependent on well irrigation. The issue right from the beginning seems to have been the supply of electricity (Balasubramaniam 1989: 112–13).[6]

Coimbatore District is one of the leading districts in terms of the number of installations of new wells and electric pumpsets since Independence; in this it is second only to North Arcot District (*Statistical Handbook of Tamilnadu 1977*). At the same time it is the district with lowest average rainfall in Tamil Nadu; only 718 mm on average per year, and that too with considerable variations. During the period 1965/66–1974/75 rainfall was only 87 per cent of normal, and in 1969 (the year preceding the collective action), rainfall was just 466 mm (Janakarajan n.d.: 13–14). At the same time, groundwater was being more exploited by the increased number of energized wells.

The breakthrough for the farmers' movement came in the spring of 1970 when it started to address the price of electricity and the repayment of government loans. The immediate reason was the sudden hike in the electricity tariff which affected a large number of farmers. In March 1970 the Tamil Nadu Electricity Board decided to increase the electricity tariff from 8 Np to 10 Np per unit of power delivered to the farmers. The 25 per cent increase in tariff met with strong opposition from the farmers in the dry areas of Coimbatore District. They quickly formed an action committee and organized a one-day hunger strike on 11 March in the towns of Coimbatore, Tirupur and Avanashi, involving around 15,000 farmers. The farmers who gathered decided not to pay the electricity bill at this new higher rate and to resist disconnection of electricity for not having paid the bills. They also asked for deferral of loan collection from institutional sources.

As the protests continued, the state government responded by arresting hundreds of farmers active in the movement. On 9 May the farmers again staged a massive rally in Coimbatore city involving thousands of bullock carts and hundreds of tractors. At some places workers from the Electricity Board were *gherao*ed (surrounded) and forced to reconnect disconnected power-lines. The government again answered with repression, and on 19 June three farmers were killed in an encounter with the police at Perumanalloor.

A month later, after the release of several leaders of the association, there were renewed negotiations resulting in the reduction of the electricity tariff to 9 Np per unit. In the history of the farmers' movement this agitation was called the 'one *paisa* agitation', since that was the result of the struggle.

'Patton Tanks of Indian Villages'
Nearly the same scenario was repeated in 1972, this time with an impact in several districts of the state. The state government, now led by M. Karunanidhi, announced an increase in the electricity

tariff from 9 to 12 Np, that is, a 33 per cent increase.[7] Again, the Coimbatore farmers answered with strong resistance. In March they published a twelve-point charter asking for a reduction in the electricity tariff and a variety of other demands, such as 're-mission of cooperative, government and private loans incurred by farmers, extension of new credit under a new credit policy, fixation of agricultural prices on the basis of cost of production and input prices', etc. (Nadkarni 1987: 65–66).

The district association declared that if the demands were not fulfilled by 15 April, they would launch a major protest of defiance by not paying their electricity bills. At this stage some of the opposition parties joined the protest, including the Congress (O) and the Communist Party of India (CPI), and an all-party group under the leadership of K. N. Kumaraswamy, a Congress MLA (member of the Legislative Assembly), was set up to head the campaign. A variety of protests were staged, including resist-ing attempts by the Electricity Department to disconnect the power-lines of those who had not paid the dues. Between 2 and 4 June supplies of milk and vegetables to the cities were stopped. Then, on 7 June,

> The Agriculturists' Association led by the Congress M.L.A., Mr K. N. Kumaraswamy organized a 12 1/2-hour 'blockade' of Coimbatore by the bullock-carts numbering between 2,000 to 3,000 and paralysed life in Coimbatore. The bullocks were taken off their yokes and the carts were parked at road junctions or across streets. Neither private cars nor any other vehicle could pass through city roads. Even pedestrians had to jump over the bullock-cart barricades to reach their destination. Permission had been granted only to take a procession of bullock-carts. But the Association took unfair advantage of it and blockaded hospitals, educational institutions and the Collectorate (The Progressive Agriculturists' Federation 1972: 11).

The bullock cart invasion made a strong impression on the government and led to the release of arrested leaders and re-newed talks, again without any results. A new all-party group was formed, led by Narayanaswami Naidu, the leader of the farmers' movement. The protests soon spread to several other districts including Tirunelveli, North Arcot and Ramanathapuram. A state

wide *bandh* (a general strike) was called on 5 July, which attracted
a very large following, also from violent groups outside the direct
control of the farmers' action groups. Looting and arson occurred at
several places and was met with a strong police response: fifteen
people were killed in the confrontations, which made the headlines all over India. (It also made the headlines outside the country:
The New York Times dubbed the bullock cart demonstration as the
'Patton tanks of the Indian villages'.)

After this confrontation something had to be done. From 13–
16 July representatives of the farmers and the political parties,
led by Naidu, held new talks with the state government, which
ended with an agreement on most points in the charter. The
electricity tariff was reduced by 1 paisa to 11 Np. All arrested
persons were released and all registered court cases against
farmers were withdrawn.

The protests of 1972 were a great success for the Coimbatore
farmers' movement, and Narayanaswami Naidu had emerged as
its undisputed leader. Naidu soon proved to be a charismatic
leader capable of organising farmers all over the state. By 1973
several state-wide conferences were held by the organization, and
on 13 November the Tamilaga Vyvasayigal Sangam, VS, (The Tamil
Nadu Agriculturists' Association, TNAA) was officially announced
with Naidu as its President. After that, the organization quickly
spread to almost all districts in Tamil Nadu.

Second Wave: 'No-Tax' Campaign

The State of Emergency of 1975–77 brought a stop to the activities
of the farmers' movement in Tamil Nadu as it did to political
activities elsewhere in the country. The DMK government under
Karunanidhi was dismissed in 1976. Under Governor's rule the
electricity tariff was again raised, this time from 11 to 16 Np per
unit, and forfeitures, that is, public auction of the property of
farmers who had not paid their electricity bills and cooperative
dues, were announced.

During the spring of 1977, however, the whole political situation
changed with the lifting of the emergency and the victory of the
Janata Party in the parliamentary elections. As soon as the

emergency ended, The Tamilaga Vyvasayigal Sangam brought out a nine-point charter of demands, again asking for a reduction in the electricity tariff: 'Electricity is to be supplied free of cost for agriculture or at least electricity tariff for lift irrigation should be equal to the water-rate levied in river irrigation.' The charter also repeated most of the demands from the original twelve-point charter of 1972, but this time asking for cancellation of all debts incurred by the farmers.

The argument was that it was the central government that was in debt to the farmers, due to the unremunerative prices it had paid them for many years, not the other way round. This was the beginning of a struggle in which the farmers, referring to Gandhi's famous 'No-Tax' slogan during the freedom struggle, refused to pay not only the electricity bills but also interest and amortization on their institutional loans. This was a struggle that would last until the end of the 1980s.

The forceful manifestation of the farmers' movement at this time appears to have put some pressure on the political parties standing for the state assembly elections. One of these parties was the newly formed DMK splinter group, the All-India Anna Dravida Munnetra Kazhagam (AIADMK), led by M. G. Ramachandran (M.G.R.), the legendary film hero. It is rumoured that he, as a challenger of the established DMK party, bent the ears of the leaders of the farmers' movement by giving some vague promises to look into their grievances. In the event, M.G.R. had a sweeping success.

After assuming office, M.G.R., however, seemed deaf to the demands of the farmers. Farmers refusing to pay up were rounded up and their property was sold in public auctions. This marked the beginning of intense struggle on the part of the VS, which was now at the height of its organizational strength, and active in nearly all districts of the state. It claimed to have organized around three million farmers all over Tamil Nadu. A great number of agitational methods were used, including 'No-Tax', hunger strikes, picketing of government offices, and also *gheraos* of personnel from the Electricity Board who were trying to disconnect the power-lines of farmers who had not paid their bills.

Again the government answered with repressive force. In April 1978, eight people were shot dead by the police. In May new talks between the VS and the government led to the reduction of the electricity tariff from 16 to 14 Np per unit. Agitations continued, however, since the other demands in the 1977 charter had not been met. On 4 April 1979, another five farmers (including two women) were killed in police shootings. A state-wide *bandh* was called, in which a sub-inspector of police was killed in Tirunelveli. Naidu was arrested, but after massive protest he was again released.

In the January 1980 parliamentary elections the AIADMK lost thirty-seven of its thirty-nine seats to an alliance between Congress and the DMK, which had received tacit support from the farmers' movement (Guruswamy 1985a: 382–83). Subsequently the AIADMK state government was dismissed by the central government. This brought a temporary lapse to the farmers' agitations. Maybe the VS was satisfied with the removal of the AIADMK from power. They had also been quite successful in their 'No-Tax' campaign and arrears on loans mounting in the institutions.[8]

In May–June of 1980 elections to the state assembly were held. Since VS was now an active force, it was courted by all the major political parties, and in a shrewd move M.G.R. and the AIADMK again promised to fulfil all their demands. In the ensuing elections, according to Balasubramaniam, 'The VS maintained what was officially a "neutral" stance but amounted to a *de facto* support for the AIADMK' (Balasubramaniam 1989: 117). The AIADMK was returned to power in the elections, and not unexpectedly, almost immediately M.G.R. began a crusade against the Vyasayigal Sangam. In a clever manoeuvre he reduced the electricity rates for small farmers[9] and wrote off their overdue loans, while arrears on loans taken out by the big farmers were deferred (Nadkarni 1987: 67).

M.G.R. accused the farmers' movement of being the champion of the rich, claiming that:

> the secret behind rich farmers' call for non-repayment of credit and their demand for the blanket writing-off of arrears was to see that the flow of institutional credit to small farmers was stopped so that they became dependent on the rich. The Chief Minister charged that the landowning class was making a determined bid to bring back the golden days of feudal land-

lordism (*The Hindu*, 26 December 1980, quoted in Nadkarni 1987: 67).

In the last week of December 1980 the state government launched its famous 'Operation Disconnection', which was a military operation to collect loans and dues from the farmers, and failing that, to disconnect electricity and auction off their property (Guruswamy 1985a: 384–85). The operation was coordinated with the arrest of a great number of movement leaders, and the police also started to attack public meetings of the Sangam with *lathis* (sticks), actions which severely humiliated the farmers. Later, in 1982, a similar campaign was launched on farmers with cooperative overdue loans and tax arrears. This came to be known as 'operation loan collection'.

The Sangam could not face the massive assaults. Many farmers were also tired of not being able to borrow afresh from their cooperatives, having refused to pay arrears as part of the protest action. All this worked against the strategy adopted by the farmers' movement. In the end the farmers' disruption of the workings of the Electricity Board and the financial institutions (cf. Piven and Cloward 1979: 24–26) had too many unforeseen consequences. During 1981 many farmers paid their dues, availing themselves of some government concessions (Balasubramaniam 1989: 117), and the VS had to 'turn a blind eye' to it, to avoid a public defeat (ibid.: 118).

On 5 September 1981, when the state government again raised the electricity rate from 16 to 24 Np per unit, the VS was almost defeated – it simply came out with a statement that it would contest the forthcoming *panchayat* elections which, however, were never held. In the meantime 'Operation Disconnection' continued. A last attempt at a big collective protest was met with the arrest of thousands of VS members. The protest was called off.

Meanwhile, the TN government tried to settle the matter with an agreement in which:

> the farmers were allowed to clear the arrears of electricity dues accumulated till then on the basis of a formula known as 'one plus one'. That is, farmers are required to pay the current month's electricity charges plus one month's due of arrears.

Accepting the agreement, farmers cleared their arrears over a period (Rajagopal and Anbazhagan 1989: 341).

According to many sources, Narayanaswami Naidu was not content with this settlement and appealed to the members of the association not to follow the agreement. This led to the first major split of the movement, since many farmers were tired of protesting and wanted to settle the matter once and for all. Thus, many of them left the organization and formed an independent association, with the same name, and with an office at Erode, headquarters of a district neighbouring Coimbatore. Later splits followed this pattern.[10]

Third Wave: Farmers' and Toilers' Party

On 20–22 May 1982, at a meeting with state and district representatives, it was decided to launch a political party. The 'Indian Farmers' and Toilers' Party' was officially announced in Madras on 7 July 1982, and its ten-point charter of demands was published in the magazine *Pachai Thundu,* edited by Dr M. R. Sivasamy from Coimbatore. The declared aim was to seek legitimacy and thus ensure protection from state government repression.

The strength of the new party was soon to be put to the test. In September 1982 there was a by-election for the Periakulam Lok Sabha seat. Out of nearly five lakh valid votes, the Farmers' Party secured only a meagre 10,261 votes, or around 2 per cent. In fact, the election was more than ever before a straight contest between the two 'Dravidian' political parties, the AIADMK and the DMK, which for the first time were contesting without any political alliances with national parties. The AIADMK won the day with a populist programme: a noon-day meal for all children, old age pensioners and destitutes; free distribution of toothpaste to the rural poor; and a promise of employment schemes – a programme and political practice that would prove successful for a long time to come.

Later on, in 1984, the Farmers' and Toilers' Party contested the assembly elections with a large number of candidates, but again with very meagre results. Guruswamy comments (1985a: 387):

The formation of the political party did not have the support of the peasants from several parts of Tamil Nadu. The differences were quite severe. What logically followed was a severe split in TNAA. ... The back of the organization at the state level stands completely broken today. Caste and other considerations have also raised their heads to weaken the peasant organization.

Perhaps Dr Sivasamy, the present leader of the party and movement, grasped the basic problem involved in the transformation of a movement into a party, when he was interviewed about the failure of the party in the mid-1980s: 'Farmers by and large did not accept it initially. You see, we had been telling them all along that they could belong to any political party and still be a part of VS for the farmers' cause' (Balasubramaniam 1989: 124).

Whatever the reasons for this political failure, further mobilization proved even more difficult when in 1985 the AIADMK decided to provide free electricity to small farmers who owned less than 5 acres of dry land or less than 2.5 acres of wet land. At the same time a flat-rate system was introduced for all other farmers, in which they had to pay Rs 50 per hp annually. The latter were asked to pay surcharges for late payments (so-called BPSC), from 1984 onwards. This policy, quite naturally, further weakened the movement, since a large part of its following consisted of middle peasants owning less than 5 acres of dry land. The flat-rate system, being very generous, was also seen by many farmers as a reason to stop agitating.

The Final Victory

By the mid-1980s the finances of the Tamil Nadu Electricity Board (TNEB) were in very bad shape and it pressed for the late payment surcharge.[11] This policy kept the various factions of the farmers' movement alive; members fasted in protest and petitioned the M.G.R. government to issue a government stay order in view of the 1981 agreement. After repeated pleas it is reported that M.G.R. was planning to waive the surcharges as a Pongal gift[12] to the farmers in January 1988, but he died in December the year before.

Before Dr Jayalalitha emerged as the new leader of the AIADMK party, President's rule was imposed and a new effort to improve the finances of the TNEB was made by the state government. This gave the farmers' movements a final lease of life. Representations were made to the state Governor, to high-level teams visiting the state, and finally to the Prime Minister of India himself. All this, however, seemed to be in vain. More than 30,000 pumpsets were reported as disconnected at this time (Rajagopal and Anbazhagan: 342) and the various farmers' movements desperately tried to get stay orders against disconnection by filing thousands of cases with the courts, in some cases going all the way to the Supreme Court.

Finally, before the assembly elections in January 1989, all opposition parties were being apprised by the Indian Farmers' and Toilers' Party about this problem. The response was overwhelming:

> Almost all the political parties included in their election manifestos the promise of a complete waiver of BPSC if they are voted to power. In fact the DMK was very critical of the Governor's rule and Congress (Indira) for not having done anything on this issue (ibid.: 342).

The DMK went further. In its election manifesto it promised that it would give free electricity to all farmers, a promise that was also kept after the DMK had gained state power.

A similar long drawn-out process of struggles by individual farmers took place with respect to loan arrears. Many cases seem to have been finally settled only in 1988 with the farmers paying accumulated interest rates in instalments.[13] Needless to say, these defaults for over a decade had landed the whole rural banking system in great difficulties.

Naidu had died in 1985, mourned by his many followers, who were by then already split into a number of warring factions. After his death the splits grew even worse, and despite its role in the campaign against electricity tariffs, the movement gradually lost its voice in Tamil politics, petering out as a powerful social movement. Naidu's successor, Dr Sivasamy, today presides over a party and an organization which has practically lost its following.[14]

How then could the farmers' movement fail in Tamil Nadu? The answer lies in the character of the issue around which it was formed, the strategy chosen, the type of political opportunity structure encountered, the results it achieved, its consequences for various classes of farmers involved, and ultimately for the whole system of groundwater-dependent farming.

Subsidy of Private Use of a Scarce Common Property Resource – a Perilous Policy

As is clear from the above account, the farmers' movement emerged as a response to the problems encountered in energized well irrigation: the price of electricity and the high cost of loans contracted for well construction and pumpsets. It was around this issue that collective action took place. All other issues were secondary to this. The way the leaders of the farmers' movement, as well as farmers at large, politicians, researchers and intellectuals generally understood and acted upon this issue was also narrowly focused on monetary aspects (Rajagopal and Anbazhagan 1989: 342).

This also seems to be the way the state government and politicians looked at the problem, that is, as a financial one. But why? The farmers already enjoyed favourable treatment from the Tamil Nadu Electricity Board (MIDS 1988: 247):

> Between 1961–62 and 1983–84, the average tariff for all categories increased by 5.4 times while it went up by 8.4 times for industry, 6.2 times for commercial, 2.2 times for domestic and 1.9 times for agricultural consumers. Agricultural tariffs in Tamilnadu are among the lowest in the country while industrial tariffs are among the highest. Supply of electricity for pumpsets is totally free for small farmers in Tamilnadu, while the tariff for larger farmers is very heavily subsidized. The agricultural tariff ... has been the single most important factor responsible for the poor financial performance of the TNEB.

Not surprisingly the return on fixed capital of the TNEB was negative after 1970 (ibid.: 246), and the Board was unable to extend the power capacity in the state.

Against this it was argued by the farmers' movement that since farmers in the wet, canal-irrigated areas, as well as farmers drawing water from public tanks, got their water practically for free, as a gift from the state,[15] why should not farmers relying on well irrigation also have it for free? If the Public Works Department could work at a loss in the general interest of the welfare of society, why couldn't the Electricity Board do so? It was the responsibility of the state government to find the necessary finance for it. Water was not generally seen as a scarce resource. In his recent book, *Economic Development of Tamil Nadu*, Perumalsamy (1990: 80) maintains that 40 per cent of the groundwater resource is untapped in the state, and that in adition to the nearly 1,200,000 wells now in use, another 250,000 wells would be needed to tap the full potential!

This way of looking at the whole problem may be criticized from many points of view. From an economic point of view it tends to overlook the viability of well irrigation, since so much of the overhead capital costs are hidden, born as it were by the state (Dhawan 1991), but the critical dimension is ecological: the increasingly disastrous consequences of private farming based on the virtual mining of a scarce natural resource. The individual use of a scarce common property resource is dangerous, because if all users follow their self-interest 'the aggregate demand for the resources [will exceed] ... its replenishment rate, leading to steeply rising marginal costs for the groups as a whole as supplies become more difficult to obtain' (Ellis 1992: 264–65).[16]

In this case, obviously, the process was fuelled by state subsidies, which could only worsen the problem:

> Both gross underpricing and flat power structure linked to horse power of the electric motor instead of actual consumption of electricity by pumpset are detrimental to the cause of groundwater stock conservation as these promote groundwater depletion in water-scarce regions (Dhawan 1991: 425).

Thus, the farmers' movement in Tamil Nadu obviously contributed to the development of a 'time-bomb', because success in the struggle for low tariffs or free electricity could only bring disaster. But why was it that the movement hardly sensed the impending danger?

Before the advent of the Industrial Revolution, well irrigation had been practised in India for centuries without any perceivable harm to nature or people. The population pressure was far less than it is today, and the cost of construction and of lifting the water with the traditional technology based on animal traction was so high that only small amounts of water were drawn. The need for a collective regulation of this common property resource, as in the case of village commons and reserve forests (cf. Blaikie *et al.* 1992) had simply not arisen.

Thus, until recently and without much reflection, groundwater-based irrigation was generally seen as one of the most effective ways of developing Indian agriculture, since much of the Green Revolution had taken place in regions where this mode of irrigation prevailed (Punjab, Haryana and Uttar Pradesh), and because, as is noted by Dhawan (1991: 425): 'experiences with the construction and operation of major surface irrigation have been rather unhappy, especially during the post-Independence era of Indian history.'

In Tamil Nadu the risk of depletion of groundwater resources has been perceived at times. For example, as mentioned above, Madduma Bandara (1977) had surveyed some areas in North Arcot in the early 1970s and reported the sinking groundwater level to government officials. Venkataramani (1974) wrote a book about the need for the further development of groundwater irrigation in Tamil Nadu despite the growing potential for new techniques in dry-land farming. He anticipated problems with a sinking groundwater table if water was wasted by individual users, but he still recommended further expansion coupled with government control through an agency that 'should be vested with powers to plan projects, deal with cases of malpractice and to ensure the optimum use of water' (Venkataramani 1974: 85). It is reported that a 'comprehensive legislation for groundwater legislation was proposed by the Tamilnadu government in 1977 but has not been proceeded with' (MIDS 1988: 182, n. 1).

Much later the book *Tamilnadu Economy* published by the Madras Institute of Development Studies (MIDS 1988: 245), clearly perceived the potential problem, i.e. the over-exploitation of the groundwater that was taking place:

> By 1985, more than a million pumpsets had been connected with power, the largest number in any state and accounting for 20 per cent of energized pumpsets in the country. Pumpset electrification, which peaked in 1965–75 has, however, decelerated

since then on account of constraints related to the availability of both power and groundwater. The large agricultural load in Tamilnadu has not been without its social and economic costs. It has led to over-exploitation of groundwater, stimulated by highly subsidized tariffs, resulting in a progressive lowering of the water table, particularly in the districts of Coimbatore, Periyar, Salem and North Arcot in which pumpsets are concentrated (MIDS 1988: 245).

There is a clear indication that the rapid growth in groundwater utilization, which has been a feature of the last three decades, cannot be sustained in the future. Groundwater is already being over-exploited with the drawal in many parts of the state being continually more than the recharge (MIDS 1988: 181).[17]

Based on this insight, the report pleads for a completely different solution, lamenting the fact that 'the horse may already be stolen':

In the context of the unplanned proliferation that has already taken place, efforts to regulate the sinking of wells in the future may largely amount to closing the stable after the horse has been stolen. The collective use of wells, either under a co-operative or under a 'nationalized' framework, remains the only solution in these circumstances. It may have to be considered, at least in the tracts most seriously affected by over-exploitation and falling water tables (MIDS 1988: 186).

The solution, according to this and later reports (see, for example, Moench 1992 and Rao 1993), lies not in the subsidizing of electricity, but in completely different ways of controlling the use of groundwater. Dhawan (1991: 428) summarizes a number of alternative frameworks within which this control may be exercised:[18]

1. development of well irrigation under government aegis;
2. development under cooperative ownership of wells;
3. development under community ownership of wells;
4. rise of market in sale/purchase of surplus well-water.

Moreover, as clearly described and analysed by Dhawan (probably the foremost expert on these questions in India), there is a need to understand the interplay between surface irrigation and groundwater irrigation in the sense that the former provides an important source of recharge of the groundwater resources. Rather than being used to its utmost, groundwater can basically only complement surface irrigation, for example, under drought conditions, when it may serve as the reserve it really is (Dhawan 1991).[19] Only when groundwater is constantly recharged can it serve as a permanent source of irrigation.

Madduma Bandara's and MIDS' reports, as well as those of others, should have served as a warning to the state government, the farmers' movement and others that something was wrong.

'United We Stand ... '

Right from its inception in 1970–72, the Tamilaga Vyvasayigal Sangam was accused of being led by powerful, capitalist landlords, while doing little for the bulk of the peasantry (see Nadkarni 1987: 61; The Progressive Agriculturists' Federation 1972). Whatever the start of the movement, however, as it continued to grow it came to involve the mass of peasants and farmers of nearly all classes and castes.

There is no mystery in this spread of the movement. The problems with well irrigation in dry areas, the issue that the Sangam developed around, concerned all farmers using wells. And as soon as it was clear that the farmers' protests were making an impact, many farmers were anxious to join – only those who joined got protection from the movement against disconnection of electricity supply. The problem with free-riders (cf. Olson 1965) was thus solved in a very concrete way. Only those who joined could refuse to pay the higher electricity tariff imposed by the government.

In its general propaganda the Sangam purported to represent the rural population as a whole, since its goals was to further the viability of agricultural production (Balasubramaniam 1989: 110). There is hardly any evidence of the participation of agricultural labourers and very poor peasants, but all available information shows that the farmers' movement with its clear definition of the issue at stake had no difficulty in mobilizing almost all other classes of farmers. In the late 1970s, K. Gopal Iyer studied a number of villages in Salem, Madurai, Trichy and Dharmapuri Districts, and found that there was massive participation by small farmers with less than 5 acres of dry land, as well as farmers with more land.[20] Likewise, Guruswamy found in his study of three villages in three different ecological settings in Coimbatore District that on average one-third of the farmers were organized by the farmers' association, representing middle peasants, rich peasants and bigger landlords, with the higher classes in the leading positions (Guruswamy 1985a: 445).[21]

When the movement grew also to include peasants and farmers in regions with more assured irrigation from tanks and canals, where the issue was more the remuneration of farming at large, the same pattern seems to have been repeated. The masses of the movement consisted of middle peasants, while the leadership came from the rich peasantry and capitalist farmers (cf. Iyer (n.d.); Guruswamy 1985a). Poor peasants joined to a lesser extent. This is also borne out by survey data which I collected in three dry and three canal-irrigated villages in Trichy District together with some colleagues in 1979–80 (Athreya *et al.* 1990). The middle peasantry had rates of membership which were higher than the average in both areas, while the membership of the poor peasants was low. In the dry area the capitalist farmers had the highest rates of membership, but since they are numerically weak as a category, this does not contradict the statement that the middle peasantry made up the mass base of the movement.

Thus, during the height of its mobilization and until the end of the 1970s the farmers' movement enjoyed a broad support among farmers, all having an interest in the issue most actively contested. Eventually, however, things came to work out quite differently. There was not only a ticking ecological time-bomb built into the issue central to the farmers' movement; there was also an explosive class element involved.

' ... Divided We Fall!'

Though all farmers reliant on wells suffer from lack of water, high investment costs (including loans), and the cost of running the pumps, some suffer more than others. Because they control less land, overhead capital costs for resource-weak poor and middle peasants tend to be higher per acre of production, than for farmers who own more land.[22] Therefore, poorer farmers generally have shallow wells and less powerful pumps compared to their more fortunate neighbours, who also sometimes escape public loan regulations about distance to nearest well, since they may have dug the wells without institutional credit. When too much water is drawn, obviously the poor farmers are the first to suffer from dry wells, and then, of course, the price of electricity becomes an academic issue. They risk going bankrupt anyway, and if unable to repay their debts, they also risk losing their land (cf. Rao 1993). There is at least some indication that this was happening in the dry areas of the state during the 1960s and 1970s (Ramachandran 1980). MIDS reports that 'affluent farmers, whose dependence on institutional credit has been much lower than that of smaller farmers, have escaped regulations based on distance criteria to which beneficiaries of institutional credit have been subject' (MIDS 1988: 181–82).

During most of the period of struggle, prices favoured the resource-rich farmers who had deep wells and powerful electric pumps. They could pump up all the water there was in their wells, while there was no or little water in neighbouring wells. It is quite clear that M.G.R. and the AIADMK understood this built-in contradiction between the various groups of farmers involved, when they started to give concessions to small farmers after gaining state power in 1980.

Even worse from the point of view of solidarity within the farmers' movement were the consequences of its strategy after 1977 not to repay institutional loans, since the consequences of this must have divided the movement for good. The great advance in institutional credit during the 1970s, which also covered small farmers and their needs, had made a large impact on agricultural production (cf. Athreya *et al.* 1990: ch. 7). Even if bigger farmers had bigger institutional loans and depended on these for their production, quite clearly the ones who had benefited the most from lower interest rates were the poorer farmers, since these loans had replaced previous borrowing from private moneylenders at very high interest rates.

As the loan arrears grew, institutions became increasingly unable to give new loans to farmers. In the beginning of the 1980s, institutional borrowing had come almost to a standstill because of massive defaults (cf. Athreya *et al.* 1990: 255–56). This tended to dry up the flow of cheap institutional credit. Yet, poorer farmers, strained by poverty and tempted by the promise of the farmers' movement, seemed to hold out. Harriss (1985: 83) reports from a field study in North Arcot villages:

> It is widely believed by people in the villages that if they hold out long enough, debts incurred as a result of failure to repay these loans will eventually be cancelled, as they have been in the past (after the state Legislative Assembly elections in 1980).

This meant that they either had to revert to a lower level of commoditization of their production (that is, depend more on family labour and on non-farm income for their reproduction), or resort to private and more usurious forms of credit. At the same time there are strong indications that eventually many rich peasants and capitalist farmers paid back their loans, availing themselves of the concessions granted by the government, and after that they could start borrowing anew. This must have been the final blow to the 'No-Tax' campaign of the farmers' movement.

To mobilize people is one thing, but to sustain a movement is another. Any producer-oriented farmers' movement worthy of the name must involve and represent the interests of the mass of farmers producing for the market. The way the VS understood and fought the issue of the economics of well irrigation and the virtual mining of groundwater that took place under its protection, in the end it seems, came to harm the interest of the resource-poor farmers in the movement.[23]

This character of the farmers' movement and its strategy also seems to have helped the state government to neutralize the movement by giving special favours to the small farmers. But, as we have seen above, the response and actions of the state were more varied than that. Therefore, a final clue to the understanding of the cause and consequences of the farmers' movement is the political system they encountered.

The Political Opportunity Structure: Competitive Populism

> Outbreaks of collective action cannot be derived from the level of deprivation that people suffer or from the disorganization of their societies; for these preconditions are more constant than the movements they supposedly cause. What varies widely from

time to time, and from place to place, are political opportunities, and social movements are more closely related to the
incentives they provide for collective action than to underlying
social or economic structures (Tarrow 1994: 81).

Clearly, it was a badly timed administrative decision on the part
of the Tamil Nadu government to increase the electricity tariff
(while farmers were suffering from severe drought conditions)
that sparked off the farmers' protests in 1970. In fact, similar
administrative decisions later ignited farmers' movements in
Punjab and Uttar Pradesh. The way the state government then
reacted with repression, further enhanced the mobilization power
of the movement. Subsequent negotiation and agreement brought
a measure of success to the farmers' agitation, which helped to
sustain it. A similar process took place in 1972.

Later on, state response in the form of negotiation, manipulation and repression reinforced the farmers' movement up to a
certain point, until its power was weakened by a clever political
strategy by M. G. Ramachandran, who pretended at first to yield to
its demands, and then split the farmers into two camps. Weakened
by this strategy and by its own policy of 'No-Tax', the Vyvasayigal
Sangam was finally broken by an escalation of state violence
which it found impossible to counteract. Yet, with all its disruptive
power broken, the farmers' movement still managed to achieve
its main aim – initially a lowering of electricity tariffs, then finally
getting it for free.

What kind of a political system is that – winning the battle and
the war, but in the end giving the bounty to the loser with severe
ecological and economic consequences?

One answer is given by Washbrook:

[A]n important feature of the contemporary Indian state is the
extent to which it intervenes in the marketplace, and deflects
these 'farmer' mobilizations into administrative channels before
they harden into expressions of overt class antagonism. Diffuse
resentments become directed at the government which mediates
them in such a way that the class forces giving rise to them are
obscured by the bureaucracy.

The possibilities of class politics in rural Tamil Nadu, then, have
been reduced by the extent to which capitalism has promoted
the almost infinite 'petit bourgeoisification' of interests in the

countryside and developed a managerial state to undertake reconciliation of the conflicts which it generates (Washbrook 1989: 219–20).

The Tamil Nadu government, especially under the leadership of M.G.R. and the AIADMK party, handled the farmers' movement with a mixture of repression, negotiation and political manipulation, which in the end led to the dissolution of the movement. But why give electricity for free, and why not rectify past mistakes by enforcing regulation of energized well irrigation?

The answer to this must be sought in the character of the political system in Tamil Nadu, especially as it developed after 1967, with the rise to prominence of a regional Tamil nationalist political party, the Dravida Munnetra Kazhagam (DMK) and its subsequent division into two rival factions. The unfolding features of this political setup have been characterized by S. Guhan and others in the following way:

> With the split in the DMK in 1972 and the ascendancy of the AIADMK in 1977, partisan politics between the two formations has become extremely intense, leading to a situation of competitive populism. (A striking illustration of this was the government announcement of free electricity to small farmers prior to the State Assembly elections in December 1984 and the retaliatory campaign promise from the DMK, its main contender, of free electricity supply to all farmers [parentheses used to mark a footnote to the quoted text].)
>
> The ruling party has had to improve upon subsidies and welfarist programmes initiated by its predecessor-in-power (subsequently its main opposition), with the latter using, or being used, by various pressure groups – farmers, government employees, teachers, traders, bus and cinema operators, the urban middle class, etc. – to advance claims and concessions from time to time. In this competitive and insecure environment, the political time horizon has shrunk at each stage to the on-coming election. Inevitably, long-term planning, a long-term fiscal policy based on equity, efficiency and economy, and fiscal discipline in general, have been the casualties (MIDS 1988: 333–34).

While this type of popular democracy, without stable class-based parties to balance the system, characterizes much of political decision-making in India, Tamil Nadu seems to represent an extreme version of it (cf. Price 1993: 502).[24]

This kind of politics together with a gradual decline of rational bureaucracy under successive AIADMK and DMK governments (cf. Washbrook 1989) have certainly created a favourable political structure for the kind of pressure generated by the farmers' movement. Its success, however, proved devastating not only to the farmers' movement itself but to the ecology and economy of Tamil Nadu state at large.

Conclusion: The Rise and Fall of the Farmers' Movement in Tamil Nadu

Summarizing on a concrete level, we can now see how the state policy of promoting and subsidizing energized well irrigation in the dry areas of Tamil Nadu laid the foundations of an impending ecological crisis. Without much foresight the farmers and their movement became victims of these circumstances.

The Tamilaga Vyvasayigal Sangam, the first 'modern' producer-oriented farmers' movement in India, emerged by a coincidence of two conditions. At the end of the 1960s a large number of farmers dependent on energized well irrigation (and heavily indebted on account of this) were affected by continuous drought conditions. The opportunity to act collectively came in 1970 when they faced a badly timed government decision to increase the price of electricity.

The farmers quickly appeared to gain a decisive power of disruption by refusing to pay electricity bills, an action that the Tamil Nadu Electricity Board was unprepared for. Attempts at disconnecting the power-lines to defaulting farmers were met with massive *gheraos*. A reaction was inevitable, however, but it took the state nearly ten years to mobilize a counter-force of severe repression. In the meantime the farmers had also started to refuse paying back institutional loans, which, however, proved to be self-defeating since after some time it meant that no fresh loans could be taken from these institutions. This in particular affected poorer farmers of the movement.

During the 1970s, Tamil politics became increasingly populist and personalized, especially after the emergence of M.G.R. on the political scene. With his shrewd manoeuvres, the farmers' movement was lured into supporting the AIADMK in the elections of 1977 and 1980, only to find that they were being tricked. 'Is it our fate to always agitate after putting someone else in power?' Narayanaswami Naidu is reported to have said in 1983 (Balasu-bramaniam 1989: 127), at the time when the political party was formed, a step that nonetheless finally broke the power of the movement.

In the end the farmers' movement lost out, unable to sustain its protests and mobilization. Paradoxically, however, when the movement started to founder their main demand was about to be satisfied. Like a Pongal gift, given by a benevolent landlord to his farm servants, in 1989 the farmers were finally granted free electricity by the DMK, one of the Tamil nationalist parties competing for the voters' favour. This was the real tragedy. It meant that farmers were free to pump. Free electricity added to the ecological crises now evident in many dry areas of Tamil Nadu and other southern states of India.

Unlike heroes in a Greek tragedy, who often sense the inner secret of their fate, there are not many indications that the leaders of the farmers' movement or other commentators ever seriously considered this ultimate consequence of their actions. Moreover, despite the presence of green movements and some awareness in the state bureaucracy, there seems to be low general public preparedness to save and rejuvenate this common property resource so badly needed for a sustainable life in the dry areas.

Acknowledgements

This research work has been undertaken with support from the University of Lund and SAREC. Special thanks goes to: Dr K. Gopal Iyer, Punjab University, Chandigarh, whose writings and personal communications I have drawn upon a great deal in this essay; Dr P.A. Guruswamy at Sri Ramakrishna Vidyalaya, Coimbatore, who generously shared with me his writings and personal experience of the movement in Coimbatore District; Dr M.R. Sivasamy, the present leader of what remains of the farmers' movement in Tamil Nadu, for many hours of discussions about the movement; Dr S. Janakarajan at the Madras Institute of Development Studies for sharing his information with me; R. Vidyasagar, Madras, for assisting in a number of interviews; and Göran Djurfeldt, Steen Folke, Barbara Harriss White, Stig Toft Madsen and Arni Sverrisson for useful comments on earlier drafts of this paper.

Notes

1.   For a general discussion of this dilemma in most economic systems, see Godelier (1972).

2.   I have used the following sources: The Progressive Agriculturists' Federation 1972; Alexander 1981a; 1981b; Moses 1982; Guruswamy 1985a; 1985b; Balasubramaniam 1986; 1989; Iyer (n.d.); Iyer and Vidyasagar 1986; Nadkarni 1987; Rajagopal and Anbazhagan 1989; Narayanan 1991; Janakarajan (n.d.). In addition to this I have followed the farmers' movement from its inception via press reports and interviews from 1970 onwards. My own fieldwork on the Tamil Nadu farmers' movement was conducted in 1979–80, 1989 and 1991.

3.   These new farmers' movements have in a short period of time become very important non-party political forces in Tamil Nadu, Punjab, Karnataka, Maharashtra and Uttar Pradesh (cf. Nadkarni 1987; Brass 1994; Lindberg 1994; 1995; 1997). They represent the upper and middle strata of the peasantry, as well as the emerging capitalist farmers, demanding better terms of production, cheaper inputs and higher output prices.

4.   This figure was given by Dr K. Gopal Iyer at the Workshop on 'The New Farmers' Movements in India in 1980s and 1990s' in New Delhi, 12–14 March 1993, organized by the Indian Council of Social Science Research (ICSSR) and the *Journal of Peasant Studies*.

5.   A *taluk* is a subdivision of a district.

6.   According to Alexander (1981a: 131), the origin lay in an attempt to get irrigation facilities extended to two villages in this area.

7.   There is some evidence that the state government was under pressure to raise tariffs: 'The Tamil Nadu government had to raise the rate of the rural power tariff from 10.8 to 12 paise from June 1972 in deference to the advice the Centre has given to states to tap the agricultural sector for mobilizing resources and with a view to making up for the quantum of loss sustained by the Electricity Board. Further the Rural Electrification Corporation of India has insisted on a return of at least 11 per cent on investment of Power Boards for being eligible for assistance and the Corporation had further made it clear that only after the rate was increased to 12 paise could the loan facility be extended' (The Progressive Agriculturists' Federation 1972: 8).

8. For example, in the Coimbatore Central Cooperative Bank arrears on short-term loans rose from 11 per cent in 1976–77 to 74 per cent in 1979–80 (Guruswamy 1985a: 379–80).

9. Defined as those farmers having less than 2.5 acres of wet land or 5 acres of dry land.

10. This information is based on my interviews with members and leaders of the Tamilnadu Farmers' Association in Erode, 21 March 1989. They had taken the same name as the mother organization, because it was not a name registered with the government. VS was still registered as the Coimbatore District Agricultural Association. When the movement split further, a number of associations came up with identical names in different regions.

11. This section is mainly based on the article by Rajagopal and Anbazhagan (1989).

12. A Pongal gift is given by a landlord to his farm servant at the time of the harvest festival (Pongal) in January.

13. Information from Dr M. R. Sivasamy (interview 13 March 1989).

14. According to Dr M. R. Sivasamy, there were in 1989 thirteen such splinter organizations (interview 13 March 1989).

15. Cf. the discussion of this in Athreya *et al.* (1990: 61 ff.).

16. This is the mechanism involved in what economists and other social scientists call 'the Prisoners' Dilemma', cf. Wade (1988).

17. For a similar report on falling groundwater tables due to over-exploitation in neighbouring Karnataka, see Folke (1995: 16–17).

18. For a general discussion of the problems involved when individuals use a scarce common property resource like groundwater, see Ellis (1992: 262–71).

19. Excessive use of groundwater for agricultural production may also endanger access to drinking water in many areas.

20. These facts were presented by Dr K. Gopal Iyer at the Workshop on 'The New Farmers' Movements in India in 1980s and 1990s' in New Delhi, 12–14 March 1993, organized by ICSSR and the *Journal of Peasant Studies.*

21. Guruswamy found that '[a]gain the participation was found to be closely related to the class position of the peasants. Thus, higher class position was strongly associated with higher participation in the movements and vice-versa' (1985a: 447). It is not quite clear, however, whether this means that middle peasants were less active than other classes.

22. This is so despite the possibility of sharing wells, and/or selling water to a neighbour in need of water.

23. Similarly, not fully understanding the class contradictions involved, the farmers' movement had difficulty in defending the farmer against merchant exploitation. This is illustrated by VS agitation against the Tirupur Cotton Market in 1980. Though the farmers' movement tried to get better state regulation and reduced commission rates, it was in the end unable to enforce its demands. This was partly because many traders, as landowners, were members of the farmers' union, and the protests were weakened by this fact, while the merchants, on their part, had no such compromises in mind. Cf. Harriss (1980, 1981a; 1981b), and Guruswamy (1985b).

24. This is not to say that the so-called populist policies of the AIADMK-led government in Tamil Nadu are only negative. On the contrary, a modicum of welfare has actually been provided by this state over the past years, such as midday meal schemes, programmes for immunization and primary health care, access to basic necessities through 'fair-price' shops, improved water supply through handpumps and drinking water wells, access to subsidized housing, etc. (cf. Djurfeldt *et al.* 1997).

References

Alexander, K.C. (1981a) *Peasant Organizations in South India*, New Delhi: Indian Social Institute.

—— (1981b) 'The Dynamics of Peasant Organisations in South India', *Social Action*, vol. 31, no. 1, pp. 35–50.

Athreya, Venkatesh, Göran Djurfeldt and Staffan Lindberg (1990) *Barriers Broken. Production Relations and Agrarian Change in Tamil Nadu*, New Delhi: Sage Publications.

Balasubramaniam, A.V. (1986) 'Tamil Nadu Farmers at the Crossroads: A Note on the Recent Formation of the "Indian Farmers' and Toilers' Party"'. In Sunil Sahasrabudhey (ed.), *The Peasant Movement Today*, New Delhi: Ashish Publishing House, pp. 40–54.

—— (1989) 'A Report on the Peasant Movement in Tamilnadu 1966–1984'. In Sunil Sahasrabudhey (ed.), *Peasant Movement in Modern India*, Allahabad: Chugh Publications, pp. 110–44.

Blaikie, Piers, John Harriss and Adam Pain (1992) 'The Management and Use of Common-Property Resources in Tamil Nadu, India'. In Daniel W. Bromley (ed.), *Making the Commons Work*, San Francisco: ICS Press, pp. 247–64.

Brass, Tom (ed.) (1994) Special Issue on New Farmers' Movements in India, *The Journal of Peasant Studies*, vol. 21, nos 3–4.

Dhawan, B.D. (1991) 'Developing Groundwater Resources. Merits and Demerits', *Economic and Political Weekly*, vol. 26, no. 8, pp. 425–29.

Djurfeldt, Göran, Staffan Lindberg and A. Rajagopal (1997) 'Coming back to Thaiyur – Health and Medicine in a Twenty-five Years' Perspective'. In J. Breman, P. Kloos and A. Saith (eds), *The Village in Asia Revisited*, Delhi: Oxford University Press, pp. 175–198.

Ellis, Frank (1992) *Agricultural Policies in Developing Countries*, Cambridge: Cambridge University Press.

Folke, Steen (1995) 'Conflicts over Natural Resources in South India – in a Political Economy Perspective', Paper to the Third Conference of the Nordic Association for South Asian Studies, Oslo, Norway, 18–22 May.

Godelier, Maurice (1972) *Rationality and Irrationality in Economics*, London: New Left Books.

Guruswamy, P.A. (1985a) 'Agrarian Structure and Peasant Movements in Coimbatore District', Unpublished Ph D Panjab University, Chandigarh.

—— (1985b) 'Tirupur Cotton Growers' Agitations, 1979–80: A Brief Case Study', *Social Action*, vol. 35, no. 1, Jan–March, pp. 39–53.

Hardin, Garret (1968) 'The Tragedy of the Commons', *Science*, vol. 162, pp. 1243–48.

Harriss, Barbara (1980) 'Inaction, Interaction and Action – Regulated Agricultural Markets in Tamilnadu', *Social Scientist*, vol. 9, no. 4, November, pp. 96–137.

—— (1981a) 'Agricultural Mercantile Politics and Policy: A Case Study of Tamil Nadu', *Economic and Political Weekly*, vol. 16, nos 10–12, annual number, pp. 441–58.

—— (1981b) *State and Market. A Report to ESCOR of the Overseas Development Administration of the U.K. Government on State Intervention in Exchange in a Dry Region of South India*, London: Overseas Development Institute.

Harriss, John (1982): *Capitalism and Peasant Farming. Agrarian Structure and Ideology in Northern Tamil Nadu*, Bombay: Oxford University Press.

—— (1985) 'What Happened to the Green Revolution in South India? Economic Trends, Household Mobility and the Politics of an "Awkward Class"', University of East Anglia, School of Development Studies, Discussion Paper No. 175.

Iyer, K. Gopal (n.d.) 'Farmers' Movement in Tamil Nadu and Punjab: A Comparative Study', Chandigarh: Panjab University, unpublished manuscript.

—— and R. Vidyasagar (1986) 'Agrarian Studies in Tamilnadu'. In A.R. Desai (ed.), *Agrarian Struggles after Independence*, Delhi: Oxford University Press, pp. 508–537.

Janakarajan, S. (n.d.) 'Agrarian Relations and Agrarian Movements in Tamil Nadu – a Comparative Study of Thanjavur and Coimbatore Districts during the Post Independence Period'. Synopsis for the application of PhD Fellowship, Madras Institute of Development Studies, Madras.

Lindberg, Staffan (1994) 'New Farmers' Movements in India as Structural Response and Collective Identity Formation: The Cases of Shetkari Sanghatana and the BKU', *The Journal of Peasant Studies*, vol. 21, Nos. 3–4, pp. 95–125.

—— (1995) 'Farmers' Movements and Cultural Nationalism in India – an Ambiguous Relationship', *Theory and Society*, vol. 24, no. 6, pp. 837–68.

—— (1997) 'Farmers' Movements and Agricultural Development in India'. In Staffan Lindberg and Arni Sverrisson (eds), *Social Movements in Development. The Challenge of Globalization and Democratization*, London: Macmillan, pp. 101–25.

Madduma Bandara, C.M. (1977) 'Hydrological Consequences of Agrarian Change'. In B. H. Farmer (ed.), *Green Revolution? Technology and Change in Rice-growing Areas of Tamil Nadu and Sri Lanka*, London: Macmillan, pp. 323–39.

MIDS (Madras Institute of Development Studies) (1988) *Tamilnadu Economy. Performance and Issues*, New Delhi: Oxford & IBH Publishing Co. Pvt. Ltd.

Moench, Marcus H. (1992) 'Chasing the Watertable. Equity and Sustainability in Groundwater Management', *Economic and Political Weekly*, vol. 27, nos 51 and 52, pp. A:171–77.

Moses, Brindavan C. (1982) 'Tamil Nadu: Verdict at Periakulam', *Economic and Political Weekly*, vol. 17, no. 41, pp. 1643–44.

Nadkarni, M.V. (1987) *Farmers' Movements in India*, New Delhi: Allied Publishers Private Limited.

Narayanan, K. Badri (1991): 'Peasant Movement and Agrarian Reforms in Tamil Nadu 1940–1989', *The Indian Journal of Labour Economics*, vol. 34, no. 2, pp. 412–20.

Olson, Mancur (1965) *The Logic of Collective Action. Public Goods and the Theory of Groups*, Cambridge, Mass.: Harvard University Press.

Perumalsamy, S. (1990) *Economic Development of Tamil Nadu*, New Delhi: S. Chand & Company Ltd.

Piven, Frances Fox and Richard A. Cloward (1979) *Poor People's Movements. Why They Succeed, How They Fail*, New York: Vintage Books.

Price, Pamela (1993) 'Democracy and Ethnic Conflict in India', *Asian Survey*, vol. 33, no. 5, pp. 493–506.

The Progressive Agriculturists' Federation (1972) *Facts about 'Farmers' Agitation' in Tamil Nadu*, Madras: Murasoli Achagam.

Rajagopal, A. and P. Anbazhagan (1989) 'Problems of Pumpset-Farmers in Tamil Nadu', *Economic and Political Weekly*, vol. 24, no. 7, pp. 341–42.

Ramachandran, V.K. (1980) 'Agricultural Labour in the Working Population of Tamilnadu', *Bulletin*, Madras Institute of Development Studies, Seminar Series, March.

Rao, D.S.K. (1993) 'Groundwater Overexploitation through Borehole Technology', *Economic and Political Weekly*, vol. 28, no. 52, pp. A: 129–34.

Statistical Handbook of Tamilnadu 1977, Madras: Department of Statistics.

Tarrow, Sidney (1994) *The Power in Movement. Social Movements, Collective Action and Politics*, Cambridge: Cambridge University Press.

Venkataramani, G. (1974) *Minor Irrigation in Tamilnadu*, Madras: Sangam Publishers, Madras Institute of Development Studies, Publication 8.

Wade, Robert (1988) 'The Management of Irrigation Systems: How to Evoke Trust and Avoid Prisoners' Dilemma?', *World Development*, vol. 16, no. 4, pp. 489–500.

Washbrook, D.A. (1989) 'Caste, Class and Dominance in Modern Tamil Nadu. Non-Brahminism, Dravidianism and Tamil Nationalism'. In Francine R. Frankel and M.S.A. Rao (eds), *Dominance and State Power in Modern India. Decline of Social Order*, Delhi: Oxford University Press, vol. 1, pp. 204–64.

11 | Nature, State and Market : Implementing International Regimes in India

Ronald Herring

> Our sacrifice to the cause of the tiger was a joke. The Forest Department could not take care of us, the animals or the forest ... They left the tiger in the hands of the poacher and left us in the hands of God. (Jagan, *Sarpanch* of Kailashpuri, a village removed from Ranthambore National Park, Rajasthan).

Introduction: The Nature Problem

Environmental protection is not a matter of better 'education' or better administration – though both are good ideas. Rather, serious protection of what is left of natural systems confronts contradictory interests – from global to local levels. At each level, authoritative resolution of conflicting interests requires governance. These contradictions among interests go to the core of political economy – questions of property rights, structures of authority and the telos of economic systems. As India goes through fundamental shifts in its developmental strategy in line with the 'Washington consensus' of greater allocative authority for markets, protection of nature[1] competes with new preferences at the level of development strategy.

The origin of state power in a normative sense is market failure. We expect states to do things markets cannot do – to provide certain public goods and to deal with the externalities of individual pursuit of interests, for example. Could states not provide these functions, it would be hard normatively to justify their extraordinary burdens on society. One special relationship among nature, state and markets is that both market failure and market success prove deleterious for ecological systems. Intervention in the name of market failure then presupposes meta-preferences different from those expressed behaviourally by individuals dealing with the commoditized pieces of natural systems.

Nature policy then almost always involves a struggle with the market; regulatory logic limiting market dynamics has been a mainstay of environmental protection. As the dynamics of natural systems refuse to respect the arbitrary boundaries of human administration, international regimes have begun to address problems considered global in scope. In international negotiations addressed to global commons issues, nation-states represent themselves as agents of societies and as holders of rights in nature. Both claims are typically problematic. States' capacity to assume such obligations is a function of the tenuous and contested nature of their domestic claims – a failure of governance.

This chapter will consider three elements of the international nature regime: the Convention on International Trade in Endangered Species; the International Tropical Timber Agreement; and the World Heritage Convention. More comprehensive treaties on biodiversity and climate change are too young to assess. It provides a snapshot of dynamics before liberalization of economic policy became the meta-agenda of Indian development strategy during the Narasimha Rao regime of 1991–96. It is too early to tell what liberalization will mean for India's quite strict *de jure* constraining of markets in nature. A major argument will be that there is a fundamental contradiction between markets and preservation at India's stage of development; how that contradiction will play out is beyond prediction.

Nature, Markets and Property: The Great Transformation

The fundamental political–economic project for societies is sorting out rules for using and distributing scarce things in the face of conflicting interests. Human interests in nature are most evident in a nature appropriated for human use; appropriated nature generates livelihoods and use values, as conceptualized in both mainstream and Marxian economic logic. Appropriation and alteration of nature for purposes of increasing human wealth and welfare are not entirely modern projects,[2] though modern means have enhanced the scope for intervention just as prior develop-mental successes have increased the fragility of systems.

A species-level learning process – the discovery of hidden interconnectedness, or ecology – has dramatically expanded not only the scale over which control of environmental processes must proceed, but the breadth of implications for economic life. To the extent that nature is perceived as 'abundant' or dangerous – as through most of human history – rigorous regimes for its protection are subjectively unnecessary. With globalization of en-vironmental understanding and policy, the definition of public goods has moved even further from the proximate users of nature – exacerbating the problem of governance.

Political conflicts over nature then begin with a definition of the telos of human intervention and control: preservation, con-servation or accumulation. The collective objective (and increasingly subjective) human interest in nature *for itself* posits imperatives of ecological integrity as a public good, threatened by depletion, independent of use values. This perception introduces a conflict between a conservationist agenda and a preservationist agenda. Internationally, the latter has been identified with rich nations, whereas the public good itself (less degraded nature) is spatially concentrated in poorer nations. Regime development at the inter-national level increasingly asserts the reality of a global [ecological] public good, and ideational commitment to its preservation. Addressing global environmental degradation has meant soft regimes around the edges of hard property rights – peripheral strands of the 'bundle of rights' we call ownership (Baden-Powell 1892: vol. I, p. 216, *passim*; Herring 1983: ch. 2).

'Defensive reactions' as a theme of underclass political behaviour derives from unresolved conflicts in what Karl Polanyi called 'the great transformation.' Polanyi noted (1957: 71):

> But land and labor are no other than the human beings them-selves of which every society consists and the natural surroundings in which it exists. To include them in the market mechanism is to subordinate the substance of society to the laws of the market.

When Polanyi conceptualized the commoditization of nature a central element in the 'great transformation' to market society, he had in mind a process much broader than mere enclosures of the classic form: 'What we call land is an element of nature inextricably interwoven with man's institutions. To isolate it and form a market out of it was perhaps the weirdest of all undertakings of our ancestors' (ibid.: 178). In his formulation, pre-market economic relations, norms and outcomes were 'embedded' or 'submerged' in social relations generally; the extraction and elevation of market-driven dynamics from their social mooring produce significant social conflicts and centrally involve the state (compare Neale 1988). There is nothing 'natural' about the market as arbiter of allocative decisions; challenges to market allocative rules evoked the use rights established by custom and common law as bases for opposition (e.g. K. S. Singh 1986; R. Guha 1989). Regulation represents the culmination of this 'double movement'.

The making of market society entails the long historical process of collapsing differentiated use rights into a system of ownership in which individual private property rights are generally bounded only by the prior claims of the state.[3] Individuated and state-guaranteed property rights almost certainly increase the probability that land will be 'developed', as Douglass North (1990) argues persuasively. Changes in property relations in the direction of greater conduciveness to 'development' simultaneously increase the likelihood of resistance from losers.

The effect of colonial law in the Indian subcontinent was to simplify, collapse and locate concretely the bundle of rights in land with the objective of creating property rights in the market sense (e.g. Logan 1887: vol. I, 670–696; Neale 1988). Simultaneously, vast tracts were 'reserved' for the state on the claim that unused 'waste' land had traditionally been 'the property of the state' (Baden-Powell 1892: vol. I, p. 236). Whether this transformation represents a qualitative shift or merely a linear projection of pre-colonial policy is a matter of dispute, given the weakness of pre-colonial environmental historiography (Guha 1995). But the transformation was extensive; as the use rights of subordinate strata inhabiting newly protected nature were nominally curtailed, a complex game of bargaining, cat-and-mouse evasion and outright confrontation resulted. Defensive reactions were set in motion by attempts of the state to claim and manage terrains previously defined by local usage (eg. R. Guha 1985, 1989; K. S. Singh 1986; Omvedt 1987).

Though internally disputed in vigorous policy debates within the colonial state (cf. Tucker 1984; Presler 1987), the marriage of revenue/developmental imperatives (timbering, plantations, mining) with an emerging scientific discourse of forest management intensified confrontation with local societies' property claims. This conflict continues, perhaps most sharply, in the resistance of upstream forest communities to the state's claim to develop hydroelectric and irrigation potential through dam construction (CSE 1986: 99–120; S. Kothari 1995a). The scope for conflict is large; the Forest Department alone administers 23 per cent of the Indian surface area (Madsen 1995: 3).

Predominance of the state in claiming property rights is buttressed by the 'tragedy of the commons', a simple and influential model that explained why maximization of individual interests in resource use could result in catastrophe. The logic of that metaphor has been used by states as legitimation for exercising control of nature in opposition to local institutional mechanisms. States are supposed to solve failures of collective action, just as they are to solve more classic forms of market failure. The argument for state authority over nature hinges on the difficulty in spontaneous provision of public goods of either conservation or preservation. It is true that our models of collective action are ambiguous even at the level of theory.[4] Nevertheless, dynamics in natural systems are the worst-case scenario for collective action since contested notions of the public good prevail; the numbers of actors are very large; monitoring is difficult; and the benefits of protection to individuals are tenuous, indirect and/or distant in time and space. The real tragedy of the *natural* commons is that the same logic of interests, short-time horizons and instrumental values that make local commons protection problematic applies, often *a fortiori*, to states themselves.

Market Solutions

One solution to the original tragedy-of-the-commons model was commoditized land as private property.[5] No rational shepherd would degrade his or her own land by overgrazing; to do so would decrease the value of the commodity. Therefore the division of common pasture into individually owned plots could be expected to avert destruction of a common resource (cf. Ostrom 1986: 8).

Market solutions to environmental problems are currently popular, and in the case of patented biota they may be ecologically friendly. But in general, individuated property rights are useful only as long as the level of exploitation does not measurably degrade the resource any further than the value of the short-term benefits of exploitation in the perception of a knowledgeable and rational rights holder. Conservation will, even in the best-case scenario, be limited to the very loose constraint that degradation does not interfere with market rationality. Market rationality, in turn, will only incidentally coincide with ecological rationality (cf. Singh 1976; Desai 1987; Nadkarni 1987). Ecosystems are large and complex; individually rational behaviours (diversion of surface water, draining of wetlands, clearing of forests, etc.) still offer the likelihood of counter-finality in a context that is extra-local and extended in time. As importantly, human lives are short in terms of the evolution of ecosystems; it is difficult to imagine a fit between short-term interests and intergenerational 'rationality', or justice, being generated by the market (Nadkarni 1987: 360–61 and *passim*).

It is for this reason that states make strong claims to authority over nature. At its core, these claims contest the market *as arbiter of value*, as Polanyi asserted. In markets, value is measured in exchange. This notion carries over in the dominant policy language of 'common property resources'; the natural is valuable insofar as it constitutes a resource, something to be exploited. This instrumental view of nature in market economics is shared by the Marxian tradition.[6] When Blaikie and Brookfield (1987: 1–7) discuss land 'degradation' in their classic text, they use the Latin etymology of 'rank', as though assigning ranks to capacities of the physical surface of the planet were unproblematic; they (knowingly) reduce 'land' to soil.[7] Reductionism is the core of developmental discourse on nature: forests become trees, or timber, or just biomass.

This instrumental and utilitarian view of nature is contested by the science of ecology. If ecology means anything, it is the irreducible interdependence of elements within systems. An ecological frame for state involvement necessarily presupposes an alternative value frame. The primary value is to preserve the integrity of nature itself: the common bio-physical systems that support and depend on a full complement of species and not merely our own (Herring 1991). As Blaikie and Brookfield (1987) understand, one person's environmental degradation is another's bonanza; drained wetlands turn into meadows over time, which is good for agriculturalists, but bad for ecological functions. Richard Eaton's (1990, 1993) study of the expanding frontier of cultivation at the expense of wetland forests in Bengal *c.* 1200–1760 illustrates this process: Islamic 'saint-entrepreneurs' made use of symbolic appeals, underwritten by the space provided by superior authorities, to mobilize for collective action, which achieved some collective good for participants (additional agricultural land) but simultaneously destroyed the mangrove wetlands in a piece-meal fashion at the margins. In terms of 'development' of 'natural resources,' destruction of the Sundarbans was a success.

Yet even in developmental logic, the notion of limits proved irresistible: the same colonial government that encouraged forest clearing in the Sundarbans later recognized that resources were not infinite; conservation was rational policy. The political argument for conservation depends on the commercial value of that which is to be conserved; conservation law in colonial India was generated by the imperatives of long-term access to forest products for export, military uses and construction of rail nets (e.g. R. Guha, 1989: 37–61).

Preservation raises a higher hurdle: the integrity of systems con-stitutes the public good, not simply the continued stream of use values to be conserved. The politics of preservation must be rooted in more tenuous values of aesthetics, risk, or species ethics (derived from the reality of species mastery). Responding collectively to the meta-commons dilemma requires recognition of interests that are temporally removed, collective in the broadest sense (species-wide), and embedded in the uncertainty of a technical discourse that can be evaluated only by a tiny elite.

The tension between an instrumentalist view of nature and an idealist argument for the value of nature *per se* shadows the tension between the commoditization of market society and pre-market or extra-market sources of values. When value is measured by use, priced in markets, nature depends for its preservation on extra-market valuation in the 'moral-economy'[8] tradition. In the absence of market power, preservationist values can become actualized only through a political process that bounds and limits markets. A common means of attaining this end is to remove elements of nature from the market in favour of management as de facto or de jure state property.

Real States and Meta-Commons Dilemmas

If rational individuals operating through markets are no solution to nature's problems, collective authority of some form wins almost by default. This has been recognized for centuries: both Thomas Hobbes and the earlier Indian political philosopher Kautilya[9] proposed a powerful state – Hobbes's Leviathan – which could impose its will on subjects for their own (common) good. As early as the *Laws of Manu*, it was recognized in Indic political thought that local claims overlap; an ecological understanding makes it clear that even effectively regulated village commons present needs for broader systems of authority – such as a state. This legitimation is commonly used to support the privileging of state property claims over those of individuals or communities for conservation or preservation.

State-centric developmental processes accentuated the critical proprietary role of the state (S. Kothari 1995a, 1995b). State-led economic change in India was accelerated by proprietary claims of colonial rule but was presaged by *vedic, puranic* and state-craft literature of India long before colonial rule (Raghunandan 1987: 545). Much of the debate at the intellectual and regime level (e.g. Guha 1990) centred on how much can be assumed about local capacity to manage local commons dilemmas, to prevent their escalation to tragedy. The dominant understanding for a very long time has been that 'villages' (and 'villagers') need Leviathan.[10]

The problem with the Leviathan solution in political theory is the absence of a guarantee, or even a likelihood, that the state will not behave in the same self-seeking, socially disregarding manner as individuals (cf. Ostrom 1986). The developmentalist state in particular derives its legitimacy from leveraging growth, producing many of the same motives, instrumentalities and outcomes of the private owner but on a vast scale. The assumption in the market-failure justification for a strong state is that will and implementation are joined in one (resolute) actor. Yet states of the subcontinental region are indeed (selectively) 'soft' (in Gunnar Myrdal's [1968] memorable formulation). Real states demonstrate not only the permeability and bureaucratic pathologies which generate 'softness', but also both vertical and horizontal incoherence; as lower levels of the state ramify into society, they become less and less distinguishable *from* society, much as blood vessels ramify into capillaries and finally disappear into tissue. Neither political will at the top, nor transmission capacity through the system, can be assumed. More importantly, real implementation must take place on the ground, where the local state exhibits the permeability, incapacity and embeddedness characteristics in extreme form.

The permeability of state to powerful interests bent on exploitation or evasion of regulation is a pervasive phenomenon in South Asia and the source of significant environmental degradation (e.g. CSE 1986: 353–82). Even assuming relative autonomy and capacity, structural pressures for taxation revenue and hard currency earnings have abetted environmental degradation throughout the subcontinent (e.g. Agarwal 1985: 363–66). But most importantly, the state is not a stable configuration; exclusion and control evoke the politics of opposition and evasion, reducing state capacity. Residuals of pre-transformation systems of property – its contested nature in particular – leave compromised the state's establishment of its own property rights in nature.

Political authority over nature in India is segmented. The political system is federal, weakening the centre's control of policy. The form of federalism itself is under continuous renegotiation – particularly in environmental matters. The centre has had an environmental ministry only since 1985; centre–state negotiations of environmental policy are often tense and indecisive. Most issues of environmental importance – water, land, forests, fisheries, public health, agriculture, wildlife – were constitutionally subjects reserved to the states before recent legislation added some to the concurrent list of joint centre–state responsibility. The Ministry of Environment and Forests' report for the World Bank on *Environmental Action Programmes* (Govt of India 1992b: 24) noted consistent reluctance in the states to strengthen their environmental protection capacity, even when funds were designated for same. Instability of governments at the centre exacerbates the weakness of segmented authority; governments in Delhi reserve their political capital for issues of great urgency, including survival.[11]

Because of these political conditions, state as a solution to market failure is problematic. Theoretically possible solutions present severe difficulties in the concrete social settings of the region (extraordinary levels of destitution, state incapacity) particularly because one must distinguish 'natural resources' from ecological systems. The politics of the environment in the region represent variable levels of intensity, but it is clear that the state in general cannot play the Leviathan role effectively. Indeed, having the state weigh in on the side of preservation may prove counter-productive, so deeply is it compromised in local political perceptions. In the case of 'Silent Valley' in South India, the centre's intervention on the side of preservation helped to shift political dynamics in the direction of local people vs. the state, periphery vs. centre and, in a curious twist, Bharat vs. India (Herring 1991).

If ecological values are difficult to sustain in states, they are equally rare in mass publics. The perception, policy and politics of conservation of a usable resource as a collective good is not nearly as problematic as that of preservation of ecosystems as a public good independent of their utility as resources. This is the classic Pinchot–Muir controversy of American historical experience; it represents an irreducible struggle between meaning systems privileging conservation in opposition to those centred on preservation, or the conflict between social ecology and 'deep' ecology (Herring 1991). At the level of politics, the 'ecological consciousness' attributed to environmental movements in India has arguably remained more in the realm of defensive reactions than in the realm of recognition of ecological imperatives as collective goods (cf. Raghunandan 1987; Baviskar 1993). Even a state seeking support for ecological values would be hard-pressed to find a stable and powerful constituency.

But governments can hardly go to international conferences and plead complexity and incapacity; international negotiations are displays of stateness. International treaties assume real state capacity on the ground. I shall discuss three international treaties to demonstrate the reasons for fragility in the state's claim to authority over nature. These treaties are linked through natural resource issues in which administrative capacity in a narrow technical sense is limited and local populations have strong normative and political claims against enforcement.

Rigging the Market for Internationally Traded Species[12]

The Convention on International Trade in Endangered Species of Flora and Fauna (CITES) addresses the global biodiversity interest by imposing constraints on trade. It applies to those discrete pieces of nature already commoditized through international channels of supply and demand. The underlying assumption is that markets are a threat to the continued existence of particular species listed in schedules which are updated as new information becomes available.

India has been especially important in the operation of CITES, ratifying the treaty early (20 July 1976) and being elected chairman of the standing committee for an unprecedented three consecutive terms, beginning in 1983 (Singh, S. 1986: 199). India's implementation of CITES is stricter than the international regime. Primary mechanisms are the Wildlife (Protection) Act of 1972, the Customs Act of 1962 and the Import–Export Policy of 1993. The Director of Wildlife Conservation is the Management Authority. Wildlife was moved from the State List to the Concurrent List by constitutional amendment in 1976, giving the Centre more control. Chapter XVI of the Import–Export Policy (Govt of India 1993), under the Foreign Trade (Development and Regulation) Act of

1992, prohibits exports of 'all forms of wildlife including parts and products' (p. 74). Wildlife is defined as 'all plants and animals'. India's CITES Annual Report of 1993 (p. 1) notes: 'With the domestic trade in wild animals already banned and virtually a complete ban of export of all forms of wildlife, there is hardly any room left for unscrupulous elements to export wildlife … in the garb of permissible items.' The legal framework is unusually comprehensive.

Legal traffic in biota is quite limited in India. Import of both animals and plants is allowed on recommendation of the Chief Wildlife Warden of a state government, subject to the provisions of CITES. Permission is essentially limited to zoological or scientific purposes. India is not a major importer; in 1993 the total number of animals imported, mostly for zoos, was seventy-one. Imports of flora are likewise minimal. Legal exports of animals have for years been very small as well, mostly to zoos.

International and domestic discourse around endangered species has exhibited a decidedly faunal bias. Exports of flora have received far less attention and are administratively more difficult. India's CITES-certified exports of flora are increasing rapidly; in 1993, the listing of exports took thirty-seven pages of the Annual Report. All exports were certified 'cultivated', and without exception for purposes of trade (as opposed to scientific uses). This increase seems to be evidence both of increased international trade in exotic plants and increased awareness of CITES regulations. Not all 'cultivated' certifications are authentic, but traders are increasingly aware that they must have them. Only a Legal Procurement Certificate (or No-Objection Certificate) is required, obtained from Divisional Forest Officers (junior officials) who find them difficult to verify. Distinguishing species and origins of plants is even more demanding than for animals.

Threats to endangered flora from trade seems to be growing but is little researched, certainly in comparison to the glamorous mega-fauna which began with and is exemplified by Project Tiger. Only six species of highly endangered flora are explicitly mentioned in the Wildlife (Protection) Act; very little is known about threats to other species. TRAFFIC-India is the leading NGO researching endangered flora, but the task is daunting. It was, for example, a TRAFFIC study of trade in agarwood which facilitated CITES listing of *Aquilaria malaccensis*. Agar, worth Rs 3,000 per kg, is traded for use in incense, perfume, medicines, writing material, occult/ceremonial purposes, timber, fumigation and many other things (Chengappa 1993; Chakraborty *et al.* 1994). *Taxus baccata*, from which taxol is made, *Clochicum luteum*, a medicinal plant, *Paphio paedilium* orchids and *Gloreosa superba* for allopathic drugs are among other illegal exports.

A severe technical problem in enforcement is the inability of customs officials and other officers to distinguish different species. WWF-India has produced a small handbook, *Wildlife Trade: A Handbook for Enforcement Staff*, (WWF-India 1994) and a more extensive loose-leaf reference guide with indigenous names of controlled species in local languages as well as Hindi and English.

Liberalization of export policy, 'reportedly necessitated by the World Bank', has greatly increased the danger to plants, sandalwood forests and coastal areas among other resources (Shekar Singh 1993: 14). Ashish Kothari (1996: 5) reports similar effects of liberalization, though CITES regulations have not been suspended. Moreover, the community censure that often attaches to the killing of animals – and to the felling of some trees – is not so easily activated for plants in general.

Illegal export of plants is a relatively new concern; animals have dominated compliance efforts. The range for the latter is great: ivory, rhino horn, tiger bone, furs of lesser cats, musk, peacock feathers, reptile skins, tortoises, etc. – the scale is impossible to estimate.[13] This international trade indicates the existence of an internal market for animal products which is illegal under the Wildlife Act of 1962.

Exports of wild animal skins and garments were banned in 1979, along with indigenous ivory. Strengthened efforts against poaching were triggered by evidence of increased killing of the flagship species, tigers, in the 1980s. India's wildlife conservation efforts were symbolized by Project Tiger from 1973 onwards. Though it is now fashionable to downplay glamorous mega-fauna, the world has lost probably 95 per cent of its tiger population this century; India remains the last best hope for avoiding extinction of this majestic animal. The central government inaugurated the Control of Poaching and Illegal Trade in Wildlife programme in 1986. The scheme included the improvement of telecommunications through a network of wireless stations and walkie-talkie sets; more vehicles for enhanced mobility; arms for protection staff; the setting up of check-posts and the introduction of rewards for information or apprehension of offenders – in effect creating slush funds for encouraging intelligence and diligence (*LSQ* 4776; 4781 26 August 1987). Nevertheless, officials both at central government and state level have been alarmed by the subsequent escalation of the trade in tiger bone with no clear resolution.[14]

In the belief that smuggling would be diminished if internal trade were more strictly controlled, a government ruling on 20 November 1986 prohibited carrying on business or trade in articles made from listed animals under Chapter VA of the Wildlife Act. Enforcement was disrupted by a legal challenge. Traders of furs and skins argued that Chapter VA violated their rights under Article 19g of the Constitution, the right to earn a livelihood. Traders tried to sell legal stocks in the interim; the government claimed that 'stocks' were a cover for continual purchases. The Delhi High Court ruled on 23 January 1987 that the government must buy the stocks at market value, which the government argued it could not do except by legitimizing the commoditization of illegal commodities.

The Ivory Traders and Manufacturers Association raised a similar challenge. A stay granted by the Court was used by nearly 300 petitioners along with the Cottage Industries Association. India has the largest number of ivory workers in the world. Ivory craftsmen and dealers mobilized; a long court battle ensued (Chengappa 1993; Panjwani 1994). Effective from 23 May 1992, a total ban on the import and domestic sale, transfer or display in any commercial place of African elephant ivory was enacted. The intent was to protect endangered Asian elephants by preventing laundering of Asian ivory as African ivory.

Both the fur traders and the ivory workers made claims resonant with objections to environmental protection worldwide: the contrary right to make a living. By 1992, the state had spoken against the livelihood argument and in favour of protection. Both stays had been vacated and the right to livelihood protection had been finally dismissed by the Supreme Court's refusal to hear the case. Much of the energy came from the NGO sector; the WWF-India was prominent in these and other legal battles to enforce both CITES and Indian law.[15]

Despite resolution of legal challenges, CITES remains difficult to enforce. Smuggling routes are difficult to monitor because of India's very long borders, many in inaccessible areas. Major CITES enforcement efforts are concentrated in the four metro-poles; smugglers avoid these points in favour of small ports such as Tuticorin, though a surprising number of seizures are still made in Delhi (for data, see TRAFFIC-India 1994). Tiger bones and parts move through Bhutan and Bangladesh to South-East and East Asia; tiger pelts and birds move west to the Persian Gulf. Monkeys and a variety of pets go to the United States. Furs and snake skins move through Nepal to Europe. Kashmir, where military conflict reduces the reach of the state, is a major fur-trading centre. Calcutta has been the major bird export nexus. Traders use the posts and rails; they pack animals into Tibet and Bangladesh, or transport them via ships to the Persian Gulf, or in luggage aboard commercial aircraft, and many other vectors. The variety of routes and techniques creates severe jurisdictional and tactical difficulties for enforcers.

Though illegal consignments are regularly seized, penalties on kingpins are extremely rare. Cases drag on for years; seized stocks remain the subject of long legal battles. It is difficult to know whether or not enforcement efforts are reducing smuggling. Certainly the seizures are increasing in volume and value – especially in 1994 – which could indicate either more traffic or better enforcement. The most knowledgeable people think it is both: more traffic because of international price movements, and somewhat better enforcement. Enforcement is improved by the small sums available to officers to buy intelligence; an improve-ment would be to match the customs' practice of 10 per cent of the haul as a reward, but seized stocks are assigned no monetary value and destroyed – again because of the principled stance of the government that there can be no price on animal parts. It is now harder to forge CITES certificates, but not impossible. Co-ordination among police, customs, wildlife wardens and at least nine other agencies involved in enforcement is improving in part because of efforts initiated by the WWF-India and the MOEF with support from the CITES Secretariat.[16]

Nevertheless, the CITES regulatory regime is limited by its commodity-denying and counter-market nature. High value products will find markets. Elephant tusks worth Rs 4,000–6,000 a kilo in India – or 200 days of employment for a landless labourer – are sold in Bangkok for $60,000 apiece. A leopard skin sells for $10,000. Tiger bones costing $90 per kg in Delhi bring $250 kg in China and East Asia. Tiger skins sell for $15,000; a single bowl of tiger penis soup, $320. Reports of payments to local people to kill tigers range from the equivalent of $5 to $300 per animal; rural wages in tiger areas are less than $1 per day. Between 1988 and 1992 tiger bones increased in price from $150 per kg to more than $250 per kg in 1992. Rhino horn which was worth in the 1970s $3,000 per kg was up to $10,000 per kg by 1985 and $17,500 in 1993. There is a saying along the Nepal border areas that you take a tiger to Nepal and come back on a motorbike.[17]

Better administration will not stop trade when stakes are high; borders are porous, enforcement personnel are spread thinly, often outnumbered and/or outgunned, and corruption is always possible in a high-value game, as we have learned universally from the trade in narcotics. The importance of CITES is its underlying recognition that simultaneous work on both demand and supply sides of the equation through international cooperation is necessary for improving the survival chances of species threatened by commoditization. Nevertheless, it remains true that a global ecological interest in biodiversity is at odds with the power of international markets and the state's fragmented and contested authority over its claimed property in nature.

Trade in Tropical Timber

The International Tropical Timber Agreement (ITTA) began as a means of promoting a stable market for tropical timber commodities. Over time, conservationist exhortations were added, along with guidelines for sustainable extraction. Parallel with the implementation of CITES, Indian law is stricter than the conservationist exhortations of the ITTA, and Indian policy rejects its commodity-promoting intent. Chapter XVI of the Import–Export Policy (1993) (Section 7) prohibits export of 'wood and wood products in the form of logs, timber, stumps, roots, barks, chips, powder, flakes, dust, pulp and charcoal'. The only explicit exception to this very thorough cataloguing is sandalwood handicrafts (Section 9). Restriction of exports, and a liberal policy towards timber imports, are meant to prevent further deforestation.[18] How well this very strict regime will survive liberalization is open to doubt (Kothari 1996).

The ITTA imposes no environmental claims on India, not only because of its commodity-promoting nature, but also because India does not (legally) export timber, with rare exceptions,[19] but only value-added products. Nevertheless, the objectives of India's forest policy have long been consonant with those of ITTA Article 1, Para. h: 'sustainable utilization and conservation' and 'ecological balance'. Both the conservationist and preservationist strands of Article 1 are pillars of India's forest policy; both are exceedingly difficult to achieve.

'Forests' now cover about 19.44 per cent of the geographical area – about 639,182 sq km. There is dispute about the net gains and losses in forest cover; the definitions of forest are problematic in any case – more administrative than biological.[20] Much of the dispute about extent of forest cover is biologically meaningless; threats to biodiversity are masked as monoculture biomass replaces endemic forest systems. There is no dispute that forest ecology is under significant threat and that the direction of change is towards destruction. India's *National Conservation Strategy* (1992: 3) concludes that the national 'forest wealth is dwindling'.

What to do about this widely perceived threat evokes intense controversy in India. In the pre-colonial period, forests were not conceptualized as limited or threatened, but rather a resource to be converted to human use values; forest-clearing for settlement and agriculture was honoured (Raghunandan 1987). The modern policy logic of forest conservation begins in the late nineteenth century as an outgrowth of European 'scientific forestry' organized for sustained yield for extraction (which increased dramatically with the demands of empire (see, for example, Guha 1985, 1989). Forests essentially became state property, with different functions. Reserved forests were used by the government for timber production; protected forests permitted limited extraction by local people for their traditional subsistence needs: fuel, fodder, and non-wood products. Continuation of this colonial system is increasingly attacked as ineffective, unjust and undemocratic (Hiremath *et al.* 1994).

The National Forest Policy of 1952 set a goal of 33 per cent forest cover for the country; states enacted their own legislation. In 1976, forests were moved from the State List of the Constitution to the Concurrent List, giving Delhi more control. Social forestry programmes for afforestation began in 1976 on recommendations from the National Commission on Agriculture.[21] In 1980, the Forest (Conservation) Act was passed to prevent deforestation and protect habitat for wildlife conservation. This controversial act prohibited conversion of any forest area to non-forest use without approval from the central government. Approved diversions for development projects had to be compensated by an equal area of afforestation. The Act spawned substantial conflicts between central government and states; a typical representation in parliament taps familiar issues:

> There is an urgent need to provide employment to the people in Maharashtra, especially in the District Nasik, but due to the Forest Conservation Act, 1980 ... all the development works in the area have been held up. Many development works which were started earlier have become stalled. Crores of rupees have already been spent on them ... I would request that a little relaxation would be provided ... so that employment could be generated and the people may not have to starve (*LSQ* M/R 377, 26 March 1990).

Amendment of the Forest (Conservation) Act in 1988 coincided with a new National Forest Policy. Noting that the 1952 Forest Policy's goal of restoring forest coverage to 33 per cent of the country had failed and that destruction of 'genetic diversity' had been extensive, the policy envisioned joint power-sharing between villagers and forestry officials, compensatory afforestation for developmental diversions of forests, and eco-restoration with joint usufruct. The biodiversity function was stressed at the expense of revenue production as the public good provided by forests. In theory, the inadequacy of the command-and-control logic of colonial forestry was appreciated, though working out new institutional arrangements in the face of suspicious subjects and recalcitrant officials will take dogged commitment and creativity (see R. Guha 1994). Experiments in process attempt to disentangle the property rights bundle in favour of local communities.

Despite official gestures towards participatory forest management, the policy to ensure sustainable use remains controversial. Politically, the contradiction is between centralized bureaucratic control and devolution to states and communities. Normatively, there is conflict over the conceptualization of forest dwellers' daily practices as 'concessions and privileges' (granted by a state) as opposed to rights inherently vested in local people. Environmentally, the conflict is between preservationist 'deep ecology' and the social ecology of development favoured by most activist NGOs (Herring 1991). Empirically, in terms of forest conservation, there are no easy conclusions and deep disagreements.[22] Conflicting claims to resource stewardship, conservation values, employment and social justice are no easier to resolve in India than in the old growth forests of the United States. Whatever the resolution at the level of policy, state proprietary claims to forests will remain contested and contingent.

Constraining Markets in Fragile Ecosystems

The World Heritage Convention (WHC) recognizes a global public good in the preservation of biologically important spaces within national terrains. It achieves this function via rigging of land markets. States remove ecologically rich and sensitive areas from their highest use value in market terms. There has been conflict surrounding the justice of different ratios of land removed; many of the most fragile and biologically rich terrains exist in areas where the demands for development are most compelling.

The aggregate protected (on paper) area in India is similar to that of the United States, just under 5 per cent, one-fifth that of Costa Rica, but more than many nations. There are levels of protection; much 'protection' is tenuous or bogus. Current research seeks to identify 'biodiversity hotspots' for special protection, given limited resources and intense competition for space. Pressures to 'denotify' protected areas for 'development' have intensified with liberalization (Kothari, A. 1996).

India's WHC natural sites are a subset of its national parks.[23] Of India's five natural heritage sites, two have been seriously threatened in recent years – Manas and Kaziranga; the north-east is rich in hotspots of both biodiversity and political rebellion.

Manas is one of India's largest (2,837 sq km) and richest protected areas, containing twenty-two known endangered species; it became a WHC site in 1986. Agitation by the Bodos for a separate state began on 2 March 1987. In addition to autonomy, their demands included an end to plantation monoculture in the area, prohibition of foreign liquor, preventing exploitation by middlemen in forest products, expulsion of ethnic Assamese and withdrawal of the paramilitary Central Reserve Police. Guerrillas of the Bodo Security Force found sanctuary in the park. Structures were burned and field officers were evacuated after a number were killed; much of the area was in effect surrendered to guerrillas. As staff departed, the 'wildlife and timber mafia' moved in without restraint. Wildlife was destroyed, including threatened species such as the swamp deer. The grasslands, which are the last refuge of the floricans, hispid hare, pygmy hog and other species, were extensively burned; timber was felled.

The state's response to Bodo demands was a typical developmentalist programme. Announced in 1990, and funded by the WWF-India, it was meant to defuse tensions through a segmentation of space and alternative livelihoods: development of the buffer zone with cooperatives, apiculture, pisciculture, and so on. A Memorandum of Settlement creating a Bodo Autonomous Council, covering 2,000 villages, was signed in 1993.[24] Nevertheless, the conflict is not resolved; guerrillas remain active, but increased staff with more fire power have re-established tenuous state control over most of the park.

Kaziranga has been threatened by both large-scale poaching and development. As in Manas, gangs of poachers outgunned forest guards. The state government blamed central government for inadequate funding; the central government countered that allocated funds were under-utilized. In 1990 Kaziranga was placed on the threatened list of the International Union for Conservation of Nature; Manas was already on the list. Kaziranga had been listed previously because of poaching and plans for rail connections; it was removed from the list and then placed on it again as plans for an oil refinery nearby were announced.[25] As in Manas, there have been cycles of threat and response, conflicts between central and state governments over responsibility, and speculation among wildlife activists that timber and poaching gangs could not thrive without political connections.

Though Manas and Kaziranga have received special attention because of international threats to their status and the especially high levels of conflict, all protected areas are susceptible to people–state conflicts. In the Sundarbans WHC site, these involve conflicts over wildlife protection – specifically, tigers that kill people. The widely publicized 'tiger widows' of the area demand compensation from the state for depredations of animals that the state has in effect declared its wards.[26]

In the Bharatpur WHC site (Keoladeo National Park), a ban on grazing of domestic buffaloes in 1982 led to conflict between officials and villagers, fatal shootings and an unanticipated biological outcome. Bharatpur presents a paradox of the preservationist mission in biological terms: its globally important biological function as a migratory bird breeding ground resulted from anthropogenic landscaped changes for the hunting pleasures of the aristocracy. Banning grazing in national parks in some sense preserves their natural integrity, but in Bharatpur the ungrazed wetland became choked with weeds and paspallum grass previously kept in check by grazing. The transition from ecologically sensitive wetland to emergent grassland (a natural process) creates a sub-optimal habitat for avifauna (many migratory, some endangered, and thus a global concern), for which the area was made a WHC site. Compromises with militant villagers have allowed the human removal of grasses. International threats to delist Bharatpur have been resisted by the government of India.[27]

World Heritage Convention 'natural' sites represent a thin claim of global property in nature. The criteria for what counts as preservation are unclear. If smuggling threatens the status of Manas, does commercial tourism threaten Yosemite, a WHC site in the United States? Certainly there is damage inflicted on the ecology of each. In India, WHC sites receive no more legal and administrative protection than other national parks. Their very richness in biological terms reflects historically their inhospitality in terms of human developmentalism: jungles, swamps, dangerous or inaccessible places. Isolation and remoteness in turn render the state's proprietary claims more difficult to assert.

Global Regimes and Micro–Macro Governance

Regulating nature severely tests state capacity. Despite consonance between global treaties and domestic policy in India, global public goods in nature prove difficult to provide locally. Unlike treaties such as the Montreal Protocol, which require innovations of states, global nature treaties are congruent with, and in some respects lag behind, Indian legal development. Compared to many nations on the periphery,[28] India has developed significant capacity to comply with the treaties it signs and has imposed significant limits on markets in nature and its commoditization.

CITES, the ITTA and the WHC are linked through issues in which local populations have strong normative and political claims against state restrictions; livelihoods are at stake. The ability of states to enforce claims on nature hinges on governance – that elusive mix of authority, transparency, representation, participation, resonance with local norms and cooperation. Institutional capability variables (how many officers, with how many vehicles, walkie-talkies, weapons, and how much organizational coherence, etc.) constitute necessary but not sufficient conditions for enforcement after some threshold capability is reached. More important are variable relationships between bearers of state power and subjects of state authority. Power capacity in and of itself is not only insufficient to enforce rights in nature, but may, in the

318

typical command-and-control routines, undermine capacity for governance.

One response to these contradictory claims is administrative segmentation of ecosystems. Creation of 'buffer zones' between people and protected nature has not generally been an effective strategy for both technical and administrative reasons. As the ecology of the 'core' area is difficult to predict or control, success in raising predator populations or degradation of forage for herbivores causes animals to leave the core and destroy livestock, crops and sometimes people. These dilemmas are serious in a political democracy; questions to the Environment Ministry in parliament frequently touch on the costs to local people of pre-serving nature red in tooth and claw.[29] Furious at the state's callousness in compensating loss, and its incapacity to control its marauding property, villagers predictably defend themselves by killing predators.

When the state is more enemy than public trust, confrontation and evasion are more likely than cooperation; governance gives way to coercion. The very remoteness of 'natural' reserves, necessary for their biodiversity function, makes them attractive to anyone who wishes to avoid the state, undermining their bio-diversity function. State incapacity to control smugglers, socially ensconced bandits, kidnappers, insurgents and drug dealers[30] merely reflects the larger phenomenon of parallel power beyond the reach of state authority and pervasive antagonistic relations of rural people to the state. Just as rural rebellion often begins in 'banditry' in remote areas, challenges to state authority often begin in, or are legitimated by, disputes over claims to natural resources, frequently connected to demands for autonomous political space.[31] This connection between subnationalism and natural-resource use, one step more radical than the 'sagebrush rebellion' over federal control of land use in the western United States, may be used instrumentally by politicians, but constitutes a predictable outcome of intrusive state power that is not locally sanctioned or leavened with participation.

States have had, and will continue to have, mixed motives in declaring authority over segments of nature; the net effect on environments is determined by a very situationally contingent mix of motives, capacity and will. The argument for a capable and activist state to enforce preservationist norms presupposes a legitimate state. In a hierarchical world economic system, legitimacy may well presuppose precisely that form of development which has devastated so much of the global environment. The growth-legitimized state cannot authentically demand sacrifices to preserve as nature space demanded by the poor for livelihoods or the rich for accumulation.

An inferior position in an unequal world system constrains both will and the capacity for state-led environmental solutions.[32] International regimes create a difficult tension. The international system simultaneously urges economic liberalization and environmental management; the magic of the market and the spectre of externalities require both urgent attention and sacrifices in the periphery. The former necessitates disengaging an intrusive state; the latter requires an activist, interventionist state. Contraction of the state's regulation of industry is counterposed to expansion of state control of nature. It is not difficult to construct the North's prescriptions on both scores as a hypocritical 'Do as we say, not as we did.' In a fairly typical response from the South, India's representative to the 1993 ITTA conference said to me: 'Having killed all their forests, they now presume to tell us how to manage ours.' Such perceptions are both rooted in history and corrosive of global governance.

There is contradiction in the demand that the international system become more a market, that it absent itself from state meddling, and the simultaneous demand that market failures and externalities (of which ecological integrity is perhaps the most egregious) be considered in global terms. Emergence of global regulatory regimes with state-like properties attempts to solve the planetary commons problem by constructing a soft global Leviathan. Of these two tendencies, global neo-liberalism is dominant, legitimated by growth, not justice or ecological integrity. To use a poignant example, globalization of markets and market reforms in the former socialist bloc have had a perverse effect on regulating trade in endangered species (under CITES). Eastern

European and Russian entry into the market operating with hard currency and fewer constraints on trade has accelerated depletion of endangered species in India.[33]

The late twentieth century witnessed a sea-change in the valence attached by mass publics and intellectuals to the relative values of state intervention and market autonomy. States came to be seen as more a part of the problem (any problem) than of the solution. State authority in nature is not immune from this intellectual reversal. Yet the character of meta-commons dilemmas makes a strong case for nested authority, certainly larger than local, despite the litany of failures. Globally, states remain the actors among whom agreements are made; absent agreements, a species-wide public good, is underprovided. The environmentally engaged nation-state becomes Janus-faced – looking to a global system of international pressures, bribes and censure that presupposes its competence, and simultaneously to local societies that distrust its effects and contest its claims. As some developments in inter-national soft law reinforce the state's obligations to manage nature, others reassert the rights of indigenous peoples to 'environmental rights' and local control.[34]

Given powerful forces of economic integration and growth pressures on states, centralized control is no guarantee of even conservation, much less preservation. Simultaneously, the 'great transformation' produces intense pressures for the commoditization of everything and the further individuation of interests.[35] This statement does not presume the romanticized notion that the ancients and locals were incapable of environmental error or destruction, which is clearly wrong,[36] but does suppose that social learning at a very local level has cybernetic advantages over centralized bureaucracy.

Global governance of the natural commons then presupposes local governance. Expansion of state claims reduces the institutional and cultural diversity of local arrangements – a perceived pre-condition for administrative rationality.[37] The state's pernicious effect on local accommodations to natural systems is both structural and cultural; centralized states reduce both the political space within which local communities can work institutional solutions to perceived problems and the authority of existing institutions. Just as reduction of biodiversity precludes options, traditional state control of nature reduces the richness of institutional and cultural diversity from which governance can be constructed.

Abbreviations

AST: Assam Tribune (Guwahati)   *MH: Maharashtra Herald* (Pune)

ET: Economic Times (Delhi)   *PIO: Pioneer* (New Delhi)

DH: Deccan Herald (Pune)   *RSQ: Rajya Sabha Questions*

HT: Hindustan Times (Delhi)   *TEL: Telegraph* (Calcutta)

IT: India Today   *TOI: Times of India*

LSQ: Lok Sabha Questions

Notes

1. For the purposes of this paper, 'nature' will be essentialized and uninterrogated. Nature will take on its meaning in ordinary discourse. Presumably everyone is aware by now that, in the words of Lukacs (1971 [1923]: 234): 'Nature is a societal category ... whatever is held to be natural at any given stage of social development, however this nature is related to man [*sic*] and whatever form his involvement with it takes, i.e. nature's form, its content, its range and its objectivity are all socially conditioned.'

2. See Raghunandan 1989; Eaton 1990; 1993; S. Guha 1995 and below.

3. The hegemonic literature on Indian ecological history tends to view the claims of the colonial state as novel, and therefore productive of resistance. Sumit Guha's (1995) work on medieval Maharashtra suggests that this is not the case.

4. The logic of collective action is ambiguous on 'small' aggregates. Villages may have more potential for collective action than much smaller aggregates in industrial society because of (a) the greater continuity of relationships over time; (b) the greater information about the character of other individuals; (c) the multidimensionality of relationships, such that 'side-payments' and sanctions can be managed in spheres other than that to which collective action directly applies.

5. There is nothing in logic which prevents privatization from meaning devolution to local corporate bodies rather than individuals; as Bromley and Chapagain (1984: 870) note, 'the matter of private control over resources refers to the ability to exclude others, not to how many individuals share in the decision making by those not excluded'. That

extremely large and complex social organizations such as business corporations should be considered individual actors in theory and law whereas villages are a priori held to be incapable of rational action does seem bizarre.

6.   Scattered exceptions may be found in the works of Marx, for example in the discussion of agriculture in *Capital*, vol. I, Raghunandan (1987: 546) points to exceptions in Engels' 'Dialectics of Nature'. Nevertheless, the weight of the Marxian tradition is clearly as indicated in the text.

7.   Tellingly, they mention 'invasion of weeds' as an indicator of land degradation (Blaikie and Brookfield 1987: 5) To be fair, it is possible to describe a biological category congruent with 'weed' (invasive, opportunistic, wide tolerance for conditions, etc.) but here I think they mean, as we usually do, a plant that is growing where a human being does not want it to grow.

8.   The moral economy tradition is something of a totem in peasant studies. It opposes 'moral' not to immoral but to amoral; that is, there exist social formations in which economic relations and outcomes are judged not by canons of markets, but by socially constructed notions of right and wrong: acceptable, unacceptable and optimal. The roots in Polanyi (1944) are clear; the term is usually associated with James Scott's early work. For the briefest possible summary, and a comparison to a leading critic's theoretical alternative, see Herring (1980).

9.   Kautilya argues in the *Artha Shastra* that 'the means of ensuring the pursuit of philosophy, the three Vedas and economics is the Rod [wielded by the King]; its administration constitutes the science of politics ... On it is dependent the orderly maintenance of worldly life ... If not used, it gives rise to the law of the fishes. For the stronger swallows the weak in the absence of the wielder of the Rod' (From Robinson 1988: preface). The doctrine of *matsyanyaya*, which Robinson calls the 'law of the fishes', implies that in a state of nature, anarchy prevails, providing the justification for a strong and interventionist state. So strongly is the state associated with 'the Rod' (*danda*) that Kautilya calls the science of politics, or kingship, *dandaniti* (a useful corrective, more rooted in realism to the more usual *rajniti*).

10.   In talking with many state managers on the reasons for success and failure in state control in preserving nature, I found a number of discrete, though sometimes co-mingling, themes. First there are the Incompetent Villagers. Robert Wade is certainly right in arguing that much has been assumed about the incapacity of Indian villages for collective action but very little has been established empirically. Second, there are the Lamentably Desperate Villagers. Being against poverty is politically correct in India. In this view, congruent with the Maslovian

hierarchy of needs and post-industrial society worldview, pervasive destitution drives villagers to if not justifiable, at least understandable, acts of ecocide. Blaikie and Brookfield (1987: 48) make the case more generically: '[P]overty is the basic cause of poor management and the consequence of poor management is deepening poverty.' In both scenarios, villagers need control from the centre.

11. During the past three years a very weak centre capitulated to state demands for weakening environmental impact statement requirements and delegating more power to the states. Likewise, the No-Development Zones (NDZs) around national parks and reserved forests were compressed (by 80 per cent) and state demands that 'non-polluting' industries be allowed even within the NDZs were met (see *Financial Express,* 2 May 1993).

12. This section, and the two that follow, borrow from Herring and Bharucha (forthcoming). Dr Bharucha is in no way implicated in my use of our arguments in that piece.

13. When questioned in parliament, the Finance Minister responded: 'Smuggling being a clandestine activity, it is not feasible to estimate the value of snake skin smuggled out of the country' (*LSQ* 3764, 19 Aug. 1987). The best data come from TRAFFIC-India. It is impossible to ascertain whether increasingly large seizures indicate increased activity or better enforcement, but seizures are increasing. In the first week of November 1994 the Indian government announced the largest ever seizure of skins and hides (in Kashmir), totalling over one thousand. Included was the largest tiger skin ever seized, 14 feet from nose to tail. A listing that a TRAFFIC researcher says may represent 10 per cent of the seizures in the country in 1993–94 covers 303 instances (TRAFFIC-India 1994).

14. Though the issue was intensively discussed at the International Tiger Symposium in Delhi in 1993, no specific guidelines to reduce the trade from India into China, including use of CITES, could be formulated. China, though invited, chose not to attend the Global Tiger Forum in India in 1994. *The New York Times* (20 November 1994) reported new agreements reached by Asian nations at the recent meeting of CITES parties in Florida to curb the tiger trade. A bilateral agreement between India and China is too new to be assessed.

15. See *Traffic Bulletin* 13: 1 May/June 1993. On the cases, *PAT* 24 May 1993; Panjwani 1994: 26–42. Some residual problems with stocks remain. As late as February 1995, a public sector corporation was still petitioning the MOEF for special dispensation to sell stocks of reptile skins, pleading financial hardship (overheard by Ron Herring in the Ministry).

16. Customs, coast-guard, navy, revenue intelligence, state wildlife officials, police, border security force, Indo–Tibetan police, railway

protection force, Department of Revenue intelligence, commerce intelligence, Controller of Import and Export, and others have come together with NGOs and activist individuals. The multiplicity of agencies renders coordination and training more difficult and complicates data collection: offenders are reported not to any central monitoring centre, but up through different administrative hierarchies.

17. Price data are only representative; there is great volatility and regional variation in prices. The data in the text were culled from a number of press accounts and TRAFFIC-India, CAT News, etc.

18. For example, *LSQ* 1763: 6 March 1987: The Finance Minister said in a typical response: 'Import of timber has been allowed with a view to conserve the country's depleting forest resources,' on Open General Licence at a concessional rate of duty of 10 per cent. Significant imports of timber (largely from South-east Asia) began in the early 1980s; in 1982–83, the value was Rs 308.47 crores; in 1983–84, Rs 162.07 crores; in 1984–85, Rs 293.70 crores (data from Directorate General of Commercial Intelligence and Statistics). Though we do not have confidence in the data, imports for 1989–91 were somewhat higher, averaging Rs 411.95 crores annually, less than US$137 million.

19. One hears unconfirmed reports of smuggling, primarily of sandalwood. Some exceptions are made for reasons of foreign policy, for example teak to the Gulf states for 'luxury consumption', as the official who had to sanction the export said. The value-added concession is legitimated as a spur to 'handicrafts' which are produced by 'weaker sectors'. By chance, a timber exporter shared our interview space with the official in charge of certifying exceptions. He explained to us (when the official stepped out) that the loophole was used by timber contractors to reduce sandalwood logs to dust and chips, claim these as by-products of handicraft production, then export same for extraction of oil. As the regulatory regime has been tightened, timber-exporting firms have virtually disappeared; the last active exporter spends much time in Delhi lobbying for exemptions.

20. The Ministry of Environments and Forests believes from its surveys that 385,000 sq km of this total represent 'dense forest'; 239,930 'open forest'; and 59,640 'scrub'. (Govt of India 1992b: 35). As to ITTA classification, officials are puzzled that oaks and pines growing in India are more 'tropical' than those growing in England or the United States. It was believed through the 1980s that forests were being destroyed at the rate of 0.3 per cent per annum. Though recent satellite images show a small increase in forest cover, this could reflect a change in imaging techniques. (See Govt of India 1991).

21. Social forestry schemes in the 6th Five-Year Plan (1980–85) covered 465 million ha; the 7th plan, 1985–90, planned for 9 million ha, and

covered 7.14 million (MOEF data). On issues of forest policy generally, see S. Singh (1986: ch. 4, pp. 27ff.).

22. In 1994 the government proposed the 'Conservation of Forests and Natural Ecosystems Bill', which became known to NGOs through leaks from the Ministry. This bill, designed to replace the 1927 Colonial Forest Act, is widely perceived to represent a strengthening of the centralized command-and-control logic. NGO resistance prevented the bill from going immediately to Parliament; an alternative NGO bill is being circulated and discussed. For commentaries by leading activists and scholars, see Hiremath *et al.* 1994; the government's draft bill is reproduced on pp. 91–222; see also R. Guha 1994; *TOI*, 1 Feb. 1995.

23. The WHC also lists 'cultural' sites of international significance. There are now 75 national parks, 421 wildlife sanctuaries and 19 tiger reserves in India.

24. 'Mafia' designation by Sanjay Deb Roy (1994: 2), the leading conservation official in the area. Also, WWF-India 1992; *Telegraph* (Calcutta), 18 Dec. 1989; *Assam Tribune*, 21 Feb. 1993; *Statesman* (Calcutta), 21 Feb. 1993; *Economic Times*, 11 June 1990; *IT*, 31 Aug. 1992; *STM*, 18 Oct. 1990; *TOI*, 12 Aug. 1989; *PAT*, 22 Jan. 1990; *AST*, 11 Jan 1993; *IED*, 9 May 1989 and interviews in the MOEF and wildlife community.

25. Accounts in *TOI*, 30 Nov. 1990; *AST*, 1 April 1990; *TEL*, 12 Dec. 1992; *NEO*, 6 April 1993; *DH*, 6 Aug. 1989; *NWT*, 27 May 1991 and interviews. The central government's position was explained in 1991 *RSQ* 394 May 1991: a centrally sponsored scheme for rhino protection, with Rs 5 crores in the 7th Plan, for more protection staff, vehicles, arms and wireless sets in addition to the centrally sponsored scheme for the control of poaching and illegal trade in wildlife. These schemes allow 50 per cent cost sharing for the state government of Assam.

26. For example, *IPS*, 25 Jan. 1990. Wildlife officials who work in the area are convinced that press reports overstate the killings, but emphasize that recurrent deaths of people and livestock from wildlife are a large and intractable problem.

27. See BNHS 1988; Madsen 1995. *Pioneer* (11 Feb. 1995) carried a front-page story on the threatened delisting, citing WHC Secretariat concern that the endangered Siberian cranes no longer visit Bharatpur. The Ministry had been in contact with the BNHS and the WWF-India to formulate a response.

28. For example, see the Blaikie and Simo study of the same accords in Cameroon, where international treaties for nature preservation are neither domestically consonant nor influential; state capacity is minimal.

29. For example, the MP from Almora said in the Lok Sabha: '[D]ue to the increase in … tigers in the Corbett National Park … and non-

availability of adequate food for them, the tigers come in the areas adjacent to this park and it creates terror in the neighbouring villages … In my constituency about 200 people have been either killed or injured by tigers during the last three years. There is terror in the villages … Sillour and Silt villages are gripped in terror.' He asked for more guards, barbed-wire fencing, and victim compensation 'as is being paid to the persons killed or injured in rail or air accidents' (*LSQ* M/R 377 (I) 27 April 1990).

30. Press reports (e.g. *TOI*, 16 July 1990) periodically mention the well-known phenomenon of drug production in protected areas. *Cannabis sativa* (marijuana) grows naturally in Corbett and Dudwa Tiger Reserves and is both cultivated and harvested wild for smuggling. When this issue was raised in parliament (*LSQ* 2896, 27 Aug. 1990), the government responded with a central scheme to assist the state in eradication. Tractors have been sent into protected areas for eradication. Drug smugglers also poach animals.

31. In addition to the discussion of the Bodo insurrection in Manas treated above, consider the position of M.S. Pal, MP for Nanital. He argued that the Forest Conservation Act (1980) had stopped development work in the Uttarakhand region of Uttar Pradesh. As a result, 'resentment among the people is growing and the feeling of a separate state is gaining momentum' (*LSQ* 066, M/R 377, 22 March 1990).

32. For example, at the White House conference on global warming in 1990, India's greenest environment minister, Ms Maneka Gandhi, argued that poor nations necessarily put development before environment; democratic institutions ensured that 'legitimate aspirations' of the poor to catch up as soon as possible to rich-nation standards could not be denied (*HT*, 19 April 1990).

33. Infiltrators for TRAFFIC-India who are British nationals, got only so far in investigating smuggling in Nepal as their accents were not Italian or Slavic (see Van Gruisen and Sinclair 1992).

34. For example, the ILO's Convention on Indigenous and Tribal Peoples in Independent Countries (ILO 169) of 1989 and debates around the UN Commission on Human Rights' Draft Declaration on the Rights of Indigenous Peoples. For discussion, see Madsen (1995: 4–7).

35. For an expanded treatment, and discussion of conference papers pointing in this direction, see Sinha and Herring, 'Common Property, Collective Action and Ecology,' *Economic and Political Weekly*, July 1993.

36. For example, Raghunandan (1987: 545) notes the case of a ninth-century Pallava king who was given the honorific *Kuduvetti* (one who clears forests) for presiding over the rapid conversion of forests to cultivated land. For similar observations based on pre-colonial Maratha

records, see Guha (1995). Eaton's (1990, 1993) 'saint entrepreneurs' were saintly precisely because their entrepreneurship destroyed forests to make fields. See also Madsen (1995: 11–17) for a critique of the Gadgil and Guha (1992) position.

37. On the effect of colonial law in this regard, see Gadgil and Guha (1992: 134 ff.). For a summary of papers connecting state intervention to common-property institution decline, see Sinha and Herring (1993); also, Schenk-Sandbergen (1988).

References

Agarwal, Anil (1985) 'Politics of Environment – II'. In *The State of India's Environment 1984–85*, New Delhi: Centre for Science and Environment.

—— (1993) 'Ecomanagement: The Best Solutions Are Home-made', *The Hindu: Survey of the Environment*, pp. 7–11.

Agarwal, Bina (1990) 'Engendering the Environment Debate: Lessons from the Indian Subcontinent', *WIDER* Conference on Environment and Development, September (Helsinki).

—— and Sunita Narain (1992) *Toward a Green World*, New Delhi: Centre for Science and Environment.

Ayyar, R.S. Vadyanatha (1976) *Manu's Land and Trade Laws*, Delhi: Oriental.

Baden-Powell, B.H. (1892) *The Land Systems of British India*, 3 vols. Oxford: The Clarendon Press.

Bandyopadhyay Jayanta and Vandana Shiva (1988) 'Political Economy of Ecology Movements', *Economic and Political Weekly*, June 11, pp. 1223–32.

Baviskar, Amita (1995) *In the Belly of the River: Tribal Conflicts over Development in the Narmada Valley*, Delhi: Oxford University Press.

Blaikie, Piers and Harold Brookfield (1987) *Land Degradation and Society*, London: Methuen.

—— and John Mope Simo (forthcoming) 'Cameroon's Environmental Accords: Signed, Sealed but Undelivered'. In Edith Brown Weiss and Harold Jacobson (eds), *Engaging Countries: Strengthening Compliance with International Accords*, Cambridge, Mass.: MIT Press.

Bombay Natural History Society (BNHS) (1988) *Ecology of Semitropical, Monsoonal Wetland in India: The Keoladeo National Park, Bharatpur, Rajasthan* Bombay: BNHS.

Bromley, Daniel W. and Devendra P. Chapagain (1984) 'The Village against the Center: Resource Depletion in South Asia', *American Journal of Agricultural Economics*, December, pp. 868–73.

Chakrabarty, Kalyan, Ashok Kumar and Vivek Menon (1994) *Trade in Agarwood*, New Delhi: TRAFFIC-India.

Chengappa, Raj (1993) 'Poaching: A Lethal Revival', *India Today*, May 31.

Cronon, William (1983) *Changes in the Land: Indians, Colonists and the Ecology of New England*, New York: Hill and Wang.

CSE (Centre for Science and Environment) (1986) *The State of India's Environment, 1984–85: The Second Citizen's Report*, New Delhi: Ravi Chopra.

Eaton, Richard M. (1990) 'Human Settlement and Colonization of the Sundarbans, 1200–1750', *Agriculture and Human Values*, vol. VII, no. 2, pp. 6–16.

—— (1993) *The Rise of Islam and the Bengal Frontier: 1204–1760*. Berkeley: University of California Press.

Elster, Jon (1985) *Making Sense of Marx*, Cambridge: Cambridge University Press.

ENVIS Centre 07, World Wide Fund for Nature–India (1993) *Annual Report*, New Delhi, submitted to the MOEF.

Far Eastern Economic Review (1993) 'Endangered Species: Targets of Asia's Affluent', August 19, pp. 23–27.

Feeny, David, Fikret Birkes, Bonnie J. McCay and James M. Acheson (1990) 'The Tragedy of the Commons: Twenty-Two Years Later', *Human Ecology*, vol. 18, no. 1.

Gadgil, Madhav and Ramachandra Guha (1992) *This Fissured Land: An Ecological History of India*, Delhi: Oxford University Press.

——, N.V. Joshi and Suresh Patil (1993) 'Power to the People: Living Close to Nature', *The Hindu: Survey of the Environment*, pp. 58–62.

Government of India (1980) Department of Science and Technology, *Report of the Committee for Recommending Legislative Measures and Administrative Machinery for Ensuring Environmental Protection.* September 15, New Delhi.

—— (1991) *The State of the Forest Report*, New Delhi: Ministry of Environment and Forest.

—— (1992a) *The Wildlife (Protection) Act, 1972* [as amended up to 1991], Dehradun: Natraj.

—— (1992b) Ministry of Environment and Forests, *Environmental Action Programmes – India* [Interim Document], November, New Delhi.

—— (1992c) Ministry of Environment and Forests, *National Conservation Strategy and Policy Statement on environment and Development*, June, New Delhi.

—— (1993) Ministry of Commerce, *Export–Import Policy 1 April–31 March 1997* [with Amendments up to 31 March 1993], New Delhi.

Guha, Ramachandra (1985) 'Forestry and Social Protest in British Kumaun, c. 1893–1921', *Subaltern Studies*, vol. IV, pp. 54–100.

—— (1989) *The Unquiet Woods: Ecological Change and Peasant Resistance in the Himalaya*, Delhi: Oxford University Press.

—— (1990) 'An Early Environmental Debate: The Making of the 1878 Forest Act', *The Indian Economic and Social History Review*, vol. 27, no. 1.

—— (1994) 'Switching on the Green Light', *Telegraph* (Calcutta), 25 Oct. 1994.

Guha, Sumit (1995) 'Kings, Commoners and the Commons'. Paper presented to the conference on Science and Technology Studies, Cornell University, New York, April 28–30.

Hardin, Garrett (1968) 'The Tragedy of the Commons', *Science*, Vol. 162, pp. 1243–48.

Herring, Ronald J. (1980) 'Review of Popkin', *The Rational Peasant*, *American Political Science Review*, vol. 74, no. 2 (June).

—— (1983) *Land to the Tiller*, New Haven: Yale University Press.

—— (1991) 'Politics of Nature: Commons Interests, Dilemmas and the State', Harvard Center for Population and Development Studies, Working Paper Series no. 106, October.

—— and Erach Bharucha (forthcoming) 'Capacity, Will and Governance: India's Compliance with International Accords'. In Edith Brown Weiss and Harold Jacobson (eds), *Engaging Countries: Strengthening Compliance with International Accords*, Cambridge, Mass.: MIT Press.

Hiremath, S.R., Kanwalli, S. and Kulkarni, S. (eds) (1994) *All About Draft Forest Bill and Forest Lands*, Dharawad: Samaj Parivartana Samudaya.

Jodha, N.S. (1985) 'Population Growth and the Decline of Common Property Resources in Rajasthan, India', *Population and Development Review*, vol. 11, no. 2 (June).

—— (1986) 'Common Property Resources and Rural Poor in Dry Regions of India', *Economic and Political Weekly*, vol. xxi, no. 27 (July).

Kothari, Ashish (1996) 'Structural Adjustment vs. India's Environment'. Paper presented at the Annual Meeting, Association for Asian Studies, Honolulu (April).

Kothari, Smitu (1995a) 'Whose Nation Is It? The Displaced as Victims of Development', *Lokayan Bulletin*, vol. 11, no. 5 (March/April), pp. 1–8.

—— (1995b) 'Developmental Displacement and Official Policies: A Critical Review', *Lokayan Bulletin*, vol. 11, no. 5 (March/April), pp. 9–28.

—— and Pramod Parajuli (1993) 'No Nature without Social Justice: A Plea for Cultural and Ecological Pluralism in India'. In Wolfgang Sachs (ed.), *Global Ecology: A New Arena of Political Conflict*, London: Zed Books.

Lukacs, Georg (1971 [1923]) *History and Class Consciousness*, London: Merlin.

Madsen, Stig Toft (1995) 'Recent Changes in India's Forest Policy'. Paper presented to the Conference on 'Rural and Urban Environments', Nordic Association for South Asian Studies (Oslo, May 18–22).

Nadkarni, M.V. (1987) 'Agricultural Development and Ecology: An Economist's View', *Indian Journal of Agricultural Economics*, vol. 42, no. 3 (July), pp. 359–75.

Nandy, Ashis (1988) *Science, Hegemony and Violence*, Delhi: Oxford University Press.

Neale, Walter C. (1988) 'Exposure and Protection: The Double Movement in the Economic History of Rural India'. Paper presented to the Second International Karl Polanyi Conference (Montreal, November).

North, Douglass (1990) *Institutions, Institutional Change and Economic Performance*, Cambridge: Cambridge University Press.

Omvedt, Gail (1987) 'India's Green Movements', *Race and Class*, vol. XXVIII, no. 4, pp. 29–38.

Ostrom, Elinor (1986) 'How Inexorable is the "Tragedy of the Commons"?' Distinguished Faculty Research Lecture, Indiana University (Bloomington, April 3).

Panjwani, Raj (1994) *Courting Wildlife*, New Delhi: WWF-India.

Polanyi, Karl (1957) *The Great Transformation*, Boston: Beacon Press.

Porter, Gareth and Janet Walsh Brown (1991) *Global Environmental Politics*, Boulder, Col.: Westview.

Raghunandan, D. (1987) 'Ecology and Consciousness', *Economic and Political Weekly*, vol. XXII, no. 13 (March 28), pp. 545–49.

Robinson, Marguerite S. (1988) *Local Politics: The Law of the Fishes*, Delhi: Oxford University Press.

Roy, S. Deb (1994) 'Manas National Park: A Status Report', New Delhi, unpublished ms.

Runge, C.F. (1986) 'Common Property and Collective Action in Economic Development', *World Development*. vol. 14.

Schenk-Sandbergen, Loes (1988) 'People, Trees and Forest in India,' Annex 2. *Report of the Mission of the Netherlands on the Identification of the Scope for Forestry Development Corporation in India*, Amsterdam.

Shiva, Vandana (1986) 'Coming Tragedy of the Commons'. *Economic and Political Weekly*, vol. 21, no. 15 (April 12), pp. 613–15.

Singh, Chhatrapati (1986) *Common Property and Common Poverty: India's Forests, Forest Dwellers and the Law*, Delhi: Oxford University Press.

Singh, K.S. (1986) 'Agrarian Dimension of Tribal Movements'. In A.R. Desai (ed.), *Agrarian Struggles in India after Independence*, Delhi: Oxford University Press.

Singh, Narindar (1976) *Economics and the Crisis of Ecology*, Delhi: Oxford University Press.

Singh, Samar (1986) *Conserving India's Natural Heritage*, Dehradun: Nataraj.

Singh, Shekar (1993) 'Eco-Funds: Budgeting for the Environment', *The Hindu: Survey of the Environment*, pp. 11–16.

Sinha, Subir and Ronald Herring (1993) 'Common Property, Collective Action and Ecology', *Economic and Political Weekly*. July.

TRAFFIC-India (1994) 'Seizures in India', New Delhi, mimeo.

Van Gruisen, Joanna and Toby Sinclair (1992) 'Fur Trade in Kathmandu: Implications for India', New Delhi: TRAFFIC-India.

Wade, Robert (1988) *Village Republics*, Cambridge: Cambridge University Press.

World Commission on Environment and Development (1987) *Our Common Future*, New Delhi: Oxford University Press.

World Wide Fund for Nature–India (1992) *Manas: The Conservation Plan 1992–93*, New Delhi: WWF-India.

—— (1993) *The Conservation Plan 1992–93*, New Delhi: WWF-India.

—— (1994) *Wildlife Trade: A Handbook for Enforcement Staff*, New Delhi: WWF-India.

Index

adaptation 2, 59–60, 77
Afghanistan 221–223
Agarwal, Anil 4, 87, 94
Ankleshwar Industrial Estate (Gujarat) 154–160
autonomy 118–119, 136

biodiversity 1, 15, 82, 227, 307, 313, 315, 316
blame 96, 124
Bodos 316
buffer zone 97, 319

canal *panchayat*s 251–254
caste 4–5, 29, 180
chher (system of silt clearance) 249–253, 262
  abolition of 257
Civic Exnoras (CEs) 127–138
class 10, 11–12, 131, 140, 283–286
  as structural asymmetry 171–177
climate change 41
Coimbatore District 269
Common Property Resources (CPR) 2, 4, 21, 80, 175–176, 179–180, 192–194, 268

Community-Based Organizations (CBOs) 114–115
Community Forest Management in Protected Areas (CFM-PA) 100–101, 107
competitive populism 13, 267, 286–288
compliance 117–118, 123
compromise 8, 68
consumerism 41
Convention on International Trade in Endangered Species of Flora and Fauna (CITES) 307–312
cooptation 119, 141
corruption 8, 12, 84, 212, 219, 223, 227, 312. *See also* moral ecology
customs (*rivaj*) 241–242, 248, 305

decentralization 14, 143
democracy 13, 266, 319
discount rate 215, 225
double movement 300
drainage 187

ecosystem people 80, 85, 88–89, 94

ecotourism 93

electricity
  free of charge 278
  price of 185, 269–290

entrepreneurs 224

environmental degradation
  definition of 166–168, 170
  mechanisms of 188–189

envy 42

Exnora International 127–129, 136–138

externalities 171, 178, 320

farming system 63

firewood 37, 79, 182

fixed-price system 211

food production 11

foreign trees 35–40, 52

forest 179–183
  coniferous 206–207
  cover 91, 200, 313–315
  contractors 3, 202, 208, 212–217, 223
  deforestation of 3, 7, 22, 32–35, 40–44, 182, 202, 218
  law 202–206, 300–301
  private or community-owned (*Guzara*) 203
  reforestation of 22, 39

Forest Cooperative Societies 217

Forest Development Cooperation (FDC) 209

formalization 136, 138

free-riders 134

Gadgil, Madhav 4–5, 88–89

garbage 10, 121–135

gender 29

global regimes for protection of nature 298, 318–322

governance 318

grazing 183, 317

great transformation 299–300

Guha, Ramachandra 4–5, 88–89

Gujar 75, 108, 220

Gujarat 150

habitus 93

Hazara Division (North-West Frontier Province) 200

hunting 27, 28, 91, 95

hydro-electric power 59, 66

income distribution 165

Indian Farmers' and Toilers' Party 276–277

indigenous knowledge 8, 45, 85, 321

Indus Basin 238

international production 151–152

International Tropical Timber Agreement (ITTA) 312–313

irrigating public 12, 13, 245

irrigation 12, 13, 236
  from glacial streams 62–63
  from inundation canals 239–241, 249
  from perennial canals 258
  from tanks 186
  from energized wells 266

ivory 310

Joint Forest Management
(JFM) 98, 315

Kali Yuga, the Degenerate
Age 40–47
Kashmir, kingdom of 70, 75
Kaziranga National Park
(Assam) 317
Keoladeo National Park
(Rajasthan) 317–318
kingdoms 7

labour union, absence of 158
land
claims 68
settlement 240
landlordism, abolition of 7, 32
legitimation 117–118, 141
liberalization 14, 297–298, 309,
313, 316
love 42, 45, 103

Madras Corporation 122–124, 138
Madras Metropolitan Area
(MMA) 119
Malakand Division (North-West
Frontier Province) 200
Manas National Park
(Assam) 316
market
definition of 177
failure 171, 177–178, 297, 320
forces 6, 146, 200, 221–222,
225, 298
rigging 307, 315
media 98
memory 7, 8, 20–21

metaphor 60, 71–73
monsoon. *See* rain
moral ecology 22, 34–35, 39–47,
76, 92. *See also* corruption

neo-classical environmental and
resource economics 168
neo-Darwinism 1
nested authority 321
net-sale system 209
Non-Governmental Organizations (NGOs) 114–115
North-West Frontier Province
(NWFP) 200–201

Operation Disconnection 275
oral history 20–22, 24

participation 117–118, 123
patronage 138
Pareto-efficiency 169
pesticides 10
definition of 147
health hazards of 148–149
marketing of 156–158
organophosphorous 153–154
production of 146, 149, 156–
158
treatment of pollution by 159
poaching 13, 23, 96, 310, 317
pollution-intensive
technologies 151–152
population
of urban India 113
of the world 11
porterage duty 70
precedence 71–73

Prosopis juliflora. See foreign trees

public realm 237

Punjab 238

raiding 65

rain 37, 40–46

Rajaji National Park (Shiwalik foothills, Uttar Pradesh) 81, 89–91, 95–97

rationality 13, 255, 266, 302, 321

regeneration 88

risk 12, 237

royalties 205, 210

Rural Litigation and Entitlement Kendra (RLEK) 82

resource-partitioning 5

sanctions
   judicial 10, 205, 311
   royal 23, 32

Sawar, kingdom of (Ajmer–Merwara District) 23

settlement history 75–77

Shah Nahr (Hoshiarpur District) 243–248

share systems 239–248, 253

Shinaiki (Gilgit District) 60

sin 38

slum dwellers 121

social capital 8, 10,

social ecology 5, 306, 315

social justice 47, 315

soil 187

solid waste. *See* garbage

smuggling 308–312

stakeholders 2, 11–12, 87, 200, 214, 227. *See also* share systems

Standard Environmental Narrative (SEN) 2–6, 179–183

state
   capacity 8, 13, 31, 34, 114, 133, 305, 308–312, 318
   legitimacy 33, 320
   necessity of 116
   origin of 297
   property in nature 227, 304, 315

state–society–market paradigm 6

state–society relations 259, 305

street beautifier 130

subaltern studies 5–6, 31, 51

subsidies 185, 267, 279

Tamil Nadu Agriculturists' Association (TNAA) 267

Tamil Nadu Electricity Board (TNEB) 268

Tamil Vyvasayigal Sangam (VS). *See* Tamil Nadu Agriculturists' Association

tigers 309–310, 317

timber
   cross–border trade 221–223, 312–313
   harvesting ban 217, 219. *See also* forest

timescales 14, 167, 302

trade-offs 7, 32, 39, 45

tragedy of the commons 80, 116, 178, 226, 266, 301–302

transaction costs 5, 171, 225

transhumance 83, 92

Transnational Corporations (TNCs) 146

trust, lack of 215

utility 168–169

value, categories of 166–167, 299, 303

Van Gujjar 9, 81–85, 91–108. *See also* Gujar

Vansh Pradip Singh (king of Sawar) 23

vilayati bambul. See foreign trees

Voluntary Organizations (VOs) 114–115

water 120
  market 73, 186
  rights to 59, 73–77
  extraction of groundwater 184–185, 269

wild pigs 7, 22–32, 45

Wade, Robert 237–238

Wilson, Edward O. 1

working plans 207–208

World Heritage Convention (WHC) 315–318

The Nordic Institute of Asian Studies (NIAS) is funded by the governments of Denmark, Finland, Iceland, Norway and Sweden via the Nordic Council of Ministers, and works to encourage and support Asian studies in the Nordic countries. In so doing, NIAS has published over one hundred books in the last thirty years, most of them in collaboration with Curzon Press.

Nordic Council of Ministers